Local Consequences of the Global Cold War

COLD WAR
INTERNATIONAL HISTORY
PROJECT SERIES

James G. Hershberg
series editor

Brothers in Arms
The Rise and Fall of the Sino-Soviet Alliance,
1945–1963
Edited by Odd Arne Westad

Economic Cold War
America's Embargo against
China and the Sino-Soviet
Alliance, 1949–1963
By Shu Guang Zhang

Confronting Vietnam
Soviet Policy toward the
Indochina Conflict, 1954–1963
By Ilya V. Gaiduk

Kim Il Sung in the Khrushchev Era
Soviet-DPRK Relations and the
Role of North Korean Despotism,
1953–1964
By Balázs Szalontai

Failed Illusions
Moscow, Washington, Budapest,
and the 1956 Hungarian Revolt
By Charles Gati

Behind the Bamboo Curtain
China, Vietnam, and the World beyond Asia
Edited by Priscilla Roberts

Local Consequences of the Global Cold War

Edited by Jeffrey A. Engel

Woodrow Wilson Center Press
Washington, D.C.

Stanford University Press
Stanford, California

EDITORIAL OFFICES
Woodrow Wilson Center Press
One Woodrow Wilson Plaza
1300 Pennsylvania Avenue, N.W.
Washington, D.C. 20004-3027
Telephone 202-691-4029
www.wilsoncenter.org

ORDER FROM
Stanford University Press
Chicago Distribution Center
11030 South Langley Avenue
Chicago, Ill. 60628
Telephone 1-800-621-2736

Library of Congress Cataloging-in-Publication Data

Local consequences of the global Cold War / edited by Jeffrey A. Engel
        p. cm. — (Cold War international history project series)
    Includes bibliographical references and index.
    ISBN 978-0-8047-5947-2 (cloth : alk. paper)
    1. Cold War—Influence.   2. Cities and towns—History.   I. Engel,
Jeffrey A.
    D840.L56 2008
    909.82'5—dc22

                                                    2007039387

**Woodrow Wilson
International
Center
for Scholars**

The Woodrow Wilson International Center for Scholars, established by Congress in 1968 and headquartered in Washington, D.C., is a living national memorial to President Wilson.

The Center is a nonpartisan institution of advanced research, supported by public and private funds, engaged in the study of national and world affairs. The Center establishes and maintains a neutral forum for free, open, and informed dialogue.

The Center's mission is to commemorate the ideals and concerns of Woodrow Wilson by providing a link between the world of ideas and the world of policy, by bringing a broad spectrum of individuals together to discuss important public policy issues, by serving to bridge cultures and viewpoints, and by seeking to find common ground.

Conclusions or opinions expressed in Center publications and programs are those of the authors and speakers and do not necessarily reflect the views of the Center staff, fellows, trustees, advisory groups, or any individuals or organizations that provide financial support to the Center.

The Center is the publisher of *The Wilson Quarterly* and home of Woodrow Wilson Center Press, *dialogue* radio and television, and the monthly newsletter "Centerpoint." For more information about the Center's activities and publications, please visit us on the web at www.wilsoncenter.org.

The Cold War International History Project

The Cold War International History Project was established by the Woodrow Wilson International Center for Scholars in 1991. The project supports the full and prompt release of historical materials by governments on all sides of the Cold War and seeks to disseminate new information and perspectives on Cold War history emerging from previously inaccessible sources on the "the other side"—the former Communist world—through publications, fellowships, and scholarly meetings and conferences. The project publishes the *Cold War International History Project Bulletin* and a working paper series, and maintains a website, cwihp.org.

At the Woodrow Wilson Center, the project is part of the History and Public Policy Program, directed by Christian F. Ostermann. The project is overseen by an advisory committee that is chaired by William Taubman (Amherst College), and includes Michael Beschloss; James H. Billington (Librarian of Congress); Warren I. Cohen (University of Maryland at Baltimore); John Lewis Gaddis (Yale University); James G. Hershberg (George Washington University); Samuel F. Wells, Jr. (Woodrow Wilson Center); and Sharon Wolchik (George Washington University).

The Cold War International History Project is supported by the Henry Luce Foundation (New York), the Korea Foundation (Seoul), the John D. and Catherine T. MacArthur Foundation (Chicago, Ill.), the Ratiu Family Foundation (London), and the Smith Richardson Foundation (Westport, Conn.).

Contents

Tables and Figures

Foreword: Bringing Diplomatic History Home

Paul Boyer

Thucydides, the first great diplomatic historian in the West, fully grasped the impossibility of understanding the relationships among nations (or, in his case, city-states) without close attention to the social and cultural loam from which these relationships emerge and evolve. His masterwork, *The Peloponnesian War,* traces the complex diplomatic maneuvering among Athens, Sparta, and the other city-states of ancient Greece; the failure of diplomacy and the outbreak of war in 431 B.C.; and the repeated but largely futile efforts of statesmen and generals to negotiate truces and armistices as the conflict unfolded.

Himself an Athenian general, Thucydides was exiled early in the war for failing to prevent the surrender of Amphipolis, a city he was defending. His disgrace is our good fortune, for he spent the rest of his life observing the conflict from behind the lines and setting down his observations and reflections in the history we still read today. This narrative is not only a masterpiece of world literature but also, in its breadth of perspective, an exemplary text for historians. Though focusing on military and diplomatic events, the arenas he knew best, he also pays attention to the social, cultural, and technological context of events, including the importance of omens and prophecies, the devastating impact of plague on wartime Athens, the respective political structures and psychological makeup of Athenians and Spartans, and even the innovations and production feats of the shipbuilders supplying the warring powers—the "military-industrial complex" of the day.

The author would like to thank Ann Boyer and Jeremi Suri for helpful suggestions relating to the style and substance of this preface.

Of particular relevance to this volume, Thucydides also records the war's social and political impact on the people of Athens and its allied cities, as the seemingly interminable conflict stretched into decades. As his narrative proceeds, the tone grows darker and more pessimistic and the focus is increasingly on home-front politics, highlighting the deepening discontent and party strife in Athens, the widespread revulsion against a government unable either to prosecute the war successfully or negotiate a peace. Thucydides died before the war's full effects became clear, but as his narrative breaks off, democracy in Athens has been discredited, an authoritarian military regime has gained power, and Athens' long decline as a center of culture and intellectual life is clearly foreshadowed. All these social, political, and cultural effects were surely not foreseen by the diplomats and statesmen who led Athens into war. Nevertheless, as Thucydides came to recognize, they must constitute a part of any comprehensive "diplomatic history" of Athens in the Age of Pericles and after.

As Jeffrey A. Engel and Katherine Carté Engel make clear in their introduction to this volume, Thucydides' successors in the field of diplomatic history have not always maintained the breadth of perspective that he brought to the task. By contrast, however, ordinary folk throughout history have always understood that actions taken by those in power, including those who shape their nations' foreign policies, have profound implications for the lives of men and women far removed from the centers of power and decisionmaking. Examples abound. When Secretary of State William Henry Seward acquired Alaska from Russia in 1867, the implications for the indigenous peoples of the region, who had established fishing and hunting settlements centuries before either the Russians or the Americans arrived, were hugely significant. For the Tlingit people of Shee Atika (today's Sitka), a post-1867 influx of Presbyterian missionaries brought a more somber and austere version of Christianity than that of the Russian priests, with their incense and icons, who for several decades had been a familiar if problematic part of the Tlingits' world. The missionaries soon opened a school, on the lines of Richard Henry Pratt's Carlisle Indian School in Pennsylvania and Samuel Chapman Armstrong's Hampton Institute in Virginia, to train native Alaskan youth in the Protestant faith, Victorian morality and dress, and the work habits of the dominant classes in the distant United States. Decades later, during World War II, the Tlingit settlement on choice lands fronting Sitka's lovely harbor was expropriated for "military reasons." After the war, the land was not returned to the Tlingit but fell into the hands of nonnative real estate developers.

One intrepid early Presbyterian missionary and educator in Sitka, the Reverend Sheldon Jackson, of Minaville, New York, devoted himself to collecting masks, carvings, totem poles, and other artifacts from the native peoples of Alaska, at least in part, apparently, to demonstrate to his coreligionists back home the natives' abject paganism, and the need for more money to convert and civilize them. (In a nice historical irony, these artifacts, now on display in the Sheldon Jackson Museum on the campus of Sheldon Jackson College in Sitka, are today considered priceless treasures of indigenous folk art and craft.)

The fate of indigenous peoples in remote Alaskan communities thousands of miles from Washington was probably not central in William Seward's mind as he negotiated the purchase treaty with the Russian minister to the United States, Baron Edouard de Stoeckl. But the implications of these negotiations for the local residents must clearly be a part of any comprehensive history of the diplomatic process by which control of Alaska shifted from Moscow to Washington.

More recent Alaskan history provides another graphic example of the larger point. In the later 1950s, as fear of radioactive fallout fueled a grassroots movement in the United States for a nuclear test ban treaty, the physicist Edward Teller, the "father of the H-bomb" and a fierce supporter of continued testing, worked strenuously to derail the movement. In his pursuit of this goal, he trumpeted the scientific knowledge and peacetime benefits to be gained from continued testing. As part of this strategy, he championed "nuclear engineering"— that is, using nuclear blasts literally to transform the landscape to serve human purposes. To illustrate the alleged promise of nuclear engineering, in 1958 Teller broached the idea of detonating multiple thermonuclear bombs at a remote site on Alaska's northwestern coast, where Ogotoruk Creek flows into the Chukchi Sea. His goal, at least for public relations purposes, was to convert the mouth of this small stream into a bustling deepwater port where oceangoing freighters could load coal mined far in the interior for shipment to Japan and elsewhere.

Bizarre as it seems in retrospect, Teller's plan, dubbed Project Chariot, was backed by the Atomic Energy Commission and gained significant support. Opposition soon emerged, however, led by a pair of intrepid local geologists concerned about the scheme's ecological impact, and by the Inupiat Indians of nearby Point Hope Peninsula (where records of human habitation stretch back at least 2,500 years), whose lands and way of life would have been devastated by the project. Project Chariot eventually collapsed, and in 1963, over Teller's objections, the United States, the Soviet Union, and the United Kingdom signed a limited nuclear test ban treaty, pledging to halt atmospheric testing.

From one perspective, Project Chariot may be seen as simply another move on the chessboard of Cold War diplomacy, as a politically powerful scientist sought to influence the course of events as strategists in Washington, Moscow,

London, and elsewhere pursued their national interests while trying to keep a lid on the nuclear arms race. From a different perspective, however, Project Chariot emerges as literally a life-and-death issue for the native peoples of the affected region, and for those concerned with the ecological implications of the planned nuclear blasts. In this instance, Teller's ploy did *not* succeed, fortunately for the environment and for the local Inupiat. But any history of Project Chariot must look not only at its global diplomatic and strategic aspects but also at its local implications.

Recent developments in many historical subfields illustrate the benefits of incorporating local perspectives. In the past, for example, scholars in the closely related fields of the history of science and the history of technology typically took an internalist approach, focusing on specific scientific discoveries and disciplines, and on specific technological inventions and innovations. This approach produced much valuable work. But as these fields evolved and the perspective broadened, historians began to probe the social and cultural factors underlying the direction of scientific and technological innovation in specific social contexts. This broader perspective also led historians to investigate the *consequences,* for society at large and for specific communities and groups, of a host of scientific and technological developments, from railroads, the telegraph, the telephone, and Darwinian theory to the theory of relativity, the internal combustion engine, the atomic bomb, and the computer. As a result, these fields of historical inquiry have been fruitfully expanded, have become more rewarding and exciting, and have yielded a rich body of knowledge about the historical processes that shape human experience.

The field of intellectual history has followed a similar trajectory, from the era of Arthur O. Lovejoy and others who traced "the history of ideas" largely abstracted from their social and cultural context, to the awareness, as John Dewey pointed out a century ago, that ideas and ideologies emerge from specific social contexts, meet specific psychological needs, serve the interests of specific groups, and have real-world consequences. Certainly communities of Jews across Europe, from Amsterdam and Oslo to Warsaw and Bucharest, understood in the 1930s and 1940s that the Nazi ideology of racism and Aryan supremacy was no mere airy abstraction, cut off from the world of action and experience. No intellectual historian seriously investigating twentieth-century racist ideology can possibly avoid confronting the Holocaust.

One could go on and on. Military history—at its best, at least—has similarly evolved from an exclusive preoccupation with battle strategies and comparative weaponry to a more comprehensive focus on the effects of war on civilian populations, local communities, and specific social and ethnoracial groups, including those far from the scenes of battle.

Political history, too, has undergone a comparable transformation. In earlier generations, political historians generally concentrated on campaign strategies, electoral outcomes, the personalities of prominent politicians, and the maneuverings of political parties. Again, this scholarship often proved illuminating and valuable in its way. Contemporary political historians, however, also pay attention to the economic, social, religious, and regional sources of political movements and controversies, and to the ramifying impact of political actions taken in national capitals or regional centers of government. In the 1930s, for example, sharecroppers and tenant farmers across the South—families like those immortalized in James Agee's prose and Walker Evans's photographs in *Let Us Now Praise Famous Men* (1941)—were often driven off the land and forced deeper into poverty by New Deal agricultural policies that paid large planters handsomely to take their acreage out of production. This of course was not a conscious goal of the New Dealers, but it was the result at the grassroots level. For historians, the familiar aphorism of the late Massachusetts representative Thomas P. (Tip) O'Neill, "All politics is local," has a resonance perhaps even broader than he intended.

In nearly every field of historical inquiry, in short, the past generation has seen a broadening of perspective, a movement beyond the narrower preoccupations of earlier times. Diplomatic historians, too, are responding to the intellectual currents that have influenced the profession as a whole.

So is all diplomatic history local? In a limited but powerful sense, yes. Just as other fields of history are taking into account the local and grassroots sources and consequences of the processes they study, so diplomatic historians are becoming more aware of how illuminating this perspective can be. By the same token, practitioners of local history can find that their work gains depth and significance as they factor in the impact of global realities that have traditionally been considered the domain of diplomatic historians. This volume, and the Yale conference from which it emerged, bear witness to this evolving reconceptualization of the field and its parameters.

Of course, some scholars will continue to practice diplomatic history in its more familiar and traditional form, and this is as it should be. We still need to know the inner histories of the negotiating strategies, hidden agendas, and personal affinities and animosities of the politicians, diplomats, and power brokers who maneuver behind closed doors as nations continue their incessant jostling for power and wealth. And we certainly continue to need historians who can shed light on the covert ways influential corporate lobbies and other interest groups help shape the foreign policy of the United States and other nations.

But we are increasingly coming to realize that diplomacy is not simply a hermetic "Great Game"—the term Rudyard Kipling used to characterize the nineteenth-century struggle of Imperial Britain and Czarist Russia for dominance in Central Asia. The consequences of diplomacy for real human beings, living in real communities, lie at the heart of what diplomatic history must be about. Fortunately, this is not a zero-sum situation. Closer attention to the local impact of diplomacy need not be at the expense of the more traditional top-down approaches that continue to be of great value. Quite the contrary: A heightened sensitivity to local effects and implications can enrich and deepen the macro-level analysis of foreign relations, adding complexity and human texture to the enterprise.

The diverse and illuminating chapters that follow illustrate the promise of this new perspective for diplomatic history. Indeed, this book represents an important contribution to ongoing debates about the nature of historical scholarship. As such, it merits close attention and reflection, not only for the fascinating specificity of the stories that unfold about the local and regional impact of Cold War diplomacy and policy initiatives but also for the new approach and perspective that these chapters represent.

Acknowledgments

This book is the product of a 2003 conference at Yale University, cohosted by International Security Studies at Yale and the Cold War International History Project of the Woodrow Wilson International Center for Scholars. Our hearty thanks go to these institutions and to the people who make them valuable assets for scholars interested in strategy and in the superpower conflict. In particular, thanks must go to Ted Bromund, Ann Carter-Drier, John Lewis Gaddis, Paul Kennedy, Minh Luong, and Monica Ward of International Security Studies, and to Mircea Munteanu and Christian Ostermann of the Cold War International History Project. Joseph Brinley of the Woodrow Wilson Center Press never wavered in his support for this project through its varied stages, the last of which were ably directed by Yamile Kahn. Alfred Imhoff provided the copyediting, and Rose Williams of the Bush School of Government and Public Service at Texas A&M University aided immeasurably with logistical support. Andrew Preston and Thomas Zeiler provided invaluable comments on the entire manuscript, and on the introduction in particular. Special thanks must go to Katherine Carté Engel, whose patience and understanding of this project, cultivated over countless hours, exceed all.

Local Consequences of the Global Cold War

Introduction: On Writing the Local within Diplomatic History—Trends, Historiography, Purpose

Jeffrey A. Engel and Katherine Carté Engel

Jake Holman sat alone, with a bullet in his chest. He was thousands of miles from home, a troubled Midwestern kid who had joined the Navy to escape a run-in with the law. Now, years later, he found himself embroiled in a Chinese revolution he understood little and cared about even less. And he was about to die, alone in the dark, with blood staining his crisp white uniform. He never even saw his assailants. They remain unseen and unknown, their well-aimed rifle hidden in the twilight shadows. He does not know why the bullet landed in his chest. He does not even know what broad force demanded his seemingly senseless sacrifice. "What happened?" he yells with his last breath. "What the hell happened?"

It is a poignant question, punctuated by the crack of a second bullet that ends Holman's pain and wonder. Asked by the actor Steve McQueen in the penultimate scene of Robert Wise's classic 1966 film *The Sand Pebbles,* it vividly demonstrates the way global affairs can wash over a single life.[1] International relations have consequences, Holman's slumping corpse reminds us, far from the stirring words of leaders or the drone of musty documents. Yet his death—had it not, of course, been fictional—would have merited hardly a footnote in most traditional diplomatic histories of China's tumultuous journey from colony to independence. It would have hardly mattered in the annals of history and would hardly have been remembered. Yet undoubtedly, the life that was not even a footnote to most mattered tremendously to him.

With the untold stories of the innumerable real-life Jake Holmans of the world in mind, the chapters that follow turn the lens of historical inquiry away from the policymakers and pundits whose exploits and words traditionally fill the histories of great power struggles, turning attention instead to the consequences of international diplomacy on regional, local, and human levels. Superficially, this would not appear a difficult task. It is considered a truism today that international relations affect lives. One need look no further than the growing globalist literature outlining the transformational power of transnational business or ideas, or to the activists' cry to "think globally, act locally," to appreciate the pervasiveness of the notion that international relations reach far beyond national borders, touching lives and communities in every city, region, and small village around the entire globe. Citizens and scholars alike recognize the penetrating power of globalism without question and therefore presume that documenting this impact would be an easy task. Yet throughout most of the last century (and surely even earlier), those scholars charged with chronicling international events for posterity—diplomatic and international historians, especially—have generally failed to demonstrate this nearly universally accepted idea in an explicit manner. Similarly, international relations scholars have more generally presumed the impact of foreign affairs rather than documenting that impact.

Recent generations of historians have worked hard to remedy this omission by demonstrating diplomacy's intrinsic links to culture, politics, and domestic concerns. Happily, the seemingly age-old criticism of diplomatic history as little more than a chronicle of "what one clerk said to another" is no longer valid after the intellectual revolution of the past generation, which transformed diplomatic history into one of the discipline's most innovative and methodologically exciting subfields. Much of this new work, however, emphasizes influences on international affairs, rather than the reverse: the impact of international affairs on people. Even among the most avante garde diplomatic historians, there remains a generally unquestioned focus on explaining how and why foreign policies developed. This is primarily done by tracking the domestic and international forces that influenced policy formation, to determine not only what international policies states chose (or ignored) but also why. This is as it should be. Without understanding the "how" and "why" of policies and events as a foundation for any diplomatic history, without this first building block, our understanding of the past would quickly crumble.

Yet there are other questions to ask as well, such as that posed and answered by the authors of the following chapters: How did those same international events alter lives back home and across the globe? How did policies formed in Washington or Moscow—policies shaped by domestic forces, culture, technology, and the like—affect lives ten thousand miles away, or just down the street, from the policymaker's office? Diplomatic history as a field has made great strides over the past generation. What it still requires despite this progress—where we think it should move in the years to come if it wishes to remain relevant in this new century's omnipresent debates on globalism—is further recognition not only that domestic forces affect international relations but also documentation of the reverse: that foreign affairs and geopolitics affect communities and lives as much as the other way round. In short, by focusing predominantly on policy formation, even though that is the necessary first step in our discipline's intellectual process, we have too frequently forgotten the Jake Holmans of the world. The chapters in this volume suggest pathways to recover such stories.[2]

Beyond illuminating heretofore unexplored tales from the Cold War, this book offers a call to our colleagues to consider explicitly and formally that which we implicitly believe to be true: that foreign affairs affect people, regions, and communities, three different perspectives here referred to by the short-hand term "local." The book reflects a process that began in April 2003, when a group of Cold War scholars—drawn from a variety of disciplines, though primarily trained as historians—gathered at Yale University to consider the topic they knew best in a wholly new light. They were asked to go a step further than their disciplines normally require by illuminating not only the words of leaders or the workings of policy but also the real-world consequences of those words and policies. The eleven chapters that make up this book are the result. Taken individually, each offers a new view of one slice of Cold War life. Collectively, they tell us something far more important: that the Cold War manifested itself in every facet of life, in industrial and developing nations alike, East and West, urban and rural, on the periphery of the international system and throughout every stratum and region of the superpowers themselves.[3]

The chapters of this volume do not represent either traditional diplomatic history or community history. They seek to combine the two by linking local events with international narratives. In this effort, the authors contribute to a long conversation among scholars about how to conceive, research, and chronicle some of history's most dramatic moments.[4] Indeed, historians from other fields have begun to best their diplomatist colleagues in demonstrating the tangible ways international affairs and globalization have affected individual lives.[5] So too have novelists and filmmakers. This introduction to the present volume investigates this past conversation, exploring how writers (historians and otherwise) have combined the local and the international, alongside a tracing of how diplomatic historians as a group have evolved over time in their ability and inclination to incorporate local actors into their own work. Its thesis is that the primary result of this evolution has been to broaden the range and number of actors studied who influence policy, without necessarily looking at policy's consequences. The chapters that follow try to remedy this omission.

This introduction will primarily be of use for those readers who want an overview of the field's own history. Many international scholars already know this story, its literature, and its main actors. Having heard our call to action, they may wish to jump directly to chapter 1. For those readers new to the field, or for those fascinated by the growth of historical study, we suggest what the contributors to this collection were asked to consider: that diplomatic historians must now reverse the traditional equation used to understand international affairs, demonstrating not only how domestic forces affected international policies but also how international affairs altered a larger range and number of lives. It might well be argued that we ask of our colleagues an unfair burden—that it is hard enough to discover why policies were made, without simultaneously being forced to consider their human impact. We plead no contest to this charge, because even if we ask the impossible, the intellectual act of posing this question might help historians stop and ponder, if only for a moment, the human consequences of the policies they study. The very act of asking such questions, in other words, might produce a different final answer. As a result, historians who pose such questions of themselves and of their work might prove that much more sensitive to the consequences of diplomacy. If we as diplomatic historians hope to remain pertinent in the increasingly frenetic marketplace of ideas in this globalized twenty-first century, we must retain this sensitivity and heightened awareness.

A Rationale for Studying Local Effects

Writers and scholars outside the traditional confines of diplomatic history have not been reticent in examining the local effects of international affairs. Many pieces of literature pluck a single soul from the stream of history, highlighting the impact of global affairs upon a solitary life or community. The searing experience of war offers a typical forum. Tim O'Brien's Vietnam novels, to cite one of innumerable examples, reveal lives permanently affected by a brutal conflict few combatants or their families could ever truly comprehend even while in its midst.[6] William Faulkner did the same for a whole region in the aftermath of defeat, shame, and reconstruction, whereas George Orwell's *1984* previewed a nation's fate amid a perpetual war, when individuals faced global forces well beyond their control or even comprehension.[7] Indeed, Orwell showed the human effects of policies explicitly designed to root out individuality itself. No single person could withstand the weight of global history if society went off the wrong track, he argued, for the weight of the state when brought to bear on a single individual was crushing and insurmountable—no single person, that is, who resided at the bottom of society's social hierarchy.[8] Those at the top, however, had the power to affect lives by the millions. "Personality made a difference," Martin Amis argued in his recent study of Joseph Stalin and the Soviet state. "In Stalin's case, the difference was an Andes of dead bodies."[9]

Novelists and essayists have thus long modeled the local impact of diplomacy, drawing conclusions about the human soul, as in the case of Amis's work, that no academic would easily publish given the lack of quantifiable provability. The social scientific method, in this case, obscures examination of terror, and of hope. In cases such as Chinua Achebe's *Things Fall Apart* (1959) and Boris Pasternak's *Dr. Zhivago* (1957), novelists have explicitly placed individuals at the center of an international system most scholars would rather quantify, schematize, or in some other way dehumanize so that they could approach it scientifically. Novelists are therefore more insightful into matters of the soul, because their burden of proof is far lower. Could Amis *prove* that Stalin's effect on Soviet history was a mountain of corpses? Would another leader have killed more, or perhaps less? Such conclusions may be moot or they may be vital; but however important, they are impossible to know with absolute certainty.[10]

Writers of literature in this sense wield an imposing advantage over academics, one that provides clear insight into the local impact of global affairs. Fiction writers and historically minded essayists delving into the past, whose numbers are far too vast to count, are free to highlight the way macro forces affect individuals; but academics who specialize in the very same topics (war, state power, etc.) have largely tended to focus on how those same macro forces combine to shape not individual lives but rather world-historical trends. World-systems analysis offers one example. Its theoretical construct—developed initially by sociologists in the late 1970s and popular with diplomatic historians over the next decade—removed individuals from its analysis of the global structures of core and periphery.[11] In a similar way, international relations theorists of all stripes (defensive and offensive realists, structuralists, etc.) have postulated as a starting point for further analysis that states will act with predictable and specifically defined self-interest regardless of individual leadership. Implicit in their arguments of international power and motive is the idea that policymakers charged with guiding a state through the international system's treacherous waters inherit a state's specific status and rank within the international hierarchy. Because all states will strive to improve their lot whatever their current or former place, improving their security and enhancing their prosperity, such realist and world-systems scholars equally argue, policymakers will act similarly given the same parameters. Human contingency—indeed, human personality—matters less in such a view to explain how and why states act than do quantifiable structural forces.

Scholars in the realist tradition, which includes both diplomatic historians and international relations theorists, operate with the same basic assumptions of policymaker rationality. Writing from what may be considered the opposite side of the academic spectrum, scholars fascinated (and persuaded) by culture and ideology's influence on decisionmaking and policy formation also presume a deterministic understanding of how their subjects act.[12] Though frequently on opposite sides of the political spectrum as well, these two groups, realists and those who emphasize ideology, share a vital if too frequently overlooked connection: a basic faith that circumstance dictates action. For realists, this is the presumption of stated values (security chief among them); for ideologists, it is the presumption of unstated values (of race, gender, etc.) so deeply embedded in a policymaker's psyche as to be unrealized and unexplored.[13] Realists own up to and even extol this presumption (and implicitly devalue those who think otherwise). As Christopher Layne has argued in a recent book, "Because the world is a competitive, potentially dangerous place, realists believe that the most basic goal of great powers is to gain security, and thus to ensure their survival."[14] In this framework, survival demands hard policies, made of tangible and quantifiable goods like steel, iron, and oil; and ideas and ideology are seen as softer qualities. Policymakers (and scholars) concerned with what Joseph Nye has called the "soft power" of culture and media and values are, to most realists, powerful in times of peace but ripe for the picking at the point of a sword.[15] Ironically, owing to their own presumption of rationality, American policymakers as a group (and as intellectual collective) have traditionally rejected the very notion that they are driven by a common ideology. These policymakers have argued that American policies are merely practical and logical in a way that those of their foreign counterparts are not. Thinking in ideological rather than purely "logical" terms, to steal a phrase from Anders Stephanson, is "always something the other guy does."[16] A slew of historians have made a good living demonstrating how this very claim itself—that American strategists have no collective ideology—suggests little more than the depth of their shared presumptions.

For our purposes, the key fact in this discussion so far is that all the major historiographic interpretations that have recently dominated scholarship on international affairs (world-systems, realism, ideology, and soft-power analysis) diminish the focus on individual responsibility for policy in favor of using a wide-angle lens to discern how policies are formed and change over time.

More to the point, none of these interpretations focuses primarily on policy outcomes, or what we might term the impact of diplomacy. None emphasizes first and foremost the economic, social, environmental, or individual impact of particular policies to explain why states and leaders choose those policies. The reasons for this focus on policy development over consequences are sound and even understandable. First, discerning the how and why of policies is, as mentioned above, the bread and butter of diplomatic history, and the necessary first step for any study. But there is a second reason for the traditional emphasis on policy formation over policy impact: The former is methodologically in line with the traditional historian's art, which favors an analysis of broad structural forces over the endless examination of unpredictable contingencies. When the looking glass is focused too closely, historians believe, the myriad contingencies and accidents of life can interfere with the scholar's perception of clear causality. Looking through a magnifying glass helps one understand the lives of the protozoa within a single drop, but it does not reveal the depth or volume of the water.

Thus—and this is at the heart of the matter—scholars of international affairs have an understandable tendency to depersonalize macrohistorical forces as a necessary precondition to writing effective history or comprehending the international system. Humans and their unique life stories are unpredictable at best, and historical narratives based only on such narrow grounds frequently appear haphazard by their very nature. As E. H. Carr, a student of foreign affairs, put it in his durable (and oft-cited) essay on the field's methodology, historians "distinguish rational and accidental causes." Though the former "lead to fruitful generalizations," the latter "teach no lessons and lead to no conclusions."[17] Most historians prefer the longer and broader view, the practiced orchestra rather than the jazz solo. Even the famed "splitters" and "lumpers" of historians, to use John Lewis Gaddis's revealing typology for the two basic types of historians, share the desire to find pattern amid the randomness because, as Carr instructs, to catalogue accidental causes is to be a mere chronicler more than a scholar.[18]

Patterns of Diplomatic Historiography

Today's historians typically eschew the search for the type of historical laws that captivated predecessors such as Henry Adams more than a century ago and that formed the basis of Carr's training. Yet the enduring scholarly tendency to favor structural analyses over accidental causes—and to favor explorations of policy formation over impact—can be traced to the broader way in which diplomatic historians have traditionally understood their field, beginning with their two greatest influences before 1900, Leopold von Ranke and Karl Marx.[19]

Von Ranke advised a generation of historians on the virtue of detached analysis under the ideal "wie es eigentlich gewesen"—in the modern vernacular, to "tell it like it was."[20] The historian should be without intellectual vice, he ordered his students, and go no further than the documents lead. His work considered relations between nation-states and the ways leaders considered the European balance of power. His analysis broke new ground and brought forth a new methodological focus on documents and archival sources (more on this just below), yet it remained at the national level. In his writings, states maneuvered like so many crashing icebergs directed by the currents of their leaders.[21] Nations reacted. Leaders pondered. Diplomats strategized and generals barked orders. But leaders and the borders they oversaw were the primary categories of analysis. Though Austria might gain or lose a province or two through affairs of war and peace, von Ranke—who influenced the first generation of diplomatic historians as arguably no other—paid little attention to how the movement of a borderline on a map affected those who lived on one side of it or the other. Having been educated in the aftermath of the Napoleonic cataclysm, he looked at societies that had been buffeted by the sweep of revolution across Europe yet had managed to survive largely intact. This structural consistency contributed to his ultimate intellectual conservatism, because despite generations of conflict, the institutions that had existed at the beginning of the century largely remained. Indeed, one might argue that diplomatic historians, even those who study ideas or interest groups, still regard the state as the sacrosanct unit of analysis. Anders Stephanson, for example, in 1998 began an extended commentary on sovereignty and space thus: "The sovereign state is the classical locus of diplomatic history, indeed its very condition of possibility. States conduct policy and diplomacy toward other, similarly territorialized entities in the name of sovereignty, without which there would be no domain of 'international relations' as we know it."[22] In a reflection of Von Ranke's influence (even as historians have moved beyond his methodologies), Stephanson does not challenge this statement throughout his essay; the state as a unit of analysis—as "the" unit of analysis—is taken as an unquestioned truth of the field.

Karl Marx also influenced later diplomatic historians, less through his ideological view than for the way he perceived of structural categories and conflict within European society. Writing during a period of social revolution that transcended borders only to be crushed by traditional centers of power, he explored the transnational proletariat but underestimated or seemed unimpressed by national distinctions within that theoretical body. He considered foreign affairs an outgrowth of class struggle within a society, and thus he stands as an intellectual godfather to any diplomatic historian captivated by the domestic drivers of foreign policy.[23] In his view, nation-states were details—constructed means of distributing power by and for the ruling elite. Because he self-consciously disapproved of traditional borders in his concern to show how international relations diffused or inflamed the transnational class struggle, he did not stop to consider why international relations diffused or inflamed classes within a specific society in a specific way. Classes linked arms beyond borders, he argued; thus it was not only unnecessary but also imprudent to focus on one locality within one nation when what mattered were the connections of class and economic interest between them all.

Both von Ranke and Marx were products of their time (as are we all), and all subsequent diplomatic historians have been influenced at least to a degree by this pair. What makes these two particularly important to consider in the context of this book is that despite their broad influence on the way modern historians understand international affairs, neither explored the way transnational forces might alter lives within or on the other side of a border. Therefore, it should come as no surprise that diplomatic history in its modern inception has focused more on the designers and perpetrators of policies than on those affected by them. Von Ranke and his followers sought a more scientific history, but what they wrote was ultimately a state-based story bounded by the narrow stretch of their sources. Ministers wrote memos to be preserved in archives; peasants did not. Individuals who made policy consequently rose to the fore of their narratives. Later historians have worked hard to broaden their sources and thus to incorporate new and previously unheard voices from the past. Yet the same types of state documents that fascinated Von Ranke's disciples remain the bedrock sources for today's diplomatic historians. Diplomatic historians may take some solace in their traditional focus on states, leaders, and transnational movements, even as they strive to incorporate the stories of individuals and localities within borders, because in doing so they are only standing on the shoulders of the first giants in their field.

The nineteenth-century Teutonic contribution to the field embodied by both Von Ranke and Marx—epitomized, again, in the former's phrase "wie es eigentlich gewesen"—was in fact an epistemological revolution wrought less by brash conceptualization than by unprecedented access to documents. A desire to understand the past not by trusting in the ex post facto explanations of leaders but rather by investigating the words they wrote and uttered at the time (and thus by denying the authors of those texts the sole right to interpret events) drove academic history's modern development. Paradoxically, however, diplomatic historians would be among the most laggard within the field of history to fully learn this lesson. When American scholars trained in Henry Baxter Adams's seminar at Johns Hopkins University at the close of the nineteenth century gained access to local records, for example—Adams having been trained in the dispassionate German style—they moved the field's attention from the highest levels of state power toward studies of power well below the state level. Adams's disciples, who included both Frederick Jackson Turner and Woodrow Wilson, exponentially broadened the range of acceptable topics within the field. Historians in subsequent generations made even greater strides in expanding their source base, and thereby increased their own range of topics and began the process of further specialization within the field of history. Diplomatic historians, however, as one such specialization, remained for the first decades of the twentieth century wedded to their traditional sources produced by elite and state-based actors. They thus began diverging from their colleagues, while other subfields dedicated to investigating social forces within society were strengthened by a steady diet of innovative materials. It was thus up to historians outside the subfield of diplomatic history to first draw attention to the local consequences of international affairs. Their sources revealed what diplomatists never thought to explore.

Broadly speaking, diplomatists failed to be influenced by the *Annales* school, named after the journal in which their work was published and first popularized in France following World War I, whose methodological approach shaped the field of academic history during the middle decades of the twentieth century (and beyond).[24] Writing amid a French society still convulsing from the loss of a better part of a generation, and further from Europe's brush with societal suicide, Marc Bloch and Lucien Febvre led a movement away from traditional political and diplomatic history in favor of what they called a "wider and more human history."[25] They sought society's structures, distinct from the structures of the international system later championed by world-systems analysis, and they tried to uncover and place the deep currents of change within the ocean of time. They rejected the waves and wind-peaks of events on the surface that so often occupied their colleagues (especially political and diplomatic historians) as just so much superficial noise. What one man (even one as clearly powerful and influential as Napoleon) did or said mattered less in this context than how French peasants lived, worked, and died. From their insight eventually grew a series of influential movements—French existentialism most proximally, but also a series of movements within the ranks of academic historians. The current influences of social and cultural history popular among contemporary historians (where the state and leaders are deemphasized in favor of "history from below") owe an intellectual debt to the *An-*

nales school, as do those who emphasize the omnipresent cultural milieu, such as the postmodernists who follow in the footsteps of Michael Foucault.[26]

Though separated by multiple generations, the chapters in the present volume are in conversation with the members of the *Annales* school for the very reasons that most diplomatic historians are not: Because the *Annales* school's engagement with history below the upper strata of society provides a model diplomatic historians might follow. To understand why, one must first appreciate that just as Marx and von Ranke were products of their time, so too were Bloch and Febvre. Their desire to deemphasize passing events (including individuals) as noise within the system can be understood at least in part as emblematic of their nation's desire to put aside the traumas of the recent past and of sacrifices that no human could comprehend or justify. They sought to make sense of such a societal spasm of pain by effectively ignoring moments of crisis and sacrifice in favor of longer durations of analysis. If everyone within sight will be long dead before the forces of history have changed, then it matters somewhat less that a generation of their countrymen lost its flower and purpose in useless charges across crater-scarred fields. The way we all live, the evolution of our *mentalité* across centuries, matters more than the awful moments when so many died. After World War I, the *Annales* scholars strove to answer the question that would come to occupy post—World War II historians of Europe, that of an individual's responsibility in an age of collective mass movements, by sweeping the actions of statesmen and peasants alike into the wider current of time. There were simply too many Jake Holmans to catalogue otherwise. The deaths of so many Holmans could not be explained one by one; but perhaps their collective lives, viewed as a whole, might have meaning.

The *Annales* scholars who first came to prominence after the Great War found their best voice after yet another societal flirtation with death a generation later. Writing while his native France roiled in the aftermath of World War II, Fernand Braudel influenced social history as has arguably no one before or since, largely by removing individual action from his understanding of the past.[27] This was a conscious act. Having come of age in the aftermath of World War I, and having been held captive by occupying German forces during World War II, Braudel in the years that followed 1945 transformed his prewar investigation of Philip II of Spain's Mediterranean policy into a broader exploration of the region as a whole. Philip's role in determining the region's history and evolution decreased in Braudel's postwar writing even as larger structural forces came to the fore. Writing later of the war's influence, he reconstructed a vision of the historian so overwhelmed by events as to be obscured to the point of insight. Clarity, in other words, came from blocking out the petty details of human life in favor of its broader strokes. "Rejecting events and the time in which events take place was a way of placing oneself to one side, sheltered, so as to get some sort of perspective," he wrote, "to be able to evaluate them better, and not wholly to believe in them. To go from the short time span, to one less short, and then to the long view (which, if it exists, must surely be the wise person's time span); and having got there, to think about everything afresh and to reconstruct everything around one: a historian could hardly not be tempted by such a prospect."[28] Thus did Braudel reject the sensory overload and inherent emotionality of detail, as a means of both alleviating cognitive dissonance and explaining larger structural trends. His solution to the problem of how to elucidate transnational forces while burdened by individual causality was to emphasize the former by explicitly deleting the latter. Everything, in this sense, was consequence.

The *Annales* scholars did not influence diplomatic historians, especially in the United States, as much as they did other segments of the field. Not only did singular events decrease in a Braudelian retelling—events and crises being the basic narrative of diplomatic tales—but the *Annales* scholars also deemphasized the powerful individuals who so often comprise a diplomatist's cast of characters. Ultimately, the rise and fall of nations themselves became mere footnotes for Febvre, who termed traditional historians a "laborious but intellectually lazy cult of the fact," when compared with the grander forces of history worth studying.[29] Braudel eliminated the state explicitly in his later writings, and thus he furthered the separation between those who would study annalistic structure from those who studied diplomacy. Without individuals, singular events, and even states, diplomatic historians had little to offer these new historical schools.

Diplomatic History in the Wake of World War II

Diplomatic history was not, of course, frozen in a mid-nineteenth-century mold as new influences swept across the twentieth-century historical landscape, and even this subfield so dedicated to high policy moved well beyond the state after 1945. Transnational history is the field's latest wave, whose practitioners combine the histories (and unique cultures and stories) of as many different states as possible to explain their reasons for conflict or cooperation. The more states studied (and by implication, the more archives visited and languages employed), the more holistic the picture of the past and, presumably, the better the project.[30] This important approach, in vogue at the time of this writing, was in fact advocated (and practiced) by predecessors. Harvard's Ernest May in particular purposefully placed American diplomacy in an international context through his multiarchival work, which was composed just as Braudel was clearing his powerful historical voice. May's influential *The World War and American Isolation, 1914–1917* (1959) highlighted the influence of domestic affairs on international policies, but it did so with an explicitly multinational focus. So too did Richard Leopold frequently chastise his fellow diplomatic historians of the late 1940s for their failure to employ multiple archives and languages.[31] Akira Iriye took up the mantle of transnational advocate in subsequent decades with his focus on the multinational diplomacy before and during World War II in Asia, beginning with *Across the Pacific: An Inner History of American–East Asian Relations* (1967), and then more fully in the purposefully transnational *Power and Culture: the Japanese-American War* (1981).[32]

The list of international history's early advocates is as long as it is distinguished. Each scholar was determined to broaden the number of national perspectives in his or her work, and thus to invoke new means of determining the reasons for state conflict and policy formation. Chief among them is Princeton's Arno J. Mayer, whose *Political Origins of the New Diplomacy* (1959) and *The Politics and Diplomacy of Peacemaking* (1968) offered explicitly transnational histories focused on how domestic pressure groups shaped World War I diplomacy.[33] Given his attention to the formation of diplomacy, it is not surprising (and hardly a justifiable critique) that the way diplomacy subsequently and in turn altered domestic affairs received less attention. Mayer's magisterial work helped set the tone for multinational studies during the tensest years of the Cold War and after. Recent examples of international history at its finest are Frederick Logevall's *Choosing War* (1999), which examined the Americanization of the Vietnam War as viewed from a host of national capitals, and Jeremi Suri's *Power and Protest: Global Revolution and the Rise of Détente* (2003), which posits that national protest movements of the late 1960s forced international policymakers to collaborate in diffusing Cold War tensions.[34] To say that what these historians have accomplished is wholly new would be incorrect; it is better to place each in a broad postwar tradition of international historians by noting that that each has taken the international historian's call to arms far beyond that of their peers.

These international historians taught that domestic affairs altered foreign policy through a process that seemed to replicate across borders, a view that would have been readily accepted by Thomas Bailey—one of the country's leading pre–Cold War diplomatic historians, the author of the widely used textbook *A Diplomatic History of the American People,* and an influence on a generation of students. It was his work on public opinion's effect on diplomacy, however—most notably in his provocative book *The Man in the Street*

(1948)—that brought his greatest fame and proffered his greatest method-ological influence.[35] Through the broad use of newspaper accounts, opinion surveys, and records from pressure groups, he echoed Braudel's critique of historians as mere chroniclers and presented an alternative to what he termed "merely presenting digests of official correspondence." He argued instead that "diplomatic affairs cannot be conducted in a vacuum . . . since they cannot be isolated from political, economic, and social developments."[36] His example of how domestic forces altered foreign policies, and his demand that the list of factors influencing high policy be broadened beyond mere diplomatic correspondence, was well learned by subsequent generations. That his work focused less on the way foreign policies in turn affected these groups, however—or, in our parlance, that he focused more on policy formation than on the consequences of diplomacy—demonstrates yet again a mental approach to the study of international relations that went from the local to the national to the international, not the other way round.

Transnational history has appeal and purpose, particularly so in this age of globalism. Yet Braudel rejected this approach well before May, Mayer, or Iriye had fully articulated it. As Kelly Mulroney has recently argued, from the first to the second edition of *La Méditerranée,* Braudel "developed an approach that sought not only to avoid the classic pitfalls of traditional political and diplomatic history, but also advanced a view fundamentally denying the notion that universal history is merely a combination of multiple national histories." Without states or individuals, and then without even the prospect of satisfying the *Anna*listic *mentalité* by building global history through a concerted combination of national tales, diplomatic historians had no place in Braudel's new landscape of postwar historical studies. In this light, it appears that just as diplomatic historians remained immune to the full influence of the *Annales* school, that school's followers shunned diplomatists' efforts to renovate their field as well.[37]

American diplomatic historians therefore diverged from their colleagues within the profession largely at the very postwar moment they sought to broaden (and thus make more relevant) their own methodological landscape of transnational or international history. Social, cultural, and political historians, catalyzed by the perception of broad change brought on by the tumultuous 1960s, used local and regional studies to examine the basic structures of society: family, life cycle, material environment, and economic organization, as well as a host of other subjects. Such studies brought heretofore unknown actors to the fore for the sake of drawing larger historical lessons, and often for the purpose of giving voice to the previously unheard or oppressed. This focused work arguably reached its zenith among the historians of colonial North

America, where easy access to deep records ensured that by the late 1970s there were, anecdotally at least, more dissertations written on colonial Massachusetts than immigrants to the colony in its first years.[38] The 1980s subsequently saw particular emphasis by historians of race and civil rights in more contemporary eras eager to compose "histories from below," wherein the focus moved from American society's power elite to the disenfranchised. Social histories of the South, for example, and especially of African American and multiracial communities within that region, were the result. Such works frequently showed communities buffeted by national or transnational forces, but they did little to explain the policymaking at the elite level that helped spawn those forces. They showed, obliquely, the local impact of world affairs, but it was not considered necessary to first consider how and why transnational forces had been formed.

During social history's Cold War development, diplomatic historians influenced by the realist writers George Kennan and Hans Morgenthau turned away from studies of those beneath the radar in favor of an explicit focus on elites. Indeed, the initial impulse toward international history detailed above broadened the number of national actors and of nations under review but did not necessarily increase the breadth and range of historical voices discussed within each country. Kennan in particular brought his impressive international experience to bear in *American Diplomacy, 1900–1950* (1951), which criticized the influence of public opinion on American policymakers and their ensuing embrace of "the legalistic-moralistic approach to international problems," as an effort to appease public whims.[39] The first is our concern here. Kennan loathed the public, calling popular understanding of foreign affairs "erratic" and "subjective," and he worried most of all that educated policymakers would play to popular passions rather than to the detached analysis that should be their focus.[40] This concern was not new with Kennan among American thinkers, of course. Fear of popular influence on policymaking occupied the authors of the Federalist Papers during the earliest years of the American republic, and made Walter Lippmann a favored analyst of the policymaking elite through five decades of the twentieth century.[41] Yet it was Kennan—himself the author of so many American policies during the early Cold War, and with his fear of popular vicissitudes—who was among the greatest influences on the writing of diplomatic history, despite his lack of formal training as a historian.

A generation of realist thinkers followed Kennan's lead in focusing on those at the pinnacle of the American power pyramid as the key to understanding policy formation. What resulted was nuanced work on decisionmaking processes and bureaucracies, but scant attention to the impact of decisions on domestic constituencies. Indeed, because realists explicitly feared undue public influence on foreign policy, implicit in their work is the idea that a good foreign policy would be little noticed by domestic interest groups. Only when something went wrong or, more cynically, only when elites fanned public emotions for the benefit of their own narrow interests would the public concern itself with international affairs.[42]

Realist writers thus largely avoided examining the local impact of foreign affairs, for two important reasons. First, they focused on the decisionmakers with every bit of the intensity that the *Annales* school devoted to discovering long durée structure. Second, they believed that too great a public influence on foreign affairs undermined the national interest. They cared about local concerns when they influenced foreign policy; but a good foreign policy, in their view, would go unnoticed by localities. Thus, whereas realists might at times demonstrate the influence of interest groups or inflamed public passions (though rarely showing this influence in a good light), the arrow of causation always went from the bottom to the top, never the other way around. This aspect of realist thinking was taken up by postrevisionist synthesizers, especially John Lewis Gaddis, whose *The United States and the Origins of the Cold War* (1972) highlighted efforts by ethnic groups in America to influence the Franklin Roosevelt administration's European policies at the close of World War II. Whether these groups did or did not succeed was a prime question for Gaddis. Left less examined was foreign policy's effect upon them. Implicit as well (throughout Gaddis's writing, in fact) was the unstated though omnipresent idea that diplomacy's effect upon those people behind the Iron Curtain—those relatives and kin of the lobbying ethnic groups in America of his first study—was always negative and harmful. Life under communist tyranny was always worse than under democratic rule, Gaddis repeatedly argued. The local impact of diplomacy in this sense need not be examined, because historians should know, prima facie, that it was full of pain and misery.[43]

The most concerted intellectual response to the realist style of diplomatic history, the New Left (often termed "revisionist") school that developed during the 1950s and blossomed in the subsequent decade, agreed with Kennan and his disciples (including the postrevisionists) on one important point: that public interests could and did influence foreign policies. Whereas realists abhorred this influence, however, New Left writers embraced (though did not necessarily endorse) popular persuasion as guidepost for understanding American foreign policy. If those writing in the oft-termed Wisconsin tradition had one dominant trend—though its first generation of practitioners almost reflexively insist they do not—it was neither their willingness to critique traditional interpretations nor their emphasis on economic factors, though both were frequent conclusions.[44] Rather, what unified the members of this group was their belief that domestic forces not only influenced but wholly drove foreign policy. The search for markets that dominated their analysis was in fact a domestically inspired search for prosperity at home through policies abroad. Likewise, in their eyes Washington's seeming inexorable quest for order was a crusade for a business-friendly global environment. Walter LaFeber's *The New Empire* (1963) explained a half-century of American involvement in Latin America through the framework of policymakers seeking domestic peace through expanded economic influence abroad.[45] Another study developed in the same graduate seminar, Robert Freeman Smith's *The United States and Cuba: Business and Diplomacy, 1917–1960* (1961) demonstrated how domestic groups on the American mainland altered Cuban development, a point reinforced for the Caribbean broadly by David Healy's influential *U.S. Expansionism: The Imperialist Urge in the 1890s* (1970).[46]

Each of these University of Wisconsin graduates argued that domestic affairs drove foreign policy, a point whose influence and potential flaw appeared most tellingly in Thomas McCormick's *The China Market* (1967). McCormick argued that American policy toward China—or, as was often the case, American policy toward other Western powers over the penetration of China—could be explained largely as a reaction to fears of an impending domestic economic collapse. America produced more than could be consumed at home, or at least so its leaders believed. Their solution was not to curtail growth, which would lead to economic misery and dissent, but rather to secure new markets for American products abroad. The untapped China market was thus a natural source of attention. *The China Market*'s causal arrow moved from domestic American affairs to international policy.[47]

New Left revisionism changed diplomatic history more by reinterpreting the motives of elite actors and domestic interest groups than by broadening the range of its subjects. The movement was best encapsulated by its most controversial advocate, William Appleman Williams, whose pointed *The Tragedy of American Diplomacy* (1959) and more substantial *Contours of American History* (1961) not only illuminated the influence of domestic factors but also emphasized that the perception of domestic actors frequently drove policy as much as any provable reality.[48] Williams feared the consequence of American diplomacy in the abstract—the impending "tragedy" that the policies developed to sustain American democracy contained the seeds of its destruction—but he never moved past the abstract to examine the impact of policies at a local level. Yet again, policy formation more than its effect was his primary concern, even if caution for long-term macro consequences was his ultimate warning.[49]

Here the movement's Wisconsin roots shine through. Frederick Jackson Turner, one of the key founders of environmental and western history and a Madison professor for more than two decades at the turn of the twentieth century, clearly recognized the link between foreign and domestic affairs. As noted above, Turner was a product of Adams's Johns Hopkins seminar, though he achieved scholarly fame largely by rejecting his mentor's narrow approach in favor of writing history in the largest terms possible.[50] His was the famous "frontier thesis," positing that the existence of the frontier had fundamentally infused American democracy and society, and that "with its going has closed the first period of American history."[51] His seminal book *The Frontier in American History* was profoundly influential. Even if most western historians discredit it today, evidence of its broad influence can be found among diplomatic historians (and within the *Annales* school as well, a rare honor for an American), especially for New Left writers who claim Turner as an intellectual forbearer. Yet from the perspective of the present volume, Turner was as typical as he was influential. He focused on the influence of domestic factors on American foreign policy. Loss of the country's long-standing outlet for products and human energy created "demands for a vigorous foreign policy, and for the extension of American influence" abroad. Foreign policy, in other words, was merely the outgrowth of domestic politics and perception.[52]

This argument that domestic affairs affect diplomacy now seems a truism, though it is in the nature of truisms to seem obvious in retrospect though radical when first proposed. Beginning with Turner's hypothesis, one can paint a grand swath through the entire study of foreign policy in the twentieth century, connecting the desire of historians to trace the domestic influences of diplomacy and the realist and New Left interpretations with the transnational work of international historians and the public opinion emphasis of Bailey. One can even draw this line back to von Ranke's concern for the diplomacy formed within each imperial court. Each generation accepted that domestic actors altered foreign policy, even if each constructed the circle of influential actors differently. Yet the arrow of the equation still went from domestic to international. Writing history in this way illuminated how and why foreign policies were formed, and it provided immeasurable space for historians to dicker over interpretations, methodologies, and ideology. But it left little room for detailing the consequences of diplomacy.

If the field as a whole has downplayed the consequences of diplomacy, in each generation scholars have offered just such a local focus, and their contributions—generally cast in broad, national terms—are important to this discussion. Influential writers from Charles Beard and Randolph Bourne in the twentieth century's first decades, to Williams in its middle and Michael Hogan and Aaron Friedberg in its last years, have either argued or noted the influence (often insidious) that foreign affairs can have on domestic society.[53] Their most frequent topic is war, hot or cold. Bourne feared that European-style nationalism catalyzed by American entry into World War I would warp American society in militaristic ways. Hogan and Friedberg highlighted this fear among the earliest Cold Warriors, showing that the "garrison" state was as much feared by conservatives like Dwight D. Eisenhower as was international communism. "If we let defense spending run wild, you get inflation, . . . then controls, . . . then a garrison state," Eisenhower fearfully prophesized, "and then we've lost the very values we were trying to defend."[54]

Beard proved the most influential (and most controversial) of historians working in this vein, though today he is more often remembered for his nuanced 1913 economic interpretation of the American Constitution.[55] He subsequently turned his pen to foreign affairs, with more mixed results.[56] His quixotic indictment of Franklin Roosevelt (as a warmonger, liar, and even as instigator of the Pearl Harbor attack) brought him into the crosshairs of conservative pundits and historians. What critics missed with their barbs, however, even when accurately dissecting the flawed specifics of his argument, was his unassailable fear that an aggressive American foreign policy could warp American society at home.[57] This was a line of argument subsequently picked up by Williams, whose *Tragedy of American Diplomacy* can be read as less an indictment of American foreign policy than as a siren-like lament for its unforeseen consequences. Important as this insight was and is, it too suffers from the diplomatic historian's most common omission. Even as Beard, Bourne, Williams, and the like wrote passionately of their fear of warped domestic institutions arising from foreign policy, none explicitly demonstrated what those domestic effects might be or had been in earlier periods.[58] However prescient, theirs was a theoretical argument. They did little to explicitly show how foreign affairs actually affected American lives, on the ground, in communities large and small.

Some who were clearly influenced by these three subsequently described the domestic social and political effects of a ramped-up Cold War foreign policy culture. Elaine Tyler May's influential *Homeward Bound: American Families in the Cold War* (1990) showed how Cold War conservatism, surely transformed by a need to protect the home front from communist influence and direct attack, made the post-1945 generation of parents a more socially conservative group than their parents. Likewise, Stephen J. Whitfield's *The Culture of the Cold War* (1991) noted the pervasive influence of Cold War thinking on American society far removed from the political wrangling of diplomats.[59] Perhaps the clearest examples of attempts to show the domestic impact of Cold War political culture came in the myriad of books written about Joseph McCarthy's red baiting during the paranoid first years of the superpower conflict. Richard M. Freeland's *The Truman Doctrine and the Origins of McCarthyism* (1974) went further than most in his documentation of the way the Harry Truman administration's foreign policies intertwined (to the detriment of civil liberties and civil political discourse, he argues) with domestic politics.[60] Lloyd Gardner's marvelously titled *Architects of Illusion* (1970) also showed how Truman's policymakers employed domestic fears of communism to their own political advantage (sewing dragon's seeds of the McCarthy era and the 1950s).[61] Yet even these superb examples of scholarship did not draw a causal link between foreign policies and specific domestic affairs—though Freeland arguably comes closest in this effort—because they instead showed the (vitally important) way in which the makers of foreign policy altered the domestic political landscape to ensure the safe passage of their international program. The grand culture of America society (politically, socially, and otherwise) was affected, but not so much by foreign policies per se as by the domestic politics of constructing foreign policy.

Perhaps not coincidentally, the revisionist historian who tried to link foreign policies and ensuing domestic events most explicitly, Frank Kofsky, was not a diplomatic historian by training. Nor, for that matter, was his work ultimately immune to the critique that it was more conspiracy theory than detached academic history. Indeed, Kofksy's *Harry S Truman and the War Scare of 1948* (1993) so embraced the moniker of "conspiracy" that he included a long afterword on the nature of conspiracies and their relation to historical analysis.[62] That he did not prove his case to the satisfaction of most historians is most likely because his conclusion—that Truman's White House orchestrated a war scare to scare money out of Congress—while not without merit, was too fantastic for most to believe. Yet it was also fundamentally about a dynamic—the domestic impact of diplomacy—that most diplomatic historians, as we have seen, are not eager to document or methodologically trained to consider.

Plan of the Book

The chapters of this book suggest several routes for considering the domestic impact of diplomacy, complementing the progressive growth of historical inquiry from states to elite policymakers to domestic constituencies and beyond. The chapters take the lesson gleaned from the revisionists and realists alike, that foreign affairs are frequently the product of national and domestic processes, and turn the equation on its head by explicitly locating the consequences of diplomacy. Each chapter sets out first the diplomacy and the international question at its heart. Each in this way offers the building block and foundation that we believe should be the first step in any diplomatic study. But each then goes a step further to demonstrate how diplomacy affected localities. This is a vital task in this new century. Both the proponents and critics of globalism agree that the pace of international change, and surely the expanse of international consciousness, have increased in recent decades. Communications advances alone ensure that the faces of those affected by foreign affairs on any one continent can be dissected nightly by viewers around the world. Thomas Friedman has recently argued that "the world is flat" and thus economically competitive—and intertwined—throughout.[63] Yet his spatial metaphor holds for our purposes as well. Water runs downhill, and diplomatic effects used to do so as well, with foreign affairs directed by elites altering the lives of citizens and subjects the world over. Those on top of the societal pyramid, in other words, directed and affected the lives of those beneath them more than the other way around. In a flat world, however, effects diffuse more broadly. All are affected by decisions made at the highest levels of power, yet dramatic increases in technology help level this playing field, so that domestic affairs and individuals throughout every stratum of society can now alter the international scene as never before. What this means is simple to state yet profound to consider: Local affairs are themselves no longer truly possible, at least not without recognition that locality itself, in an age of instantaneous communication and globalized identity, can know no definitive geographic bounds.

This volume shows how the Cold War was just such a global phenomenon, without real geographic bounds, in the sense that peoples the world over felt its impact. One might even state, without necessarily applying the emotional power this word typically carries, that all were victims of Cold War diplomacy as well. As Catherine Stock argues in chapter 9, nuclear weapons and the threat of global destruction have ensured that there is no nowhere anymore. There was no safe place to hide from the Cold War's reach. In the world that exists following the close of that conflict, global and local affairs remain inherently intertwined—and so too must diplomatic history.

Part I of the book focuses on daily lives. In chapter 1, Hiroshi Kitamura begins our rethinking of this process with his investigation of Japanese culture and cinema during the period of American occupation. He demonstrates the way American values were purposefully transmitted through film, and then consciously revised by their Japanese recipients, as a means of altering Japanese society to best fit American needs. In chapter 2, Jeremi Suri follows with a penetrating analysis of student life and consciousness in Berlin, the epicenter of the Cold War. His subjects altered their politics and activities almost daily based upon foreign affairs. In chapter 3, Thomas Borstelmann demonstrates how the ways of life in an entire region, in this case the American South, fundamentally changed with the Cold War's cultural and economic tides. Collectively, each of these chapters demonstrates how the Cold War, that global superpower affair, altered daily lives across continents.

The Cold War also affected whole regions, especially economically, as the next set of chapters shows. It was the era that spawned the term "military-industrial complex," and nothing so signified the Cold War coordination between government and commerce as the broad and lucrative aviation industry. Part II of the book explores the military impact of the military-industrial complex. As Richard Kirkendall demonstrates in chapter 4, this industry also came to define the entire Pacific Northwest, whose fate became intertwined with the fortunes of its largest employer, and America's largest single Cold War exporter, the Boeing Corporation. The history of the region simply cannot accurately be told without reference to this company and time. The same could be said of Los Angeles, which, as Michael Oden argues in chapter 5, was famous for Hollywood, but whose real engine of prosperity was aerospace and the defense industry. What Dwight D. Eisenhower famously termed the "military-industrial complex"—as a warning against the very incursions against individual liberty foretold by Beard and Williams and so many of the writers mentioned above—was the bread-and-butter of the Southern California economy. If California represented the golden American dream, therefore, as Oden shows, it was a dream forged in the very crucible of war and Cold War.

Indeed, aviation and the aerospace needs of the defense industry in particular dominated life throughout the territory of each superpower, and—by means of comparison with Kirkendall and Oden—in chapter 6 Anita Seth illuminates how Siberia's Novosibirsk was transformed during the Cold War from a sleepy river town into a world-class industrial zone. Whether in a command or a capitalist economy, in other words, the Cold War provided economic life and livelihoods. Preparation for the superpower war that never happened, and for the peripheral and proxy fights that did, put food on the table throughout the industrially developed world, making economic impact a visible symbol of the way superpower diplomacy affected localities.

Such dramatic infusions of state investment, and the industrial changes they wrought, frequently left a human and environmental mark. Part III explores the environmental costs. Practical matters dominated the discussion of the Cold War's impact on Scotland, as Alan Dobson and Charlie Whitham explain in chapter 7, where they trace the high diplomacy and local impact of London's decision to locate American missile submarines deep in the heart of Scotland.

In chapter 8, Arvid Nelson offers an assessment of the early Cold War environmental consequences of East German land policies, noting that politics (and frequently politics alone) drove land use techniques in this ideologically infused era. Policies formed for Cold War practicalities, in other words, created environmental hazards that few in East Germany had predicted, and that even fewer at the time cared to prevent. From the very mud of the loch to Whitehall, these two chapters show that Cold War diplomacy left its mark, and as long as isotopes decay in Scotland and soil continues to erode in Saxony, it will continue to do so.

Nuclear weaponry altered life on the American plains as well, as Catherine Stock shows in chapter 9. Life was never the same in the Dakotas after the U.S. Air Force and its thousands of missiles arrived. With these weapons of mass destruction came tens of thousands of soldiers and airmen, their dollars altering the plains as much as their roads, radios, and other improvements made twentieth-century life finally possible in a region long considered a laggard in American development. The New Deal may well have brought the Dakotas into the twentieth century (economically, at least); but the Cold War helped this region, arguably as far removed from the Soviet threat as any part of the United States, keep pace with the rest of the nation.

Part IV of the book explores the impact of superpower affairs in the developing world, in Angola according to Jeremy Ball in chapter 10, and in East Timor as demonstrated by Luís Nuno Rodrigues in chapter 11. Superpower diplomacy fell with full force on each of these developing regions. There can be no more stark examples of the local impact of diplomacy than the thousands whose lives were forever changed—and the thousands whose lives were lost—in lands far removed from Washington and Moscow. Lives on the Cold War's periphery, each author shows, became like so many chess pieces to leaders in each superpower capital. Indeed, it is perhaps here that the local effects of diplomacy offer some of their greatest lessons to scholars, by connecting the domestic histories (and historians) of one nation to the international history (and, likewise, historians) of another.

The local impact of diplomacy was everywhere during the Cold War. It influenced life throughout disparate American regions and in Siberia; in the heart of Berlin's most cosmopolitan zone and in the agricultural and forest zones of East Germany only miles away; and from the movie theaters of Tokyo to the movie studios of Los Angeles. Diplomatic historians have long known that domestic affairs, even local affairs, alter foreign policy. From their nineteenth-century origins through the divergent interpretive models of the twentieth century, scholars have shown well how policies are formed, expanding the cast of influential characters all the while. At this start of the twenty-first century, in an age of thinking globally but acting locally, this book shows the reverse as well.

Notes

1. Wise based his movie on Richard McKenna's 1962 novel of the same name. It was McKenna's only full-length novel. See *The Sand Pebbles* (Annapolis, 2000).

2. Historiographical surveys of American foreign relations abound. For a recent treatment, see Michael J. Hogan and Thomas Paterson, eds., *Explaining the History of American Foreign Relations* (New York: Cambridge University Press, 2004), esp. "Introduction," 1–9, and Frank Costigliola and Thomas G. Paterson, "Defining and Doing the History of United States Foreign Relations: A Primer," 10–34. Other useful surveys include Alexander DeConde, *American Diplomatic History in Transformation* (Washington, D.C.: American Historical Association, 1976); Charles Neu, "The Changing Interpretive Structure of American Foreign Policy," in *Twentieth-Century Foreign Policy,* ed. John Braeman, Robert Bremner, and David Brody (Columbus: Ohio State University Press, 1971); Thomas J. McCormick, "The State of American Diplomatic History," in *The State of American History,* ed. Herbert Bass (Chicago: Quadrangle Books, 1970) 119–40; Jerald A. Combs, *American Diplomatic History: Two Centuries of Changing Interpretations* (Berkeley: University of California Press, 1983); Michael J. Hogan, ed., *Paths to Power: The Historiography of American Foreign Relations to 1941* (New York: Cambridge University Press, 2000); and Michael J. Hogan, ed., *America in the World: The Historiography of American Foreign Relations since 1941* (New York: Cambridge University Press, 1995).

3. This was stated at the conference "Lives and Consequences: The Local Impact of the Cold War," sponsored by International Security Studies, Yale University, and the Cold War International History Project of the Woodrow Wilson International Center for Scholars, April 25–26, 2003.

4. Diplomatic historians have not been wholly ignorant of diplomacy's domestic and local effects, and this point will be reinforced in the text below; it is simply an avenue that demands greater attention. For useful examples—and this is hardly an exhaustive list—of the intermingling of international and local history, see Jessica Gienow-Hecht, *Transmission Impossible: American Journalism as Cultural Diplomacy in Postwar Germany, 1945–1955* (Baton Rouge: Louisiana State University Press, 1999); John Dower, *Embracing Defeat: Japan in the Wake of World War II* (New York, W. W. Norton, 2000); Petre Goedde, *GIs and Germans: Culture, Gender, and Foreign Relations, 1945–1949* (New Haven, Conn.: Yale University Press, 2003); and Elizabeth Cobbs Hoffman, *All You Need Is Love: The Peace Corps and the Spirit of the 1960s* (Cambridge, Mass.: Harvard University Press, 1998). Each demonstrates the effects of American policies on foreign (for the first three, subjugated) peoples, or as Hoffman described, they offer a "new diplomatic history" whose goal is at least in part to "do justice to the real life of a foreign people as they contemplated how to handle, resist, emulate, and manipulate the United States"; "Diplomatic History and the Meaning of Life: Toward a Global American History," *Diplomatic History* 21, no. 4 (Fall 1997): 499–518.

5. Some of the best work exploring diplomacy's local and human effects within

the United States comes from disciplines outside of traditional diplomatic history. See, e.g., Paul Boyer, *By the Bomb's Early Light: American Thought and Culture at the Dawn of the Cold War* (Chapel Hill: University of North Carolina Press, 1994); Elaine Tyler May, *Homeward Bound: American Families in the Cold War Era* (New York: Basic Books, 1990); and Mary Dudziak, *Cold War Civil Rights: Race and the Image of American Democracy* (Princeton, N.J.: Princeton University Press, 2002).

6. O'Brien's works are numerous—see, e.g., *The Things They Carried* (Boston: Hougton Mifflin, 1990); *If I Die in a Combat Zone: Box Me Up and Ship Me Home* (New York: Broadway Books, 1999); and *In the Lake of the Woods* (Boston: Houghton Mifflin, 1994).

7. The best example of diplomacy's localized effect in Faulkner's writing can be seen in *The Unvanquished* (1938), the only one of his novels to deal with historical memory in the midst of a conflict, rather than generations later.

8. For a recent treatment of Orwell's thinking in a globalized age, see Scott Lucas, *The Betrayal of Dissent: Beyond Orwell, Hitchens, and the New American Century* (London: Pluto Books, 2004).

9. Martin Amis, *Koba the Dread* (New York: Talk Miramax Books, 2002), 137.

10. Historians never tire of discussing the evolution of their progression and its methodological progressions (a point this chapter reinforces). For a recent treatment of the utility of scientific methodologies to historical practice, see John Lewis Gaddis, *The Landscape of History: How Historians Map the Past* (New York: Oxford University Press, 2002).

11. This literature is best described by Thomas J. McCormick, "World Systems," in *Explaining the History of American Foreign Relations,* ed. Hogan and Paterson, 149–62. Classic statements include Immanuel Wallerstein, *The Modern World System* (New York: Academic Press, 1974); and Fernand Braudel, *Afterthoughts on Material Civilization and Capitalism* (Baltimore: Johns Hopkins University Press, 1977). Braudel's thought is discussed at length in the text below.

12. Among the best of realist representations are E. H. Carr, *The Twenty Years' Crisis* (London: Macmillan, 1940); Hans J. Morgenthau, *Politics among Nations: The Struggle for Power and Peace* (New York: Random House, 1973); Norman A. Graebner, *America as a World Power: A Realist Appraisal from Wilson to Reagan* (Wilmington, Del.: Scholarly Resources, 1984); George F. Kennan, *American Diplomacy, 1900–1950* (Chicago: University of Chicago Press, 1951); Kenneth Waltz, *Theory of International Politics* (Boston: McGraw Hill, 1979); and John Mearsheimer, *The Tragedy of Great Power Politics* (New York: W. W. Norton, 2003). John Lamberton Harper, *American Machiavelli: Alexander Hamilton and the Origins of U.S. Foreign Policy* (New York: Cambridge University Press, 2004), discusses realism and American foreign policy at the country's founding. For a discussion of realism's utility to the historical profession, see Jerald A. Combs, "Norman A. Graebner and the Realist View of American Diplomatic History," *Diplomatic History* 11, no. 2 (Summer 1987): 251–64. Realism and Kennan's contributions are discussed at length in the text below.

13. A useful introduction to ideology and American foreign policy is Michael Hunt's aptly named *Ideology and U.S. Foreign Policy* (New Haven, Conn.: Yale University Press, 1988), and his "Ideology" in "A Roundtable: Explaining the History of American Foreign Relations," *Journal of American History* 77 (June 1990): 108–15.

14. Christopher Layne, *The Peace of Illusions: American Grand Strategy from 1940 to the Present* (Ithaca, N.Y.: Cornell University Press, 2006), 15.

15. Joseph Nye, *Soft Power: The Means to Success in World Politics* (New York: PublicAffairs, 2004).

16. Anders Stephanson, "Rethinking Cold War History," *Review of International Studies* 24 (January 1998): 122. See also Anders Stephanson, "Ideology and Neorealist Mirrors," *Diplomatic History* 17 (Spring 1993): 285–95; and Odd Arne Westad, "The New International History of the Cold War," *Diplomatic History* 24 (Fall 2000): 553–54.

17. E. H. Carr, *What Is History?* (New York: Alfred A. Knopf, 1962), 140–41.

18. John Lewis Gaddis, *Strategies of Containment* (New York: Oxford University Press, 2005), 1. Gaddis takes this typology from J. H. Hexter, *On Historians* (Cambridge, Mass.: Harvard University Press, 1979), 241–43.

19. On the development of historical analysis within Germany during this period—an influence still being felt in American circles today—see David Telman, "Clio Ascendant: The Historical Profession in 19th Century Germany," Ph.D. dissertation, Cornell University, 1993. For a discussion of von Ranke's divergent influence in Europe and the United States—including the important point that von Ranke saw continuity as the end result of change, whereas Marx predicted further change—see Felix Gilberg, "Leopold Von Ranke and the American Philosophical Society," *Proceedings of the American Philosophical Society* 130, no. 3 (1986): 362–66.

20. Useful introductions to von Ranke, in English, include Roger Wines, *Leopold Von Ranke: The Secret of World History* (New York: Fordham University Press, 1981); Georg Iggers and James Powell, eds., *Leopold Von Ranke and the Shaping of Historical Discipline* (Syracuse: Syracuse University Press,, 1990); and Leonard Krieger, *Ranke: The Meaning of History* (Chicago: University of Chicago Press, 1977).

21. A foremost international relations scholar, John Mearsheimer, helped shape the field at the onset of the twenty-first century by arguing that states were like so many billiard balls on a table in *The Tragedy of Great Power Politics*. Whether one can view the top 10 percent or the top half of a structure, the point of each seems to be their tendency to crash.

22. Anders Stephanson, "Diplomatic History in the Expanded Field," *Diplomatic History* 22, no. 4 (Fall 1998): 595–603. "The geopolitical role of the state has in fact changed little between the seventeenth century and the present," he argues, "chiefly because of the historically contingent advent in the nineteenth century of the popular nation-state" (602–3).

23. On Marx in this context, see David R. Task, "Writings on American Foreign Relations: 1957 to the Present," in *Twentieth-Century American Foreign Policy*, ed. John Braeman et al. (Columbus: Ohio State University Press, 1971), 60.

24. Discussion of the *Annales* is plentiful. For a useful overview, see Traian Stoianavitch, *French Historical Method: The Annales Paradigm* (Ithaca, N.Y.: Cornell University Press, 1976).

25. French historians were not alone in searching for "structural" meaning in society after the Great War. Lewis Namier and R. H. Tawney both rejected narrative history while writing in Britain in the 1930s, while Karl Lamprecht reached the same conclusion at the turn of the century, well before the killing fields of France. For a discussion of the search among historians for social focus before and after the *Annales,*

see Peter Burke, "Overture: The New History, Its Past and Its Future," in *New Perspectives on Historical Writing,* ed. Peter Burke (University Park: Pennsylvania State University Press, 1992), 1–24. For "wider," see Peter Burke, *History and Social Theory* (Ithaca, N.Y.: Cornell University Press, 1993), 15–17.

26. See Jim Sharpe's aptly titled "History from Below," in *New Perspectives on Historical Writing,* ed. Burke, 24–41; Frederick Krantz, ed., *History from Below: Studies in Popular Protest and Popular Ideology* (Oxford: Oxford University Press, 1988); E. P. Thompson, "History from Below," *Times Literary Supplement,* April 7, 1966, 279–80; and E. P. Thompson, *The Making of the English Working Class* (New York: Pantheon Books, 1965). On the utility of postmodern and Foucaudian thought to diplomatic historians, a useful beginning is Emily S. Rosenberg, "Revising Dollar Diplomacy: Narratives of Money and Manliness," *Diplomatic History* 22, no. 2 (Spring 1998): 155–76, especially n. 2, which Andrew J. Rotter has dubbed "the single most useful footnote in the brief history of 'culturalist' U.S. foreign relations; see Andrew J. Rotter, "Saidism without Said: Orientalism and U.S. Diplomatic History," *American Historical Review* 105, no. 5 (October 2000): 1205.

27. See Fernand Braudel, *On History* (Chicago: University of Chicago Press, 1980); Samuel Kinser, "Annaliste Paradigm? The Geohistorical Structure of Fernand Braudel," *American Historical Review* 86, no. 1 (February 1981): 63–105; and J. H. Hexter, "Fernand Braudel and the Monde Braudellien," *Journal of Modern History* 44, no. 4 (December 1972): 480–539.

28. Braudel, "History and the Social Sciences: The *Longue Durée,*" in *On History,* 47–48.

29. Walter LaFeber, "Ah, If We Had Studied It More Carefully: The Fortunes of American Diplomatic History," *Prologue* 11 (Summer 1979): 121. History was not only a record of the past, Braudel argued, but also an interpretation of the present as well. This was a view in direct contradiction to von Ranke's doctrine of detachment.

30. For recent calls for international history, see Michael J. Hogan, "The Next Big Thing: The Future of Diplomatic History in a Global Age," *Diplomatic History* 28, no. 1 (January 2004): 1–21; and Michael Hunt, "Internationalizing U.S. Diplomatic History: A Practical Agenda," *Diplomatic History* 15, no. 1 (Winter 1991): 1–15.

31. McCormick, "State of Diplomatic History," 122; Ernest May, *The World War and American Isolation, 1914–1917* (Cambridge, Mass.: Harvard University Press, 1957).

32. Akira Iriye, "The Internationalization of History," *American Historical Review* 94 (February 1989): 1–10. See also Akira Iriye, *Across the Pacific: An Inner History of American—East Asian Relations* (New York: Harcourt, Brace & World, 1967); and Akira Iriye, *Power and Culture* (Cambridge, Mass.: Harvard University Press, 1981). On culture, see Akira Iriye, "Culture and Power: International Relations as Intercultural Relations," *Diplomatic History* 3 (Spring 1979), 115–28; Christopher Thorne, *Border Crossings: Studies in International History* (New York: Columbia University Press, 1988); and Jessica Gienow-Hecht and Frank Schumacher, *Culture and International History* (New York: Berghan Books, 2003).

33. Arno J. Mayer, *Political Origins of the New Diplomacy* (New Haven, Conn.: Yale University Press, 1959); Arno J. Mayer, *The Politics and Diplomacy of Peacemaking* (London: Weidenfeld & Nicolson, 1968).

34. Fredrik Logevall, *Choosing War* (Berkeley: University of California Press,

1999); Jeremi Suri, *Power and Protest: Global Revolution and the Rise of Détente* (Cambridge, Mass.: Harvard University Press, 2003).

35. Thomas A. Bailey, *A Diplomatic History of the American People* (New York: F. S. Crofts & Co., 1940); Thomas A. Bailey, *The Man in the Street* (New York: Macmillan, 1948).

36. Bailey, *Diplomatic History,* xi.

37. Kelly Mulroney, "Discovering Fernand Braudel's Historical Context," *History and Theory* 37, no. 2 (May 1998): 265.

38. Charles Cohen has termed this factoid an "urban myth," though one useful for understanding the stranglehold on colonial history held by Northeastern universities (with clear access to records) throughout much of the country's past. Cohen to J. A. Engel, private correspondence, August 25, 2005. For a discussion of the influence and consequences of the *Annales* school on early American history, see Jack P. Greene and J. R. Pole, "Reconstructing British-American Colonial History: An Introduction" in *Colonial British America: Essays in the New History of the Early Modern Era,* ed. Jack P. Greene and J. R. Pole (Baltimore: Johns Hopkins University Press, 1984), 1–17, esp. 6–8.

39. David F. Trask, "Writings on American Foreign Relations: 1957 to the Present," in *Twentieth-Century Foreign Policy,* ed. Braeman et al., 61. Also see Kennan, *American Diplomacy.*

40. Trask, "Writings on American Foreign Relations."

41. For the evolution of Lippmann's foreign policy views, including his fear of popular interest in foreign affairs, see Ronald Steel, *Walter Lippmann and the American Century* (New York: Vintage Books, 1980).

42. Such a view has long dominated discussion of secretive intelligence services, and it continues to dominate their discussion and formation to this day; successes in foreign policy and intelligence are rarely known to the public—which perhaps, the argument runs, would not appreciate them anyway—but failures alone shape public perceptions of these institutions.

43. John Lewis Gaddis, *The United States and the Origins of the Cold War* (New York: Columbia University Press, 1972). Gaddis made the case for postrevisionism most explicitly in "The Emerging Postrevisionist Synthesis on the Origins of the Cold War," *Diplomatic History* 7, no. 2 (Summer 1983): 171–90, and he then broadened the conceptual approach's utility in "New Conceptual Approaches to the Study of American Foreign Relations: Interdisciplinary Perspectives," *Diplomatic History* 14, no. 3 (Summer 1990): 404–23. Thomas McCormick offered the most cogent rebuttal to the latter in "Something Old, Something New: John Gaddis's 'New Conceptual Approaches,'" *Diplomatic History* 14, no. 3 (Summer 1990): 425–32. For critiques of postrevisionism, see Lloyd C. Gardner, "Responses to John Lewis Gaddis," *Diplomatic History* 7, no. 2 (Summer 1983): 190–204; and Bruce Cummings, "'Revising Postrevisionism,' or The Poverty of Theory in Diplomatic History," *Diplomatic History* 17, no. 4 (Fall 1993): 539–69.

44. This is so named for the influence of teachers and products of Madison's history program on this line of reasoning. See Walter LaFeber, "Fred Harvey Harrington, Teacher and Friend: An Appreciation," in *Behind the Throne: Servants of Power to Imperial Presidents, 1898–1968,* ed. Thomas J. McCormick and Walter LaFeber (Madison: University of Wisconsin Press, 1993), 3–20.

45. Walter LaFeber, *The New Empire* (Ithaca, N.Y.: Cornell University Press, 1963).

46. Robert Freeman Smith, *The United States and Cuba: Business and Diplomacy, 1917–1960* (New York: Bookman Associates, 1960). David Healy, *U.S. Expansionism: The Imperialist Urge of the 1890s* (Madison: University of Wisconsin Press, 1970).

47. Thomas J. McCormick, *The China Market: America's Quest for Informal Empire, 1893–1901* (Chicago: Quadrangle Books, 1967).

48. William Appleman Williams, *The Tragedy of American Diplomacy* (Cleveland: World Publishing, 1959); William Appleman Williams, *Contours of American History* (Cleveland: World Publishing, 1961).

49. *Diplomatic History* 25, no. 2 (Spring 2001), explores Williams's influence on the field. See also Bradford Perkins, "The Tragedy of American Diplomacy: Twenty-Five Years After," *Reviews in American History* 12, no. 2 (March 1984): 1–18; Gary R. Hess, "After the Tumult: The Wisconsin School's Tribute to William Appleman Williams," *Diplomatic History* 12, no. 4 (Fall 1988): 483–99; Henry W. Berger, "Introduction," in *A William Appleman Williams Reader*, ed. Henry W. Berger (Chicago: Ivan R. Dee, 1992), 11–33; and Paul Buhle and Edward Rice-Maximin, *William Appleman Williams: The Tragedy of Empire* (New York: Routlege, 1995).

50. John Higham, "Herbert Baxter Adams and the Study of Local History," *American Historical Review* 89, no. 5 (December 1984): 1225–39.

51. Frederick Jackson Turner, *The Frontier in American History* (New York: H. Holt and Company, 1937), 32–37.

52. Walter LaFeber, *The American Age* (New York: W. W. Norton, 1994), 185.

53. Beard is discussed further below. See Randolph Bourne and Olaf Hanson, eds., *Randolph Bourne: The Radical Will* (Berkeley: University of California Press, 1992); Randolph S. Bourne and Carl Resek, eds., *War and the Intellectuals: Collected Essays, 1915–1919* (Indianapolis: Hackett Books, 1999); Bruce Clayton, *Forgotten Prophet: The Life of Randolph Bourne* (Columbia: University of Missouri Press, 1998); Michael Hogan, *A Cross of Iron: Harry S Truman and the Origins of the National Security State* (New York: Cambridge University Press, 2000); and Aaron Friedberg, *In the Shadow of the Garrison State* (Princeton, N.J.: Princeton University Press, 2000).

54. Hogan, *Cross of Iron*, esp. 23–69. See also Michael Sherry, *In the Shadow of War: The United States since the 1930s* (New Haven, Conn.: Yale University Press, 1997), 194.

55. Howard K. Beale, ed., *Charles A. Beard: An Appraisal* (Lexington: University of Kentucky Press, 1955); Elias Berg, *The Historical Thinking of Charles A. Beard* (Stockholm: Almquist & Wiksell, 1957); Thomas Kennedy, *Charles A. Beard and American Foreign Policy* (Gainesville: University of Florida Press, 1975); Ellen Nore, *Charles A. Beard: An Intellectual Biography* (Carbondale: Southern Illinois University Press, 1983). Williams considered Beard particularly influential to his own work, and thus commented frequently on Beard's legacy. See, e.g., "Charles A. Beard and the Constitution: A Critical Analysis of 'An Economic Interpretation of the Constitution,'" *William and Mary Quarterly* 14, no. 3 (July 1957): 442–48; and his review of Bernard C. Borning, *The Political and Social Thought of Charles A. Beard* (Seattle: University of Washington Press, 1962), in *Journal of Southern History* 29, no. 2 (May 1963): 252–54.

56. John Patrick Diggins sums up the dichotomous nature of Beard's reputation: "Perhaps no historian has been so esteemed in one period, and so systematically criti-

cized in another as Charles A. Beard"; Diggins, "Power and Authority in American History: The Case of Charles A. Beard and His Critics," *American Historical Review* 86, no. 4 (October 1981): 701–30.

57. Campbell Craig, "The Not So Strange Career of Charles Beard," *Diplomatic History* 25, no. 2 (January 2001): 251–74.

58. On the mingling of local and international history in Beard's work, see Arthur Lloyd Skop, "The Primacy of Domestic Politics: Eckhard Kehr and the Intellectual Development of Charles A. Beard," *History and Theory* 13, no. 2 (May 1974): 119–131. See also Lloyd R. Sorenson, "Charles A. Beard and German Historiographical Thought," *Mississippi Valley Historical Review* 42, no. 2 (September 1955): 274–87.

59. Stephen J. Whitfield, *The Culture of the Cold War* (Baltimore: Johns Hopkins University Press, 1991).

60. Richard M. Freeland, *The Truman Doctrine and the Origins of McCarthyism* (New York: Alfred A. Knopf, 1972).

61. Lloyd C. Gardner, *Architects of illusion: Men and Ideas in American Foreign Policy, 1941–1949* (Chicago: Quadrangle Books, 1970).

62. Frank Kofsky, *Harry S Truman and the War Scare of 1948* (New York: St. Martin's Press, 1993).

63. Thomas Friedman, *The World Is Flat: A Brief History of the Twenty-First Century* (New York: Farrar, Straus & Giroux, 2005).

Part I. Daily Lives

1. Exhibition and Entertainment: Hollywood and the American Reconstruction of Defeated Japan

Hiroshi Kitamura

The years immediately following World War II dramatically altered the course of Japanese history. Following its unconditional surrender to the Allied forces, the nation witnessed the arrival of General Douglas MacArthur's Supreme Command for the Allied Powers (SCAP), the United States—led occupation forces in the Far East. During its six and a half years in Japan, SCAP implemented a series of far-reaching reforms—in such areas as politics, law, business, labor, and education—to demilitarize and democratize the former enemy. The blanket attempt to revamp the Japanese nation intensified as Cold War tensions brewed in East Asia. Within a year after MacArthur deplaned at Atsugi Airfield, the occupiers began to confront left-wing movements in the economically ailing nation. Despite policy contradictions and political controversies under this "reverse course," the occupation, on the whole, exemplified America's consistent effort to exercise hegemonic authority over the defeated population.[1] By 1952, when the Allied headquarters ceased its operation, the former imperial giant had metamorphosed into a political, economic,

The author expresses gratitude to Hidano Atsushi, Seth Fein, Makino Mamoru, Yamada Noboru, Andrew Preston, Walter Skya, Gaddis Smith, and Jeremi Suri for their critical suggestions and research assistance with this chapter. Jeffrey A. Engel deserves special thanks for his consistent faith in and support of the author's work. Japanese-language resources were obtained at the National Diet Library, Waseda University, and the Gordon Prange Collection at the University of Maryland, College Park. Following Japanese convention, the names of Japanese authors cited appear with the last name first, except for works written in English.

and strategic ally of the United States. From this vantage point, the occupation of Japan was nothing short of a "pronounced success."[2]

This chapter examines the prominent role culture played in facilitating America's reconstruction of Japan. I do so by examining Hollywood's trade in the war-shattered nation. Japan's unconditional surrender ended the four-year hiatus of America's transpacific film trade, and it cracked open a movie market that had flourished before the air raids and island-hopping campaigns. Backed by the U.S. government and military forces, the U.S. film industry launched a large-scale campaign to expand its patronage in cities and towns across the country. This cinematic campaign not only doubled the share of American products in a market tightly controlled by local studios before the war. By transforming Japan into one of the industry's "best market[s]," it also helped solidify America's economic and cultural prominence in the years to follow.[3]

Hollywood's transpacific expansion is a subject that deserves closer scholarly attention. English-language accounts on this process are sparse; even John Dower's *Embracing Defeat: Japan in the Wake of World War II*, an outstanding synthesis of the occupation, lacks a sustained discussion of the U.S. film industry's early postwar campaign.[4] In the Japanese language, Tanikawa Takeshi's *Amerika eiga to senryo seisaku* (American films and occupation policy) seeks to demonstrate the continuities and disjunctures between the U.S. State Department's film policies formulated during World War II and their implementation by SCAP during the occupation years. A pioneering and useful account, Tanikawa's book is largely a study of official policymaking and state-level discourse. This leaves us wondering about the impact of Hollywood's penetration on the "ground level," as well as the response of the local population to the policies and programs implemented from above.[5]

This chapter is an attempt to explain Hollywood's interactive relationship with the groups and individuals on the "ground level." More specifically, it discusses the reconstruction of American film exhibition in defeated Japan. This business of Hollywood exhibition was manifested through a collaborative and pragmatic relationship between the Central Motion Picture Exchange (CMPE), the U.S. film industry's Far Eastern outpost, and hundreds of film exhibitors—particularly independent theaters—that mushroomed across the nation. Eager to differentiate its product from those of other cinemas and leisure enterprises, the CMPE called upon its affiliates to expand and refine the quality of film presentation. Many local theaters responded in favor of the CMPE's intentions. Determined to survive and succeed in a competitive business field, Japanese exhibitors helped construct a flamboyant, conspicuous, and distinctly "American" entertainment culture from the ground up.[6]

34

This entertainment culture expanded in part through the collective efforts of the CMPE and its affiliated exhibitors, but also through a renewed relationship between Hollywood and SCAP in the context of the Cold War. The growing threat of left-wing activism prompted SCAP to establish a film importation policy that would privilege Hollywood entertainment at the expense of other national cinemas—especially Soviet films. Meanwhile, the U.S. film industry also adopted an anticommunist position to defend its business from political attacks. The CMPE assisted SCAP's ideological battle by disseminating feature films and newsreels embedded with anticommunist themes. This Cold War corporatism between SCAP and the CMPE solidified the place of Hollywood entertainment in early postwar Japan.

The birth and growth of Hollywood entertainment illustrate the expansion of American power in early postwar Japan. This process was partly shaped by the collaborative endeavors of U.S. industrial and occupation forces, but it also required the active engagement of hundreds of local exhibitors that rose from the ashes of war. The negotiation and interaction of these diverse institutions yielded a conspicuous entertainment culture, which would enthrall everyday consumers in the face of defeat. Ultimately, the will and desire of these separate agents not only elevated U.S. cinema into a major contender against Japanese cinema—which had dominated the overseas share in the local market before the war—but also facilitated Japan's integration into a U.S.-centered international system. Hardly a trivial institution, Hollywood, in this regard, was a "chosen instrument" that enhanced America's overseas influence in the wider world.[7]

The Revival of American Film Exhibition

The American film campaign in occupied Japan stemmed from a set of corporatist negotiations between the U.S. government, SCAP, and Hollywood. During the midst of World War II—a war that shut down many of the industry's overseas markets—U.S. film studios approached the State Department to formulate plans for their global trade after the war. Washington responded favorably. Expressing "desires to cooperate fully" with the industry, leaders of the two entities developed ideas to best enhance Hollywood's international business—eventually resulting in the founding of the Motion Picture Export Association (MPEA), a legal cartel of eight major U.S. studios.[8] In the meantime, U.S. companies participated in the plans to occupy Japan. Eager to utilize the movies to disseminate pro-American and democratic values, SCAP's Civil Information and Education Section (CIE) assisted the founding of a distribution office for MPEA products. That apparatus became the CMPE.

Founded in February 1946, it would eventually distribute over 500 feature films across the war-torn nation.

The CMPE's objectives in occupied Japan were twofold. The first was to further the business interests of major Hollywood studios. During the early stages of its operation, the CMPE ran a modest distribution campaign from a one-room office in the heart of Tokyo. Soon, however, it developed into a bureaucratically structured, "scientifically managed" company that parceled its labor into several departments—accounting, publicity, production (which took on subtitling), sales, and general affairs—and opened office in four other cities: Nagoya, Osaka, Sapporo, and Fukuoka. Managed by Charles Mayer, a former representative of 20th Century–Fox, the expanded CMPE carried out a large-scale business campaign to "amuse and entertain" the mass audiences.[9] Until its liquidation in December 1951, the CMPE would thrive as the dominant distributor of American movies in Japan.

The second objective was to assist SCAP's efforts to reconstruct Japan. While pursuing its commercial opportunities, the CMPE made it clear that its other role was to "bring to the Japanese people a means of seeing democracy at work."[10] The distributor submitted synopses, reviews, and film prints to the censors of SCAP, and it complied with their requests by editing and withdrawing certain feature films from release. The CMPE also screened feature films together with newsreels, "as if its distribution had been mandatory."[11] Mayer's company also cohosted educational events with the CIE Information Center—the America Houses of Japan.[12] The corporatist partnership was strong during the first fifteen months, when the CMPE operated under the direction of CIE, but remained central throughout the occupation. In October 1951, two months before the CMPE's liquidation, Donald Nugent of CIE praised Mayer for his "outstanding service in the achievement of Occupation objectives."[13]

One of the company's key tasks to succeed in Japan was to establish control over the sites of film exhibition. Unlike in the United States, where the vertically integrated U.S. studios owned most of the sites for film presentation, MPEA's affiliates lacked that luxury in Japan. They turned to direct negotiations in the field of exhibition, which was undergoing an unprecedented boom. Following a war that destroyed hundreds of theaters across the nation, exhibitors—both old and new—opened their businesses in open lots, empty basements, and one-floor spaces of department stores. Only a year after the war, there were as many as 500 new theaters mushrooming in the field. By 1951, the nation had about 3,600 venues—far exceeding the number of theaters in prewar Japan.[14] The "theater craze" of this vibrant era expanded the infrastructure of filmic presentation. It created a volatile but competitive market that enhanced the CMPE's business opportunities in the field.

The CMPE's initial dealings with theaters followed historical convention.[15] During the first few months, it relied primarily on the large theater chains Toho and Shochiku. This deal offered at least two advantages. First, the two chains possessed control over a nationwide network through which Hollywood could disseminate its feature films. By securing distribution arrangements with the country's largest circuits, U.S. studios could reach far beyond the big metropolitan centers and enhance the exposure of American cinema in the remote hinterlands. Second, the CMPE could gain an advantageous position in the most competitive big-city markets. Because these chains owned prestige theaters like the Musashinokan (owned by Toho) and the Hogakuza (Shochiku), both located in the heart of Tokyo, the CMPE could distinguish its products by way of these high-end venues.

But this relationship with the big chains soured quickly. Despite the popularity of the U.S. industry's initial postwar releases, Toho and Shochiku found the CMPE's arrangements too demanding. Part of the problem was the 50 percent rental fee, which was 5 to 15 percent higher than what Japanese studios normally imposed on their exhibitors.[16] An equally troubling demand concerned screen time. As film producers themselves, Toho and Shochiku saved a large proportion of their venues for their own filmic products. The CMPE, however, requested that the two chains allot half the screen time (in all their venues) to Hollywood movies.[17] This baffled the two exhibitors. The head of Shochiku, for instance, insisted that his company had already offered a big favor by sparing its "first-class" houses for American films, at the risk of creating an impression that the quality of its own films was "second rate."[18] Conflicting interests soon led to the breakup of this relationship in mid-October 1946.[19] The CMPE now had to find new affiliates to thrive in a competitive theater market.

The solution was to arrange business with two alternative theater bodies. One was the midsized Nikkatsu chain. Before World War II, Nikkatsu was film producer, as was Toho and Shochiku, and it was often known for its fast-paced period films, or *jidaigeki.* During the war, Nikkatsu temporarily abandoned film production and operated exclusively as an exhibitor.[20] While the CMPE was still distributing through Toho and Shochiku, Nikkatsu agreed to handle Hollywood cinema in a mixed program that shared screen time with Japanese films, mostly produced by the Daiei studio.[21] Following its breakup with Toho and Shochiku, the CMPE approached Nikkatsu for extensive deals.[22] In an agreement that went into effect on May 1, 1947, Nikkatsu, the owner of forty-two large venues, agreed to supply twenty-nine theaters exclusively for American feature films (ten theaters continued to display Japanese films; three showed half-and-half).[23]

The other theater body was the independents. The war's disruption of the movie business, the relative low costs required to run a stand-alone theater, and an inflation that elevated the value of the exhibition business all contributed to the growth of the independent field in the early aftermath of defeat. The owners of these venues included experienced veterans repairing their war-damaged structures, as well as aspiring newcomers who invested in this business for quick cash.[24] The emergence of these small-time venues ultimately favored the CMPE. Charles Mayer, the CMPE's managing director, expressed enthusiasm in working with independently owned theaters, convinced that their initiatives would foster an open market condition akin to Germany's.[25] Following the contract termination with Toho and Shochiku, the CMPE quickly shifted its attention to "get the best independent theatre of every city."[26]

Reforming Exhibition

The CMPE's goal in courting exhibitors was simply to maximize the number of affiliates. It was equally important to secure venues that were equipped with top-notch facilities and respectable services, which would increase the drawing capacity of the filmic products. The deal with Nikkatsu gave some hope to the CMPE, because the exhibitor was known to pour "large sums of money" to construct "large theaters" during the early postwar years.[27] Independent exhibition, however, was a different story. Even though the theaters under this category were increasing rather dramatically in number, their quality generally appeared low. In the fall of 1946, *Asahi shinbun* noted that most of these independent businesses were saddled with "poor theater facilities" and were "hardly comparable to the theaters of Toho and Shochiku."[28] Mayer complained that most of these theaters lacked the ability to "draw the upper classes."[29]

Disappointed but hardly discouraged, the CMPE engaged in a widespread effort to "educate the Japanese people in methods of theatre operation."[30] Its methods for "education" were threefold. First, the distributor dispatched sales and publicity agents to theaters across the nation. In selling the product to managers, they introduced various strategies for betterment. Second, the company distributed *MPEA News,* a monthly newsletter, to offer instructions, ideas, and advice. Third, the CMPE organized a series of workshops and forums with local theater managers. In these meetings, the "nation's exhibitors from every province [were] invited to sit down with distributors, air grievances and offer suggestions for improvement in service and operations."[31] To theaters that met its standards, the CMPE awarded first-run status, usually supplying high-grade and prestige films to them before other rivals. Lesser exhibitors became second- or third-run theaters, which typically received damaged and worn-out prints after the screenings ended in the first-run houses. The highest status was the road show, which involved the regional and national premieres of top-grade products.[32] This overall system was what an MPEA official called a "superior theater principle."[33] Or the motto read: "Good movies to good theaters."[34]

The content of these "instructions" began with sanitation. To the CMPE's dismay, the hygiene of theaters during this time was generally poor and uninspiring. Surveys conducted during the occupation years commonly pointed out that theaters suffered from poor ventilation, high humidity (during summers), and uncomfortable temperatures (hot in the summer, cold in the winter).[35] It was not rare to encounter rats, mice, fleas, and ticks; and poor maintenance forced SCAP to sterilize the theaters in Tokyo to prevent the spread of typhus and other contagious diseases.[36] *Newsweek* went so far as to say that the poor sanitary conditions of Japanese theaters were attributable to the "Jap fish diet." The reporter disdainfully wrote that movie houses smelled like "an octopus which has been chased 10 miles over a dusty road on a hot day and is perspiring freely."[37]

Dismayed at the lack of cleanliness, the CMPE advised theater owners to tidy up their venues. Sanitation was a relatively easy task, the distributor stressed, because it "did not cost money." In *MPEA News*, the company called upon its affiliates to sweep the floors, wash the front entrances, and keep other areas of the theater clean. An equal amount of care should fall on projection maintenance, the CMPE noted, to improve the quality of image and sound. Toilets, furthermore, had to be kept clean to prevent unpleasant smells from infiltrating the main halls.[38] If theaters could not afford to buy soap, they could at least refresh the air a few times a day, particularly during the hot summer days.[39]

Advertising was another area that necessitated hands-on instruction. Although the distributor did manufacture posters, flyers, billboards, and other promotional materials, the CMPE also relied on the exhibitors' own initiative to publicize the feature film. The divorce from Toho and Shochiku posed a problem, because independent theaters usually lacked the resources to generate large-scale promotion campaigns.[40] In an effort to develop the initiative of its affiliates, the CMPE repeatedly addressed the significance of extensive publicity; Mayer once noted that "promotion . . . is the most important [aspect of] the movie business."[41] The distributor often hosted publicity contests and honored the best theaters with modest rewards.[42]

According to the CMPE, several areas in the advertising field required instruction. As a first step, the distributor urged owners to dress up the theaters with flamboyant imagery, while decorating the interior with posters, still photos, sketches, and other material (figures 1.1 and 1.2). The emphasis of this endeavor was more than visibility. While asking its affiliates to hype the products, the CMPE called for clear and straightforward promotion. One practice that troubled the distributor was the simultaneous publicity of the current and future releases on the same marquee. In response, the CMPE agents urged theaters to publicize the featured film on the marquee or at the front entrance, while advertising the forthcoming pictures indoors.[43] Another disturbing practice involved "vulgarity." Realizing that exhibitors would sometimes misrepresent film content by hyping eroticism and sexuality, the CMPE explicitly stressed that exhibitors perform respectable publicity to represent Hollywood as a refined entertainment. Violators suffered serious consequences, typically losing distribution arrangements.[44]

The distributor also addressed other means of movie promotion. For example, the CMPE preached the effectiveness of movie programs—"cultural guides," the distributor called them—and urged theaters to distribute them to consumers free of charge.[45] Poster and still photo exhibits were also effective and welcome, according to the CMPE.[46] Agreeing to loan display materials for free, the distributor encouraged its affiliates to use their lobbies, hallways, storefronts, cafés, and other open spaces to showcase Hollywood fare.[47] In addition, the CMPE advanced the idea of organizing public lectures on the films. Such events could multiply attention if the exhibitor worked with schools, companies, and cultural organizations.[48] Finally, the milieu in the theater became a subject for change. The CMPE asked theaters to carefully select the appropriate music for intermissions, and to avoid the use of regional dialects in their announcements over the public address system.[49]

Moreover, the CMPE's "education" addressed social order. Since the prewar decades, movie theaters had typically been chaotic spaces. When a popular film came to town, it was not rare to see the floors packed with standing spectators. The crowding of theater space was largely a result of the "packing-in" (*tsumekomi*) or "flowing-in" (*nagashikomi*) system, in which exhibitors allowed audiences to fill the theater space regardless of seating capacity. This practice troubled the CMPE for three simple reasons: hygiene, safety, and fan enjoyment. "Audiences," wrote the CMPE, "purchase tickets to enjoy the movie, not to learn how to survive in packed trains."[50] At various public occasions, Mayer spoke of the "responsibility of the exhibitor"—which addressed a need to render theater space comfortable for ticket holders to enjoy

Figure 1.1. Posters inside a Japanese Theater Publicizing the American Movie *State Fair*

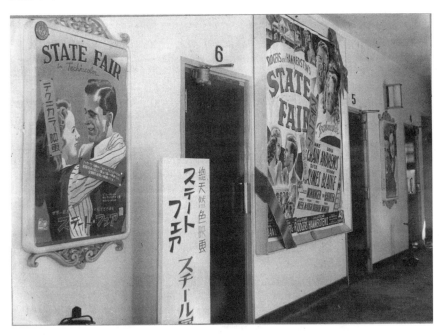

Source: Photograph courtesy of Oi Misuru.

the cinematic experience. The remark implied criticism against profit-driven exhibitors and their shameless desires to collect cash at the expense of viewer comfort.[51]

Finally, the CMPE recommended that exhibitors upgrade their hardware. In *MPEA News,* the CMPE supplied various tips and suggestions to improve the physical conditions and appearances of the venues. The "correct structure" of a movie theater, the CMPE argued, consisted of the use of durable material for doors and floors. External walls, roofs, stairs, gutters, and windows required special coating that would prevent corrosion. To prevent fires, theaters needed to design emergency hallways and exits, and also to apply fireproof paint on curtains, ornaments, and stage equipment every six months.[52] Exhibitors, furthermore, had to carefully select their seats to assure the viewer's comfort.[53] In a supplementary leaflet, the CMPE recommended seats with plastic fiber surfaces and slide-back functions. The floors needed to provide slight inclina-

Figure 1.2. Exterior of a Japanese Theater Showing Ads for American Movies

Source: Photograph courtesy of Oi Mitsuru.

tions to clear the sight for all viewers. "Seats are the life of the theater," the article underscored.[54]

The Flowering of Entertainment Culture

The deals that the CMPE proposed to exhibitors were not a bargain. Hollywood's methods and policies occasionally elicited complaints from local agents and exhibitors. One prominent film handler complained that the American film policy toward Japan, particularly the 50 percent rental fee, was simply "exorbitant."[55] Many, however, chose to do business with the CMPE. Two months after the breakup with Toho and Shochiku, the number of theaters that screened Hollywood movies was 275.[56] In May 1947, 728 movie houses displayed Hollywood features.[57] This expansion of American film exhibition was also a geographic phenomenon. *Eiga geino nenkan* observed that "the number of American-movie spectators consistently increased in regional cities." The business of Hollywood cinema, the film-and-entertainment almanac concluded, was stretching "nationwide."[58]

Three reasons account for the exhibitors' decision to choose Hollywood. First, American cinema granted stability. Exhibitors were aware that the CMPE was armed with stockpiles of ready-to-release films, which could assure an uninterrupted stream of feature films, so crucial to sustaining the business. Second, Hollywood cinema was a fresh and marketable commodity. It boasted a wide array of filmic genres—from shoot-'em-up westerns to romantic comedies to serious melodramas—that could draw the attention of diverse audience groups. It also offered an element of prestige. By exploiting Hollywood's status as a producer of high-end cinema, especially in contrast to local cinematic products, which many deemed as "vulgar" and "lowbrow," exhibitors could use the U.S. cinema's respected status to differentiate product.[59] Third, the general public appeared to express a strong fascination with and interest in American culture. After the war, the public also expressed a strong interest in American ideas, values, and popular culture.[60] This anticipation of high demand rendered Hollywood an attractive business product.

The high market value of Hollywood entertainment did not simply draw the interest of independent exhibitors from around the nation. It also inspired collaborations among many of these businesses. In an effort to boost their own publicity efforts, theaters exchanged information and know-how through meetings and organized activities. The CMPE's newsletters and gatherings also cultivated a shared sense of community among these diverse exhibitors. In Tokyo, a group of independent exhibitors founded the Federation of American Film Exhibitors (Amerika eiga fukirikan rengokai). This organization, soon renamed the American Film Club (Amerika eiga kurabu), generated publicity programs in conjunction with the distributor.[61] Coordinated activities materialized in other cities as well.[62] Many of these disparate exhibitors were connected through social and informational exchanges, and they took part in developing a widespread entertainment culture on the ground.

The content of this entertainment culture was, not surprisingly, complex. It consisted of a hodge-podge of expressions and presentations that differed from exhibitor to exhibitor, particularly depending on location, budget, status, reputation, and personnel. But despite the internal differences, several expressive characteristics shaped a common entertainment culture that boosted Hollywood's presence in defeated Japan. To add further, this entertainment culture was a celebration of American values in its own way. In this sense, Japanese film exhibitors were active agents in shaping American culture through their business activities.

This shared culture partly consisted of flamboyant exteriors. Colorful and eye-catching, the marquees and front entrances usually displayed large inscriptions of the film's title. A wide variety of icons and images—from a bare-chested Johnny Weissmuler howling in the jungle to a grim-faced Victor Mature drawing a six-gun to the jubilant faces of Deanna Durbin and June Allyson—hyped the film's genres and stars.[63] Other Hollywood symbols illuminated these spaces as well. These included Oscar statues, logos of the MPEA and its affiliated studios, and "Home of American Movies" signs—which the CMPE allowed for display only by contract. This epitaph signaled the fact that the theater exclusively screened Hollywood products. *Motion Picture Herald* observed that a number of first-run houses in Japan had been "sold on the prestige value of setting up permanent display fronts with [this] identification."[64]

Theaters showing American movies also engaged in common forms of advertising. Because exhibitors could not depend entirely on the CMPE's own publicity campaigns, they worked hard themselves to draw the attention of local audiences. Exhibitors employed multiple strategies. For instance, they posted block advertisements in newspapers and magazines, touting the new releases as well as the stars in them. Posters and panels of a similar nature appeared in diverse public spaces, from open billboards to the outside walls of moving streetcars.[65] Many theater owners dressed up their motorbikes, automobiles, even horse-pulled wagons and stagecoaches, with eye-catching ballyhoo. These vehicles, often equipped with loudspeakers, sprinkled flyers across the city while announcing the latest releases.[66] Costumed publicists, placards in hand, circled the downtown neighborhoods. It was not rare to spot a costumed tiger on the streets when films like *The Man-Eater of Kumaon* were in town, or a band of baseball players coasting on their bicycles, promoting *The Pride of the Yankees* or *The Stratton Story*.[67]

Exhibitors also arranged special screenings in conjunction with the CMPE and community organizations. Theaters hosted these events to draw public attention. Using films like *Fighting Father Dunne* (a biographical picture about a Catholic priest's devotion to helping displaced children), *Sister Kenny* (a biopic on Elizabeth Kenny, an Australian nurse who labored to find a cure for polio), and *Random Harvest* (a critically acclaimed melodrama about a World

War I veteran), exhibitors welcomed school teachers, college professors, doctors, public officials, intellectuals, artists, SCAP personnel, and, on special occasions, the imperial family.[68] Scores of theaters welcomed young children and students to their "movie classrooms." Relying on films with child protagonists such as *The Boy with Green Hair, Rusty's Birthday,* and *Deep Waters,* theaters arranged morning shows with schools and educational institutions, to offer a "sociological" resource about American culture and life to the youth.[69] Some screenings were "English-language classrooms." For such events, theaters distributed copies of dialogues to participants, and they showed the films twice: once without subtitles, and the second time with transliteration. Through such arrangements, audiences gained a "fun" opportunity to learn and study the victors' language.[70]

Theaters also altered their seating practices in developing this entertainment culture. Instead of continuing with the packing-in system, many exhibitors—especially road show and prominent first-run venues—began to adopt restricted seating policies, prioritizing audience comfort and climate construction over overcrowded exhibition.[71] This differed from the practices of most Japanese movie theaters. One exhibitor remarked that the reason was the "difference in the quality of audiences."[72] Furthermore, theaters encouraged heterosocial movie viewing by adding love chairs and calling them "romance seats." This practice, invented by an exhibitor of American movies in Osaka, immediately attracted widespread attention.[73] It not only created a media frenzy; soon, exhibitors in Tokyo, Sendai, Ube, Morioka, and other cities were adopting this seating practice.[74] In a new social climate in which wholesome Hollywood romances were being mainstreamed, the selling of a romantic experience was sensational and appealing. Other theaters began selling "romance tickets" for couples.[75]

Foreign Cinemas and Cold War Contexts

Hollywood's entertainment culture grew at a time when the Cold War was penetrating the fabric of defeated Japan. Ideological tensions in Japan had surfaced as early as May 1946, a time when labor unionism and left-wing activities were growing in the economically ailing nation.[76] The fear of communist infiltration and working-class uprisings inspired MacArthur's infamous strike ban in January 1947 as well as George Kennan's visit to Japan in March 1948. In this changing climate that scholars and contemporaries have referred to as the "reverse course," SCAP put forth a get-tough policy against political oppositions and labor uprisings. The occupiers consequently supported the conservative power elites and orchestrated the Red Purge in 1950. By this time, the Cold War was in full swing across the Pacific. Japan had become a prominent site of the global Manichean struggle.[77]

The growth of left-wing politics posed two main challenges to Hollywood entertainment. First, it nourished a critical outlook against Hollywood. *Akahata,* the flagship newspaper of the Communist Party in Japan, regularly denounced U.S. films as "unrealistic," "vulgar," and "half-baked" products.[78] Workers' publications alerted readers to the "politics" embedded in the seemingly innocuous Hollywood entertainment.[79] Second, it cultivated the public's attention and interest in Soviet cinema. Only a few months after the CMPE launched its operation, the Soviets screened *Sportivny Parad,* following SCAP's official clearance and approval.[80] Advertised as a "modern masterpiece," this color production about a sports parade in Moscow caught the attention of film critics and broader audiences.[81]

SCAP responded to the changing political and cultural circumstances.[82] In the summer and fall of 1946, it discussed plans to establish a blanket rule to increase and regulate foreign film imports. The end result was Circular 12, "Admission of Foreign Magazines, Books, Motion Pictures, News and Photograph Services, et Cetera, and Their Dissemination in Japan." Issued December 5, 1946, this key document outlined the basic principles for a diverse range of media products. The occupiers opened the market for foreign film companies under the following conditions: (1) Only one distributor per nation can engage in business. (2) Each company can distribute as many as the maximum number of films its host country brought to Japan in any given year prior to the war. (3) SCAP will reserve the right to monitor film content, in order to judge its "suitability in furthering the information and education objective of the Occupation," (4) Screenings of these products are acceptable only within "normal commercial channels."[83]

On the surface, Circular 12 welcomed foreign film distributors to open their businesses with Japan. Following the announcement of this policy, as many as fourteen distributors applied with hopes of carving their niches in this movie market.[84] But as a "control procedure" that allowed the occupiers to inspect and censor the narrative products for "information and education" purposes, this new rule reinforced SCAP's intentions to privilege Hollywood over other foreign cinemas.[85] In particular, Circular 12 was designed to contain communism.[86] SCAP personnel would contend that the new policy was a means of "prevent [ing the] dissemination of anti-American propaganda in Japan by the Soviet Union."[87] The Cold War implications of Circular 12 were evident to outside observers as well. On December 14, 1946, the *New York Times* reached

Table 1.1. National Origins of Distributors of Foreign Films in Japan, 1946–1950

Nation	1946	1947	1948	1949	1950	Total
United States	39	72	70	91	85	357
France	0	0	15	34	11	60
United Kingdom	0	1	18	24	14	57
Italy	0	0	0	2	3	5
Soviet Union	0		9	2	2	15
Argentina	0	0	0	0	2	2

Source: Jiji tsushin sha, *Eiga nenkan 1951* (Tokyo: Jiji tsushin sha, 1950), 194.

an "inescapable . . . conclusion that [the SCAP] headquarters is determined to check the flow of Soviet propaganda."[88]

SCAP's policy toward foreign cinema yielded a lopsided distribution pattern (see table 1.1). It allowed a growing number of British and French films to reach the screens, but their quantity was far limited in contrast to Hollywood products. Italian cinema, which SCAP admitted as "outstanding . . . artistic productions," was even shorter in number. The occupiers worried that the realism and grim endings of these narratives would make them prone to "exploitation by Japanese communists."[89] Unspecified "political considerations" hindered the entry of Chinese cinema.[90] Germany suffered as well. In 1950, a Japanese film importer approached SCAP to ask for permission to handle West German cinema. SCAP rejected the request, in part because Germany was "technically . . . still an enemy country," but also out of fear that the endorsement of West German cinemas would give an excuse for communist-infused East Germans to demand a distribution license.[91]

The occupiers took a particularly stringent attitude toward Soviet cinema. Invoking Circular 12, SCAP argued that the annual quota for Soviet films would be no more than six.[92] MacArthur's headquarters also took extra time to scrutinize the products. Whereas the films submitted by the United States were usually examined in a matter of weeks, Soviet productions could remain in SCAP's hands for over a year.[93] For the screening of Moscow's productions, occupation censors commonly invited members of the Civil Intelligence Section (G-2), a higher echelon within SCAP's bureaucratic hierarchy.[94] Soviet representatives would repeatedly complain that a "majority" of the films were denied without "any explanations," but to no avail.[95] In 1951, SCAP bluntly reiterated its commitment to "obstruct" the presentation of Soviet films because of "their propaganda content and . . . the propaganda purposes to which they are put by Japanese communists."[96]

SCAP's film policy played a significant role in expanding Hollywood entertainment in defeated Japan. Its regulation of foreign film imports hindered non-U.S. distributors' efforts to thrive in this competitive market. Because the British, French, Italian, and Soviets were unable to fill the bills individually, they joined forces and distributed their products through "Western film" (*yoga*) theaters, whose visibility and outreach were mostly limited to the venues in big cities.[97] In this sense, Circular 12 largely prevented non-U.S. importers from forming their "national" entertainment cultures in the field of film exhibition. In contrast, the occupiers allowed and encouraged Hollywood to multiply its share in Japan. Armed with a large stockpile of films, the CMPE rapidly developed a nationwide network for cinematic presentation. Its entertainment culture thrived amid an unprecedented theater boom. By 1951, some 1,100 exhibitors displayed American products. By this time, Hollywood had risen on par with Japanese cinema, with which it would enjoy a "co-prosperity" during the 1950s.

Hollywood's Anticommunism

In the meantime, Hollywood supported SCAP's (and the U.S. government's) Cold War mission by reshaping its entertainment culture from within. Back in the United States, the growing outcry against left-wing activists in the movie colony prompted studio heads to announce the Waldorf Statement in November 1947, which promised the removal of communists and fellow travelers from the motion picture industry. To the studios, this anticommunist position was a means of protecting its business from political criticism and federal pressure.[98] In the months that followed, film companies not only blacklisted suspected communists and left-wing affiliates. They also produced a growing number of anticommunist film narratives that would take part in shaping the Cold War culture of the midcentury. By late 1951, the industry had catalogued at least twenty-one motion pictures that would support the "anti-communist fight."[99]

Shortly following the studios' turn to anticommunism in the United States, the CMPE expressed its intention to assist SCAP's Cold War endeavors in defeated Japan.[100] The CMPE did this in part by displaying newsreels infused with Cold War topics. The Korean War, for example, became a popular subject in CIE newsreels and United News episodes. American-movie exhibitors hyped the information value of these narratives on billboards at the main entrances, rendering contemporary news as yet another source of attraction.[101] The CMPE informed SCAP that Mayer has instructed the company to "use all of the 'anti-communist' sequences" in their newsreels.[102] Japanese theaters appear to have endorsed Hollywood's political turn. One exhibitor noted that the shortage of American movies would cause "upheavals and turmoils in thought, and giving way to the invasion of communistic trend of thought through Soviet pictures."[103]

In addition, the CMPE distributed a handful of feature films that portrayed the ideological struggle of the two superpowers. Perhaps the first Cold War film for Japan was *The Iron Curtain*. Based on an actual spy case in Canada, the 20th Century—Fox film traced a Soviet defector who supplies secret information to the Canadian Embassy. Facing the Soviets' relentless efforts to assassinate him, the protagonist decides to cooperate with the Western Allies in order to have his wife and newborn child live in a free "democratic" country. Following SCAP's scrutiny and approval of this product, *The Iron Curtain* garnered public attention as a road show picture.[104] Exhibitors coordinated special events to boost attention.[105] In Sapporo, for example, an anticommunist rally took place in conjunction with Nikkatsu's screening of this controversial film. The Toyoza in Hiroshima invited a local politician for a speech at a special screening, and distributed postcards inscribed with the film's content to schools and other organizations.[106]

The Big Lift was another Cold War film that reached the theaters in the Japanese market. Using the Berlin Blockade as a backdrop, it focused on a doomed romance between an American flight engineer and a German heroine, who tries to coax him into a marriage in order to begin a new life in the United States. A film that portrays the dangers of the Soviet zone and the benevolence of the Americans, this 20th Century—Fox product, in the words of the CMPE, was a "textbook of democracy."[107] In Tokyo, it received road show billing, and it "scored positive results."[108] Exhibitors circulated a colorful pamphlet, which underscored the "absolute significance" of the film "at times when the Cold War is greatly intensifying [and] about to blanket Japan."[109] Theater owners treated this film as a politically serious and instructive product. In Fukuoka, the Nikkatsu Theater hosted a charity event with this film. Municipal representatives, U.S. military officials, and general audiences sat side by side at this event. One U.S. officer who experienced the airlift in Germany lectured on his personal experiences.[110]

The story of *The Red Danube* took place in occupied Vienna. Like *The Big Lift,* it revolved around yet another tragic romance, this time between an American soldier and a Russian ballerina. The film highlights the U.S. allies' efforts to curtail the Russians' subversive endeavors in a tension-ridden city, and it also portrays an Austrian convent's efforts to help displaced foreigners. Most important, the Soviets in the film turn out to be cruel and ruthless toward their own citizens. In Japan, the CMPE promoted this product as an "anticommunist film" that denounced Russian exploits "from the standpoint of Christian humanitarianism."[111] One theater in Tokyo boasted that the film was a "tragic love story" that would "appeal to the wisdom and emotion of women . . . at the height of a Red storm in our country."[112] Perhaps not as prominent as the aforementioned Cold War films, this product also began as a road show picture and reached regional theaters in subsequent weeks.[113]

Two other ideologically charged films entered the Japanese market. One was *The Woman on Pier 13,* a thriller in which a newly married couple break up because of the husband's past membership with the Communist Party. Originally titled *I Married a Communist,* this Robert Stevenson film ends with the male protagonist's tragic death in front of his forgiving wife. The Cold War picture, the CMPE stated, was a "powerful tale" peppered with "fear and terror."[114] *Ninotchka* was a prewar production that made it to Japan in the winter of 1949.[115] The narrative centered on three Russian male agents who indulge in Paris nightlife while on a mission to sell their confiscated jewelry. The heroine, Ninotchka, who arrives from Moscow to monitor their actions, falls in love with a French gentleman, and she eventually chooses him over her country. The CMPE hyped the director Ernst Lubitsch's skills in producing a "tender and witty" film but asserted that its main theme was a "satire against Bolshevism."[116]

Conclusion

The occupation of Japan was a hegemonic process that affected the war-shattered society at all levels. SCAP's policies and programs transcended high-level spheres and penetrated deeply into the fabric of everyday life. Hollywood was a vital instrument designed to do just that. Through collaboration with MacArthur's headquarters, U.S. studios generated a large-scale distribution campaign in cities and towns across the nation. The key to their success was the reconstruction of an exhibition network to show American movies. The Central Motion Picture Exchange established a working relationship with a growing body of independent theaters, and it also pressed for improvements in the quality of film exhibition. Theaters responded with eye-catching promotion, special events, and unique seating practices. The interactive relationship between distributor and exhibitor gave rise to a unique entertainment culture that celebrated American culture through the movies.

This entertainment culture blossomed in defeated Japan also through Cold War corporatism. Responding to the growing threat of left-wing activism, SCAP opened the local media market to foreign distributors in ways that favored Hollywood, while marginalizing Soviet and left-wing cinemas. Hollywood studios also embraced anticommunism. They collaborated with SCAP by disseminating newsreels and feature films that foregrounded Cold War themes. By the end of the occupation, Hollywood's entertainment culture not only controlled much of the foreign film market but also stood on par with Japanese cinema—the dominant national cinema during the prewar decades.

The expansion of Hollywood entertainment illustrates an interactive process through which the United States consolidated its power and presence in postwar Japan. This dynamic phenomenon was shaped by a combination of multiple elements, including Hollywood's rigorous operation; the voluntary engagement of local exhibitors; SCAP's cooperation; and, most important, the collaboration of the three parties. The confluence of these separate agents helped produce a widespread entertainment culture, which was quickly mainstreamed in a society that was undergoing a dramatic transformation. In this way, Hollywood reinforced American power by drawing Japan into an American orbit. It ultimately served as a cultural instrument that, through its economic practices, facilitated Japan's incorporation into the larger international system centered on the United States.

Notes

1. On hegemony, see Thomas J. McCormick, *America's Half-Century: United States Foreign Policy in the Cold War and After,* 2nd ed. (Baltimore: Johns Hopkins University Press, 1995), esp. 1–16; T. J. Jackson Lears, "The Concept of Cultural Hegemony: Problems and Possibilities," *American Historical Review* 90, no. 3 (June 1985), 567–93; and Ernesto Laclau and Chantal Mouffe, *Hegemony and Socialist Strategy,* 2nd ed. (New York: Verso, 2001).

2. John Dower, "A Warning from History: Don't Expect Democracy in Iraq," *Boston Review* 28, no. 1 (March 2003), http://bostonreview.mit.edu/BR28.1/dower.html.

3. *Variety,* November 21, 1951, 3.

4. Dower's discussion of foreign cinema is sporadic. John Dower, *Embracing Defeat: Japan in the Wake of World War II* (New York: W. W. Norton and New Press, 1999), 195, 252.

5. Tanikawa Takeshi, *Amerika eiga to senryo seisaku* (Kyoto: Kyoto University Press, 2002).

6. I rely on Richard Maltby's definition of "entertainment" as a "commercial commodity, produced and consumed as part of a capitalist industrial system." In this sense, entertainment signifies the film text as well as contextual resources, e.g., advertisements and the physical and social atmosphere of the theaters. See Richard Maltby, *Hollywood Cinema,* 2nd ed. (Malden, Mass.: Blackwell, 2003), 56.

7. Emily Rosenberg, *Spreading the American Dream: American Cultural and Economic Expansion, 1890–1945* (New York: Hill & Wang, 1982), 59–62.

8. A. A. Berle to American Diplomatic officers, February 22, 1944, 800.4061 Motion Pictures/409A, Records of U.S. Department of State, record group 59, National Archives II, College Park, Md. (hereafter State Department Records, NA).

9. Central Motion Picture Exchange (CMPE), *M.P.E.A.-Japan,* June 1, 1947, 1, Hidano Atsushi Collection, Tokyo.

10. CMPE, *M.P.E.A.-Japan,* June 1, 1947, 1.

11. Charles Mayer to Commander in Chief, July 7, 1950, box 5081, folder 13, Records of the Supreme Commander for the Allied Powers, National Archives II, College Park, Md. (hereafter SCAP Records, NA).

12. Mayer to Donald Nugent, July 27, 1950, CIE (B)-08391, Records of the Supreme Commander for the Allied Powers, National Diet Library, Tokyo; "Item for Next Issue of Information Centres Bulletin," undated, box 5207, folder 8, SCAP Records, NA. On the America House, see Reinhold Wagnleitner, *Coca-Colonization and the Cold War: The Cultural Mission of the United States in Austria after the Second World War* (Chapel Hill: University of North Carolina Press, 1994), 128–39.

13. Nugent to DCS/SCAP, October 9, 1951, box 5088, folder 15, SCAP Records, NA.

14. Kinema junpo sha, ed., *Kinema junpo eiga 40-nen zen kiroku* (Tokyo: Kinema junpo sha, 1986), 6.

15. Donald Kirihara, *Patterns of Time: Mizoguchi and the 1930s* (Madison: University of Wisconsin Press, 1992), 39–57.

16. Daiei charged Nikkatsu 45 percent rental and supplied 50 percent of advertisement costs. Japanese films rented out at a flat rate. Civil Censorship Detachment (CCD) Memorandum, May 13, 1947, box 8603, folder 7, SCAP Records, NA. According to Joseph Anderson and Donald Richie, the usual share of an American distributor was 35 percent. Anderson and Richie, *The Japanese Film: Art and Industry,* expanded ed. (Princeton, N.J.: Princeton University Press, 1982), 173.

17. Walter Mihata to Chief, Motion Picture Section, September 16, 1946, box 8520, folder 8, SCAP Records, NA.

18. *Kinema junpo,* May 1, 1946, 16.

19. *Film Daily,* October 16, 1946.

20. Nikkatsu kabushiki gaisha, ed., *Nikkatsu 50-nen shi* (Tokyo: Nikkatsu kabushiki gaisha, 1962), 57–58.

21. *Kinema junpo,* June 15, 1946, 18.

22. *Sentoraru nyusu,* 2, undated, 1.

23. CCD Memorandum, May 13, 1947, box 8603, folder 7, SCAP Records, NA.

24. *Kinema junpo,* June 1, 1946, 9; Jiji tsushin sha, *Eiga nenkan 1950-nen ban* (Tokyo: Jiji tsushin sha, 1949), 71–72.

25. Mayer to Civil Information and Education Section, January 12, 1948, box 5066, folder 2, SCAP Records, NA.

26. CMPE, *M.P.E.A.-Japan,* June 1, 1947, 9.

27. Jiji tsushin sha, *Eiga geino nenkan 1947-nendo ban* (Tokyo: Jiji tsushin sha, 1947), 56–57; *Zenkoku eigakan shinbun,* February 1, 1948.

28. *Asahi shinbun,* November 3, 1946.

29. *Sentoraru nyusu,* 2, undated, 1.

30. Motion Picture Export Association, "Minutes of a Special Meeting of the Board of Directors of Motion Picture Export Association, Inc.," September 29, 1948, Gradwell Sears Papers, box 7, folder 1, United Artists Collection, Wisconsin Center for Film and Theater Research, Madison.

31. *MPEA Newsletter,* December 1949, 4–5.

32. See the following forum: "Rodosho no kenkyu," *Kinema junpo,* August 15, 1955, 39–47.
33. Jiji tsushin sha, *Eiga Nenkan 1950-nen ban,* 52. *MPEA News,* no. 14, undated, 1.
34. *Zenkoku Eigakan Shinbun,* October 15, 1947.
35. *Kinema junpo,* October 15, 1948, 41.
36. *Nihon bunka tsushin,* February 20, 1947.
37. *Newsweek,* February 18, 1946, 97–98.
38. *Sentoraru nyusu,* 4, undated, 1.
39. *MPEA News,* no. 22 (July 1948), 1.
40. Jiji tsushin sha, *Eiga geino nenkan 1947-nendo ban,* 59.
41. *MPEA News,* no. 10, undated, 1.
42. *MPEA News,* no. 18, undated, 1; *MPEA News,* no. 17, undated, 1; *MPEA News,* no. 47, August 1, 1950, 6; *MPEA News,* no. 27, January 1, 1949, 4; *Rengo tsushin,* 1007, November 13, 1949.
43. *Sentoraru nyusu,* no. 7, undated, 4. CMPE-Nagoya agent Toshiharu Komaki recalls that he instructed local exhibitors in person, to normalize this strategy. Interview with Komaki, September 26, 1999, Kamakura, Japan.
44. *MPEA News,* no. 21, undated, 4.
45. *Sentoraru nyusu* no. 2, undated, 1; *Sentoraru nyusu,* no. 3, undated, 2; *MPEA News,* no. 10, undated, 4.
46. *MPEA News,* no. 24, October 1, 1948, 4; *MPEA News,* no. 25, November 1, 1948, 4.
47. *MPEA News,* no. 41, February 1, 1950, 1.
48. *MPEA News,* no. 28, February 1, 1949, 4.
49. *Sentoraru nyusu,* no. 2, undated, 1; interview with Komaki, September 26, 1999.
50. *Sentoraru nyusu,* no. 4, undated,1.
51. *Nihon bunka tsushin,* April 24, 1947.
52. *MPEA News,* no. 8, undated, 1.
53. *Sentoraru nyusu,* no. 7, undated, 1.
54. *MPEA News,* no. 33, June 1, 1949, supplement.
55. *Variety,* April 4, 1951, 7.
56. *Sentotaru nyusu,* no. 4, undated, 4.
57. CCD Memorandum, May 13, 1947, box 8603, folder 7, SCAP Records, NA.
58. Jiji tsushin sha, *Eiga geino nenkan 1947-nendo ban,* 57.
59. This trend to denounce Japanese cinema continued into the 1950s. See, e.g., Kitamura, "National Cinema, National Reception: Japanese Film Critics and the 1950s," paper presented at Annual Conference of American Historical Association, Philadelphia, January 8, 2006.
60. See, e.g., Yasuda Tsuneo, "Amerikanizeshon no hikari to kage," Nakamura Masanori, Amakawa Akira, Yun Koncha, Igarashi Takeshi, eds., *Sengo nihon senryo to sengo kaikaku: Sengo shiso to shakai ishiki* (Tokyo: Iwanami shoten, 1995), 251–85.
61. *Kinema junpo,* January 1, 1949, 41. *Zenkoku eigakan shinbun,* December 1, 1947. *Zenkoku eigakan shinbun,* February 1, 1949. *Kinema junpo,* March 1, 1949, 41. Also see *Rengo tsushin* 1102, February 25, 1949.
62. Jiji tsushin sha, *Eiga geino nenkan 1947-nendo ban,* 59.

63. *MPEA News*, no. 45, June 1, 1950, supplement.

64. *Motion Picture Herald*, July 19, 1947, 52.

65. *MPEA News*, no. 51, December 5, 1950, 6.

66. *MPEA News*, no. 34, July 1, 1949, supplement; *MPEA News*, no. 46, July 1, 1950, supplement; *MPEA News*, no. 51, December 5, 1950, supplement; *MPEA News*, no. 48, September 5, 1950, supplement; *MPEA News*, no. 47, August 1, 1950.

67. *MPEA News*, no. 39, December 1, 1949, supplement; *MPEA News*, no. 44, May 10, 1950; *MPEA News*, no. 48, September 5, 1950, supplement.

68. *MPEA News*, no. 14, undated, 1; *MPEA News*, no. 40, January 1, 1950, 6; *MPEA News*, no. 43, April 5, 1950, 5; *MPEA News*, no. 49, December 5, 1950, 5, 6; *MPEA News*, no. 50, November 5, 1950, 6; Kitamura, "'Home of American Movies': The Marunouchi Subaruza and the Making of Hollywood's Audiences in Occupied Tokyo, 1946-9," in *Hollywood Abroad: Audiences and Cultural Exchange*, ed. Melvyn Stokes and Richard Maltby (London: British Film Institute, 2004), 109–11.

69. *MPEA News*, no. 46, July 1, 1950.

70. *MPEA News*, no. 54, March–April 1951, 4; *MPEA News*, no. 49, December 5, 1950, 5, 6.

71. *Zenkoku eigakan shinbun*, May 15, 1948; *Eiga no tomo*, October 1949, 39; *MPEA News*, no. 26, December 1, 1948, 4; *Eiga no tomo*, February 1950, 60–61; *MPEA News*, no. 28, February 1, 1949, 4.

72. *Zenkoku eigakan shinbun*, June 1, 1948.

73. *Eiga no tomo*, January 1950, 51; *MPEA News*, no. 27, January 1, 1948, 4; *Zenkoku eigakan shinbun*, November 1, 1947; *Subaru Theatre News*, no. 11, November 1, 1947, 32; Kitamura, "'Home of American Movies,'" 113.

74. *MPEA News*, no. 36, August 1, 1949, 4; *MPEA News*, no. 46, July 1 1950, 6.

75. *MPEA News*, no. 39, December 1, 1949, 4.

76. Takemae Eiji, *Senryo sengo shi* (Tokyo: Iwanami shoten, 1992), 201; Joe Moore, *Japanese Workers and the Struggle for Power, 1945–1947* (Madison: University of Wisconsin Press, 1983).

77. Takemae Eiji, *Inside GHQ: The Allied Occupation of Japan and Its Legacy* (New York: Continuum, 2002), 457–515; Hirata Tetsuo, *Reddo paaji no shiteki kyumei* (Tokyo: Shinnihon shuppansha, 2002).

78. *Akahata*, June 25, 1947, 2; *Akahata*, August 30, 1946, 2; *Akahata*, January 22, 1948, 2.

79. *Eien rodosha wikuri*, August 4, 1948, 1.

80. Jiji tsushin sha, *Eiga geino nenkan, 1947-nendo ban*, 88.

81. *Eiga geino nenkan 1947-nendo ban*, 87; *Akahata*, November 9, 1946, 2.

82. The following two works also deal with SCAP's Cold War film policy: Kyoko Hirano, *Mr. Smith Goes to Tokyo: Japanese Cinema under the American Occupation, 1945–1952* (Washington, D.C.: Smithsonian Institution Press, 1992), 241–57; Tanikawa, *Amerika eiga to senryo seisaku*, 387–410.

83. "Admission of Foreign Magazines, Books, Motion Pictures, News and Photograph Services, et Cetera, and Their Dissemination in Japan," attached to an unrestricted memorandum by the U.S. Political Adviser for Japan, December 12, 1946, 894.916/12-1246, State Department Records, NA.

84. John B. Cooley to K. Derevyanko, March 20, 1947, box 5062, folder 15, SCAP Records, NA.

85. Bratton to Willoughby, November 18, 1946, box 8520, folder 8, SCAP Records, NA.

86. Nugent to C of S, March 22, 1949, box 5096, folder 8, SCAP Records, NA.

87. J.J.C., "Request for Information on Censorship by CMPE," January 20, 1947, box 8579, folder 26, SCAP Records, NA.

88. *New York Times,* December 14, 1946.

89. Nugent to Diplomatic Section, March 21, 1951, box 5088, folder 16, SCAP Records, NA.

90. RWA Memorandum, January 10, 1949, box 5072, folder 2, SCAP Records, NA; Donald Nugent to DS, December 31, 1948, box 5072, folder 2, SCAP Records, NA; Diplomatic Section Memorandum, December 14, 1948, box 5072, folder 2, SCAP Records, NA.

91. Nugent Memorandum, February 18, 1950, box 5081, folder 13, SCAP Records, NA.

92. Nugent to N. I. Agueev, April 28, 1948, box 5066, folder 2, SCAP Records, NA; Nugent to C/S, "Entry of Soviet Films into Japan," July 1, 1948, box 5066, folder 2, SCAP Records, NA.

93. A. P. Kislenko to D. Hickey, April 27, 1951, box 5088, folder 16, SCAP Records, NA.

94. See, e.g., Harry Slott, "Russian Film Ali Sher Navoi," April 4, 1949, box 5305, folder 3, SCAP Records, NA; Harry Slott, "Russian Feature Film *Train Going East,*" May 31, 1949, box 5305, folder 3, SCAP Records, NA.

95. Kislenko to Hickey, April 27, 1951, box 5088, folder 16, SCAP Records, NA.

96. Nugent to C/S, May 9, 1951, box 5088, folder 16, SCAP Records, NA.

97. *Zenkoku eigakan shinbun,* September 1, 1948. These European film exhibitors also joined arms to coordinate their activities. See, e.g., *Zenkoku eigakan shinbun,* May 1, 1949.

98. Jon Lewis, *Hollywood v. Hard Core: How the Struggle over Censorship Saved the Modern Film Industry* (New York: New York University Press, 2002), 11–49.

99. "American Motion Pictures with Anti-Communist Themes and other Industry Services via Film in the Anti-Communist Fight," undated (circa 1951), "American Films Abroad" folder, Special Collections, Margaret Herrick Library, Los Angeles (hereafter MHL).

100. G-2 to CCD, June 30, 1949, box 8603, folder 24, SCAP Records, NA; Cross-referenced memo, January 4, 1949, roll 14, MPAA General Correspondences, Special Collections, MHL.

101. *MPEA News,* no. 52, January 1, 1951, supplement.

102. CCD Memorandum, October 12, 1948, box 8578, folder 33, SCAP Records, NA.

103. Yasukichi Ozasa to MacArthur, July 5, 1949, box 595, SCAP Records, NA.

104. *MPEA News,* no. 36, August 1, 1949, supplement; *MPEA News,* no. 39, December 1, 1949, 4; *MPEA News,* no. 40, January 1, 1950, supplement.

105. *MPEA News,* no. 41, February 1, 1950, 6.

106. *MPEA News,* no. 40, January 1, 1950, 5.

107. *MPEA News,* no. 52, January 1, 1951, 2.

108. *Kinema junpo,* February 15, 1951, 86.

109. *Amerika eiga sendensha* (The big lift), pamphlet, undated.

110. *MPEA News,* no. 53, February 1, 1951, 8; *MPEA News,* no. 54, March–April 1951, 4.

111. *Red Danube* press sheet, undated.

112. Toyoko Hikokan, *Red Danube* flyer, undated. Also see Kindai eiga sha, *Gaikoku eiga no sengo 50-nen: Chirashi daizenshu Part 1* (Tokyo: Kindai eiga sha, 1995), 16.

113. *MPEA News,* no. 53, February 1, 1951, 5. *MPEA News,* no. 54, March–April 1951, 3.

114. *The Woman on Pier 13* press sheet, undated.

115. *MPEA News,* no. 41, February 1, 1950, 6.

116. *MPEA News,* no. 38, November 5, 1949, 2.

2. The Cultural Contradictions of Cold War Education: West Berlin and the Youth Revolt of the 1960s

Jeremi Suri

The history of the Cold War in the 1960s is a history of disillusionment and unintended consequences. Writing in the aftermath of this turbulent decade, the sociologist Daniel Bell observed that the promises of liberal capitalism in the twentieth century—individual enterprise, extensive wealth creation, and technological progress—had produced their own internal detractors. Many of the young beneficiaries of capitalist enterprise, wealth, and technology in the most prosperous Western societies no longer wished to support this system of relations. Raised in privilege, Bell's students at Harvard and other universities felt free to reject dominant political and economic institutions in search of cultural alternatives that emphasized more transcendent values. The very successes of capitalism undermined its hold on the minds of young men and women who took their high standard of living for granted. Modern societies confronted, in Bell's famous phrase, "the cultural contradictions of capitalism."[1]

Bell's analysis remains powerful, but it suffers from a neglect of the Cold War context that framed the development of capitalist institutions after 1945. Soviet-American rivalry transformed capitalism. Confronted by a communist adversary that appeared capable of endless "crash" production programs, the U.S. government and its allies pushed for rapid advances in science and technology. To stay ahead of Soviet slave labor, Americans emphasized innovation, with generous federal support. Recent studies of the U.S. "military-industrial complex" have focused on this point, particularly as it relates to the ways American policymakers contributed to a culture of inventiveness rather than enforced regimentation in the industrial facilities, military institutions, and universities funded for anticommunist purposes.[2]

The inventiveness financed during the Cold War gave the United States a tremendous long-term advantage in its competition with the Soviet Union. Over time, Moscow failed to keep pace with technological advances in the West. A consciousness of this shortcoming, as much as its material effects, contributed to the collapse of the communist bloc by the end of the twentieth century.[3] As early as the 1960s, the Soviet leader Nikita Khrushchev understood this problem and sought to redress it with rapid—and frequently erratic—action on many fronts.[4]

America's comparative advantage in international competition, however, had a complicated domestic side. The programs that encouraged U.S. and West European innovation also inspired rebellion against the leadership of these societies. Sophisticated citizens could build better cars and rockets, but they now desired better politicians as well. By the second half of the 1960s, the residents of the United States and its closest allies felt secure enough from international dangers to turn their attention to far-reaching reforms at home. Bell lamented that this revolt of the privileged was a cultural contradiction of capitalism. Integrating the international context with the local experience of popular unrest, we can more accurately call this a *cultural contradiction of the Cold War.* Soviet-American rivalry contributed to domestic activities that both supported international competition and undermined existing political authorities.

The Expansion of Higher Education in the Cold War

Higher education is a particularly appropriate place to look for evidence of the cultural contradiction that accompanied Cold War competition. Between 1955 and 1965, the number of students enrolled in higher education at least doubled in the United States, France, and West Germany. In Great Britain, university enrollments grew by nearly as much: 98 percent. This dramatic growth continued through 1970, as is shown in table 2.1.[5]

Policymakers in Washington, Paris, London, and Bonn financed this massive expansion in higher education because they believed that a learned and technically proficient citizenry was necessary to outcompete the Soviet command economy. James Conant—the former president of Harvard University, ambassador to West Germany, and scientific adviser to Presidents Franklin Roosevelt and Harry Truman—pushed this point during the late 1950s. Writing to President Dwight D. Eisenhower soon after the Soviet Sputnik satellite

Table 2.1. Total Enrollment in Higher Education, Selected Countries, 1955–1970

Year	United States	West Germany	France	United Kingdom
1955	2,812,000	133,884	152,246	85,200
1960	3,789,000	203,335	216,426	107,700
1965	5,921,000	279,345	368,154	168,600
1970	8,581,000	386,244	602,712	228,000

Sources: United States: U.S. Department of Health, Education, and Welfare, *Projections of Educational Statistics to 1975–76* (Washington, D.C.: U.S. Government Printing Office, 1966), 5, 102. U.S. Department of Health, Education, and Welfare, *Projections of Educational Statistics to 1980–81* (Washington, D.C.: U.S. Government Printing Office, 1972), 23, 158. West Germany: *Statistisches Jahrbuch für die Bundesrepublik Deutschland* (Stuttgart: W. Kolhhammer, 1956–71), 1956, 91; 1961, 106; 1966, 102; 1971, 81. Hansgert Peisert and Gerhild Framhein, *Systems of Education: Federal Republic of Germany* (New York: International Council of Educational Development, 1978), 14. Hedwig Rudolph and Rudolf Husemann, *Hochschulpolitik zwischen Expansion und Restriktion: Ein Vergleich der Entwicklung in der Bundesrepublik Deutschland und der Deutschen Demokratischen Republik* (Frankfurt: Campus Verlag, 1984), 134. France: Pierre Bourdieu and Jean Claude Passeron, *Les Héritiers: Les Étudiants et la Culture* (Paris: Éditions de Minuit, 1964), 120–21. Jürgen Schriewer, *Die Französischen Universitäten, 1945–68* (Bad Heilbrunn: Julius Klinkhardt, 1972), 561. Alain Bienaymé, *Systems of Higher Education: France* (New York: International Council for Educational Development, 1978), 4–5. H. D. Lewis, *The French Educational System* (London: Croom Helm, 1985), 101. United Kingdom: W. A. C. Stewart, *Higher Education in Postwar Britain* (London: Macmillan, 1989), 268, 271–72.

launch of October 1957 raised public fears of American scientific inferiority, he criticized the "present complacency and the confusion" that he saw surrounding government policy on education.[6] During the early 1960s, Conant spearheaded a series of collaborative projects underwritten by national governments and the Ford Foundation to create a "worldwide education revolution," centered on the United States and Western Europe. This endeavor encouraged democratic governments to see a national interest in developing what Conant called "the potentialities of all youth to fit them for employment in a highly industrialized society."[7] Conant's work made higher education a central element of Cold War policy on both sides of the Atlantic.[8]

Conant and his followers, however, overlooked the ways in which higher education provided a setting and a set of skills—what I have elsewhere called a "language" and an "infrastructure"—for dissident behavior.[9] The newly educated American and European youths who were trained to challenge their Soviet counterparts rapidly emerged as critics of their own societies. For the children of middle-class families—many the first generation of college students in their families—university campuses offered an intensive exposure to heretical ideas about social justice, economic redistribution, and cultural change. In place of the traditional canons of study that many leaders (including Conant) expected would instill patriotic virtue, students gravitated to the exciting ideas of intellectual critics like Michael Harrington, C. Wright Mills, and Herbert Marcuse.[10] These writers encouraged their young readers to attack the "false promises" of democratic governments that tolerated poverty, social repression, and militarism. Students persuaded by this simple yet alluring message could easily organize discussion groups and demonstrations thanks to the density on college campuses and the relative freedom of movement in these settings.

To the dismay of the very leaders who sponsored the expansion of higher education, university students undermined the domestic foundations for Cold War foreign policy in the late 1960s. In spite of its initial efforts to blame communist infiltrators of one kind or another for social unrest, the Central Intelligence Agency concluded that the "worldwide phenomenon" of "restless youth" was an outgrowth of structural changes within societies promoting higher education for the purposes of international competition:

> The proximate causes are rooted in the university: . . . The confidence of the agitators in the likelihood of their being able to expand a limited protest rests—sometimes fragilely—on a growing base of student cynicism with respect to the relevance of social institutions and to the apparent gap between promise and performance.[11]

West Berlin, the Cold War, and the Free University

West Berlin and its famous institution of higher learning, the Free University, were a microcosm for the contradictions in Cold War education. Located at the geographic center of the Cold War, the Free University symbolized the creative advantages of West against East. The violent protests organized by students during the late 1960s also revealed the threat that this institution posed to the cohesion of Western societies. The Free University was a Frankenstein that turned on its creators. Like the monster in Mary Shelley's novel, it pointed to a wider series of unintended local disruptions triggered by international political and social transformations.[12]

The Free University emerged from a series of student-led initiatives in West Berlin. Unlike any other German institution of higher learning, this was an institution founded in November 1948 as a response to public demand among citizens who found themselves alienated from the Soviet-dominated Humboldt University in East Berlin. Contrary to the rigid administration of its counterpart, the Free University encouraged experimental courses and creative pedagogy. Students in the Western institution had extensive voice in admissions and curricular decisions. The Free University was, at least in its earliest years, an experiment in democratic education, within a hardening context of Cold War conflict.

The West German and American governments, as well as prominent anti-communist institutions—particularly the Ford Foundation—funded the Free University because they recognized its attraction for men and women in the East. This institution was an integral part of the Western alliance's "magnet" strategy in West Berlin, and Europe in general. Policymakers in Washington and Bonn expected that the dynamic and democratic environment created by the Free University would attract the most ambitious and innovative minds from both Western and Eastern Europe. Drawn to the vigor and excitement of this institution, citizens from Soviet-dominated nations would now reject the grey and regimented life they endured under communist authority. In this sense, government-sponsored higher education in West Berlin was a sophisticated form of Cold War subversion.[13]

During its first decade, the Free University served the purposes of its Cold War sponsors with remarkable success. Between 1949 and 1961, more than one-third of the student population at the university came from East Germany. East-West contacts in this setting allowed Western authorities a unique opportunity to exert informal influence over some of the best and brightest emerging from the communist milieu. The virtues of the relatively open and democratic society in West Germany became evident, even as many students remained critical of American foreign policy. Most significant, the fact that students from East Germany had to travel outside the communist milieu for a dynamic intellectual and social discourse highlighted the shortcomings of the Soviet-dominated states.[14]

The East German construction of the Berlin Wall in August 1961 marked a turning point for the Free University, the Cold War, and the local experiences of West and East German students. The forced separation of the two Germanys turned the dynamic and cosmopolitan environment around the Free University rigid and tense, like the Soviet-American rivalry in Central Europe at this time. East German students could no longer travel by street car (S-Bahn) to the Western university. West German and American-sponsored anticommunist propaganda became more dominant within the Free University. Because the West German government was apprehensive about Soviet-sponsored subversion in this period of crisis, it began to discourage, and even repress, potentially dissident experimental ideas. The Free University was now isolated from the East and smothered by its Western sponsors.[15]

Cold War conflict in the 1960s undermined the hopes for a truly open and democratic model of education at the Free University. This model always served the political interests of Washington and Bonn, but it also maintained a recognized legitimacy from the space it offered for relatively uninhibited interactions between the citizens of different societies before 1961. Though relations among students between West and East were a definite "magnet" for American-sponsored interests, they also created an important degree of stability in Central Europe. Knowledge and contact across Cold War divides humanized the Soviet-American conflict.[16]

The Berlin Wall enforced clear and rigid boundaries, but it also created new sources of internal instability. The Free University no longer served as an environment where diverse political groups came together in a consensual and relatively open setting. Like the city of West Berlin, the Free University suffered from a pervasive sense of social abnormality. Here were a city and a university surrounded by a wall, preaching open and democratic education. The Free University benefited from generous funding and privileges to showcase the virtues of freedom in the West, but it also received increasing government pressure to repress communist points of view. West Berlin and the Free University became social pressure cookers for anxiety, discontent, and, very soon, angry protest against the isolating structures of the Cold War.[17]

The Free University and the Revolt against the Cold War
In the context of tightening Cold War divisions during the 1960s, the Free University developed as the "Berkeley of West Germany."[18] It symbolized the remarkable political and economic accomplishments of the Federal Republic, while cultivating radical dissent. Students in West Berlin revolted against the division of the city, the government in Bonn, and the Cold War in general. By the late 1960s, "most active groups among the student body," according to the West German philosopher Jürgen Habermas, "desire[d] the immediate overthrow of social structures." Radical students became "the backbone of an extraparliamentary opposition that seeks new forms of organization in clubs and informal centers, and a social basis wider than the university."[19]

West German youth dissent grew particularly disruptive in late 1966. Students blamed the American government for prolonging the division of Germany and supporting a "Grand Coalition" of the dominant West German parties—the Christian Democratic Union and the Social Democratic Party—that constrained political debate. In December, groups of young men and women demonstrated throughout West Berlin, including the crowded shopping area known as the Kurfürstendamm. One student leaflet pledged to restore "democracy, a socialist alternative, [and] a new left party" in West Germany. The protesters proclaimed their opposition to the "bankruptcy of the established parties."[20]

Altercations between students and law enforcement officers in West Berlin, including alleged incidents of police brutality, escalated through the end of

1966 and the early months of 1967. In January 1967, West Berlin authorities entered the offices of the Sozialistische Deutsche Studentenbund—one of the leading West German youth groups.[21] They searched through the organization's materials, confiscated membership files, and accused the group of conducting illegal antigovernment activities. This heavy-handed police behavior had the contradictory effect of strengthening public support for the student protesters throughout West Germany. In addition, it contributed to a more confrontational climate, especially within West Berlin and around the Free University. The social tension in this old Prussian city now approximated the polarized atmosphere of Berkeley.[22]

West German authorities worried not only about the mounting protests of the New Left. They also confronted a resurgent nationalist right. In 1967 and 1968, the Nationaldemokratische Partei Deutschlands (NPD) won between 7 and 9.8 percent of the vote in local elections. Friedrich Thielen and Adolf von Thadden—the leaders of the NPD—called for a strong, independent, and re-united Germany, free of the "alien" interests that had allegedly corrupted the states on both sides of the Berlin Wall. "Our nation" (*Volk*), the NPD Manifesto proclaimed, "is being merged into two antagonistic systems." "Territorially alien powers are assuming the guardianship of the peoples (*Völker*) of Europe and jointly maintaining the division of Germany and of Europe for their own political aims."[23]

Like the students on the left, the NPD attacked what it called the "unrestrained materialism" that harmed the people's spiritual and moral health (*Volksgesundheit*). The party's 28,000 members condemned the Grand Coalition for repressing traditional German family and community traditions. Instead of increased federal aid to universities, the NPD argued that the "youth want and need decent, clean standards to look up to." The NPD demanded a strong central government that would eliminate "public immorality."[24]

In retrospect, the challenge from the nationalist right appears quite tame. The NPD never crossed the critical 5 percent threshold in national elections required for seating in the West German Bundestag. During the late 1960s, however, worries about the party animated radical students and government officials responsible for protecting the social order. Protesters at the Free University renounced the alleged return of "fascists" to German politics.[25] Policymakers feared that continued student radicalism would inspire more counterdemonstrations on the right. Excessive police repression of left-leaning protesters could also legitimize the militant rhetoric of the NPD. Student demonstrations at the Free University posed a very difficult dilemma for a society scarred by memories of both the Weimar period of social disorder and the Nazi years of excessive state power.[26]

Washington's attempts to secure West German financial and moral support for the war in Vietnam added another layer to the troubles around the Free University. Repeatedly, American leaders argued that the sanctity of anticommunist commitments in Southeast Asia was vital for the international credibility of the North Atlantic Treaty Organization (NATO). If the United States allowed communist advances in Vietnam, then that would allegedly encourage enemy incursions in Europe as well. American representatives like Secretary of State Dean Rusk argued that Bonn's aid for U.S. efforts in Vietnam was a matter of West German security and obligation to its most important ally.[27]

Student protesters in West Berlin turned this argument on its head. They contended that America's support for South Vietnamese dictators discredited the democratic claims of the anticommunist states. The war in Southeast Asia was not an isolated, faraway event for the men and women attending the Free University. They felt the presence of military forces—both Warsaw Pact and NATO—all around them. They feared that the indiscriminate and brutal violence exhibited by the allegedly most advanced societies in Vietnam would reverberate in their contested territory. The dogmatic reaction of local police and university officials to the protests of late 1966 only heightened these student anxieties. "Today Vietnam, tomorrow us," the protesters predicted.[28]

The "America House" in West Berlin—established to build cultural contacts between the United States and West Germany—became a favored target for demonstrations and physical attacks in 1967. Early in the year, members of the Sozialistische Deutsche Studentenbund defaced the building, throwing makeshift water balloons filled with red paint at its glass and concrete exterior. They accused the United States of propagating imperialism through its cultural, economic, and military programs overseas. Protesters argued that Washington acted as an "occupying" power in West Germany, stifling creative, sometimes socialist-inspired, reforms. The America House found itself under student siege for much of the next decade.[29]

U.S. Vice President Hubert Humphrey visited the city on April 6, 1967, seeking to reinvigorate German-American friendship after the first attacks on the U.S. cultural center. Humphrey hoped to arouse the same public displays of goodwill that had greeted President John F. Kennedy's "Ich bin ein Berliner" speech in June 1963. Kennedy had also spoken to an enthusiastic Free University audience about the "unity of the West" and future work for a "peaceful reunification of Germany."[30]

Humphrey's appearance in West Berlin succeeded only in extinguishing the still lingering legacy of Kennedy's earlier trip. Before Humphrey's arrival, rumors spread of an assassination attempt organized by some of the West German students who had attacked the America House. The police in West Berlin arrested eleven young people and tightened security on the eve of the vice president's visit.[31] Kennedy had traveled in a topless car, mingled with crowds, and delivered his famous oration from an open platform. Humphrey, in contrast, gave a short, nondescript speech to the Berlin House of Representatives, avoiding any uncontrolled contact with citizens on the street.[32]

During Humphrey's short time in West Berlin, more than 2,000 students demonstrated against American policies at the city offices of *Der Spiegel*—a popular pro-American newsweekly. The vice president was so dismayed by his treatment overseas, especially in West Berlin, that he lashed out against his critics. In a National Security Council meeting soon after his return to Washington, he uncharacteristically interjected that the "Europeans have rejected the world after the loss of their colonies. They resent U.S. power. . . . The Europeans are selfish. We should challenge them to participate in the world outside their borders. We must keep pounding at them on this problem."[33]

Humphrey correctly identified the rising anti-American sentiment in West Berlin. Protesters had seized the initiative in the streets—they were now the ones pressuring state officials. Student demonstrations continued after the vice president's visit, including a sit-in of more than 300 men and women at the meeting of the Free University's Academic Senate on April 19, 1967. For the first time in its history, the rector of the school had to call police on to the campus. Fears of disorder and excessive reaction rose yet again as university officials struggled to punish disruptive individuals while avoiding additional provocation.[34]

In June, another foreign visitor inspired disruptive activity in West Berlin. Mohammed Reza Pahlavi—the shah of Iran—made a dramatic state visit. The Persian dictator and his glamorous wife traveled around West Germany in an attempt to foster closer economic and cultural ties between the two societies. Leaders in both states saw themselves as emerging "middle" powers, poised to challenge Soviet and American global dominance, as well as growing Chinese power in Asia. During an extended discussion, the shah and West German Chancellor Kurt Georg Kiesinger emphasized new opportunities for joint projects in weapons development and industrial production. West Germany would provide technical know-how and some capital. The Iranians would supply their own capital, labor, and, of course, oil. Working together, the two states hoped to escape the limits of the bipolar international system.[35]

For residents of West Berlin, however, it appeared that deeper relations with the shah would only prolong the injustices of the Cold War world. Within the Free University, a number of Iranian émigrés publicized the frequent domestic brutalities of the government in Tehran.[36] The shah's security forces beat, tortured, and often murdered critics at home. No one could question the authority of the absolute ruler. The shah and his close associates accumulated and flaunted ostentatious riches while the majority of the country's citizens were mired in poverty.[37]

The Iranian leader was an anticommunist and a modernizer who maintained friendly relations with the Western powers in an important strategic area, but he was hardly a democrat. In the rush to build deeper economic and cultural ties with the shah, the Federal Republic—like the United States and other Western nations—neglected the Iranian leader's grave domestic shortcomings.[38] "We Germans," one student leaflet proclaimed, "have, with the help of the other great powers, supported a dictator. We cannot legitimize such a dictator with assistance and heartfelt reception." "Through our demonstration," the protesters announced, "we want to direct your attention to the true conditions in Iran."[39]

The domestic brutalities perpetrated in Iran, with Western aid, were not isolated occurrences. Students in West Berlin recognized that communist containment, economic development, and concerns for international stability frequently led democratic leaders to underwrite domestic violence. In Southeast Asia and Latin America, this was so common by the 1960s as to almost escape notice. In Europe—including West Germany—the widespread acceptance of the divided status quo on the continent reflected a choice for security over self-determination. "Iran is for us," the protesting students explained, "just one example of the difficult problems in the developing countries today." The "realities" of international politics appeared to smother real democracy. By demonstrating against the Iranian shah, the American vice president, and other allies, members of the Free University hoped that they could inspire greater international concern for "basic democratic rights."[40] Though they did not completely overlook the violence of "leftist" regimes—especially those in the Soviet bloc—protesters focused their attention on the brutalities of "rightwing" anticommunists.

The Free University and the Allure of Global Revolution

The shah arrived in West Berlin on June 2, 1967. Throughout the day, protesting students trailed his entourage, shouting "freedom for Iranians" and "Shah, Shah, Charlatan," as well as other cruder epithets. In the evening, as the foreign guests traveled to the city Opera House for a performance of Mozart's *Magic Flute,* more than 800 men and women attempted to block the streets. An army of police officers and the shah's personal bodyguards reacted to the aggressive crowd with force. After the delayed dignitaries finally reached their destination, the Iranian personnel accompanying the entourage used large sticks and other projectiles to beat upon the protesters. The West Berlin police, according to reports in *Der Spiegel,* acted similarly.[41]

Amid the disorder on the Berlin streets, a plainclothes police officer fired two shots at approximately 20 minutes after 8 o'clock. Benno Ohnesorg, a twenty-six-year-old Free University student, fell to the ground and died soon thereafter. By almost all accounts, Ohnesorg was only a peripheral participant in the demonstrations. No one provided evidence that he directly provoked the West Berlin police in any way. According to the bishop of his church, Ohnesorg was "not a fanatic" but a good citizen who was active in the student religious community.[42]

Ohnesorg's murder threw the city into virtual chaos. According to a prominent newsweekly, the anguish exhibited by students and other sympathetic citizens after the incident rivaled the emotions unleashed by the construction of the Berlin Wall almost six years earlier.[43] The mayor of West Berlin, Heinrich Albertz, gave an address on television the next day, pleading for "security and order." He accused an extreme minority of "terrorizing" the population.[44]

This student minority only grew in size and unruliness during the coming days. More than 4,000 men and women gathered on June 3, 1967, to condemn the entire West Berlin city government for Ohnesorg's death. The angry protesters demanded the resignation of the mayor, the police chief, and other officials.[45] Accused of authorizing widespread brutality, Mayor Albertz soon resigned. The city of West Berlin never regained the "security and order" that government and university officials demanded. A frustrated Chancellor Kiesinger lamented that the youth of his nation had fallen victim to an "international sickness" that infected all the major states.[46] The West German government struggled to repress proliferating student demonstrations without provoking more radicalism, or an NPD-advocated reaction.

In the second half of 1967, one fiery student emerged as the chief agitator for protest activity in West Berlin. Rudolf "Rudi" Dutschke came from the province of Brandenburg in East Germany. The Communist government had barred him from higher education when he refused to participate in mandatory military service during the late 1950s. As a consequence, he attended the Free University—the only postsecondary institution from which he was not barred. After the construction of the Berlin Wall, he fled to the Western half of the city, continuing his studies in sociology, philosophy, and political science at the Free University.

Unlike most other students in Western Europe and the United States, Dutschke understood the domestic cruelties of the Soviet bloc firsthand. In West Berlin, however, he found many of the promised freedoms unfulfilled. He took particular aim at the "manipulation" of power that allowed dominant political and economic groups to make policy without popular consent. He blamed government "bureaucracy" for prolonging Cold War divisions in Europe, supporting dictators around the world, employing violence in Southeast Asia, and neglecting inequalities between rich and poor. The established political institutions in West Germany "blocked" necessary reforms, according to this analysis.[47] "We must always make more people conscious and politically mobilized," he announced. Active students would harass established elites, creating the foundation for what he called an "anti-authoritarian camp."[48]

Sit-ins, demonstrations, and organized student heckling prohibited regular instruction at the Free University during late 1967 and early 1968.[49] Dutschke's followers did much more than voice radical rhetoric. At times, student activity became explicitly violent. Men and women began to identify themselves as members of an "academic proletariat" that, in Marxist terms, required the use of force against its oppressors.[50] During protest marches, students hurled tomatoes, rocks, and even bricks at the police.[51] Dutschke was careful never to advocate student violence, but when pressed he refused to condemn it.[52]

Free University students saw themselves as players in a larger global revolution. In his diary, Dutschke wrote with relish about the development of an international movement against both American and Soviet domination. He intentionally overlooked the domestic abuses of Mao Zedong, Che Guevara, and Fidel Castro because these figures publicly challenged the Cold War status quo. They were vanguards for radical change in image, if not reality.[53] Following Mao's inspiration, in particular, Dutschke called on students around the world to lead a "long march" through the institutions of society, overturning established centers of power from within and without. "The third front is set up," Dutschke wrote in his diary. Like guerilla fighters in Bolivia and South Vietnam, men and women in West Germany would wage a militant struggle to smash the existing order.[54]

In this context, the Vietnam War provided both an inspiration and an opportunity for the student protesters in West Berlin. Dutschke and others saw the fierce fighting around the time of the Tet Offensive as overriding confirmation of the destruction that followed from Western attempts to foster "development" in the developing world.[55] In South Vietnam, American bombs and guns protected an unpopular, corrupt government that looked more like the shah of Iran's dictatorship than a democratic state. America and its West European allies had become "imperialists," according to this analysis. Vietnamese villagers and German students would struggle as a united "third front" to "revolutionize the masses."[56]

American setbacks in Vietnam opened the possibility of successful resistance from both the periphery and within. "Comrades, Anti-authoritarians, People!" Dutschke exclaimed, "we have an historic opening." "Real solidarity with the Vietnamese revolution comes from the actual weakening and upheaval in the centers of imperialism." Students, natives, and guerilla fighters had all become proletarians under the domination of repressive "fascists." The time for a global "emancipatory struggle and national self-determination" had arrived.[57] After Tet, the tide of history appeared to move in favor of the weak and downtrodden.

On February 17–18, 1968, students at the Free University organized an "International Vietnam Congress," using the war to bring 10,000 protesters and intellectuals together from all across Western Europe.[58] Reform through existing institutions had become "hopeless," Dutschke remarked in his diary. "We must do something else." "We will make the Vietnam Congress," he wrote, "into an international manifestation of solidarity with the bombed and struggling people."[59] Accordingly, he addressed the attendees of the Congress, calling for "revolutionary struggle" against the domination of the great powers in Asia, Latin America, and other parts of the world.[60]

Demonstrations throughout West Berlin and the rest of West Germany grew more confrontational after February 1968. The government proposed a set of "emergency laws" permitting expanded police powers to control unruly crowds. Students besieged government buildings, foreign embassies, and the offices of university administrators. Instead of sitting in, men and women now staged "go-ins," which included physical harassment and deliberate property damage. Almost all institutions of authority came under attack, including communist-supported organizations that appeared hesitant to join the student radicals.[61]

On the afternoon of April 11, 1968, an unemployed worker—Josef Bachmann—shot Dutschke three times at close range. Dutschke miraculously survived, but he never fully recovered before his death in 1979. Students immediately blamed the government and the press for encouraging the attack.[62] That night, more than 5,000 young men and women marched to the center of West Berlin, angrily condemning the entire "system." The next day, another 5,000 students protested in front of City Hall. Demonstrations with even larger numbers continued, reaching a crescendo during the month of May. When the West German *Bundestag* passed the long-debated "emergency laws" for public order on May 30, 1968, protesters demanded popular "agitation" to undermine the existing regime. The student revolt had, by this time, become a self-conscious "guerilla" struggle.[63]

The men and women who took to the streets did not achieve the radical changes they sought. They did, however, reorient West German society. Before 1968, West Berlin was a Cold War frontier, an outpost of communist containment. The East Germans and the Soviets constituted the greatest threat to the city. After 1968, the most pressing danger to West Berlin and the Federal Republic came from within. Moscow did not want war but expanded trade and economic assistance from the West.[64] University students who received more aid and privileges from the state than other citizens were now the main enemies of order. They continuously attacked the government through words, demonstrations, and, in some cases, acts of terror. Throughout the next decade, extreme "extra-parliamentary opposition" would remain a source of violence and uncertainty for the West German leadership.[65]

Conclusions

The geographic position of West Berlin reflected the conflict between the capitalist and communist states after World War II. This was a Cold War city. The Free University came into existence as a Cold War university sponsored, by its American and West German benefactors, as a "magnet" for citizens in the Soviet bloc. The Free University offered a model of democratic education that highlighted the inventiveness and openness of the West, in contrast to the regimented and authoritarian East.

The tightening of Cold War divisions in the 1960s, especially following the construction of the Berlin Wall in 1961, transformed West Berlin and the Free University from places of hope into sites of despair. Privileged students, receiving generous government support to showcase the virtues of the West German regime, felt betrayed by the makers of foreign policy on both sides of the Wall. Students at the Free University, and many other institutions of higher learning around the world, revolted against the Cold War. In West Berlin, students pursued a vision of global revolution that appears naive in retrospect. The rhetoric of Rudi Dutschke and the Sozialistische Deutsche Studentenbund commanded a wide following in the late 1960s because of the profound disillusionment born of the lived Cold War experience in an isolated, and sometimes besieged, urban community. Students were desperate for a new vision that promised something other than permanent Cold War isolation and conflict.

The history of the Free University and the West German youth revolt in the 1960s underscores the cultural contradictions of Cold War education. As Daniel Bell suggested, the successes of American-sponsored enterprise, wealth, and technology gave students in West Berlin the freedom to rebel. After all, the citizens of the more regimented, impoverished, and technologically deficient Soviet bloc could not even contemplate public protests on the order of those around the Free University. Policymakers in Washington and Bonn built a vibrant university community in West Berlin to showcase the superiority of their societies. The large cohort of bright-eyed students who came to West Berlin, however, matured into a combustible source of violent protest when they discovered that the international rhetoric of Cold War freedoms did not match the reality of Cold War isolation. The geopolitics of West Berlin made the Free University an important instrument of American influence in Europe, but the social life of West Berlin made the university a source of violent anti-Americanism. The Free University embodied a profound cultural contradiction.

American and West German leaders remade the political and social landscape of West Berlin through their support for the Free University. At the international level, the new institution contributed many valuable resources to the policy of communist containment. At the local level, the student community around the Free University challenged the values underpinning this policy dogma. The Cold War, in this sense, created a dialectical relationship between the international and the local. As with all dialectics, this one produced many surprising outcomes—most notably, the worldwide turbulence of the late 1960s and its lingering wounds. The cultural contradictions of Cold War education have been carried into a post–Cold War world.

Notes

1. Daniel Bell, *The Cultural Contradictions of Capitalism* (New York: Basic Books, 1996; orig. pub. 1976), esp. 33–84.

2. Michael Hogan, *A Cross of Iron: Harry S. Truman and the Origins of the National Security State, 1945–1954* (New York: Cambridge University Press, 1998); Aaron L. Friedberg, *In the Shadow of the Garrison State: America's Anti-Statism and Its Cold War Grand Strategy* (Princeton, N.J.: Princeton University Press, 2000).

3. See Jeremi Suri, "Explaining the End of the Cold War: A New Historical Consensus?" *Journal of Cold War Studies* 4 (Fall 2002): 60–92.

4. See William Taubman, *Khrushchev: The Man and His Era* (New York: W. W. Norton, 2003), 507–77; John Lewis Gaddis, *We Now Know: Rethinking Cold War History* (New York: Oxford University Press, 1997), 261–66.

5. For a detailed discussion of these statistics, and their sources and implications, see Jeremi Suri, *Power and Protest: Global Revolution and the Rise of Détente* (Cambridge, Mass: Harvard University Press, 2003), 89–94, 269–71.

6. James Conant to Dwight Eisenhower, February 23, 1959, folder G: Correspondence, 1957–64, box 129, Personal Papers of James B. Conant, Harvard University Archives, Nathan Pusey Library, Cambridge, Mass. (hereafter Conant Papers). See also James Killian to James Conant, November 25, 1959, folder K: Correspondence, 1957–64, box 131, Conant Papers. On Conant's role as a science and policy adviser in

the Roosevelt, Truman, and Eisenhower administrations, see James G. Hershberg, *James B. Conant: Harvard to Hiroshima and the Making of the Nuclear Age* (New York: Alfred A. Knopf, 1993), 208–390, 687–705.

7. James B. Conant, *Shaping Educational Policy* (New York: McGraw-Hill, 1964), 2–8, 109–34.

8. See Suri, *Power and Protest,* 89–92.

9. Ibid., 88.

10. On the reading habits of student activists, see "References of Interest," folder 10, reel 1, series 1, SDS Papers, State Historical Society of Wisconsin, Madison; Abé Peck, *Uncovering the Sixties: The Life and Times of the Underground Press* (New York: Pantheon Books, 1985), 38–39. Gretchen Dutschke, *Rudi Dutschke: Eine Biographie* (Cologne: Kiepenheuer & Witsch, 1996), 37–47; Rolf Wiggershaus, *The Frankfurt School: Its History, Theories, and Political Significance,* trans. Michael Robertson (Cambridge, Mass.: MIT Press, 1994), 609–36; Tom Hayden, *Reunion: A Memoir* (New York: Random House, 1988), 77–81; Todd Gitlin, *The Sixties: Years of Hope, Days of Rage* (New York: Bantam Books, 1987), 11–44, 246–47; and Suri, *Power and Protest,* 94–129.

11. U.S. Central Intelligence Agency report, "Restless Youth," September 1968, Folder: Youth and Student Movements, box 13, files of Walt W. Rostow, National Security File, Lyndon Baines Johnson Library, Austin.

12. Mary Wollstonecraft Shelley, *Frankenstein, or, The Modern Prometheus,* ed., Marilyn Butler (New York: Oxford University Press, 1998). Shelley initially published her novel in 1818.

13. On American attempts to attract East European citizens and states away from Soviet control, see Melvyn P. Leffler, *A Preponderance of Power: National Security, The Truman Administration, and the Cold War* (Stanford, Calif.: Stanford University Press, 1992), 235–37; John Lewis Gaddis, *Strategies of Containment: A Critical Appraisal of Postwar American National Security Policy* (New York: Oxford University Press, 1982), 65–71.

14. See James F. Tent, *The Free University of Berlin: A Political History* (Bloomington: Indiana University Press, 1988), 1–176.

15. Ibid., 277–320.

16. On this general point, see Matthew Evangelista, *Unarmed Forces: The Transnational Movement to End the Cold War* (Ithaca, N.Y.: Cornell University Press, 1999); and Robert D. English, *Russia and the Idea of the West: Gorbachev, Intellectuals, and the End of the Cold War* (New York: Columbia University Press, 2000).

17. See Alexandra Richie, *Faust's Metropolis: A History of Berlin* (New York: Carroll & Graf, 1998), 770–78. West Berlin and the Free University also attracted many dissident West German youths because residents of the city benefited from military service exemptions.

18. Jürgen Habermas, "Student Protest in the Federal Republic of Germany," reprinted in *Toward a Rational Society: Student Protest, Science, and Politics,* by Jürgen Habermas, trans., Jeremy J. Shapiro (Boston: Beacon Press, 1970), 15. Habermas originally delivered this lecture in November 1967.

19. Habermas, "Student Protest," 18.

20. "Protest!" circa November—December 1966, folder: Berlin, 1966–67, box 87,

German Subject Collection, Hoover Institution Archives, Stanford, Calif. (hereafter German Collection). See also Rolf Uesseler, *Die 68er: APO, Marx und freie Liebe* (Munich: Wilhelm Heyne Verlag, 1998), 192–207; Gerhard Bauß, *Die Studentenbewegung der sechziger Jahre* (Cologne: Pahl-Rugenstein Verlag, 1977), 34–41.

21. American writers often confuse the Sozialistische Deutsche Studentenbund in West Germany with Students for a Democratic Society in the United States. Both used the initials "SDS." The two groups were very different in origin, and they never created deep organizational ties. The Sozialistische Deutsche Studentenbund, initially formed in September 1946, remained closely associated with the Social Democratic Party (SPD) in Western Germany until 1960. From 1960 through 1970, the Sozialistische Deutsche Studentenbund acted as an independent student group, growing progressively more radical in its criticism of the established West German parties. Torn by internal disputes, the Sozialistische Deutsche Studentenbund dissolved itself in 1970. Students for Democratic Society, in contrast, emerged only in 1959–60 without any party affiliation. It had no explicit socialist tradition, and it began as a very moderate organization committed to "participatory democracy," civil rights, and nuclear disarmament. During the course of the 1960s, Students for a Democratic Society grew more extreme in its criticism of established political institutions in the United States. The organization moved far to the ideological left—the "New Left"—but it never embraced socialist traditions in the way that the German student group did. Students for a Democratic Society also disbanded in the early 1970s, torn by internal strife. On the history of the Sozialistische Deutsche Studentenbund, see Jürgen Briem, *Der SDS: Die Geschichte des bedeutendsten Studentenverbandes der BRD seit 1945* (Frankfurt: Päd.extra Buchverlag, 1976). On the history of Students for a Democratic Society, see Kirkpatrick Sale, *SDS* (New York: Random House, 1973).

22. See Tent, *Free University of Berlin,* 321–22; Richie, *Faust's Metropolis,* 779.

23. "The Manifesto of the NPD," first promulgated in 1965, reprinted and translated in Ivor Montagu, in *Germany's New Nazis* (London: Panther Books, 1967), 127–31; quotation on 127. See also Fred Richards, *Die NPD: Alternative oder Wiederkehr?* (Munich: Günter Olzog Verlag, 1967), 126–29; David Nagle, *The National Democratic Party: Right Radicalism in the Federal Republic of Germany* (Berkeley: University of California Press, 1970), 35–122; David Childs, "The Far Right in Germany since 1945," in *Neo-Fascism in Europe,* ed. Luciano Cheles, Ronnie Ferguson, and Michalina Vaughan (London: Longman, 1991), 72.

24. "Manifesto of the NPD," 128–31; Patrick Moreau, *Les Héritiers due IIIe Reich: L'extrême Droite Allemands de 1945 à nos Jours* (Paris: Éditions du Seuil, 1994), 7–14, 76–78, 91–94; David P. Conradt, *The West German Party System: An Ecological Analysis of Social Structure and Voting Behavior, 1961–1969* (London: Sage, 1972), 38–42.

25. See "Akademisches Proletariat?" folder: Berlin 1966–67, box 87, German Collection; Uesseler, *Die 68er,* 65–84.

26. See "Stand der Deutschlandfrage," May 24, 1965, band 5, IIA1–80.00, Politisches Archiv des Auswärtigen Amts, Bonn (hereafter AA); Klaus Hildebrand, *Von Erhard zur Großen Koalition, 1963–1969* (Stuttgart: Deutsche Verlags-Anstalt, 1984), 202–18, 283–301, 365–83.

27. See "Telegram from Secretary of State Dean Rusk to the Department of State,

December 14, 1965," in *Foreign Relations of the United States,* ed. U.S. Department of State (Washington, D.C.: U.S. Government Printing Office, 1964–68) (hereafter *FRUS*), 13:283–84. For a detailed discussion of U.S.–West German government relations during this period and the issues of "off-set payments" for American soldiers in Europe and nuclear nonproliferation, as well as the Vietnam War, see Thomas Alan Schwartz, *Lyndon Johnson and Europe: In the Shadow of Vietnam* (Cambridge, Mass: Harvard University Press, 2003).

28. Aufruf, c. 1967, folder: Berlin, 1967, box 87, German Collection.

29. See Richie, *Faust's Metropolis,* 779.

30. See John F. Kennedy, Remarks in the Rudolph Wilde Platz, Berlin, June 26, 1963, Public Papers of the President, John F. Kennedy, 1963, 524–25; John F. Kennedy, Address at the Free University of Berlin, June 26, 1963, Public Papers of the President, John F. Kennedy, 1963, 526–29, quotations on 529. See also Richie, *Faust's Metropolis,* 771–73; Tent, *Free University of Berlin,* 281.

31. See Tent, *Free University of Berlin,* 322; "11 Seized in Berlin in a reported Plot to Kill Humphrey," *New York Times,* April 6, 1967.

32. For the text of Humphrey's speech, see *Department of State Bulletin* 56 (May 1, 1967): 680–81. On Humphrey's West European tour between March 28 and April 8, 1967, see Carl Solberg, *Hubert Humphrey: A Biography* (New York: W. W. Norton, 1984), 304–6.

33. "Summary Notes of the 569th Meeting of the National Security Council, May 3, 1967," in *FRUS,* 13:572–73. These quotations are from Bromley Smith's summary of Humphrey's remarks. Humphrey's comments were uncharacteristic because he had a long record in the U.S. Senate as an active internationalist, confident in the future prospects of transatlantic political partnership. See Solberg, *Hubert Humphrey,* 181–98.

34. See Tent, *Free University of Berlin,* 322–23.

35. See "Gespräch des Bundeskanzlers Kiesinger mit Schah Reza Pahlevi, May 28, 1967," in *Akten zur Auswärtigen Politik der Bundesrepublik Deutschland, 1967* (hereafter *AAPBD*) (Munich: R. Oldenbourg Verlag, 1998), 2:797–808. See also Aufzeichnung des Staatssekretärs Rolf Lahr, January 4, 1967, in *AAPBD,* 1:19–22. On the early development of West German "Weltpolitik"—expansion of influence in the developing world—see Karl Carstens an Ludwig Erhard, October 4, 1963, band 159, B2—Büro Staatssekretäre, AA; Karl Carstens an Willy Brandt, December 5, 1966, mappe 641, N1337—Karl Carstens Nachlaß, Bundesarchiv, Koblenz, Germany.

36. See Tent, *Free University of Berlin,* 323.

37. James Bill argues that the shah of Iran pursued a policy of controlled "reform from above." He sought to modernize the Iranian economy by encouraging land reform and industrial development, according to Bill, while also retaining tight control on political behavior. The growth of vocal opposition groups within Iran during the 1960s motivated the shah to use force against domestic challengers. The shah would not allow domestic reformers to challenge his dictatorship. See James A. Bill, *The Eagle and the Lion: The Tragedy of American-Iranian Relations* (New Haven, Conn.: Yale University Press, 1988), 141–49, 161–69.

38. Ibid., 169–76.

39. "Warum Wir demonstrieren," in "Dokumente des 2 Juni 1967 und der Zeit danach," folder: Berlin, 1967, box 87, German Collection.

40. Ibid.

41. See the eyewitness accounts in *Der Spiegel,* June 12, 1967. See also Uesseler, *Die 68er,* 244–55; and Tent, *Free University of Berlin,* 323–24.

42. See *Der Spiegel,* June 12, 1967.

43. Ibid.

44. Heinrich Albertz, "Sicherheit und Ordnung müssen gewährleistet bleiben," in "Dokumente des 2 Juni 1967 und der Zeit danach."

45. Anzeige, in "Dokumente des 2 Juni 1967 und der Zeit danach."

46. "Gespräch des Bundeskanzlers Kiesinger mit dem iranischen Botschafter Malek, June 15, 1967," in *AAPBD,* 2:911–17; quotation on 916.

47. See Rudi Dutschke, "Mallet, Marcuse 'Formierte Gesellschaft' und politische Praxis der Linken hier und anderswo" (1965), in *Frankfurter Schule und Studentenbewegung: Von der Flaschenpost zum Molotowcocktail, 1946–1995,* ed. Wolfgang Kraushaar (Hamburg: Rogner and Bernhard, 1998), 2:186–87.

48. See Rudi Dutschke interview in *Der Spiegel,* July 10, 1967.

49. Radical students formed a parallel "Critical University," offering their own seminars and ad hoc courses. See "Kritische Universität: Provisorisches Verzeichnis," Wintersemester 1967/68, folder: Berlin, 1967, box 87, German Collection.

50. See "Akademisches Proletariat?" c. late 1967, folder: Berlin, 1966–67, box 87, German Collection; "Zur Situation an der FU," December 6, 1967, folder: Berlin, 1966–67, box 87, German Collection.

51. See Uesseler, *Die 68er,* 256–96; and Tent, *Free University of Berlin,* 328–32.

52. See Rudi Dutschke, "Professor Habermas, Ihr begriffloser Objektivismus erschlägt das zu emanzipierende Subjekt," June 9, 1967, in *Frankfurter Schule und Studentenbewegung,* ed. Kraushaar, 251–53; Wiggershaus, *Frankfurt School,* 617–19.

53. "Rudi Dutschkes Tagebuch" (June 17, 1967), in *Mein langer Marsch: Reden, Schriften und Tagebücher aus zwanzig Jahren* by Rudi Dutschkes Tagebuch (Hamburg: Rowohlt, 1980), 70.

54. Ibid. See also Jeffrey Herf, "War, Peace, and the Intellectuals: The West German Peace Movement," *International Security* 10 (Spring 1986): 172–74.

55. On the Tet Offensive and its international implications, see George C. Herring, "Tet and the Crisis of Hegemony," in *1968: The World Transformed,* ed. Carole Fink, Philipp Gassert, and Detlef Junker (New York: Cambridge University Press, 1998), 31–53; Robert D. Schulzinger, *A Time for War: The United States and Vietnam, 1941–1975* (New York: Oxford University Press, 1997), 259–73; Don Oberdorfer, *Tet!* (New York: Doubleday, 1971); and Suri, *Power and Protest,* 161–63, 164–212.

56. Dutschke, "Rebellion der Studenten" (1968), in *Mein langer Marsch,* 68–69.

57. Ibid.

58. See Einladung, January 30, 1968, folder: Berlin, 1968, box 88, German Collection; Erklärung zur Internationalen Vietnamkonferenz—Westberlin, February 17–18, 1968, folder: Berlin, 1968, box 88, German Collection; Bauß, *Die Studentenbewegung der sechziger Jahre,* 95.

59. Dutschke, "Tagebuch, Januar 1968," in *Mein langer Marsch,* 122.

60. See Dutschke, *Mein langer Marsch,* 71–72.

61. See Offener Brief an die Regierung der Volksrepublik Polen, March 12, 1968, folder: Berlin, 1968, box 88, German Collection.

62. "Freunde und Genossen!" April 11, 1968, folder: Berlin, 1968, box 88, German Collection.

￼g

Jeremi Suri

63. See *Aktuell* 1 (April 12, 1968), folder: Periodicals, *Aktuell*–Berlin, box 86, German Collection; "Report from the Rector of the Free University," folder: Berlin, 1968, box 87, German Collection.

64. See Suri, *Power and Protest,* 245–58.

65. See Stefan Aust, *Der Baader Meinhof Komplex* (Hamburg: Hoffmann und Campe Verlag, 1985), 103–320; and A. D. Moses, "The State and the Student Movement in West Germany, 1967–77," in *Student Protest: The Sixties and After,* ed. Gerard J. DeGroot (New York: Longman, 1998), 144–49. Jeffrey Herf argues that the youth revolt in the late 1960s gave rise to a West German peace movement that refused to acknowledge serious security threats from the Soviet Union during the 1970s and early 1980s. See Herf, "War, Peace, and the Intellectuals," 172–200.

3. The Cold War and the American South

Thomas Borstelmann

"**O**ur economy is no longer agricultural," the eminent Southern writer William Faulkner observed in 1956. "Our economy is the Federal Government. We no longer farm in Mississippi cotton-fields. We farm now in Washington corridors and Congressional committee-rooms."[1] Faulkner understood that in the era of the Cold War, the American South was changing in essential ways. This poorest, most rural, and most isolated of American regions was on the way to becoming the modern Sunbelt, with the explosive growth and vast new wealth of cities like Houston, Atlanta, Orlando, and Charlotte, and the policies of the federal government were crucial to this development. Historic patterns of emigration out of the region slowed and reversed by 1970, as both whites and blacks began to pour into the states of the former Confederacy. Southern politics realigned, too. The introduction of democracy through the inclusion of African American voters after 1965 led to the demise of the old single-party Democratic South, white flight to the Republican Party, competitive two-party elections, and—by the 1990s—Southern leadership of both major parties on the national stage. Like the region's economy and politics, the South's race relations underwent a fundamental transformation with the overthrow of segregation. The contours and possibilities of contemporary African American life in the South, despite enduring discrimination, would be almost unrecognizable to a black Southern adult from 1930.

To what extent can these changes be attributed to the Cold War? Implied in this question is the counterfactual query of how much might have changed in the second half of the twentieth century anyway, without an extended global competition and conflict between the United States and the Soviet Union. Might the creation of the modern American South have progressed in fairly similar fashion either way? Counterfactual scenarios make historians leery for good reason, as they lead away from archives and evidence and toward the realm of informed guesswork. But they can be helpful sometimes in sharpening the questions we ask. In some areas, such as popular culture, Southern history since World War II has little clear, direct connection to the Cold War. Southern influences on American popular music, from Muddy Waters and Elvis Presley to Willie Nelson and Loretta Lynn, derive from domestic developments, not from events in Moscow or the developing world. Similarly, the extraordinary popularity of stock car racing and the rise of such Southern-based corporations as Coca-Cola, Pepsi-Cola, and Kentucky Fried Chicken do not stem from U.S. foreign engagements.

Such corporations did, however, benefit from the expansion of American influence abroad. They moved swiftly into foreign markets, surging outward from their regional roots into nations and neighborhoods from China to Buenos Aires. Similarly, Ted Turner's creation of the Atlanta-based Cable News Network (CNN)—which banned the word "foreign" from its broadcasts, because it sought to be a global network—could never have been so successful without the sustained U.S. involvement around the globe required by the Cold War. Memphis-based Holiday Inns laid the basis for modern hotel chains in the 1950s by building along the new interstate highways, a vast federal construction project funded in part for emergency transportation purposes linked to the Cold War.[2] So even when developments in the South appeared unconnected to events abroad, a closer examination can often uncover intriguing links.

What exactly do we mean by the South? In this postmodern era of constructed and deconstructed categories and sometimes uncertain realities, it is wise to be precise. Malcolm X, rejecting the complacent assumption of many white Northerners that racial discrimination and violence were primarily Southern phenomena, declared that the South was "anywhere south of the Canadian border."[3] The sociologist John Shelton Reed offered a more environmental definition based on where the persistent imported vine kudzu grows, which matches almost precisely the slaveholding areas at the start of the Civil War. Such a map aligns closely with maps based on percentages of telephone listings that include "Dixie" or "Southern"—in other words, how much people seem to identify themselves as Southern.[4] Another defining cultural variable, apparently not yet researched except impressionistically, would be the sweet tea line: where, on a trip from north to south, one begins—when not specifically requesting it—in a restaurant to be served iced tea with sugar already in it. Perhaps the most important aspect of the modern South, though, is its diversity. It was long the nation's most distinctive region due to its history of secession, enduring slavery and formal segregation, poverty, and rural character.[5] But now more than ever, there are many Souths, and it is not always clear what links the suburban sprawl of Atlanta and North Carolina's Research Triangle, the grinding rural poverty of the Mississippi Delta counties, the Latin American—oriented commerce of urban Miami, and the oil and gas industries hub of Houston. "South" is used here advisedly, recognizing the diversity within the singular term.[6]

From the New Deal through the Cold War

The New Deal and World War II set critical precedents for the intervention of the federal government in the development of the South's economy after 1945. When Franklin Roosevelt in 1938 declared the South to be "the Nation's No. 1 economic problem," the region's per capita income slumbered at half that of the standard of the rest of the nation—a mark that was already well battered by the persistence of the Great Depression.[7] Black Southerners, who from the earliest days of slavery had headed north in pursuit of better opportunities, continued their World War I—era pattern of migrating to northern cities for higher wages and greater freedom.[8] Roosevelt's large electoral majority included most Southern political leaders, who shared the president's political party allegiance and who welcomed the New Deal's unprecedented federal involvement in the region's desperate economy. From subsidizing farmers to bringing electricity to remote rural areas like the Texas hill country, Roosevelt's administration accustomed many Southerners to depending on a government that had once waged war against their grandfathers. Nothing embodied the U.S. government's new role in Dixie as fully as the vast Tennessee Valley Authority, which produced hydroelectricity, reduced flooding, and encouraged agricultural and commercial development across a wide swath of the upper South.[9] Roosevelt himself, though a thoroughgoing Northerner from the Hudson River valley, spent considerable time south of the Mason-Dixon Line at his favorite retreat in Warm Springs, Georgia, where he died in 1945.

Significant as it was, the expansion of federal influence into the South in the 1930s paled beside the full-scale flood of Washington dollars that washed into the region with the onset of World War II. Nine of the largest ten Army training camps were carved out of Southern pine forests, under orders from government officials impressed by the region's available land, easily accessible coast, and mild winters, and encouraged by the South's powerful congressional bloc.[10] From Texas to Florida to Virginia, installations for the Army, Navy, and Marines appeared everywhere; in a matter of months beginning in 1940, sprawling new Fort Bragg and Camp Lejeune began to reshape a sizable chunk of the economy of rural eastern North Carolina. Construction jobs proliferated, as did contracts for provisioning the vast new facilities and the hundreds of thousands of personnel stationed there. Ports and shipbuilding centers expanded almost beyond recognition between 1940 and 1944, including Charleston, Norfolk, and Mobile, whose populations grew by 38, 45, and 65 percent, respectively. In the war years alone, 3.2 million people left rural areas of the South, headed for cities and jobs on either side of the Mason-Dixon Line.[11]

Such rapid growth inevitably brought social problems with it. The South had never had a strong infrastructure of schools, municipal services, and transportation systems, and the existing facilities were often overwhelmed in the early years of the wartime buildup.[12] Several million Americans from other parts of the country were trained as soldiers at the new Southern bases. "Most of us had never met Southerners before," one New Yorker remembered, and they did not always like what they found. "A chigger-infested land of petulant senior officers" is how a Chicago native recalled Camp Forrest in Tennessee. Regional differences remained vibrant before World War II, and another New Yorker observed how each side was "continually amazed at each other's inability to speak English."[13] African American draftees from the North encountered the more bitter and dangerous reality of being formally segregated, often for the first time in their lives. Tensions mounted rapidly between black soldiers unaccustomed to such ritualized disrespect and white Southerners who expected greater subservience, both on military bases and in surrounding communities. Bonds sometimes formed across the color line, especially in combat abroad, but the military's firm segregation policies discouraged them. More common was the outbreak of armed white violence against black soldiers across Dixie throughout the war years.[14]

After the defeat of Germany and Japan in 1945, the troops returned home, but the old plantation-based economy of the Southern states continued to change. Technological innovation encouraged the mechanization of Southern agriculture. The development and widespread use by 1950 of mechanical cotton pickers, in conjunction with new chemical weed killers, dramatically improved the efficiency of cotton farming and proportionately reduced the number of jobs available for agricultural workers. Southerners left the land, and they left the South. In the 1950s alone, 5.5 million rural folk moved off their farms, and 3.5 million migrated out of the region.[15] In 1940, 43 percent of Southerners farmed for a living; in 1970, only 7 percent did so; by 2000, that figure had dropped to 3 percent.[16] The northward flow of unskilled Southern laborers, particularly African Americans, contributed to the ongoing reshaping of black communities in such cities as Detroit and Chicago.[17]

Other technological innovations stimulated the development of nonagricultural aspects of Southern commerce, in both the manufacturing and service sectors. None was more important than air-conditioning. Few buildings were air-conditioned in 1945, but by the end of the Cold War period in 1990, it would have been difficult to find a Southern business without this increasingly crucial system of indoor climate control. Most residents of the South encountered air-conditioning in commercial enterprises for the first time in the 1950s and 1960s, and by the 1970s most homeowners in the middle class and upward had installed it. A brief counterfactual scenario can suggest how important this innovation was for the postwar South: Can we imagine the contemporary scale and success of the banking industry of Charlotte, the oil and gas industries of Houston, or the manufacturing and commerce of Atlanta—in August—without air-conditioning? Washington has always been a Southern city in climate, as summer tourists walking on the Mall are invariably reminded, and it used to empty out in the summer when lawmakers and government officials—and any other residents who could afford it—sought refuge in cooler places. Air-conditioning facilitated the constant hum of government in the Cold War era, when national security managers wrestling with continuous international challenges could not afford leisurely summer schedules. Keeping cool, literally, helps them keep cool under the pressure of global crises. Florida's spectacular growth offers one other example of the significance of indoor climate control. Bolstered by retirees and tourism, both dependent on the new availability of air-conditioning, the Sunshine State raced from twentieth on the list of most populated states in 1950 to third in 2000.[18]

The creation of what the Republican analyst Kevin Phillips by 1969 dubbed the Sunbelt—meaning the Southwest as well as the Southeast—also fit in the broader pattern that we have come to call globalization. Improvements in communication and transportation made it easier for American corporations, long centered in the industrial states of the Northeast and Midwest, to look farther afield for potentially profitable new opportunities. Regions with lower taxes, fewer local governmental regulations, fewer unions, and lower labor costs—poorer places—became increasingly attractive alternative sites for manufacturers. Eventually, those regions would be primarily abroad, from the northern borderlands of Mexico to the varied nations of East Asia. But the first stop on the road to globalization for many U.S. corporations was the American South. Universal Manufacturing of Paterson, New Jersey, for example, moved its factory to rural Simpson County, Mississippi, in 1963, before ultimately shifting its production south across the Rio Grande River in 1987, and the Radio Corporation of America (RCA) followed a similar route for its plants, from New Jersey to Indiana to Mississippi, and ultimately to Mexico.[19]

Technological breakthroughs such as mechanical cotton pickers and long-term global shifts in the mobility of capital were not directly tied to the Cold War. They would have influenced Southern life in significant ways after 1945 regardless of Joseph Stalin's actions in Eastern Europe or the communist revolutions in China, Vietnam, and elsewhere. But at least as important as these other factors for the postwar South was the specific stimulus provided by federal government spending related to the crisis-ridden competition with the Soviet Union. Indeed, the late 1940s and early 1950s witnessed a fundamental reorientation of the U.S. government toward the new priority of containing communist influence on an open-ended basis.[20] Powerful new agencies that focused on international affairs, from the Department of Defense to the Central Intelligence Agency and the National Security Council, embodied this new national security state.[21] Their vast budgets and spending programs brought the influence of the Cold War home to all parts of the United States, including the South.

Following an initial drop with demobilization at the end of World War II, U.S. defense expenditures shot up after the outbreak of the Korean War in 1950. The decision of President Harry Truman to defend South Korea quadrupled American military expenses, and the defense budget continued to grow throughout the next four decades. The decision to go to war on the Korean Peninsula, made on the basis of national security considerations, helped shape the development of American society and politics at home in important ways, locking into place Washington's new international priorities. The Truman administration dropped its earlier initiatives of social reform, in areas such as health care and racial discrimination, as it focused on winning a war. Other Sunbelt states like California benefited enormously from the new scale of military spending, and so did Dixie.[22]

Most of the military bases built in the South during World War II remained in operation during the Cold War and even expanded, making hundreds of thousands of soldiers with steady paychecks a permanent part of the peacetime Southern landscape. Contracts for military supplies from uniforms to food and for facilities maintenance assured work and profits to thousands of Southerners in surrounding communities. The South's share of military contracts tripled between 1951 and 1980, promoted by the region's influential members of Congress. Representative Carl Vinson and Senator Richard Russell, chairmen, respectively, of the House and Senate Armed Services committees, made defense the largest employer in their home state of Georgia. Vinson knew a good thing. He teased his successor as committee chair, Mendel Rivers of South Carolina, about the extent of military dollars flowing into Charleston, including "an Air Force base, a naval base, a Polaris Missile maintenance center, a naval shipyard and ballistic submarine training station, a naval hospital, a Coast Guard station, a mine warfare center, and the Sixth Naval District Headquarters." Vinson concluded: "You put anything else down there in your district, Mendel, it's gonna sink."[23]

Specific expenditures related to the Cold War transformed important parts of the South. The World War II Manhattan Project had built an entire town at Oak Ridge, Tennessee. The expansion of the nation's nuclear arsenal during the Cold War kept in continuous operation such plants as the Savannah River complex near Barnwell, South Carolina, and the uranium enrichment facility in Paducah, Kentucky, although the poisonous nature of the materials handled in those plants eventually came back to haunt many of the workers in the form of sharply elevated cancer rates. In response to the Soviet launching of the beach-ball-sized Sputnik satellite in 1957, the U.S. government established the National Aeronautics and Space Administration (NASA), which poured $25 billion into the Apollo program between 1961 and 1972 to put a man on the moon.[24] Lyndon Johnson and other Southern leaders in Congress made sure that NASA invested heavily in the South, from its launch site at Cape Canaveral, Florida, to its vast facilities in Huntsville, Alabama, and its command center in Texas. The first phrase spoken on the moon, after all, was not "the Eagle has landed" but "Houston?" The historian Bruce Schulman has argued persuasively that Cold War expenditures allowed a new Southern political economy of "development through federal investments, as southern New Dealers had envisioned, but without liberal politics or redistributionist economic policy—without support for welfare, labor, [or] blacks."[25]

William Faulkner's suggestion that the South now farmed the federal government rather than the land implied a certain success in the endeavor, one rooted in the region's disproportional power in Washington. This influence was most evident in Congress, the arm of the U.S. government responsible for the appropriation of federal funds. Simple Southern charm was not the cause. The seniority system in the Senate and the House of Representatives gave extraordinary power to long-serving committee chairmen, and the single-party character of Southern politics until the 1970s assured political victors from the region that they would have unusual longevity in Washington. Incumbent Democrats rarely faced primary challengers, and the weakness in the South of the Republican Party—the party of Lincoln, of the North—made the outcome of most general elections fairly predictable. As the United States set forth into the Cold War era, Southern Democrats held a majority of the chairmanships of the major congressional committees, including those overseeing the Armed Services. "So marked and so constant is this high degree of Southern dominion," noted one observer in the mid-1950s, "that the Senate might be described as the South's unending revenge upon the North for Gettysburg." Dixie Democrats' staunchly promilitary nationalism helped them build and sustain close ties to the Pentagon and to major military contractors, all of which redounded to the economic benefit of their districts back home.[26]

Such wily Southern legislators as Russell wielded their disproportionate influence in the early decades of the Cold War to shape Southern society in other ways as well. The same power that tapped into the rich pipeline of anticommunist military dollars also went to work obstructing and delaying progressive efforts at social reform that aimed to bring the South more into line with the rest of the nation. This was nowhere clearer than with regard to labor organizing and civil rights. The onset of the Cold War in 1946–47 encouraged Americans to define themselves against anything that hinted of socialism, including any collective action by workers that was not emphatically anticommunist. The Taft-Hartley Act of 1947 hemmed in union organizing, and the Congress of Industrial Organizations (CIO) purged its most left-leaning member unions. The CIO's Operation Dixie, launched in 1946 to organize a large swath of mostly unorganized Southern factories, was soundly defeated by 1949, as employers and Southern political leaders played on the anxieties of white workers by associating labor unions with interracial socializing and desegregation.[27] The fervent anticommunism of the early Cold War meshed well with the South's historic hostility to the labor movement. Eager to woo outside investors and manufacturers, Southern leaders emphasized the region's anti-union traditions and passed right-to-work laws in each state of the former Confederacy by 1954.[28]

The years from 1950 to 1954 marked the apex of anticommunist enthusiasm in the United States. American soldiers fought Communist Chinese and North Koreans on the Korean Peninsula while Senator Joseph McCarthy and his allies battered the nation's political system at home with highly publicized persecutions of suspected subversives.[29] The nation's most conservative region, the South, shared fully in the national drama of fear and uncertainty, for the Cold War served to exacerbate long-standing conservative and even reactionary trends among white Southerners.[30] Conservatives in 1950 targeted the reelection efforts of two of the South's leading liberals, defeating Senator Claude Pepper of Florida and Senator Frank Porter Graham of North Carolina. In these campaigns, segregationists accused Pepper and Graham of being "soft" on communism, but they made clear that their real concern was that the two liberals were "soft" on racial equality—the greater and more imminent threat to many white Southerners.

Graham's opponents in particular stoked white fears of racial integration and miscegenation. The victorious segregationist candidate Willis Smith, the chairman of the Duke University board of trustees, and his campaign publicity director, a young Raleigh journalist named Jesse Helms, encouraged their supporters to label Graham—a former president of the University of North Carolina—as a communist dupe and a proponent of the "mingling of the races." The latter was the trump card. Graham's support for school desegregation was caricatured on fliers with pictures of African American soldiers dancing with white Englishwomen in London during the war, under such captions as "Remember, these . . . could be your sisters or daughters" and "WAKE UP WHITE PEOPLE." On the very day that North Korean troops poured across the 38th parallel into South Korea, white North Carolinians took the advice of Helms and his comrades and voted to defeat Graham in the Democratic primary.[31]

Domestic Consequences of the Cold War

The Cold War competition between the United States and the Soviet Union for the goodwill and loyalty of the nonwhite peoples of the developing world—the majority of the Earth's population—would ultimately provide an important stimulus for racial reform and the delegitimation of racial prejudice and discrimination in the American South.[32] But these developments gathered speed only in the late 1950s, after the most virulent stage of anticommunist political repression had passed. For the first decade after 1945, most white Southerners successfully resisted the logic of allowing colorblind freedom and democracy in the nation claiming to be the leader of the free world. One of the most significant changes in American politics after World War II was the emergence of the Democratic Party as the party of racial equality and desegregation. When Harry Truman initiated this shift during his 1948 reelection campaign by ordering an end to segregation in the U.S. armed forces and proposing a modest package of civil rights legislation, the "solid South" fractured. Large numbers of Southern Democrats bolted the party to support instead the independent candidacy of "Dixiecrat" Strom Thurmond of South Carolina. As the national Democratic Party continued to move toward a more progressive position on racial issues, its unhappy Southern members by the 1960s began to migrate to the Republican Party, first in a trickle for Barry Goldwater in 1964 and then in a flood by 1980 for Ronald Reagan. A few years later, Trent Lott of Mississippi, soon to be the Senate majority leader, declared that "the spirit of Jefferson Davis lives in the 1984 Republican platform"—a complete reversal of the original purpose of the Republican Party of Lincoln's day.[33] By the 2000 presidential election, Dixie was once again the solid South, but it was solidly Republican.

The Cold War's greatest influence on the American South came in the reshaping of its race relations. Though it was too often hidden behind the emphasis placed on the conflict between communism and capitalist democracy, the struggle to overthrow white supremacy and colonialism was the highest political priority of the majority of the world's people in the first two decades after World War II. National liberation movements swept European colonial rulers from Asia and then from most of Africa by 1965. In precisely the same years, African Americans and their white allies challenged—sometimes at great personal cost—the system of legalized segregation south of the Mason-Dixon Line, leading to its dismantling with the Civil Rights Act of 1964 and the Voting Rights Act of 1965. These movements had close connections, for African American freedom fighters understood themselves as part of a global struggle against racial hierarchies and inequality.[34] So, too, did the U.S. government recognize that its goal of a noncommunist, free-trading world order depended in no small part on its ability to sustain an alliance of the white nations of the "first world" with the nonwhite nations of the "third world" against the communist nations of the "second world."[35] The State Department in 1963 called this "the global U.S. strategy of fostering a cooperative community of free nations across the North-South dividing lines of race and wealth."[36] That strategy could not succeed without the preservation of social peace inside the United States itself. Yet in the early 1960s, white violence against civil rights workers in the South was reaching epidemic proportions. For the Cold Warriors who directed U.S. foreign policy, it finally became clear that Jim Crow had to go.[37]

Growing turmoil along the color line from the 1940s to the 1960s exposed an essential difference in priorities between Southerners and the U.S. government. Southerners, both white and black, remained focused on the rising freedom struggle at home, a conflict that increasingly pervaded their neighborhoods, workplaces, and schools. Issues of racial equality and desegregation dominated community politics and family lives in deeply personal ways. The conflict between civil rights workers and their segregationist opponents forced Southerners of all colors to make often painful decisions about what they believed in and how much they would be willing to risk for those beliefs.

By contrast with this local perspective, officials in Washington wrestled with what seemed like continual crises abroad from the Congo to Berlin to Cuba, with the threat of nuclear annihilation, and with full-scale wars in Korea and Vietnam. National security managers varied in their attitudes about race reform in the South, but not about the region's immediate political duty. They urged Southerners on both sides of the civil rights issue to calm down and slow down. Valuing stability and unity above all, they sought gradual reform that would not rock the national boat. Historians have often noted the contrast between the globalist perspective of American Cold Warriors and the local concerns of political leaders in newly independent nations in the developing world, with the differences in priorities leading to misunderstandings and perhaps avoidable conflicts. A similar gap in perspective frequently separated Washington from its own constituents in Dixie.[38]

Postwar presidents tended to agree, to varying extents, that racial discrimination was "our Achilles' heel before the world," as Senator Henry Cabot Lodge of Massachusetts put it.[39] Their elemental problem lay in their inability to wall off white American racial attitudes and practices—in the nation as a whole, but in the South in particular—from the rest of the world and its non-white majority. The United States was too permeable a society for outside observers not to see and understand what was going on along the color line. Indeed, the very idea of such a "containment" policy toward domestic racism cut directly against the grain of postwar U.S. foreign policy, which sought to assert American leadership around the globe, thus exposing more rather than less of Americans and American life to other nations. The American practice of the Cold War was grounded in the central belief that the liberal, democratic, capitalist order of the United States represented a more humane and attractive society than that of communist states. Hiding one's flaws was a tactic of totalitarian states, not free ones. Jim Crow laws could not be effectively hidden, and the political price of harboring them was going up fast.[40]

Faced with the Cold War logic of promoting greater democracy among the multihued peoples of the world, white Southerners understood themselves to be part of what Governor George Wallace of Alabama accurately called an "international white minority." The status of that white minority seemed newly uncertain. Gone were the comfortable days of white imperialists ruling the globe, a social order that white Southerners mirrored in their own communities, an order they had known and benefited from so long that it seemed to them as natural as air. Now was instead the time of the new United Nations and its growing majority of nonwhite nations, along with a U.S. government whose officials treated these African and Asian representatives as equals. Wallace in 1963 railed against the "international racism of the liberals" of the John F. Kennedy administration that sought "to persecute the international white minority to the whim of the international colored majority."[41]

Segregationists continued to identify with their white counterparts in southern Africa, the final holdout of legal racial discrimination by the mid-1960s. Conservative white Southerners admired apartheid South Africa and freshly independent white-ruled Rhodesia. By contrast, they heartily condemned the political instability of certain newly independent African nations such as the Congo, attributing the unrest to what they considered the inherent irresponsibility of black people anywhere. The self-interest of this worldview, however, with its real target of civil rights activists at home, and its sheer inaccuracy—in the face of foreign white meddling in the Congo and of evident stability in Tanzania, Botswana, and other black-ruled states—was increasingly obvious. Few observers doubted that white rule in its last redoubts was in greater peril than ever before.[42]

Like their segregationist opponents, the activists in the struggle for Southern freedom also understood themselves as part of a larger international movement. They found hope where George Wallace and his compatriots found despair. From Martin Luther King Jr. to Malcolm X, African Americans took inspiration from the success of peoples of color across the globe in throwing off the shackles of white rule.[43] They seized on the political language of the Cold War to make plain that the South's segregation mocked the U.S. claim to be the leader of the free world. The placard worn by one black marcher in the Birmingham protests of 1963 zeroed in on the hypocrisy of racial discrimination in the Cold War: "Khrushchev can eat here—why can't we?"[44] Who was the real enemy of white Americans, anyway—might they actually have more in common with white Soviets than with their own black fellow citizens? This recalled a similar question regarding America's previous enemy, the Nazis. German prisoners in transit across the South to prisoner of war camps during World War II had at times been allowed in eat in restaurants while the black U.S. soldiers guarding them had been forced to remain outside. Who was really the enemy for white Southerners?[45]

By contrast, white Southerners tried to use the Soviet Union as a different foil, arguing that communist approval of racial equality showed how wrong that equality must be. If communists were indeed the nation's mortal enemies, they insisted, then why should Americans want to agree with them on any issue? "Who cares what the Reds say?" demanded Georgia governor Herman Talmadge. "Who cares what *Pravda* prints?"[46] The problem for U.S. policymakers, however, was that many people in the newly independent nations of the developing world did seem to care; they did pay attention to communists as well as capitalists. The crucial 1954 *Brown v. Board of Education* school desegregation decision by the U.S. Supreme Court, built in part on a U.S. Justice Department brief emphasizing the importance of racial equality for American foreign relations, indicated that antiracist freedom fighters had the better part of this Cold War argument.

The Cold War impinged directly on the South in a new way in the late 1950s when diplomats from newly independent African nations like Ghana began traveling regularly between the United Nations in New York and their embassies in Washington. A lack of decent housing for people of color and the constant threat of harassment and violence made the city of Washington a tough assignment, even more so for a person assigned to represent his country with dignity. In a mirror image of how most American diplomats viewed positions in Africa, African ambassadors and their families and staffs found the American capital—the nerve center of the "free world"—to be a true hardship post.[47] Daily life in Washington for a dark-skinned official could be grindingly burdensome, from finding housing for one's family and schools for one's children to using public facilities such as restaurants and theaters and walking the streets around the nation's monuments to freedom. At least U.S. officials in the Eisenhower and especially Kennedy administrations were sympathetic and tried to help ease their transition to the city.

But getting there was not simple. After crossing the Delaware River on southbound Highway 40 from New Jersey to Delaware and Maryland, African visitors were regularly refused service in restaurants and humiliated.[48] Officials from the nation of Mali complained that "movements of African diplomats assigned to New York and Washington are reduced, for these two cities, to a corridor constituted by Route 40 and the New Jersey Turnpike, which link the two cities. And their movements are free only if they do not get out of their automobiles."[49] Washington, surrounded by segregationist states, seemed to be for African visitors what West Berlin, surrounded by communist East Germany, was for Western visitors: an isolated citadel deep in hostile territory, safely reachable only by air or by two restricted highways off which one dared not venture.

What difference did this new problem make for life below the Mason-Dixon Line? U.S. officials registered genuine anxiety about the negative implications for American influence abroad of the representatives of the world's large nonwhite majority being treated with such disrespect. "Racial incidents have produced extremely negative reactions" overseas, admitted Secretary of State Dean Rusk.[50] He and his staff sought solutions. In part, they tried to minimize publicity. Pedro Sanjuan of the State Department's protocol office noted optimistically that there had been "close to ninety major incidents involving African diplomats brought to our attention in the past two years," but that "through our efforts, almost all of them have been kept out of the pages of the newspapers." Another State Department official suggested that Africans might be protected from the typical treatment of dark-skinned people by wearing "a suitable unique type of pin or button" to distinguish them from ordinary African Americans who, apparently, would remain acceptable targets of discrimination.[51]

Thomas Borstelmann

The Cold Warriors responsible for the nation's foreign relations also began to promote reform at home. They built on the precedent of Harry Truman's President's Committee on Civil Rights, which in 1947 had demanded domestic racial reform to shore up the nation's foreign policy. Sanjuan lobbied the Maryland state legislature to enact a law to desegregate public accommodations, urging them to "give us the weapons to conduct this war of human dignity" against worldwide communism. More dramatically, both Eisenhower and Kennedy sent U.S. troops into Southern communities to restore order against violent white mobs seeking to prevent school desegregation. At Little Rock's Central High School in 1957 and the University of Mississippi in 1962, Eisenhower and Kennedy, respectively, reluctantly decided that federal force was required. They did so in part because of the extraordinary international attention focused on the two incidents, and the considerable embarrassment being attached to the nation's Cold War campaign for greater freedom and equality. For a national government whose highest priorities lay in waging the Cold War during an era of rising racial equality, the South's Jim Crow practices were rapidly losing their acceptability.[52]

The reluctance and caution with which Cold War presidents encouraged racial change in the South reflected not only political calculations and ideological moderateness but also an array of personal connections to Dixie. Truman, Lyndon Johnson, and Jimmy Carter all grew up in former slaveholding states; Eisenhower vacationed extensively in Georgia; Nixon used a "Southern strategy" to win election to the White House; Reagan opened his 1980 campaign by declaring his support for "states' rights" in Philadelphia, Mississippi; and George H. W. Bush moved to Texas as a young man and considered it home thereafter. These men viewed segregationist officials not as dire enemies in a struggle for justice in the American South but rather as a stubborn, backward-looking, but respected part of the nation's leadership.

Nonetheless, these presidents all agreed to varying extents that the nation's Cold War priorities abroad required white Southerners, as well as other white Americans, to change their racial practices. Truman and Eisenhower initiated this process by ending legal segregation in areas of clear federal—as opposed to state—authority: the armed forces, the civil service, and the national capital. Intense resistance to the implementation of the *Brown v. Board of Education* decision forced Eisenhower and Kennedy to send federal troops into Arkansas and Mississippi. Continued violence against civil rights activists persuaded Johnson to push the Civil Rights Act and the Voting Rights Act through Congress. Such interventions in Southern life were seen as unfortunately necessary to minimize the diplomatic costs to the nation of global condemnation of racial violence in Dixie.

90

Conclusions

The far-reaching changes that swept through the American South in the three decades after 1945 cannot be fully understood apart from the international context of the Cold War. The civil rights movement was embedded in the larger story of decolonization and the Cold War contest for global leadership and the meaning of "freedom." An illuminating example came in the choice of a secretary of state, responsible for the nation's foreign relations. Sixteen years after Truman easily appointed a white supremacist, James Byrnes, to the post, Kennedy found in 1961 that the segregationist voting record of his own preferred candidate, Senator J. William Fulbright, made him politically unacceptable. Kennedy solved this dilemma by choosing Rusk, a racial liberal from the Deep South whose grandfathers had both served in the Confederate Army. Rusk made excellent use of his roots in a testy public exchange on racial discrimination's impact on U.S. foreign relations, reminding Dixie senators that he was at least as "Southern" as they were. When Senator Strom Thurmond asked provocatively, "Mr. Secretary, aren't you lending support to the communist line?" Rusk dissented with indignation, underlining that he spoke as the American secretary of state. "Mr. Secretary," Thurmond persisted, "I'm not sure that you understood my question. I am from South Carolina." "Senator," Rusk responded, "I understood your question. I am from Georgia."[53]

One of the foremost themes of American diplomacy in the Cold War was the expansion of the power and reach of the federal government. Washington's newly long arm reached around the globe, helping bolster certain governments while subverting others, and helping restructure world political alliances. That same long arm also reached into Dixie, reshaping the contours of the region's economy and race relations. The U.S. government did not go eagerly into the South. It was forced to do so, in response to the sustained efforts of civil rights organizers and the brutality those efforts provoked from their segregationist opponents. The nation's Cold Warriors could not lead the international "free world" to stability and prosperity until they had their own house in order.

Pushed along by the international pressures of decolonization and Cold War competition, the magnitude of the changes in the states of the former Confederacy was occasionally startling. Fifty years after his presidential candidacy as an arch-segregationist Dixiecrat in 1948, Strom Thurmond could be found not only pursuing and capturing black votes in South Carolina but also beaming broadly for the world media while arm-in-arm with South African president Nelson Mandela, the former antiapartheid guerrilla and Communist Party ally.[54] We can acknowledge the enduring presence of discrimination and de facto segregation in much of the South—and the rest of the nation—and still recognize how different the region had become by the end of the Cold War from at its beginning. And from the forge of those often painful changes emerged the strongest presidential supporters of racial equality in American history: Harry Truman, Jimmy Carter, Bill Clinton, and especially Lyndon Johnson—Southerners all.

Notes

1. Faulkner is quoted by Bruce J. Schulman, *From Cotton Belt to Sunbelt: Federal Policy, Economic Development, and the Transformation of the South, 1938–1980* (New York: Oxford University Press, 1991), 135, 153.

2. David Halberstam, *The Fifties* (New York: Ballantine, 1993), 173–79; Tom Lewis, *Divided Highways: Building the Interstate Highways, Transforming American Life* (New York: Penguin, 1999).

3. John Egerton, *The Americanization of Dixie: The Southernization of America* (New York: Harper & Row, 1974), epigraph.

4. John Shelton Reed, *My Tears Spoiled My Aim, and Other Reflections on Southern Culture* (Columbia: University of Missouri Press, 1993), 8, 23, 27.

5. Mississippi was at the heart of this understanding of the region. See, e.g., James W. Silver, *Mississippi: The Closed Society* (New York: Harcourt Brace, 1964).

6. An insightful journalistic study of the contemporary South is Peter Applebome, *Dixie Rising: How the South Is Shaping American Values, Politics, and Culture* (New York: Harcourt Brace, 1996).

7. Schulman, *From Cotton Belt to Sunbelt*, 3.

8. Nicholas Lemann, *The Promised Land: The Great Black Migration and How It Changed America* (New York: Alfred A. Knopf, 1991), 3–58.

9. Dewey W. Grantham, *The South in Modern America: A Region at Odds* (New York: HarperCollins, 1994), 153–57. See also James C. Cobb and Michael V. Namarato, eds., *The New Deal and the South* (Jackson: University Press of Mississippi, 1984).

10. Morton Sosna, "Introduction," in *Remaking Dixie: The Impact of World War II on the American South,* ed. Neil R. McMillen (Jackson: University Press of Mississippi, 1997), xvi.

11. Pete Daniel, "Going Among Strangers: Southern Reactions to World War II," *Journal of American History* 77 (December 1990): 886, 898.

12. Ibid., 899–911.

13. Morton Sosna, "The GIs' South and the North-South Dialogue during World War II," in *Developing Dixie: Modernization in a Traditional Society,* ed. Winfred B. Moore, Jr., Joseph F. Tripp, and Lyon G. Tyler Jr. (New York: Greenwood Press, 1988), 313, 315, 318.

14. Neil R. McMillen, "Fighting for What We Didn't Have: How Mississippi's Black Veterans Remember World War II," in *Remaking Dixie,* ed. McMillen, 93–110; Harvard Sitkoff, "Racial Militancy and Interracial Violence in the Second World War," *Journal of American History* 58 (December 1971): 667–81; James Albert Burran, "Racial Violence in the South during World War II," Ph.D. dissertation, University of Tennessee, 1977; Charles D. Chamberlain, *Victory at Home: Manpower and Race in the American South during World War II* (Athens: University of Georgia Press, 2003).

15. Numan V. Bartley, *The New South, 1945–1980* (Baton Rouge: Louisiana State

University Press, 1995), 124–26; Jack Temple Kirby, *Rural Worlds Lost: The American South, 1920–1960* (Baton Rouge: Louisiana State University Press, 1987); Gavin Wright, *Old South, New South: Revolutions in the Southern Economy since the Civil War* (New York: Basic Books, 1986).

16. Nancy MacLean, "From the Benighted South to the Sunbelt: The South in the Twentieth Century," in *Perspectives on Modern America: Making Sense of the Twentieth Century,* ed. Harvard Sitkoff (New York: Oxford University Press, 2001), 221; Joseph A. Fry, *Dixie Looks Abroad: The South and U.S. Foreign Relations, 1789–1973* (Baton Rouge: Louisiana State University Press, 2002), 224.

17. See, e.g., Thomas J. Sugrue, *The Origins of the Urban Crisis: Race and Inequality in Postwar Detroit* (Princeton, N.J.: Princeton University Press, 1996); Arnold R. Hirsch, *Making the Second Ghetto: Race and Housing in Chicago, 1940–1960* (New York: Cambridge University Press, 1983).

18. For an insightful discussion, see Gail Cooper, *Air-Conditioning America: Engineers and the Controlled Environment, 1900–1960* (Baltimore: Johns Hopkins University Press, 1998).

19. William M. Adler, *Mollie's Job: A Story of Life and Work on the Global Assembly Line* (New York: Scribner, 2000); Jefferson R. Cowie, *Capital Moves: RCA's Seventy-Year Quest for Cheap Labor* (Ithaca, N.Y.: Cornell University Press, 1999).

20. Melvyn P. Leffler, *A Preponderance of Power: National Security, the Truman Administration, and the Cold War* (Stanford, Calif.: Stanford University Press, 1992); Arnold A. Offner, *Another Such Victory: President Truman and the Cold War, 1945–1953* (Stanford, Calif.: Stanford University Press, 2002).

21. Michael J. Hogan, *A Cross of Iron: Harry S. Truman and the Origins of the National Security State, 1945–1954* (New York: Cambridge University Press, 1998).

22. Ann Markusen, Scott Campbell, Peter Hall, and Sabina Deitrick, *The Rise of the Gunbelt: The Military Remapping of Industrial America* (New York: Oxford University Press, 1991).

23. Schulman, *From Cotton Belt to Sunbelt,* 146.

24. NASA Web site, http://spacelink.nasa.gov/Instructional.Materials/NASA.Edu cational.Products/The.Apollo.Program/The.Apollo.Program.pdf.

25. Schulman, *From Cotton Belt to Sunbelt,* 149 (quotation), 151; Fry, *Dixie Looks Abroad,* 237–40.

26. Nicol C. Rae, *Southern Democrats* (New York: Oxford University Press, 1994), 36–40, quotation on 38; Fry, *Dixie Looks Abroad,* 222–24. For a perceptive critique of this problem of Southern dominance on Capitol Hill, written at the onset of the Cold War era, see W. E. B. Du Bois, *Color and Democracy: Colonies and Peace* (New York: Harcourt, Brace, 1945).

27. Barbara S. Griffith, *The Crisis of American Labor: Operation Dixie and the Defeat of the CIO* (Philadelphia: Temple University Press, 1988); Bartley, *New South,* 57–62.

28. Schulman, *From Cotton Belt to Sunbelt,* 161–64.

29. Ellen Schrecker, *Many Are The Crimes: McCarthyism in America* (Boston: Little, Brown, 1998); Richard Gid Powers, *Not without Honor: The History of American Anticommunism* (New York: Free Press, 1995).

30. John Egerton, *Speak Now against The Day: The Generation before the Civil Rights Movement in the South* (New York: Alfred A. Knopf, 1994); Patricia Sullivan,

Days of Hope: Race and Democracy in the New Deal Era (Chapel Hill: University of North Carolina Press, 1996).

31. Julian M. Pleasants and Augustus Burns III, *Frank Porter Graham and the 1950 Senate Race in North Carolina* (Chapel Hill: University of North Carolina Press, 1990); David R. Goldfield, *Black, White, and Southern: Race Relations and Southern Culture, 1940 to the Present* (Baton Rouge: Louisiana State University Press, 1990), 67–70.

32. Mary L. Dudziak, "Desegregation as a Cold War Imperative," *Stanford Law Review* 41 (November 1988): 61–120.

33. MacLean, "From the Benighted South to the Sunbelt," 203. Lott's public enthusiasm for slave-owning and segregationist heroes of the old South eventually caught up with him in December 2002, when he was forced to step down as Senate majority leader after expressing anew his wish that Thurmond had been elected president in 1948.

34. Penny M. Von Eschen, *Race against Empire: Black Americans and Anticolonialism, 1937–1957* (Ithaca, N.Y.: Cornell University Press, 1997); Brenda Gayle Plummer, *Rising Wind: Black Americans and U.S. Foreign Affairs, 1935–1960* (Chapel Hill: University of North Carolina Press, 1996); James H. Meriwether, *Proudly We Can Be Africans: Black Americans and Africa, 1935–1961* (Chapel Hill: University of North Carolina Press, 2002).

35. Thomas Borstelmann, *The Cold War and the Color Line: American Race Relations in the Global Arena* (Cambridge, Mass.: Harvard University Press, 2001); Mary L. Dudziak, *Cold War Civil Rights: Race and the Image of American Democracy* (Princeton, N.J.: Princeton University Press, 2000).

36. "Problems of Southern Africa, State Department Paper, March 25, 1963," in *Foreign Relations of the United States, 1961–1963* (Washington, D.C.: U.S. Government Printing Office, 1995), 21:495.

37. Thomas Borstelmann, "'Hedging Our Bets and Buying Time': John Kennedy and Racial Revolutions in the American South and Southern Africa," *Diplomatic History* 24 (Summer 2000): 435–63.

38. See, e.g., Richard Reeves, *President Kennedy: Profile of Power* (New York: Simon & Schuster, 1993), 59–60.

39. Minutes of meeting of U.S. delegation to UN, November 10, 1950, *Foreign Relations of the United States, 1950* (Washington, D.C.: U.S. Government Printing Office, 1976), 2:564–69.

40. Borstelmann, *Cold War and the Color Line;* Dudziak, *Cold War Civil Rights.*

41. Dan T. Carter, *From George Wallace to Newt Gingrich: Race in the Conservative Counterrevolution, 1963–1994* (Baton Rouge: Louisiana State University Press, 1996), 3.

42. Thomas Noer, "Segregationists and the World: The Foreign Policy of the White Resistance," in *Window on Freedom: Race, Civil Rights, and Foreign Affairs, 1945–1988,* ed. Brenda Gayle Plummer (Chapel Hill: University of North Carolina Press, 2003), 141–62; Gerald Horne, *From the Barrel of a Gun: The United States and the War against Zimbabwe, 1965–1980* (Chapel Hill: University of North Carolina Press, 2001); William Minter, *King Solomon's Mines Revisited: Western Interests and the Burdened History of Southern Africa* (New York: Basic Books, 1986); Thomas J. Noer,

Cold War and Black Liberation: The United States and White Rule in Africa, 1948–1968 (Columbia: University of Missouri Press, 1985).

43. James H. Cone, "Martin Luther King, Jr., and the Third World," *Journal of American History* 74 (September 1987): 455–67; Gerald Horne, "Race from Power: U.S. Foreign Policy and the General Crisis of 'White Supremacy,'" *Diplomatic History* 23 (Summer 1999): 437–61; Timothy B. Tyson, *Radio Free Dixie: Robert F. Williams and the Roots of Black Power* (Chapel Hill: University of North Carolina Press, 1999); Catherine Fosl, *Subversive Southerner: Anne Braden and the Struggle for Racial Justice in the Cold War South* (New York: Palgrave Macmillan, 2003); Meriwether, *Proudly We Can Be Africans.*

44. Taylor Branch, *Parting The Waters: America in the King Years, 1954–63* (New York: Simon & Schuster, 1988), photograph 60, following p. 688.

45. Borstelmann, *Cold War and the Color Line,* 43.

46. Herman Talmadge, *You And Segregation* (Birmingham: Vulcan Press, 1955), cited in Dudziak, "Desegregation as a Cold War Imperative," 117.

47. Michael Krenn, "The Unwelcome Mat: African Diplomats in Washington, D.C., during the Kennedy Years," in *Window on Freedom,* ed. Plummer, 163–80; Renee Romano, "No Diplomatic Immunity: African Diplomats, the State Department, and Civil Rights, 1961–1964," *Journal of American History* 87 (September 2000): 546–80; Timothy P. Maga, "Battling the Ugly American at Home: The Special Protocol Service and the New Frontier, 1961–63," *Diplomacy and Statecraft* 3 (1993): 126–42.

48. "Troubled Route," *Time,* October 13, 1961.

49. Pedro Sanjuan to chief of protocol, September 21, 1961, enclosed in Battle to Dutton, September 29, 1961, National Security File, box 2, John F. Kennedy Library, Boston.

50. Mary L. Dudziak, "Birmingham, Addis Ababa, and the Image of America: International Influence on U.S. Civil Rights Politics in the Kennedy Administration," in *Window on Freedom,* ed. Plummer, 191.

51. Krenn, "Unwelcome Mat," 168–70.

52. Mary L. Dudziak, "The Little Rock Crisis and Foreign Affairs: Race, Resistance, and the Image of American Democracy," *Southern California Law Review* 70 (September 1997): 1641–1716; Borstelmann, "Hedging Our Bets."

53. Thomas J. Schoenbaum, *Waging Peace and War: Dean Rusk in the Truman, Kennedy, and Johnson Years* (New York: Simon & Schuster, 1988), 282–83.

54. *New York Times,* September 24, 1998.

Part II. The Industrial Impact of the Military-Industrial Complex

4. The Impact of the Early Cold War on an American City: The Aerospace Industry in Seattle

Richard S. Kirkendall

The Cold War had a powerful impact on Seattle. It could do so because the city had a resource that enabled it to make large contributions to the war. The resource was the Boeing Company; it knew how to build bombers, having demonstrated that during World War II, and the Cold War generated new demands for bombers. The company responded with the B-47 and the B-52 bombers and, by doing so, gained the know-how and financial strength it needed to become more important than ever before in the production of commercial airliners. As a consequence, Boeing grew and prospered, and as it did, it also promoted a variety of changes in the city and beyond. Seattle became a very different place in various ways, including its size, its shape, its politics, and its image.

Before World War II, Seattle was a city of only modest size with a weak economic base. Growing slowly for two decades, from 315,312 in 1920 to 365,583 in 1930 and only 368,302 in 1940, it was mainly a commercial center with a busy port through which flowed trade with Asia and other parts of the world. In manufacturing, it was a place of little significance with no large firms. The areas close to the city's boundaries, including the islands in Puget Sound, the region on the east side of Lake Washington, and the valley south of the city, were dominated by small farms and small communities. In these areas, some loggers cut great trees; farther away, logging ruled, as it had in the region since the 1950s, and throughout western Washington, the forest products industry was the economy's major feature.[1] As one scholar has written, "Two-thirds of the state's jobs were timber-related, and Washington was the leading lumber-producing state in the country."[2] In the city, sports fans could root for the teams of the University of Washington and other schools and colleges, but if they preferred professionals, only the Rainiers, a baseball squad, was available, and it competed in a minor league.

Boeing and the Industrialization of Seattle

The Boeing Company, which had been a part of the scene since 1916, was Seattle's largest manufacturer. Yet it usually employed fewer than 2,000 people, and often less than 1,000. Selling mainly in the military market during the 1920s and 1930s, it faced stiff competition in the commercial market from the Douglas Corporation, a Southern California firm, for the sale of airliners. Boeing brought to market a new airliner, the 247 in 1933, but Douglas introduced a larger and faster plane, the DC-3, the next year and quickly became the leader in the industry. The Seattle company, which sold fewer than 100 247s, introduced the Clipper in 1938, a giant and luxurious flying boat built for oceanic travel, but sold only 12. Boeing enjoyed even less success in 1939 and 1940 with the Stratoliner, even though it was larger, more comfortable, and faster than the DC-3.[3]

Boeing did turn out another plane during these years that attracted a group of champions. It was the B-17, a four-engine bomber that took to the air in 1935. The airmen in the U.S. Army, including the leader there, Henry "Hap" Arnold, welcomed it as capable of demonstrating their theory of what airpower could accomplish in modern war. They competed with the ground and sea forces for scarce dollars and sought to persuade the top men in the Army as well as Congress to spend money on the big bombers. Although the airmen staged dramatic stunts designed to demonstrate that the plane could reach remote targets and operate effectively against naval ships, they failed during the early years of the new plane to build much support in crucial political arenas and become a big market for Boeing.[4]

Boeing was a high-technology firm, but it seems unlikely that many Americans in the 1930s envisioned Seattle as a site of rapid technological advance. Instead, more of them thought of it as a place of radical politics, a major part of what Jim Farley, Franklin Roosevelt's top political adviser at the time, may have labeled "the Soviet of Washington." With much of the workforce unemployed, the city and the state housed a militant left that ranged from communists to anticorporate progressives, included the Congress of Industrial Organizations and the longshoremen's union, and influenced the Democratic Party. For a time, the prominent Washington Commonwealth Federation challenged capitalism with a call for "production-for-use," not profit.[5]

At the polls, Homer Bone of Tacoma was the most successful progressive. After a career as a Socialist, a leader of the Farmer-Labor Party, a backer of "Old Bob" La Follette in 1924, and an unsuccessful candidate for Congress in 1928 as an anti-Hoover Republican, he had switched to the Democrats in 1932. He did so after the party, by nominating Roosevelt, persuaded him that it had become the progressive party. After he was elected to the U.S. Senate in 1932, he championed a variety of measures designed to reduce the power of corporate giants in American life. The Boeing Company was one of his targets. He charged that it made exorbitant profits from its business with the Navy and the Army, but his attack on the company did not prevent him from winning re-election by a wide margin in 1938.[6]

Under the impact of World War II, Seattle began to move away from this past. It suddenly became an important center for manufacturing. Money from the federal government poured in, much of it for ships, most of it for airplanes, stimulating competition for workers between Boeing and the naval shipyard on the west side of Puget Sound. People moved in, many of them from the Midwest and the South, increasing the population of Seattle by over 25 percent and more than tripling the number of nearby Renton's residents. Women joined the workforce in large numbers, and blacks became a somewhat larger part of the city's population. These demographic changes generated transportation and housing problems, racial tension, and conflict.[7]

Because it knew how to build bombers, Boeing became the main participant in Seattle's sudden industrial development. Operating government-built plants in Renton at the south end of Lake Washington and in Wichita, as well as previously established facilities just beyond Seattle's southern edge, it increased its labor force from 4,000 when the war began to nearly 50,000 by 1944. These workers turned out thousands of B-17s and B-29s, the latter an even bigger plane with a greater range, ideal for the vast distances of the Pacific Ocean. The company became the biggest manufacturer in a state where manufacturing was far more important than it had been before the war. Other parts of the state, including a new aluminum industry in Spokane, also benefited from the Boeing boom.[8]

The bombers contributed to the defeat of Germany and Japan and enhanced Boeing's reputation, but the boom did not last. On September 5, 1945, the Army canceled orders for more B-29s, forcing the company to fire nearly half its workers. In response, Senator Warren Magnuson, Bone's successor, went into action in meetings with military officials; Seattle's mayor, the president of the city's Chamber of Commerce, and a spokesman for organized labor, among others, made appeals, and the chamber sponsored a mass meeting in downtown Seattle. The protestors emphasized Boeing's contributions to victory in the war and called for reinstatement of the canceled orders so that the company could make a smooth transition to peacetime production. The uprising indicated that support for the company now ran across class lines and that many people believed Seattle's welfare now depended on Boeing's economic health.

The efforts did not succeed. The firm cut employment in Seattle to a fifth of what it had been at the wartime peak and closed the plants in Renton and Wichita. Although it introduced a new airliner, the four-engine Stratocruiser, and began to receive orders, Boeing lost money in 1946.[9]

The troubled company continued to have friends in the city of Washington, including Magnuson and the uniformed airmen. By 1947, American airpower had declined sharply from its wartime level. The United States had only small bomber force, consisting mainly of B-29s, and a small number of atomic bombs. Three planes—Boeing's B-50; an improved version of the B-29 designed to deliver A-bombs; and Convair's B-50, a gigantic intercontinental bomber—were being developed. The airmen, however, had a plan for the development of a large air force served by a healthy, technologically advanced aircraft industry and justified by a theory proclaiming the superiority of airpower to all other forms of military force. In 1947, they obtained independence from the Army with the establishment of the U.S. Air Force. The Republican-controlled Congress found the airpower theory attractive, for it seemed to promise military security at low cost. In the spring of 1948, they cooperated with the new secretary of the Air Force, Stuart Symington, a Democrat, and gave his branch of the armed forces more money in the 1949 budget than President Harry Truman, also a Democrat, had requested.

This Republican response to the beginning of the Cold War, one of several responses by the party in 1947–48, benefited Boeing and Seattle. The company obtained new orders and appeared likely to move out of it slump. During 1948, it reopened plants in Renton and Wichita, began deliveries of and received additional orders for the B-50, and initiated production of the B-47. By the summer of 1949, the firm employed more than 25,000 people in metropolitan Seattle.[10]

The B-47, the Stratojet, was Boeing's—and the new Strategic Air Command's (SAC's)—first jet bomber. Featuring swept-back wings as well as jet engines, it was "almost fighter-like in its flying qualities," one historian of aircraft, Walter J. Boyne, has written, and, for Boeing, "the foundation stone of the future." Benefiting from the Cold War's first Berlin crisis, the company obtained contracts for ten of the new planes in September 1948 and for eighty-seven more two months later and began deliveries in 1951. Many more would be built, more of them by Boeing, though in Wichita rather than Seattle, and the plane would be a major component of American airpower in the middle and late 1950s.[11]

By the summer of 1949, however, the company—and Seattle—faced a new set of problems. Truman, who had enjoyed a surprising victory in the election of 1948, and Congress, now controlled by his party, cut the military budget for fiscal year 1950, and the Stratocruiser failed to produce a profit, for Douglas continued to be a tough competitor in the commercial field. What was even more alarming, Air Force leaders threatened to force the company to shift all bomber production to Wichita. In 1948, they had insisted that the B-47 must be produced there, and now, in the summer of 1949, an officer suggested publicly that the Air Force regard Seattle as vulnerable to attack because it was too close to the Soviet Union.

The threat generated a huge "Battle for Seattle." Senator Magnuson, aided by two Democratic U.S. representatives, Hugh Mitchell of Seattle and Henry Jackson of Everett, provided leadership in the nation's capital while the Seattle Chamber of Commerce led at home. Other participants included the Republican governors of Washington, Oregon, and California; Washington's Republican senator, Harry Cain of Tacoma; major elements of organized labor; and a wide variety of groups from around the metropolitan area, state, and region. The participants expressed a strong sense of dependence on military spending and the Boeing Company, and they persuaded the Air Force to offer repeated assurances that it would continue to call upon the company to produce bombers in Seattle.[12]

Despite those assurances, the future of Boeing and its city did not seem secure. By the spring of 1950, the company's workforce in and near Seattle had dropped below 20,000 and seemed likely to fall to 10,000 by the end of the year.[13] Perhaps the company would not survive. If so, Seattle might not continue to prosper and grow.

There was, however, yet another possibility. Perhaps the Cold War could push the company and Seattle on an upward course. Even before the B-36 had entered service with SAC in 1948, Boeing had begun work on an alternative, later designated the B-52. Drawing upon their experience with the B-47, representatives of the company and the Air Force agreed in October 1948 that the new plane should be large, powered by eight jet engines, and have swept-back wings. At the same time as older American planes delivered supplies to Berlin, the firm received a substantial increase in money for the development of a radically new bomber.

In 1949, naval officers, quite unintentionally, helped Boeing strengthen its tie with the Air Force. The officers criticized the B-36, the piston-driven aircraft that was displacing Boeing-built planes as SAC's heavy bomber, charging that the new plane was too slow for its mission and there had been irregularities in its procurement. Perhaps the plane Boeing was developing could serve the interests of the Air Force in its continuing competition with the Navy. By 1950, however, the company and its champions could not be sure that the plan for the new plane was adequate or that the Air Force would get the money needed to buy it.[14]

In the midst of these uncertainties, the Cold War entered a new stage with the outbreak of the Korean War and pushed the project forward. In this new stage, the Truman administration and the Congress tripled the military budget, giving substantial increases to each branch of the armed forces, and Boeing acquired new contracts and purchases from the Air Force and enjoyed profits again. By the summer of 1951, the company had increased employment in the Seattle area to 28,000 so as to deliver on contracts for a military transport (the C-97), guided missiles, a device for inflight refueling, the B-50, and also the B-52. The company had nearly as many people at work in Wichita, but after the Air Force issued a contract for B-52s and called for the work to be done in Seattle, Magnuson concluded that the Air Force did not now regard the city as "expendable."[15]

The decision to produce the new jet bomber was a triumph for SAC's commander, General Curtis LeMay, as well as for the company and the city. Since the formation of SAC in 1946, he had supported Boeing's plans for a new bomber, and when the decision was reached in 1948 to make it a large jet plane, he knew it was the plane he wanted. He then pressed for its production and for a halt to further development of the B-47. In the summer of 1949, the Soviet Union's first test of an atomic device strengthened his case. The United States, he argued, must build a delivery system that was superior to Soviet bombers and thereby capable of maintaining American supremacy in the new weapons of mass destruction. A superior American force would dissuade the Soviet Union from moving militarily against the United States and its allies.

To win out, LeMay had to overcome opposition from both inside and outside the Air Force. When funds were still tight, budget officers proposed that the Air Force should rely upon the B-36 and the B-47 and not spend money on an expensive new bomber. However, he wanted greater speed than the B-36 could supply and greater range and bomb-carrying capacity than could be obtained from the B-47. He wanted a plane that would enable SAC to participate more effectively in the Cold War and had confidence that the proposed bomber would be that plane.

The Korean War enabled LeMay to argue his case more effectively. Early in 1951, he gained the support he needed from General Hoyt Vandenberg, the Air Force chief of staff, and Thomas Finletter, the secretary of the Air Force.

Earlier, the secretary, faced with many demands for scarce funds, had resisted LeMay's pressure. But in February 1951, with military monies now abundant, the Air Force and the company signed a contract for thirteen planes, although the B-52 had not yet been flight tested. The next year, in July, with the military budget still at a high level, the Air Force contracted for a much larger number.[16]

The B-52 became the company's main product for several years and the successor to the B-17 and the B-29 as the firm's major contribution to American air power. To do the huge job, the company changed itself, developed a large network of subcontractors, and used a facility at Moses Lake in central Washington for flight tests. By the time deliveries to SAC began in 1955, the Dwight D. Eisenhower administration had adopted a "New Look" in national defense policy that promised "massive retaliation" and relied heavily on airpower. The new policy raised the production plan for the bomber from 282 to 744 and moved SAC, which had employed only 37,000 people when it came into existence in 1946, to a force of well over 260,000. Because of the plane's superior qualities, SAC retired the B-47 and the B-36 in the late 1950s and early 1960s. Then spurred by fears of a "missile gap" that might enable the Soviet Union to attack the United States effectively, the command dispersed the B-52 fleet over a large number of bases around the United States. In later years, Boeing and the Air Force would give this bomber a long life by continuously modifying it and enabling it to deliver more than atomic and nuclear weapons.[17]

By 1962, the last year in the production history of the B-52, Boeing had delivered 744 of the giant planes to its customer. Only 277 had been built in Seattle, all of them by 1958. The rest had been assembled in Wichita, providing employment for the large, well-qualified workforce that had been making B-47s in Kansas. The change, however, did not alarm nor hurt Washington State, for there the firm had other products to turn out, including missiles, tankers, and transports for the military. Even more important, the company needed production space and a labor force for a new kind of commercial airliner.[18]

Boeing could produce that airliner, the jet-powered 707, because it was building jet bombers. The Cold War, especially what it had become by the 1950s, gave the company the opportunity to build the bombers, and their construction encouraged the company to gamble on the development of the new airliner. William Allen, the president of the firm, and his lieutenants had been thinking of a jet airliner since the late 1940s but had been restrained by several factors, including the huge costs. Now, they moved in the new situation created by the escalation of the Cold War. In April 1952, a week after the first test flight of the B-52, Allen proposed the move, and his board of directors accepted his proposal. They could move forward because their work on bombers gave the company experience with the development and production of large jet planes and the essential financial resources.[19] Boeing's "hugely successful" jet airliners, two historians wrote a decade ago, "might well be entirely responsible for transforming the name of Boeing into one that is instantly recognizable around the world—but it was the bombers, in particular, the B-52, that made it all possible in the first place."[20]

The experience and resources enabled Boeing to displace Douglas as the leader in the commercial market. Both companies developed jet airliners and obtained their first contracts for them in 1955, but the 707 flew faster than the DC-8, chiefly because of the sweep of the wings, and the Seattle-based company made its first deliveries in 1958 while the Southern California firm did not begin deliveries until 1959. Eventually, Boeing would deliver about 1,000 707s while Douglas would sell only 556 DC-8s. Furthermore, early in the 1960s, this firm that had been threatened with extinction only a short time before added a second commercial jet, the 727, to its fleet and went on to success with it, selling nearly 2,000 in twenty years.[21]

In the late 1950s and early 1960s, the escalating Cold War benefited Boeing and Seattle in still other ways. While persuading his board to build the commercial jet, Allen had pointed to the money being made in sales to the military and suggested that he could sell the new plane as a transport and a tanker to the same customer. Two years later, before selling a 707 to an airline, Boeing obtained an order from the Air Force for the tanker, designated the KC-135. It would replace the KC-97, a plane that had contributed to Boeing's survival, and by refueling jet bombers in the air, the new jet tanker would extend their range. In 1956, the company made its first deliveries, and over the course of the next decade, it sold well over 800 KC-135s to the Air Force. In addition, as concern about Soviet offensive capabilities mounted, Boeing also obtained contracts in 1957 and 1958 for the Bomarc, an air-defense missile, and the Minuteman, an intercontinental ballistic missile. Seattle-area plants produced all these planes and missiles, including the 707 and the 727.[22]

Having been made possible by the escalation of the Cold War, the production of these new military and commercial products had a powerful impact on Seattle and the surrounding area. To do the jobs, Boeing more than doubled its workforce in Seattle and Renton during the 1950s while employment with other local manufacturers stagnated. "In 1947," one historian points out, "Boeing had employed about one out of every five manufacturing workers in King County; ten years later it employed one out of every two. In 1960, . . . about 13 percent of the civilian labor force worked for Boeing."[23] "Everywhere you went, you ran into somebody who did work or had worked at Boeing," a writer raised in Renton recalled.[24] In 1957, *Business Week* labeled Metropolitan Seattle "a one-industry town." By 1958, employment at Boeing had risen to 60,000 in metropolitan Seattle; by the mid-1960s, it had soared above 100,000, more than twice as high as it had reached during World War II and one-fifth of the labor force of King County.[25]

Boeing stimulated the growth of nearby areas even more than the central city. While Seattle, which pursued a policy of "aggressive annexations," grew from 467,591 in 1950 to 557,087 in 1960, its surrounding county, King, expanded from 732,942 to more than 935,000 by 1960. On the east side of Lake Washington, Bellevue did not incorporate until 1953, grew to nearly 13,000 people in 1960, and more than doubled in population in the 1960s. Many of its people worked for the company and its suppliers. The Kent-Auburn area south of the central city and close to Renton urbanized rapidly in the 1960s.[26]

Cold War Politics

While they stimulated population growth and created a metropolis with sizable suburbs, the Cold War and the Boeing Company also influenced the politics of Seattle and Washington State. The beginning of the war in 1946 opened an opportunity for a militant anticommunist, Albert Canwell of Spokane. Since the longshoremen's strike of 1934 and the rise of Harry Bridges, and perhaps even earlier, he had identified with the anticommunist movement in the state that emerged and gained strength in response to the prominence of the left. As a journalist, a private investigator, and a deputy sheriff in Spokane Country, he had gathered information on the people who alarmed him. He had tapped telephones and rooms; worked for and with representative of major corporations, including Boeing; and collaborated with anticommunist organizations around the state and nation, including the "Red Squad" of the Seattle Police Department. His reputation as an antiradical investigator encouraged a conservative Spokane journalist, Ashley Holden of the *Spokesman-Review*, to persuade him to run for the legislature and give him favorable publicity in 1946. After his election, another journalist, Fred Niendorff of the *Seattle Post-Intelligencer*, drafted a resolution that the legislature endorsed authorizing the establishment of a special committee on "Un-American Activities." Canwell chaired it, though he was only a freshman legislator, and Niendorff gave him close, detailed, and favorable coverage.

Canwell was eager to put what he thought he knew to good use. Recognizing that Washington housed facilities of great importance in the Cold War, including Boeing, and believing that the state occupied a crucial position on the route communist invaders would take, he was sure the Soviet Union had placed agents in all the important spots. He intended to unmask communist "fronts," such as the American Civil Liberties Union, as well as Communist Party members, and he began by focusing on the Washington State Pension Union, the University of Washington, and the Seattle Repertory Playhouse. Refusing to allow defense lawyers to do anything but quietly advise their clients, he asked the individuals he targeted to testify only to their membership in the party and the people they had known in it. Rather than ask them to tell of their activities, he assumed they did what all communists did and turned to ex-members of the party to testify about its nature. They told him what he already believed to be true: The Soviet Union controlled the American Communist Party, and its members engaged in subversive activities.

The legislator sought only to throw a spotlight on his targets and relied upon others to take action against them. In Seattle, some key people behaved as he anticipated. The patrons of the Repertory Playhouse deserted it, forcing it out of business; the new president of the University of Washington, Raymond B. Allen, and the regents fired three tenured members of the faculty for membership in the Communist Party, destroying their academic careers.

Allen had an ambitious goal. He hoped to use the new economic strength that World War II had brought to Washington State to build a great national university. He knew he could not succeed without strong public support, and he assumed that Washingtonians would not back the university if communists served on the faculty. He also thought he could not recruit talented faculty members if academics believed the university did not respect academic freedom. So carving out a new conception that fitted the culture of the Cold War, he argued that communists were not free people and thus did not deserve to hold academic posts.[27]

Canwell and other promoters of the "Red Scare" in Washington State hoped to change the state's political culture, and the once-strong left did wither under this and other pressures from the Cold War. In 1948, much of what remained of it in Seattle and elsewhere around the state supported Henry A. Wallace and his effort to end the contest between the United States and the Soviet Union but failed badly. By the 1950s, the movement had little strength outside Harry Bridge's longshoremen's union, and in the 1960s, that union surrendered its militancy, accepted the containerization of the waterfront, and brought its members into the middle class.[28]

Although it contributed to the destruction of the left, Canwell's brand of anticommunism did not flourish for long. He failed to move up in state politics or enjoy further electoral or legislative victories. Instead, the great successes in the politics of Washington State during most of the Cold War were two liberals, Warren Magnuson of Seattle and Henry Jackson of Everett. Neither worried much about communists in the state and nation, but both supported America's anticommunist foreign and military polices.[29]

Early in his career, Magnuson was a man of the left, but he moved away from that. At the 1936 state convention of the Democratic Party, he had worked successfully for passage of a platform that called for "production for use, not profit," a slogan of the Washington Commonwealth Federation, then the most prominent of the organizations on the left wing of the state's political spectrum. After he was elected to the U.S. House of Representatives from Seattle that year, he supported Senator Bone's public power and antiwar policies, but his new responsibilities moved him close to other players in the politics of the state. He served on the House Naval Affairs Committee at a time when the Bremerton Naval Shipyard, not Boeing, was the largest employer in his district, and he worked for a naval buildup with the shipyard as a heavy participant. He also formed close and mutually rewarding ties with a private firm, Northwest Airlines, and beginning in 1940, encouraged the Army to buy Boeing's B-17s. Naval ships and big bombers, he believed, could keep war away from the United States.

World War II moved Magnuson away from Bone's isolationism. He voted for Lend-Lease early in 1941, but later that year he voted against extending the draft. And until the Japanese attacked Pearl Harbor, he continued to oppose American entry into the war. Then, after serving briefly as a naval officer, he began to insist that the United States must participate in a United Nations Organization and not repeat the mistake the nation had made when it refused to join the League of Nations. After the war, he supported such features of the new internationalism as the Marshall Plan. By then, he had replaced Bone in the U.S. Senate.

By then also, Magnuson had become deeply interested in the Boeing Company. Before the war ended, he had feared that its end would result in the collapse of the aircraft industry, and he did what he could to prevent that collapse. As we have seen, he responded when the Army Air Forces slashed orders for B-29s in September 1945 and, four years later, he provided leadership in Washington in the campaign to talk the Air Force out of shifting bomber production to Wichita.

Obviously, by this time, a senator from Washington State with a base in Seattle had to do what he could to help Boeing and maintain its connection with the city. In advance of the "Battle for Seattle," he had warned local leaders that the Air Force might try to shift bomber production to Wichita. After the battle began, he took advantage of his easy access to the White House, the Department of Defense, and the Department of the Air Force. He met frequently with military officials and others in the capital, including his friend Harry Truman, and he brought Secretary Symington to Seattle for a discussion of the issue. He also stepped up his efforts to strengthen western defenses so as to undermine the argument about Seattle's vulnerability to attack. Satisfied with the outcome, he concluded that the "vulnerable Seattle" argument had been defeated and that the military was committed to an adequate defense of the West Coast.[30]

Magnuson did not, however, become a major participant in the Cold War. Instead, he emphasized domestic issues and his ability to "deliver" for his constituents, including Republican businessmen as well as Democratic labor leaders. He focused much of his interest in aviation on the commercial side, helping Northwest Airlines obtain authorization for a route between Seattle and Tokyo, encouraging airlines to purchase 707s, and providing leadership in the Senate in the fight for government loans for a Boeing-developed Supersonic Transport.[31] To accomplish his purposes, he relied heavily on his position in the Commerce Committee, which he chaired for more than twenty-five years, beginning in 1955.

Magnuson had rejected his predecessor's anticorporate progressivism, but he had not become merely Boeing's agent in the Senate. Instead, as the Battle for Seattle suggests, he was an agent of his community and sought to keep that corporation there and use it as means of developing the place. Boeing could prosper in Wichita, but Seattle, in his view, needed the firm.

Washington's senior senator was satisfied to have his Democratic colleague in the Senate, Henry Jackson, be the state's specialist on foreign and military matters. Jackson moved up to the Senate in 1952 after twelve years in the House of Representatives. In the House, he had cast one of his first votes with the isolationists, voting against Lend-Lease. But World War II changed him. It persuaded him that the United States had made great mistakes—isolationism and military weakness—and must not repeat them. He regarded Truman's foreign policies as evidence that the nation had learned the lessons that recent history taught, and as a congressman, he consistently supported national defense with an emphasis on air power. He supported the Air Force in the budget battles of 1948 and 1949, cooperated with Magnuson in the Battle for Seattle, made much of this in his highly successful campaign for reelection in 1950, and backed the military buildup of the early 1950s. In his campaign for the Senate, he called for more, especially more and more powerful bombs. He regarded such weapons as the centerpiece of American defense forces, insisted that the United States must continue to have more bombs than the Soviet Union, and maintained that reliance on them would be less expensive than reliance on the weapons of the Army and Navy. He implied that Boeing-built

110

bombers, both those in the air and those on the drawing board, were a major element of American strength. Although some Democrats in 1952 were overwhelmed by charges that they were "soft on communism," he was invulnerable to them, and he defeated a Republican incumbent, Harry Cain, in an election year that favored members of Cain's party.[32]

In the Senate, Jackson quickly earned recognition as a leading critic of the Eisenhower administration's defense policies. His major committee assignments—the Senate Armed Forces Committee and the Joint Committee on Atomic Energy—reflected his strong interest in national defense. From this base, he charged that the administration underestimated the Soviet threat, placed economic considerations ahead of national security, and refused to spend enough money on security. He had confidence that the nation could spend much more for defense without sacrificing domestic programs or damaging the economy.

Jackson, like Magnuson, rejected the anticorporate progressivism that had flourished in the state during the 1930s. Instead, he proved to be a good friend of one corporation, the Boeing Company, cooperating with company officials in their quests for profitable contracts and championing their products. He promoted all the company's contributions to national defense during the 1950s: the B-52, the KC-135, the Bomarc, and the Minuteman. Regarding Boeing as a company of vital importance that served the economy of Seattle and Washington State and the security of the nation, he boasted during his reelection campaign in 1958 that he had served the local interest in jobs as well as the national interest in a stronger defense.[33]

That year, critics began to call Jackson "the senator from Boeing." This label did not originate with Republicans, including William Bantz of Spokane, his foe in the general election. Defending Eisenhower's policies against Jackson's criticisms, Bantz found nothing wrong with serving Boeing's interests. Instead, he insisted that Boeing's superior work, not Jackson, explained the company's success and warned that the Democratic Party's proposal for a state income tax might drive Boeing from the state.

Alice Franklin Bryant of Seattle, Jackson's opponent in the Democratic primary, did not introduce the label, although she did come rather close to doing so. She insisted that his efforts on behalf of B-52s was evidence of a "single-track militaristic mind" and charged that his activities favored "those who profit from the threat of war—General Electric at Hanford and Boeing at Seattle." Her point of view resembled Bone's in the 1930s, although she did insist that she wanted Boeing to prosper. She hoped it would do so by shifting out of bombers and missiles and into passenger planes.

The label in fact originated with other Democrats in western Washington.

They regarded Jackson as a militaristic warmonger who was hurting the party as well as endangering the nation with his emphasis on a military buildup. They began to call him "the senator from Boeing" early in the election year. For them, this was more than a label; it was a charge. Their point of view resembled Bone's in the 1930s—the idea that big business corrupts politics and produces war.

The charge actually seriously exaggerated Jackson's connections with Boeing. He had a complex agenda that included support for the Army and the Navy as well as the Air Force, nonmilitary approaches to the Soviet challenge such as economic aid, and a number of domestic programs beginning with public power. Furthermore, he opposed Boeing management on the proposal for a "right-to-work" law in 1958. Allen backed it, regarding it as needed to make unions "responsible." He had to contend with the Machinists, a union that had purged communists from its ranks early in World War II and become the major liberal union in Seattle as Boeing grew. Like many Seattle businessmen, he had preferred the more conservative Dave Beck and his Teamsters, but Beck had failed to displace the Machinists during and after the Machinists' strike in 1948.[34] Enjoying a good relationship with that union, Jackson opposed the right-to-work proposal. He feared it would disrupt what he regarded as the good system of labor-management relations that had developed since the 1930s. Although he did not share Bone's hostility toward corporations, he also did not endorse Allen's negative opinion of labor unions. He favored what the American economic system had become under the pressures of Depression and war: a system composed of big business, big labor, and big government.

Jackson would come to resent being called "the senator from Boeing." It challenged his conception of himself as serving both the national interest and a number of local interests. It also implied that a "munitions maker" controlled him.[35]

Yet the charge did not hurt the senator in Washington State, at least not in these early days of the Cold War. He overwhelmed Alice Bryant in the 1958 primary and defeated Bill Bantz by a wide margin. President Eisenhower's warning against the "military-industrial complex" in his Farewell Address in 1961 gave the charge greater respectability. When Jackson attacked the decision to award a contract for a fighter plane, the TFX, to General Dynamics of Texas rather than Boeing of Washington State, his critics made use of the slogan. As Jackson's biographer noted: "The TXF controversy fueled the slowly but burgeoning perception of those critical of Jackson's Cold War views that he was 'the Senator from Boeing,' in thrall to the so-called military-industrial complex."[36] Yet, this widened use of term did not harm him at home. He won again, and by wide margins, in 1964. Jackson, it seems quite obvious, faithfully represented what the political culture of his state had become under the pressure of the Cold War.

The World's Fair and the SuperSonics

By the 1960s, Americans outside as well as inside the city saw Seattle, largely because of Boeing, as occupying a cutting edge and as very important for the Cold War. The city's World's Fair of 1962, the Century 21 Exposition, offered abundant testimony on this point. The original promoters of the fair, who represented downtown business, had some negative thoughts about the company. Because its assembly plants were located outside the city and many of its workers lived and shopped in the rapidly developing suburbs, it did not give downtown as much support as its representatives wanted. Furthermore, because the employment it offered fluctuated over a wide range, it failed to supply the city's economy with a steady base. The people who spoke out for downtown hoped a fair, located close to them, would revitalize their area and attract new industries to Seattle, making the economy more diversified.

People outside the city, mainly representatives of the national government and the scientific community, moved in with other ideas about what a fair should be and do. Their design highlighted the great importance of science and technology in this era of the Cold War and its race for supremacy in space, and they made the fair a participant in the war and the promoter of an optimistic vision. From their point of view, the presence of Boeing, with its jets and missiles, made Seattle an ideal location for such a fair. When visitors arrived, they encountered the company frequently as they roamed the fairgrounds. According to John Findlay, the fair's historian, the grounds "became a virtual advertisement of everything for which Boeing stood." For visitors, people "more attuned to the suburbs and Boeing than to the problem downtown, the science pavilion, the World of Tomorrow, the Monorail, and the Space Needle [the parts devoted to science and technology] were the most popular features of the fair."

The fair not only reflected and influenced how outsiders perceived Seattle; it also affected how the people in the metropolis saw their place, and the impact did not stop with the closing of the expedition. Among other benefits, it left behind facilities that could be used for the arts and sports, and people in the city took advantage of these opportunities to upgrade Seattle's offerings in those areas. "In the months preceding the exposition, some residents thought of Seattle as a small, remote, relatively unsophisticated community, struggling against long odds to become 'a major world's fair host city,'" Findlay has writ-

Richard S. Kirkendall

ten. "After basking in the success of the fair and the praise of the nation in 1962, the metropolis perceived itself as maturing, not simply in terms of economic and physical growth, but also by developing the amenities that characterize cosmopolitan living and major-league status." The exposition left behind facilities that were used to upgrade Seattle's offerings in the arts and sports. One new user of the space, the SuperSonics, Seattle's first major-league athletic team, joined the National Basketball Association five years after Century 21 closed down. The well-chosen name linked the team with the fair, Boeing, and the Cold War. As the team began to compete, Magnuson carried on the battle for a subsidy that would enable the company to build a new transport plane capable of supersonic speeds.[37]

Between the mid-1940s and the mid-1960s, the Cold War transformed Seattle, making it very different from what it had been only a generation before. Because of the presence of the Boeing Company, the city could participate in the war and do so in large ways. During World War II, Boeing had already demonstrated that it had large capabilities. But after the war, it needed support from another powerful force to survive and prosper. The Cold War became that force. By creating a demand for new bombers, the Cold War enabled Boeing to avoid collapse and enjoy success. It supplied the bombers, and by doing so, it acquired the resources needed to build a new kind of commercial airliner. The building of these new military and commercial planes had a powerful impact on the city and its neighboring cities, changing the size, the shape, the politics and the image of the metropolis.

Notes

1. Richard C. Berner, *Seattle 1921–1940: From Boom to Bust* (Seattle: Charles Press, 1992), 4–5, 172–74, 205, 302; chaps. 4, 8, 10.

2. T. M. Sell, *Wings of Power: Boeing and the Politics of Growth in the Northwest* (Seattle: University of Washington Press, 2001), 16.

3. Berner, *Seattle 1921–1940,* 172–73, 176–77. Boeing Historical Archives, *Year by Year: 75 Years of Boeing History 1916–1991* (Seattle: Boeing Historical Archives, 1991), 9–46.

4. DeWitt S. Copp, *A Few Great Captains: The Men and Events That Shaped the Development of U.S. Air Power* (Garden City, N.Y.: Doubleday, 1980). Jeffrey S. Underwood, *The Wings of Democracy: The Influence of Air Power on the Roosevelt Administration, 1933–1941* (College Station: Texas A&M University Press, 1991).

5. Berner, *Seattle 1921–1940,* chap. 1 and 304, 308, 311, 320, 321, 323, 325, 326, 329, 332–48, 356–62, 375–76, 399–402, 407–8, 410–15, 436–43, 454. John Gunther's *Inside U.S.A.* (New York: Harper & Brothers, 1947), 47, is one source for Farley's comment. Gunther was not sure that Farley actually said this, but he was sure that Washington's politics at the time were unusually "progressive," and he admired the state for that.

6. Richard S. Kirkendall, "Two Senators and the Boeing Company: The Transformation of Washington's Political Culture, *Columbia* 11 (Winter 1997–98): 38–40. Bone's papers, housed at the University of Puget Sound, are a major source for this chapter.

7. Richard C. Berner, *Seattle Transformed: World War II to Cold War* (Seattle: Charles Press, 1999), 48–51, 54, 60–62, 68–79, 91–93, 118–34, 251.

8. Robert E. Ficken and Charles P. LeWarne, *Washington: A Centennial History* (Seattle: University of Washington Press, 1988), chap. 8. Berner, *Seattle Transformed,* 46, 57.

9. Richard S. Kirkendall, "The Boeing Company and the Military-Metropolitan-Industrial Complex, 1945–1953," *Pacific Northwest Quarterly* 85 (October 1994): 138–39. This paper rests heavily on the papers of Warren Magnuson, of Hugh Mitchell, and of Henry Jackson, all of which are available at the Allen Library of the University of Washington.

10. Ibid., 139–40, 143. Robert F. Door and Lindsay Peacock, *B-52 Stratofortress: Boeing's Cold War Warrior* (London: Osprey, 1995), 10–12.

11. Boyne, *Boeing B-52: A Documentary History* (London: Jane's, 1982), 27–29, 32–39. Dorr and Peacock, *B-52,* 12. Kirkendall, "Boeing," 143.

12. Kirkendall, "Boeing," 143–47.

13. Ibid., 143–44.

14. Ibid., 146–47; Boyne, *B-52,* 44–52; Door and Peacock, *B-52,* 17–21.

15. Kirkendall, "Boeing," 147–48.

16. Ibid., 148; Dorr and Peacock, *B-52,* 14–15, 21–22; Boyne, *B-52,* 52–53, 63.

17. Boyne, *B-52,* 53–57, 59, 62–64, 67, 89, 103–23; Dorr and Peacock, *B-52,* 12, 13, 23–25, 32, 41, 54, 73, 74, 77–94, 256.

18. Boyne, *B-52,* 67–68; Dorr and Peacock, *B-52,* 54, 58–59, 61, 77, 83, 90, 231.

19. Kirkendall, "Boeing," 148–49; Boeing Historical Archives, *Year by Year,* 73.

20. Dorr and Peacock, *B-52,* 44.

21. Kirkendall, "Boeing," 149. Boeing Historical Archives, *Year by Year,* 80, 87–88, 91–92, 94–95.

22. Kirkendall, "Boeing," 149. Boeing Historical Archives, *Year by Year,* 75–79, 81–84, 87.

23. John M. Findlay, *Magic Lands: Western Cityscapes and American Culture after 1940* (Berkeley: University of California Press, 1992), 219.

24. Sell, *Wings of Power,* ix.

25. *Business Week,* April 25, 1957; Findlay, *Magic Kingdoms,* 257; Sell, *Wings of Power,* 25, 31.

26. Berner, *Seattle Transformed,* 7. Findlay, *Magic Kingdoms,* 218, 220. Lorraine McConaghy, "No Ordinary Place: Three Postwar Suburbs and Their Critics," Ph.D. dissertation, University of Washington, 1973.

27. Richard S. Kirkendall, "Foreword," in *All Powers Necessary and Convenient: A Play of Fact and Speculation* by Mark Jenkins (Seattle: University of Washington Press, 2000), xiii–xviii. Jenkins' play focuses on Canwell and was performed in 1998 in the Playhouse Theater of the University of Washington. Also see Vern Countryman, *Un-American Activities in the State of Washington: The Work of the Canwell Committee* (Ithaca, N.Y.: Cornell University Press, 1951), Charles M. Gates, *The First Century at the University of Washington, 1861–1961* (Seattle: University of Washington

Press, 1961); Jane Sanders, *Cold War on the Campus: Academic Freedom at the University of Washington, 1946–64* (Seattle: University of Washington Press, 1979; Melvin Rader, *False Witness* (Seattle: University of Washington Press, 1979); Barry B. Witham, "The Playhouse and the Committee," in *The Performance of Power: Theatrical Discourse and Politics,* ed. Sue-Ellen Case and Janelle Reinelt (Iowa City: University of Iowa Press, 1991); Berner, *Seattle 1921–1940,* chaps. 16–20 and 399–402, 407–15, 436–42; Berner, *Seattle Transformed,* 51–54, 107–12, 203–4, 207–10, 227–34; and *Albert F. Canwell: An Oral History,* interviewed by Timothy Frederick (Olympia: Washington State Oral History Program, 1997).

28. Berner, *Seattle Transformed,* 217, 219, 223–24, 226, 234–35, 244, 252–53. As Martin Jugum, a veteran of Bridges' union, liked to say to the Labor Studies Center at the University of Washington, "Harry made us middle class!"

29. The following discussion of the senators draws upon two valuable biographies: Shelby Scates, *Warren G. Magnuson and the Shaping of Twentieth-Century America* (Seattle: University of Washington Press, 1997); and Robert G. Kaufman, *Henry M. Jackson: A Life in Politics* (Seattle: University of Washington Press, 2000).

30. Kirkendall, "Boeing," 144–46.

31. Mel Horwich, *Clipped Wings: The American SST Conflict* (Cambridge, Mass.: MIT Press, 1982).

32. Kirkendall, "Boeing," 149.

33. Kirkendall, "Two Senators," 41–42. Jackson's papers contributed to this article.

34. Berner, *Seattle 1920–1941,* 22, 25; Berner, *Seattle Transformed,* 51–54, 215–22. Kirkendall, "Boeing," 140–43.

35. Kirkendall, "Two Senators," 42–43.

36. Kaufman, *Jackson,* 145.

37. This discussion of the fair depends upon Findlay, *Magic Kingdoms,* chap. 5; the quotations can be found on 228, 241, and 264. As Horwich shows in *Clipped Wings,* Magnuson eventually failed in the new climate of the 1970s, with less influence by the Cold War and more by concern about the environment.

5. When the Movie's Over: The Post–Cold War Restructuring of Los Angeles

Michael Oden

Los Angeles occupies a unique place in American hearts and minds. The influence of this metropolitan region on the nation's economy, politics, and culture has been profound, particularly during the post–World War II period. LA-generated movies and related cultural/commercial trends are prominent in the national psyche—from optimistic forms such as beach culture, leisure wear, Disneyland, sports cars, and pop music to the darker elements of film noir and communist witch hunts. More prosaically, the region's entertainment complex is one of the few consistently successful U.S. trading sectors, drawing in export income from the sale of cultural products across the globe. Los Angeles and its surrounding areas were also the cradle of a "new" Republican Party that grew up first around Richard Nixon and subsequently around tax revolts and the more aggressive conservative vision of Ronald Reagan. Los Angeles has served as totem to a national faith (or delusion) in reinvention and overcoming the odds. Anything seems possible if a vibrant automobile-dependent metropolitan region of close to 16 million people could burgeon in an arid coastal enclave distant from adequate sources of freshwater.

Yet for over sixty years, there was another Los Angeles less embedded in the popular imagination and generally removed from the gaze of outsiders. From the 1940s until the mid-1990s, the Los Angeles basin hosted the largest defense aerospace and electronics complex in the world. It was in this local network of defense firms, laboratories, and government facilities, more than anywhere else, that the great strategic, technical, and industrial competition with the Soviet Union was fought out. In the 1980s, the last great Cold War peak in military production activity, the "person on the street" would have

likely not known that hundreds of thousands Los Angeles residents were employed in the production of bombers, missiles, surveillance satellites, and the
like. It would have been equally surprising if the layperson had known that this
metropolitan region was the largest center of manufacturing employment in
the United States, dwarfing Chicago, Detroit, and Philadelphia. Yet military-
industrial Los Angeles had at least as profound an influence on the post—
World War II world as the region's more renowned and glamorous sectors.

This "other" Los Angeles did have notoriety within the more insular defense
and intelligence worlds. The area sported its own formidable hit parade of defense firms and weapon systems. The great companies that grew up around
Cold War defense demand were unusually concentrated in the region. Lockheed, Northrop, McDonnell Douglas, Hughes, Rockwell, TRW, and Litton all
had corporate or division headquarters and huge research and production facilities in the region. These establishments spawned many of the most critical
weapons systems of the Cold War, including the U-2 and Blackhawk spy
planes of Lockheed's Skunk Works in Burbank, the surveillance and communication satellites of Hughes in Los Angeles, intercontinental ballistic missile
(ICBM) development at the local TRW and Rockwell facilities, and the more
recent stealth fighters and bombers of Lockheed and Northrop.

This chapter focuses on this other Los Angeles, documenting how the Cold
War profoundly shaped this iconic place in the American landscape. Much of
the argument here is based on a kind of historical "quasi-experiment." The
powerful influence of the Cold War on the economic and social life of the region is partly disclosed by analyzing the profound changes that occurred in the
1990s, after the Warsaw Pact disintegrated. Nevertheless, the chapter is organized around a somewhat linear/chronological history of the influence of
the Cold War on the growth and development of the LA region.

The first section very briefly details how the foundations of the LA defense
agglomeration were built in the pre–World War II period through a determined
economic development planning effort by local leaders and regional boosters.
This section documents the buildup of regional research institutions and the
careful recruitment of Air Corps/Air Force leaders during and after World War
II. This effort created the capability and institutional networks that allowed the
region to become a "first mover" in jet propulsion and rocketry—the dominant emerging military technologies of the postwar era. In the second section,
the shift of U.S. national security strategy at the end of the Korean War, sometimes labeled the "New Look," is designated as the key historical event that
secured the primacy of "aerial weaponry" in Cold War military competition.
The third section documents how this broad shift in security policy defined a
new trajectory of technological development and competition in military re-

search and production that Los Angeles was uniquely positioned to exploit. The fourth section analyzes the profound effects of the Cold War's end on the region's economy, workforce, and social structure. The dense agglomeration of defense firms and federal institutions in Los Angeles were linked to strategic Cold War missions; hence, the termination of the Cold War hit the LA complex especially hard. The final section advances several speculative propositions about how the downsizing and restructuring of the LA defense economy changed the region's class and ethnic structure and may have contributed to its durable political transformation.

Creating the Seedbed of the LA Defense Aerospace Complex, 1920–1953

The rise of the Los Angeles aerospace complex is documented by a rich and surprisingly comprehensive literature.[1] Indeed, this literature is perhaps underappreciated in terms of its implications for economic history and the processes of regional industrial development in the United States. There is a consensus that the creation and subsequent growth of the LA aerospace complex had more to do with civic and government actions than with the operation of market forces or classic firm location calculus.[2] It would, however, be inaccurate to say that the development of the early LA manufacturing base was purely state led. Rather, the development of the manufacturing base (which was primarily aircraft oriented) "grew out of the efforts of World War I and interwar city builders to find an economic niche for their rapidly growing and dynamic but unstable cities and military men hoping to arrest the decline of their services."[3]

Los Angeles was not an initial center of innovation in the emergent aircraft industry. Cities in the industrial heartland, such as Dayton, Buffalo, and Detroit, were the sites of early innovation and development. However, like the personal computer industry in the late 1970s, the aircraft industry in the 1920s was still characterized by a number of small, fragile, innovative firms. A number of figures fascinated with flying and several legendary local innovators such as Glenn Martin, the Lockheed brothers, and Jack Northrop were located in the LA area in the 1920s.[4] Initially, the industry did not, however, take root, and many fledgling local aircraft operations sold out to Midwestern firms.[5]

Enter the promethean civic figure of Harry Chandler, publisher of the *Los Angeles Times*. Chandler, who had huge real estate and business interests in Southern California in addition to the newspaper, was obsessed with diversifying the economic base of the region. To this end, he tasked his star reporter Bill Henry to conduct a detailed analysis of the nascent aircraft industry across the nation.[6] Convinced that aircraft manufacturing was a growth industry of the future, Chandler and the LA civic elite launched a courtship and recruitment campaign during the 1920s and 1930s, beginning with the successful luring of Donald Douglas from Cleveland with financial incentives.[7] This recruitment effort continued with the development of numerous airport facilities in the region, and the open space surrounding these airfields became the sites that attracted other manufacturers (with land costs often subsidized) to the region.[8] In the early 1930s, for example, Northrop and North American (later Rockwell) were attracted by cheap land and airfield access in the area that later became Los Angeles International Airport.[9]

Los Angeles boosters assiduously courted the key firms that would anchor the complex—Douglas and Lockheed in the 1920s and North American and Hughes in the 1930s—with offers of start-up capital and cheap land. Local support seems to have been a dominant factor, rather than climate or the presence of a preexisting pool of skilled labor or suppliers.[10] This initial foundation was crucial, because later entrants were spun off from these early anchor companies—Northrop from Lockheed and Douglas, TRW from Hughes.[11] Hence, local support in attracting the seed companies was a critical factor in establishing the new industry in the region.

But another local initiative, also spearheaded by Chandler and his cohort of civic leaders, was equally important to the later evolution of the complex. In the 1920s, Los Angeles did not have notable major universities or research institutions and lacked an institutional research and development (R&D) base in basic sciences and engineering. This disadvantaged the region in competition for the emerging high-technology industries of the 1920s: aircraft, chemicals, and electronics. It was hard to compete against regions such as New York City, Boston, or even southern Michigan that had well-developed universities and private research institutions. As the aircraft sector was transformed from a small-scale craft industry into an industry based on design innovation and larger-scale production techniques, links to science and technology became a crucial asset.

The LA civic elite set about in the early 1920s to create a first-class science and engineering institution and transformed the small Throop Institute into the California Institute of Technology. Lead scientists such as the physicist Robert Millikan and the aerospace pioneer Theodore von Karman were recruited from the East Coast and from Europe with rich inducements.[12] With durable commitment and energy over decades, Cal Tech and its later offshoot the Jet Propulsion Laboratory were built into premier science and engineering institutions with leading strengths in aeronautics and rocketry.

The profound influence of these institutions on the development of the LA complex is well documented by Lotchin.[13] An early and very fruitful partner-ship between Cal Tech and Douglas Aircraft began in the late 1920s. With von Karman newly on board, Cal Tech built one of the world's biggest and most so-phisticated wind tunnels in 1929. Working closely with Cal Tech scientists and exploiting the wind tunnel, Douglas engineers tested and perfected early pro-totypes of the Douglas DC-3. The DC-3 beat out competitors such as Boeing's 247 to become the dominant commercial aircraft of the 1930s. The mass pro-duction of this plane in Los Angeles cemented the region's place as an emerg-ing aircraft center. In addition, von Karman and his Cal Tech group began ex-perimentation on rockets as early as 1936.[14] In 1939, the institution received what is widely claimed to be the first government-sponsored project on rock-etry from the U.S. Army Air Corps. In sum, even before World War II brought significant economies of scale to the Los Angeles complex, regional support institutions helped to give Los Angeles the inside track on the future. The care-fully constructed alliance between local industry, the Air Corps, and Cal Tech helped create unique relationships and specific research capabilities in jet propulsion and rocketry, positioning Los Angeles well for the postwar period.

Despite real successes and important antecedents of subsequent develop-ment, the aerospace industry did not reshape the region in the 1930s. With mil-itary spending low and the commercial airline industry still in its infancy, the level of demand and production was not yet on a scale to generate a major new economic base for the region. However, World War II definitely cata-pulted Los Angeles into the leading ranks in the aircraft industry.[15] The desire for a decentralized production capacity and the significance of the Pacific front prompted a massive expansion of West Coast production. The wholesale re-cruitment of defense workers and their transportation to Southern California for war work was underwritten by the federal government, setting off publicly subsidized migration streams of skilled labor that persisted into the postwar period.[16] Of the top five producers of World War II aircraft, three were in Los Angeles (North American, Douglas, Lockheed) and a fourth (Consolidated-Vultee) was in San Diego.[17]

The massive World War II buildup set off other forces that accelerated re-gional growth and development. The war led to infrastructural improvements in the Port of Los Angeles, fostering its later development as a major ship-ping and transportation nexus for pacific trade. The most powerful effect was the huge population migration set off by the war, which added to a stream of Depression era migration to the region. The war brought in tens of thousands to participate in war production, augmenting local demand and associated transportation and service industries. Many war workers stayed on and touted the region's unique amenities to relatives in other areas. War-related economic development and migration created a critical mass of regionalized demand and economic activity, drawing other industries and services to Southern California.

The immediate postwar period brought crisis, with orders for companies like North American falling as much as 90 percent in a single year. Unlike some Midwestern participants in war work such as Ford and General Motors, Los Angeles–based companies were highly specialized and had no prior experience in consumer markets that could compensate for falling military demand. Ironically, this dependency encouraged them to pursue their government clients even more vigorously, while Midwestern companies like Ford and Bell & Howell shut down their Liberator bomber and military optics plants to pursue attractive and cash-rich commercial markets.[18]

In training their sights on Washington, Los Angeles aerospace companies were in a certain sense betting on a major shift in the geopolitical environment. Even as George Kennan's telegraphs and articles began to awaken the national leadership to the reality of the Soviet threat, Los Angeles and nearby aerospace companies were vigorously positioning themselves for potential military projects. Tentative pilot projects on an ICBM were carried out by Convair (formerly Consolidated) in San Diego in 1946. The Army Air Corps pulled the plug on this project a year later, yet Los Angeles built upon historic relationships within the Army Air Corps as the Air Force was established as an independent service in 1947.[19] Also, Cal Tech scientists were active on many prominent strategic and scientific study committees set up in the late 1940s and early 1950s to appraise emerging military threats and the potential of new military technologies.

With the drafting of NSC-68—document number 68 from the U.S. National Security Council—and the onset of the Korean War, Los Angeles aerospace firms began to benefit from a new flow of Air Force and other military procurement money, breaking the severe drought of the late 1940s. By 1952, nearly 160,000 personnel were employed in the aircraft and parts business in Los Angeles.[20] Still, it was entirely unclear if the region would become the preeminent center of the Cold War military aerospace enterprise. The Seattle rival Boeing won the biggest plum of the early Cold War buildup, the B-52 heavy bomber. In the early 1950s, LA firms were relegated to more conventional types of production, such as troop transport aircraft, and participated as major subcontractors on fighter and bomber projects centered elsewhere.

It was really the decision in 1952 to energetically pursue ballistic missiles, leading to the crash ICBM program initiated in 1954, that made Los Angeles the star of the Cold War military complex. The prominence of atmospheric warfare in the Cold War struggle, elevated by the reassessment of security strategy in President Dwight D. Eisenhower's New Look, uniquely favored the LA defense research and production complex. Underlying these changes in strategy and doctrine was the realization that military competition with the Soviets required that the United States retain significant qualitative superiority in major strategic and tactical weapons systems. This reality promoted the intense technological competition that characterized the entire Cold War era. The institutions and capacities of the LA complex allowed it to benefit from every major phase of the technological arms race in aerospace from ICBMs to spy planes, from satellites to the Strategic Defense Initiative.

The specific turns in Cold War strategy and policy that stimulated the LA defense industry are detailed briefly below. But as the New Look changes were implemented, Los Angeles firms and political leaders scrambled to position themselves though a new round of institution building and collaboration. Air Force brass looking for sophisticated assessments of threats and military responses, Cal Tech leaders such as von Karman, and Douglas Aircraft personnel worked together to build up the Santa Monica–based RAND Corporation. Originally housed at Douglas Aircraft, RAND became an independent entity in 1948. By the 1950s, RAND was playing a major role in formulating Cold War strategic and procurement strategy for the Air Force. Furthermore, in 1954 the centrality of the LA aerospace complex was ratified by the Air Force's decision to locate the new and uniquely important Western Development Division of its Air Research and Development Command in Inglewood.

The status of Los Angeles as an Air Force center paid off dramatically as this service branch won its struggle with the Army to become the Pentagon's lead service for ICBM deployment. As the Cold War waxed, LA companies successfully repositioned themselves for the missile and satellite age, supported by the local research base that had been patiently built up since the 1930s. By 1961, Lockheed, Douglas, Northrop, and North American relied on missiles for between 39 and 79 percent of their business.[21] In addition to building platforms like strategic bombers, ICBMs, and communication satellites, the LA complex bred extensive defense electronics and avionics sectors to produce the payloads and subsystems that accounted for a larger and larger share of total weapons system costs. The leadership in rocketry, space systems, and electronics established by LA firms and research institutions furthermore allowed the region to become a leading center for National Aeronautics and Space Administration procurement in the 1960s.[22]

In light of this trajectory, the postwar ups and downs of the Los Angeles economy were driven more by geopolitical than civilian business cycles, underscoring the importance of the aerospace complex to the local economy. Despite defense-related downturns in the 1970s, the region continued on a high growth path into the 1980s, when the Reagan buildup once again recharged its aerospace industries. In the post–World War II era, its economic base was clearly dominated by two industries: movies and aerospace. Along the way, Los Angeles did develop other successful industry specializations. Apparel developed and grew in the 1970s, specializing in a distinctive women's sportswear based on "LA style."[23] In the 1980s, Los Angeles also grew to be the largest banking and financial services center on the West Coast, an important locus for East Asian banking and finance. But the crucial and persistent importance of the defense aerospace complex came into sharp relief in the 1990s as the Cold War ended. The 1990s were the first down decade for Los Angeles since the 1930s. Because the termination of the Cold War era effectively ended one of the most spectacular booms ever experienced by an urban region, the era's significance for explaining the Los Angeles miracle comes into stark relief.

The Technological Imperative of the Cold War and the Rise of the LA Defense Complex

Several aerospace analysts have identified the New Look as a fundamental shift in strategic and military strategy that uniquely benefited Los Angeles. The added reliance on the nuclear arsenal, the notion of exploiting advantages to respond asymmetrically to Soviet or Chinese threats, and the reluctance to sustain a full mobilization of huge land armies and navies to fully contain Soviet ambitions were seen to favor air power, surveillance, and rocketry.[24] And these were exactly the military requirements that the Los Angeles complex was best positioned to meet.[25] What is missing from these very good accounts is a precise explanation of why specific military priorities emerged out of the New Look and how this particular shift in strategy set off a more long-term dynamic that continued to feed the LA complex throughout the Cold War era.

Before the Cold War, the United States had historically relied upon a concept that Richard Samuels has termed "rich nation, strong army."[26] Mobilizing its diverse, advanced industrial base and its huge resource and labor power endowment, the United States could outproduce and wear down any adversary in a large-scale war of attrition. At the conclusion of each conflict, military spending was slashed. Companies drawn into war production moved back into new or preexisting commercial markets, taking with them government-supplied capital equipment, technical advances, and knowledge gained in war production.

Political and military establishments tend to formulate current strategy on the basis of past experiences. This nostrum certainly captures the initial post–World War II builddown and the first call to Cold War rearmament embodied in NSC-68 and operationalized through the Korean conflict. The drawdown of forces in 1946 was what the United States had always done when wars were over. The across-the-board buildup and general mobilization of land, air, and naval forces prompted by the Korean War and the strategic buildup was likewise how the United States had always responded to major military threats. However, the far-ranging global commitments embodied in NSC-68 could be seen to imply a World War II–level mobilization that was not achievable over the long term in the absence of total war.[27] As Eisenhower and his secretary of state, John Foster Dulles, recognized, if the struggle with the communist bloc was to remain a cold war, a strategy requiring a lower level of military resource allocation had to be crafted.[28]

The difficult experience of the Korean War also shaped changes in strategy that strongly affected military requirements. The massive and surprisingly successful Chinese intervention into Korea gave pause to those who thought that the United States could outman and outproduce any opponent. The national security establishment became much less confident that size and industrial capacity could be relied upon to ensure superiority against the huge nation-states of the Soviet Union and China, capable of commanding resources with few domestic counterpressures. This reality was an important factor prompting the U.S. security establishment to coalesce around a New Look strategy that relied upon a sophisticated nuclear deterrent and technological superiority to significantly "multiply" the capability of conventional forces.[29]

Clearly, this approach created a powerful technological imperative for high performance from weapon system designers and producers. At the same time, strategies related to the New Look still required a defense industry base that could rapidly ramp up in response to the outbreak of major regional or superpower conflicts. But more to the point, because the new strategy was highly dependent upon maintaining technological superiority, it required a national science and technology base and linked complex of defense firms that could meet unanticipated military and technological challenges from the Soviets.

In this context, the profound effect of the Sputnik launch on both expert and broader public opinion can be better appreciated. It was feared in the mid-1950s that massive Soviet arms factories could quantitatively outproduce the United States and that the Soviet and Chinese armies could dwarf U.S. and allied force numbers. Sputnik was a classic case of "disruptive change" in the security environment. If the Soviets were now obtaining superior technical capability, thought to be the remaining strong suit of the West, then a dire security crisis was indeed upon the nation.[30] As Eisenhower's science adviser, Herbert York, noted, "Of all the symbols in the mythology and terror which has propelled the arms race, Sputnik is the most dramatic."[31]

The New Look strategy and Eisenhower's struggle against a permanent large-scale mobilization, or what Eisenhower termed a "garrison state," has been widely interpreted as trying to get containment on the cheap.[32] Democrats and factions of the national security establishment proffered this argument through various scares, gaps, and crises, continuing most famously with the "missile gap" of the 1960 election. However, an argument can be made that the New Look period actually involved historically high levels of military spending and military preparedness. The Eisenhower administration did significantly reduce the Army budget, but this was primarily due to a demobilization of Korean troops and a decision that maintaining a large domestic Army was not a priority to respond to Soviet actions.[33] Redeployments to the North Atlantic Treaty Organization (NATO) continued, and forces remained in Korea and Japan. There was a recognition that the United States was not prepared to instigate a large land battle in Asia with the Chinese or in Europe with the Red Army. The response to the Hungarian uprising in 1956 illustrated the latter point.[34] However, the commitment to NATO and continued high levels of military spending do suggest that the administration was certainly prepared to respond to a serious attack on the heart of Europe.

From 1955 to 1959, defense spending as a share of gross domestic product averaged 9.7 percent, a level of resource allocation to the military that was only surpassed in the Korean War and World War II.[35] As noted above, the Air Force was the big winner under New Look priorities, with money pouring into the Strategic Air Command and the ICBM development programs. In particular, two crucial national security programs received the highest priority in the New Look period, and they happened to be dominated by Los Angeles firms and research organizations.

First, the New Look strategy of deterrence and massive retaliation fundamentally required the creation of a surveillance capacity to identify targets in the Soviet Union and to monitor Soviet military developments. The Soviet Union was a closed and a uniquely extensive territory. Conventional intelligence practices had failed to provide reliable and comprehensive information on Soviet facilities, installations, and military activities. As a result, a crash program to develop a high-flying spy aircraft was launched in Lockheed's famous Skunk Works in 1954.[36] The U-2 overflights, beginning in the summer of 1956, provided the first comprehensive assessment of Soviet military installations and military capacity. At the same time Los Angeles firms, again led by Lockheed, were leaders in the Discovery/Corona spy satellite development, another crash program to replace U-2 intelligence endangered by improved Soviet surface-to-air capability in the late 1950s. Ironically, it was the Discovery/Corona spy satellite films that proved to Robert McNamara, secretary of defense in the 1960s, that the vaunted missile gap was a myth, just as feverish spending going into ICBM development was leading to the first deployment of the Atlas system, another product with Southern California roots.[37]

The story of the ICBM program and the role of Los Angeles firms is a long one, but two points are worth noting. First, the LA-based Air Force teams had to beat out the Army and Werner Von Braun's team at Huntsville, Alabama, to become the lead force in missile warfare. Markusen argues that the Army "arsenal system" failed to win the ICBM battle because it lacked advanced production capacity and had less political punch than the big private Air Force contactors in California.[38] The ICBM program went to the Air Force and was run out of the Air Force's Western Development Division in LA. Although Atlas rockets were produced by Convair in San Diego, employing over 6,000 workers at their Kearney Mesa site, Cal Tech graduates Simon Ramo and Dean Wooldridge headed the ICBM development team and systems engineering. Ramo and Wooldridge, under the auspices of their newly formed company TRW, were overseeing 220 prime contractors and thousands of subcontractors on ICBM development by 1957.[39]

The second point is that the missile race with the Soviets was very real and presaged many subsequent "races" to maintain technological superiority. It was extremely difficult to determine in the short term that the rocket that launched Sputnik was not also being mass produced to launch nuclear warheads. There was profound uncertainty; intelligence first suggested that the work of Pyotr Kapista on the hydrogen/liquid-fueled engines that launched Sputnik was related to the development of a supersonic bomber.[40] Though subsequent U-2 intelligence found no evidence of significant ICBM deployment in the late 1950s, there were still doubts, especially given Nikita Khrushchev's bluster. Not until 1961 did it become clear that the early generation of Soviet missiles was seriously flawed and could not be accurately targeted.[41] Nevertheless, to meet this threat—perceived to be mortal—the Air Force carried out a true crash program. In this crash ICBM program, centered in Southern California, no resources—scientific, financial, or physical—were be spared to overcome the technical obstacles to develop and deploy this strategic weapons system.

More important to the centrality of the LA defense complex, this ICBM program became the model for numerous other crash programs characterizing the technological imperative of the Cold War arms race. The Los Angeles research and production complex was particularly well positioned to leverage its research and production strengths and institutional contacts to obtain leadership on many leading-edge aerospace projects throughout the Cold War era. For nearly forty years, the LA complex fed on advanced strategic projects, including bomber projects (B-1, B-2) space projects (ICBMs, surveillance, and military communications), missiles (ICBMs, submarine-launched ballistic missiles, cruise missiles), and advanced electronics and communications (put on countless weapons platforms). In sum, the shift signaled by the New Look created the technological imperatives in military production that allowed the LA complex to achieve preeminence in the design and production of strategic weaponry during the 1950s and to sustain this leadership position through the end of the Cold War.

The Post–Cold War Collapse

Since the late 1980s, Los Angeles has experienced one of the most abrupt economic reversals ever visited upon a major American city. The inflow of defense dollars has shrunk dramatically, and the region's expensive real estate, environmental costs, and relatively high salary norms have made retention and/or reliance on growth in other economic sectors problematic. As the Cold War came to a close, employment in Los Angeles County's aerospace, electronics, and instruments industries fell by over 50 percent.[42] Between 1989 and 1996, the LA region suffered dramatic declines in aerospace and electronics employment and a less dramatic but still significant decline in defense-related R&D and service activity. It is not an exaggeration to say that the end of the Cold War stripped Los Angeles of much of its manufacturing base and the cadres of blue-collar production workers and white-collar engineers that constituted the region's middle class. Though the 1990s are remembered as boom times in many parts of the United States, for Los Angeles the decade was one of stagnation and growing social polarization.

With current high levels of military spending since the September, 11, 2001, terrorist attacks, it is important to recall that real spending for defense fell by roughly one-third between 1989 and 1996, while defense purchases from the private sector dropped by $66 billion or 35 percent.[43] Before the extent of the post–Cold War economic shock on LA is detailed, it is important to draw upon the arguments offered above to explain why the region was peculiarly vulnerable to defense reductions.

From its long history as a leader in high technology defense development, Los Angeles possessed a uniquely dense agglomeration of institutions and companies that captured a disproportionate share of both prime and subcontracts.[44] Though other defense-dependent regions hosted two or even three top prime contractor facilities, in 1990 the headquarters or major facilities of eight of the top twenty-five defense contractors were in Los Angeles County.[45] In 1988, before the cutbacks hit, Los Angeles County was the site of thirty-one such facilities, each employing over 1,000 employees in its defense aerospace and electronics industries. These major facilities were linked to hundreds of smaller subcontractors and suppliers and surrounded by major research institutions and large Air Force command and procurement centers.[46]

As late as 1992, Los Angeles County received far and away the largest volume of Defense Department prime contracts. It has further been noted that prime contract award totals underestimated regional defense activity because Los Angeles contractors are heavily involved in "black budget" projects not registered in the data.[47] Because of the sheer extent of this industrial and research base, Los Angeles was strongly affected both by direct contract reductions to local facilities and by national defense reductions, which reduced the stream of subcontracts coming from defense prime contractors located outside the region.

In addition, the diverse and multilayered character of the military high-technology sector did not provide immunity to cancellations in individual programs. Again based upon its history, the LA military sectors were dominated by large firms that were strongly tied to Air Force Cold War projects.[48] Even though there were over 1,000 firms with some participation in defense markets, the core LA aerospace complex was dominated by giant aircraft, missile, and search-and-navigation equipment companies.[49] Many of the weapons system contracts that occupied large LA contractors were geared to specific Cold War missions. LA contractors were never leaders in key tactical systems, such as tanks, shipbuilding, or even fighter aircraft. The F-117-A stealth fighter, Peacekeeper and Trident missiles, and the B-2 bomber were among the region's big Cold War programs that were terminated or scaled back in the early 1990s.[50] Significant cutbacks in R&D were also felt from the scaling back of research on the Strategic Defense Initiative, even though elements of this program survived and ultimately grew.

As a number of Cold War programs were terminated and new defense and commercial work failed to materialize, the region's big companies began a process of drastic consolidation and relocation. The relative dearth of major new procurement programs during the 1990s, particularly in strategic bomber and Defense Department missile and space programs, made it less important to be linked to the intertwined research, production, testing, and supply architecture that Los Angeles offered. The fact that few R&D projects moved to large-scale production in the 1990s allowed contractors to move mature pro-

Table 5.1. Key Defense Industry Employment, Los Angeles–Long Beach Metropolitan Statistical Area, 1988–1996

Sector	Employment		Job Change 1988–96	Percentage Change 1988–96
	1988	1996		
Electronics and communications	37,482	26,600	−10,882	−29.0
Aircraft and aircraft parts	95,902	50,815	−45,087	−47.0
Guided missiles and space vehicles	59,235	18,062	−41,173	−69.5
Instruments	51,718	23,937	−27,781	−53.7
Engineering and research services	38,792	34,995	−3,797	−9.8
Total	283,129	154,409	−128,720	−45.5

Source: U.S. Department of the Census, County Business Patterns, 1988 and 1996.

duction lines away from the R&D institutions and internal teams centered in costly Los Angeles.[51]

When defense cuts and the onset of recession hit at the end of 1990, it became clear that economic growth, even in Southern California, was a reversible phenomenon. It is not an overstatement to say that in 1990 the Los Angeles economy fell over a cliff. Table 5.1 details job losses in the core LA defense sectors. This does not include related job losses in sectors such as primary metals, fabricated metals, or computer services that constituted the supply base of the core defense industries. Employment in defense-related industries collapsed across the board. Between 1988 and 1996, aircraft manufacturing shed 45,000 jobs (−47 percent), missiles and space vehicles over 41,000 (−69 percent), instruments and related products nearly 28,000 (−54 percent), and electronics and communications equipment 10,800 (−29 percent). The inflow of defense contracts that had sustained LA's growth through most of the postwar era had dried up. It is interesting that the research end of the complex (in table 5.1, engineering and research services) was less devastated by post–Cold War reductions. As suggested above, many of the area's large defense contracts moved production facilities to other sites, while retaining key corporate and R&D activities in Los Angeles. Yet because of the closure and relocation of major defense manufacturing facilities, most of these jobs will not come back, even with the recent spurt in defense spending.

The fact that many of the layoffs in manufacturing facilities are permanent is suggested by the enormous losses suffered by the region's major aerospace trade unions. The represented membership of the United Auto Workers, International Association of Machinists, and International Brotherhood of Electrical Workers at defense aerospace facilities went from 62,000 in the late 1980s to 18,300 by the end of 1994.[52] The dynamics of the restructuring process, with massive declines in both the defense and the nondefense durable goods sectors, have caused many of the occupations in which defense workers are concentrated to decline in the region. The relocation of defense production to lower-cost sites has permanently removed strata of well-paying union jobs from the LA economy. This not only meant the loss of high-skilled workers but also contributed to a further deterioration in wage and workplace standards across the region.

There is evidence that jobs in the middle-income wage strata began to decline as a share of total employment in the region during the 1979–87 period.[53] However, there is strong evidence that the post–Cold War collapse in manufacturing employment stimulated a greater polarization of the region's job and wage structure. Table 5.2 shows losses in defense-related occupations. The loss of highly paid managerial and professional (especially engineering) jobs and skilled middle-wage production jobs is confirmed by these data.

The five occupations with the greatest job losses were high-wage engineering and production occupations. These included punch machine setters, electrical and electronic engineers, precision aircraft assemblers, aeronautical en-

Table 5.2. Occupations with Largest Job Losses in Aerospace and Defense-Related High Technology, Los Angeles–Long Beach Metropolitan Statistical Area, 1988–1994

Occupational Employment Statistics (OES) Occupation Title	Employment Change, 1988–94
Punch machine setters	−9,914
Electrical and electronic engineers	−7,628
Aircraft assemblers–precision	−5,772
Aeronautical and astronautical engineers	−5,698
Engineering, mathematics, and natural science managers	−5,203
Engineers, not elsewhere classified	−5,038
Industrial engineers	−4,541
Electrical and electronic engineering technicians	−4,393
Management support workers, not elsewhere classified	−4,111
Electrical and electronic equipment assemblers	−3,577
Precision inspectors, testers, and graders	−3,204
Assemblers and fabricators	−3,085
Other professional, paraprofessional, and technical workers	−2,862
Secretaries, general	−2,849
Systems analysts, electronic data processing	−2,561
Machinists	−2,518
Production planning and expediting clerks	−2,445

Source: The OES industry-occupation matrixes, prepared by the California Employment Development Department, provide data on employment in detailed OES occupations by four-digit Standard Industrial Classification (SIC) code in Los Angeles County for 1992, as well as the percentage distribution of each industry's employment by detailed occupation. For each occupation, estimates of employment in the aerospace and defense high-technology industries were calculated for 1988 and 1994. The percentage of employment accounted for by each occupation in each four-digit SIC aerospace industry code were multiplied by the 1988 and 1994 employment totals in the aerospace occupations to derive an estimate of employment by occupation.

131

gineers, and engineers (not elsewhere classified). Over 31,000 engineers and technicians joined the ranks of the unemployed in the worst years of post–Cold War downsizing, while employment losses were also high in a range of skilled machining and assembly occupations.

The match between occupations that are growing in the LA region and the skills and wages of the occupations that defense workers are leaving was poor during the 1990s. The occupations projected to offer the greatest number of absolute job openings in the 1990s were concentrated in retail trade, office support services, and, to a lesser extent, management, health care, and professional services (i.e., accountants and lawyers).[54]

In addition to being concentrated in higher-skill occupations, defense workers differed from other workers in ways that were relevant to their chances for reemployment in jobs with comparable wages. Controlling for occupation, the average defense worker was older than nondefense manufacturing workers and had slightly higher levels of educational attainment.[55] But defense aerospace workers earned wage premiums that cannot be fully explained by skills or demographics. Though defense aerospace workers earned about 18 percent more than employees in nondefense durable goods industries nationwide, only one-third of this differential is attributable to the higher skill and age profiles of the workforce.[56] In Los Angeles, this wage premium may be attributable to the fact that defense workers tend to work for larger companies offering higher wages and are probably more likely to be unionized than workers in the rest of the economy.

A RAND study of defense aerospace workers in California covering the 1989–94 period indicated that close to one-third of workers who experienced unemployment since 1989 dropped out of the workforce and either left the state or remain unemployed in 1994.[57] Another 27 percent, though still in the labor force, did not find permanent, secure jobs, and when they did work earned roughly 14 percent less than in their former jobs. Because California's defense aerospace workers are heavily concentrated in Los Angeles, this is a rough proxy measure of the experience of the region's unemployed.

These serious job and income declines spread out from major defense manufacturing facilities to locally based service and trade sectors. As real estate values began to fall in the early 1990s and segments of the local financial system became shaky, the nondurable manufacturing, trade, and finance, insurance, and real estate sectors all contracted in the early 1990s. The region as a whole registered net aggregate employment losses from 1990 through mid-1994, even as national employment grew from the bottom of the 1991 recession. The depth of the post–Cold War reductions and the prior dependence of the LA economy on Cold War projects is reinforced by the astonishing fact that

Figure 5.1. Los Angeles County Nonfarm Employment, 1988–2000 (millions of jobs)

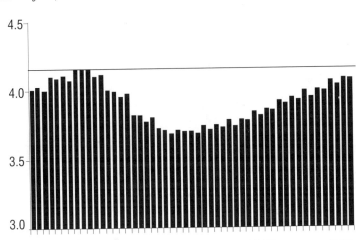

Source: Los Angeles County, *Los Angeles County Economic Forecast,* 2002.

total nonfarm employment in 2000 had yet to recover to the 4.1 million job level of 1990 (figure 5.1).[58]

The severe contraction of employment caused by defense downsizing reversed a sixty-year-long secular boom in Los Angeles that drew aspiring migrants from across the United States. Though international migration, particularly from Mexico and Central America, remained strongly positive throughout the 1990s, there was a major out-migration of U.S. citizens. As figure 5.2 shows, in the peak year of 1993, there was a net domestic out-migration of nearly 250,000 from Los Angeles County. Domestic migration to Los Angeles remained negative throughout the 1990s.[59]

If the Cold War in some sense created modern Los Angeles, drawing workers from the South and Midwest and engineering talent from the great Eastern and Midwestern engineering schools to LA's defense factories and laboratories, the termination of the Cold War erased the image of the region as a place of boundless opportunity. Or perhaps it would be more accurate to say that the impact of defense cutbacks fundamentally changed the character and dynamism of the region. With the dramatic downsizing of the defense aerospace manufacturing base, the remaining strengths of the LA economy were its huge entertainment complex and low-wage service and apparel manufacturing sector. The movie business boomed and grew locally during the 1990s, providing

Figure 5.2. Net Immigration versus Domestic Migration, Los Angeles County, 1991–1999 (thousands)

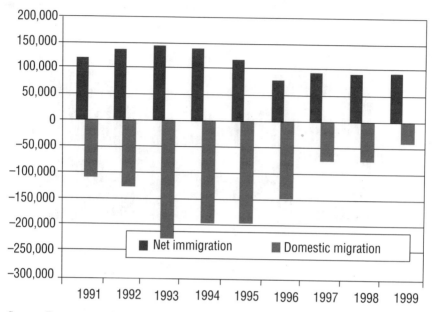

Source: Department of Finance, State of California, *Updated Revised Historical County Population Estimates and Components of Change, July 1, 1990–99* (Sacramento: State of California, 2003).

some floor for a declining overall economy. But the movie industry has a very polarized wage structure, with working actors, producers, and other industry personnel making high wages, while and aspiring actors and support personnel occupy low-wage, often temporary jobs. The other growing segments of the regional economy were linked to low-wage immigrant labor. As a result, Los Angeles is now a different, more polarized place, much less a beacon of opportunity for talented and skilled people from across the nation.

Conclusion: Signs of the Post–Cold War Transformation

In *Falling Down,* a Warner Brothers film released in March 1993, Michael Douglas plays a defense engineer whose career is terminated by post–Cold War defense industry downsizing. With his family falling apart and his job prospects nil, the still-patriotic engineer played by Douglas ventures onto the streets of Los Angeles to find an unexpected, alien world. He encounters ethnic gangs, rude service workers who will not make his hamburger to order, and throngs of people speaking in foreign tongues. Cracking up under the pressure, he launches his own personal military intervention to recover a past time and make things right. The resulting killing spree changes little; street punks are replaced by other street punks, the foreign invasion continues, and job and family are not recovered.

For many, like the character in *Falling Down*, the loss of a good defense-related job was a shattering experience. As the evidence shows, laid-off defense workers were exposed to a world where the demand for aerospace engineers and skilled blue-collar trades had dried up. The technological imperative that fueled the LA defense business dissipated with the end of the Cold War. There was no place to go, and many were forced to leave this expensive region to develop new skills and try new trades in other locales.

The stripping out of hundreds of thousands of defense workers also contributed to the amazing political transformation of Los Angeles and California during the 1990s. Since the 1950s, California has been viewed as a swing state, with a staunchly Republican south that often outweighs its more Democratic north. Many of the powerful figures of the Republican Party in the post–World War II era emerged from a Southern California base. The region was also a seedbed for central ideological trends in the Republican Party, from "Red scare" anticommunism to the antitax and antigovernment sentiments that still animate the party. Southern California Republicans could always count on the cadres of white-collar defense engineers and blue-collar production workers (who were likely to vote for prodefense Republicans, despite suggestions of union leaders) to gain majorities. This crucial political base was undermined by the post–Cold War downsizing of the defense industry and out-migration of redundant workers.

The loss of the formerly safely Republican Orange County seat of Representative "B-1" Bob Dornan to Loretta Sanchez, a Hispanic Democrat, epitomized the root causes of Republican Party losses across Southern California. White, middle-class defense workers left the region to be replaced by Hispanic immigrants who are more friendly to the Democrats, thanks in part to the Republican embrace of anti-immigrant initiatives in the 1990s. Now the region and the state are seen as a strong bastion of the Democratic Party, providing congressional seats, electoral votes, and entertainment industry money. In 2002, 56 percent of Los Angeles County voted for the incumbent Democratic governor Grey Davis, while 35 percent voted for the Republican Bill Simon.[60]

At the same time, Los Angeles has become more like the rest of America. As the national debate on growing inequality in income distribution and political power suggests, the loss of middle-class jobs in manufacturing and the growth of high-technology commercial industries has intensified social polarization. In many ways, Los Angeles in the 1990s was a perfect "case" experiment to evaluate these trends. The region lost its middle-class manufacturing job base in a few years versus a few decades. The big issues associated with growing inequality—separation and alienation between classes and ethnic groups, decline in social solidarity, and the like—are clearly being played out in the local politics of the region, with recent movements in the San Fernando Valley and even Hollywood to secede from the City of Los Angeles.

It remains to be seen if the current post-9/11 run-up in military spending might recreate the "old" Los Angeles by resurrecting the region's defense industries. Though defense spending has climbed back up to its Cold War levels, it is unlikely that the LA defense economy will recover its former status. The new high-tech thrust in the antiterrorism campaign requires a different kind organization, technology, and industrial base than did the "big platform" of the Cold War. The defense sector remains firmly rooted in Los Angeles, with R&D spending and money for special projects flowing to firms still headquartered in the region. However, the remnants of the great LA aerospace complex are concentrated in corporate project management and R&D teams, not in large-scale production. The great factories that produced the landmark systems that met the Soviet threat have been torn down and will remain silent.

Notes

1. William G. Cunningham, *The Aircraft Industry: A Study in Industrial Location* (Los Angeles: Morrison, 1951); Theodore Von Karman, *The Wind and Beyond: Theodore von Karman, Pioneer in Aviation and Pathfinder in Space* (Boston: Little, Brown, 1967); Michael H. Armacost, *The Politics of Weapons Innovation: The Thor-Jupiter Controversy* (New York: Columbia University Press, 1969); Gene R. Simonson, "Missiles and Creative Destruction in the American Aircraft Industry, 1956–61," in *The History of the American Aircraft Industry: An Anthology,* by Gene R. Simonson (Cambridge, Mass.: MIT Press, 1968); J. Leland Atwood, *North American Rockwell: Storehouse of High Technology* (New York: Newcomen Society in North America, 1970); William A. Schoneberger, *California Wings: A History of Aviation in the Golden State* (Woodland Hills, Calif.: Windsor Publications, 1984); Ann Markusen, Peter Hall, Scott Campbell, and Sabina Deitrick, *The Rise of the Gunbelt* (New York: Oxford University Press, 1991); Roger Lotchin, *Fortress California, 1910–1961: From Warfare to Welfare* (New York: Oxford University Press, 1992); Ann Markusen and Joel Yudken, *Dismantling the Cold War Economy* (New York: Basic Books, 1992); Michael Oden, Ann Markusen, Dan Flaming, and Mark Drayse, *Post Cold War Frontiers: Defense Downsizing and Conversion in Los Angeles,* Working Paper 105 (New Brunswick, N.J.: Center for Urban Policy Research, Rutgers University, 1996).

2. Markusen et al., *Rise of the Gunbelt;* Lotchin, *Fortress California.*

3. Lotchin, *Fortress California,* xv.

4. Schoneburger, *California Wings.*

5. Markusen et al., *Rise of the Gunbelt*.

6. Robert Gottlieb and Irene Wolt, *Thinking Big: The Story of the Los Angeles Times, Its Publishers, and Their Influence on Southern California* (New York: Putnam, 1977).

7. Lotchin, *Fortress California*.

8. Paul D. Friedman, "Fear of Flying: The Development of the Los Angeles International Airport and the Rise of Public Protest over Jet Aircraft Noise," master's thesis, University of California, Santa Barbara, 1978.

9. Markusen et al., *Rise of the Gunbelt*.

10. Lotchin, *Fortress California*; Markusen et al., *Rise of the Gunbelt*.

11. Schoneburger, *California Wings*; Donald L. Bartlett and James B. Steele, *Empire: The Life, Legend, and Madness of Howard Hughes* (New York: W. W. Norton, 1979); Edward M. Ainsworth, *Memories in the City of Dreams: A Tribute to Harry Chandler, Gran Benefactor de la Cuidad* (privately printed, Los Angeles, 1959); Marshall Berges, *The Life and Times of Los Angeles: A Newspaper, a Family and a City* (New York: Athenaeum, 1984); Gottlieb and Woldt, *Thinking Big;* Remi Nadeau, *Los Angeles: From Mission to Modern City* (New York: Longman, 1960).

12. Lotchin, *Fortress California*.

13. Ibid.

14. Von Karman, *Wind and Beyond*.

15. William Cunningham, *The Aircraft Industry: A Study in Industrial Location* (Los Angeles: Morrison, 1951); Markusen et al., *Rise of the Gunbelt;* Oden et al., *Post Cold War Frontiers*.

16. Sabina Deitrick, "Military Spending and Migration into California," Department of City and Regional Planning, University of California, Berkeley, 1984; Scott Campbell, "Interregional Migration of Defense Scientists and Engineers to the Gunbelt during the 1990s," *Economic Geography* 69, no. 2 (1993): 204–23; Mark Ellis, Richard Barff, and Ann Markusen, "Defense Spending and Interregional Labor Migration," *Economic Geography* 29, no. 2 (1993): 1–22.

17. Markusen et al., *Rise of the Gunbelt*.

18. Ibid.

19. Ibid.

20. Lotchin, *Fortress California*.

21. Simonson, "Missiles and Creative Destruction."

22. Allen J. Scott, "The Technopoles of Southern California," *Environment and Planning–A* 22 (1990): 1575–1605.

23. David Friedman et al., "Report of the New Economy Project," Report to the Community Redevelopment Agency, Los Angeles Community Development Department, Los Angeles Department of Water and Power, September 16, 1994.

24. John Lewis Gaddis, *Strategies of Containment: A Critical Appraisal of Postwar National Security Policy* (New York: Oxford University Press, 1982); Michael Sherry, *In the Shadow of War: The United Sates since the 1930s* (New Haven, Conn.: Yale University Press, 1995).

25. Markusen et al., *Rise of the Gunbelt;* Lotchin, *Fortress California*.

26. Richard Samuels, *Rich Nation, Strong Army: National Security and the Technological Transformation of Japan* (Ithaca, N.Y.: Cornell University Press, 1994).

27. Gaddis, *Strategies of Containment*.

Michael Oden

28. Ibid.

29. Warner Schilling et al., *Strategy, Politics and Defense Budgets* (New York: Columbia University Press, 1962).

30. Coit Blacker, *Reluctant Warriors* (New York W. H. Freeman, 1987).

31. Herbert York, *Race to Oblivion: A Participant View of the Arms Race* (New York: Simon & Schuster, 1970), 106.

32. H. W. Brands, "The Age of Vulnerability: Eisenhower and the National Insecurity State," *American Historical Review* 94 (1989): 963–89.

33. Gaddis, *Strategies of Containment.*

34. Sherry, *In the Shadow of War.*

35. Michael Oden, "Military Spending, Military Power, and Postwar Economic Performance," doctoral dissertation, New School for Social Research, 1992.

36. Ben Rich and Leo Janos, *Skunk Works* (Boston: Little, Brown, 1994).

37. Nick Koltz, *Wild Blue Yonder* (New York: Pantheon Books, 1988).

38. Markusen et al., *Rise of the Gunbelt.*

39. Ibid.

40. Rich and Janos, *Skunk Works.*

41. Koltz, *Wild Blue Yonder.*

42. Unpublished data for 1982–94, Labor Market Information Division, Employment Development Department, State of California, Sacramento, 1995.

43. U.S. Department of Defense, *Defense Budget Estimates for FY 1997* (Washington, D.C.: Office of the Undersecretary of Defense–Comptroller, 1996).

44. Robert Atkinson, "Defense Spending Cuts and Regional Economic Impact: An Overview," *Economic Geography* 69, no. 2, April (1993): 107–22; Michael Dardia, "Is Small Beautiful? Firm Size and Job Losses in the Military Industrial Base," paper presented at Economic Roundtable, RAND Graduate School, Los Angeles, October 1992.

45. Department of Information, Operations, and Reports, U.S. Department of Defense, *Prime Contract Awards by State County, Contractor, and Place, FY 1992* (Arlington Va.: U.S. Department of Defense, 1992).

46. Robin Law et al., "Defense-less Territory: Workers, Communities, and the Decline of Military Production in Los Angeles," Department of Geography, University of Southern California, Los Angeles, 1992; Allen J. Scott, "The Technopoles of Southern California," *Environment and Planning–A* 22 (1990): 1575–1605.

47. Oden et al., *Post Cold War Frontiers.*

48. Economic Roundtable, *An Economic Adjustment Action Plan for the Los Angeles County Aerospace Industry,* Report to the Community Development Commission of Los Angeles County (Los Angeles: Economic Roundtable, 1992).

49. Ibid.

50. Ibid.

51. Oden et al., *Post Cold War Frontiers.*

52. Ibid.

53. Paul Schimek, "Earnings Polarization and the Proliferation of Low-Wage Work," in *The Widening Divide: Income Inequality and Poverty in Los Angeles,* ed. Paul Ong (Los Angeles: Research Group on the New York Economy, 1989), 25–52.

54. Oden et al., *Post Cold War Frontiers.*

55. Robert Schoeni et al., *Life after Cutbacks: Tracking California's Aerospace*

Workers (Santa Monica, Calif.: RAND Corporation, 1996); Law et al., "Defense-less Territory."

56. Schoeni et al., *Life after Cutbacks.*

57. Ibid.

58. Los Angeles County, *Los Angeles County Economic Forecast,* 2002, http:// www.dot.ca.gov/hq/tpp/offices/.

59. Department of Finance, State of California, *Updated Revised Historical County Population Estimates and Components of Change, July 1, 1990–99* (Sacramento: State of California, 2003).

60. Public Policy Institute of California, *Just the Facts, Los Angeles County,* March 2003, available at http://www.ppic.org.

6. Cold War Frontier: Building the Defense Complex in Novosibirsk

Anita Seth

On July 29, 1959, Richard Nixon arrived in Novosibirsk, the emerging capital of Siberia, after a long flight on a Soviet Tu-104 jetliner from Leningrad. It was his last stop on a trip historians remember mainly for the way it began, with the famous kitchen debate with Soviet premier Nikita Khrushchev. The decision of Soviet officials to showcase Novosibirsk to the American vice president, and Nixon's willingness to fly halfway across the Soviet Union for a day-long visit, marked the city's rise from a provincial trading stop to one of the foremost centers of Soviet industry. Nixon's itinerary included stops at a new hydroelectric station along the Ob River and the construction site of the Siberian Division of the Russian Academy of Sciences, capped off by a performance of *Swan Lake* at the local ballet. None of these attractions (including the ballet performance) would have been available to Nixon had he visited just two decades before.

Both Nixon and the *New York Times* correspondent Harrison Salisbury, who accompanied him on the trip, thought they recognized in Novosibirsk a frontier reminiscent of the American West.[1] Salisbury in particular believed that the new Siberia could provide the basis for a post-Stalinist Soviet society based on industrial development and scientific progress. He admired the "independent opinion" he found among Siberians and later argued that "if the Soviet Union could harness this free and independent spirit of Siberia to the new program of science and education and power, it would create a force which would give the whole of Russia a new vitality the equal of many, many Sputniks."[2]

The relationship, between technological progress in Novosibirsk on the one hand and freedom on the other, was more complex than Salisbury was willing to recognize. Just as the stereotypical rugged, individualistic spirit of the American West was in fact rooted in massive government spending and military force, the bustling Siberian city that impressed the visiting American heavily depended on centrally planned military production. The evidence of rapid development, which seemed to Salisbury a sign of freedom from Moscow, in fact marked the expansion of central authorities' involvement in Siberia.

At the same time, processes that strengthened the bonds between Novosibirsk and Moscow did increase the power of local voices. The rapid development of Novosibirsk as an engine of Soviet military production helped local interests to lay claim to resources, and even empowered a group of scientists in the suburb of Akademgorodok to question government policy during the 1960s. Indeed, the word "frontier" accurately captures both the vitality and instability of a city on the rise, as well as the inability of authorities to keep up with economic and social change.

This chapter demonstrates the layering of successive rounds of defense investment that built Novosibirsk into a defense city, and how at each stage existing defense facilities were used to argue for expanding local military production and research capabilities. First, it underlines the importance of World War II in establishing the institutions and trends that carried over into the 1950s and 1960s. Second, it highlights the growing ties between local officials and the central government in Moscow and the place of defense industries in building these networks. Third and finally, it examines the founding of the Soviet Academy of Sciences' Siberian Division as it relates to the increasing emphasis during the Cold War on science as a key factor in both military and economic competition.

Novosibirsk as a Cold War City

Today, Novosibirsk is the financial hub of Siberia and the third largest city in Russia after Moscow and Saint Petersburg, with over 1.5 million residents. It is located about 3,000 kilometers east of Moscow on the banks of the Ob River, one of the great Siberian north-south rivers. A tiny onion dome on a downtown traffic island is said to mark the geographic center of the former Soviet Union.

Long before the advent of its scientific and industrial development, Novosibirsk served as an important Siberian outpost. The city was founded in 1893, when tsarist authorities planning the route of the Trans-Siberian rail line chose to bypass Tomsk, the largest existing city in the region, to build a bridge across the Ob several hundred kilometers to the southwest. The resulting community of construction workers slowly grew into a trading and financial center by virtue of its location at the nexus of the train line and river transport.[3]

This location as a transportation crossroads became decisive again in 1941, following the German invasion of the Soviet Union. The mass evacuation of industry from the western part of the country profoundly altered the city's previous reliance on trade and agriculture, and tipped the balance from light industry, which dominated the prewar economy, to heavy industry and large-scale manufacturing. Although some of the factories and their personnel were relocated immediately following the war, what remained provided the nucleus for the local Cold War economy.

Over the next two decades, Novosibirsk became a center of both research and production for some of the key technologies of the Cold War arms race. By the late 1950s, fourteen major defense plants in Novosibirsk produced everything from conventional explosives to aircraft, electronics, optics, and rocketry.[4] The Chkalov aircraft factory, for example, produced MiG-15 and MiG-17 fighter jets that fought in the first hot conflict of the Cold War in Korea. The enormous Kombinat No. 179 was a leading producer of explosives and small-scale rocketry, while the city's electronics and radio factories were by the late 1950s "the most important providers of military communications technology," as noted by one military official, who predicted that "the role of this collection of factories, because of their geographic and economic position, will increase in the future."[5] Novosibirsk was also on its way to becoming an internationally known center of scientific research, with ten factory-based research institutes, the newly opened Novosibirsk State University, and the Siberian Division of the Russian Academy of Sciences, which by the mid-1960s housed fourteen top-level scientific institutes. Military research was dominant at most of these institutions.

This chapter's discussion of Novosibirsk's development is part of a larger project, which compares the growth of the aerospace industries in Novosibirsk and Los Angeles from World War II through the Cold War arms buildup. It outlines how the defense sector influenced political, economic, and social development in these two cities, and it seeks to explain how a largely parallel process of weapons buildup functioned within two economic and political systems that considered themselves diametrically opposed to each other. Looking comparatively at centers of defense production on either side of the Cold War divide allows an examination of common experiences that cut across national and ideological boundaries. It also highlights things that are otherwise taken for granted, making visible the familiar in a foreign context and prompting a reinterrogation of things that seems natural or obvious in each society. For example, suburbanization and consumerism, quintessential American developments of the 1950s, have their analogs in Soviet society. Similarly, local officials on both sides of the Iron Curtain sought (often with success) to leverage defense production for improvements in infrastructure or social services, and they saw continuing military production as the key to obtaining financial and social security for their cities.[6] In contrast, although nuclear weapons technology had the similar effect of propelling production of new delivery systems in both countries, public portrayals of the nuclear threat in the 1940s and 1950s were starkly different in the United States and the Soviet Union.

The field of Cold War history, almost by definition, has focused on decisionmakers in the capitals of the major powers. Expanded access to former Soviet bloc archives in the 1990s tended to reinforce the top-down bias in Cold War studies, as newly available documents provided the basis for revised interpretations of major Cold War crises. But beyond looking for what Soviet top officials said to each other and to other world leaders, it is now possible (and declassification has been more complete) to learn how local leaders interacted with Moscow, what information ordinary people were receiving about international crises, and how they experienced the heightening Cold War conflict in their daily lives.

Novosibirsk provides an ideal provincial vantage point for examining this local aspect of the Cold War because its development was so clearly tied to the rise of U.S.-Soviet tensions. Unlike the military production centers in the Urals, which trace their roots back to tsarist times and to Joseph Stalin's crash industrialization projects, heavy industry in Novosibirsk expanded primarily after World War II and especially with the trends toward technology-based military production and economic decentralization in the late 1950s under Khrushchev.

The growth of higher education, the economic experimentation of the Khrushchev era, the increased prestige of scientists, and even investments in public transportation within Novosibirsk can be tied back to military production and the exigencies of the Cold War. Demands for technological development led to the establishment of Novosibirsk State University and dozens of smaller local institutions in the 1950s. Defense ministries built day care facilities and movie theaters as part of their administration of adjacent factories. Even sidewalks and tramcars were sought and procured on the basis of Novosibirsk's ties to defense production. By understanding how the residents of Novosibirsk contributed to strengthening Soviet power in the Cold War through military production, and to accelerating its demise through the critiques of Soviet authorities in the 1960s, the study of Novosibirsk also helps uncover dynamics of the Cold War that are lost in a state-focused history.

Anita Seth

World War II and the Establishment of the Novosibirsk Defense Complex

It is difficult to overstate the impact of World War II on Soviet politics and society. The area that fell under German occupation contained one-third of the Soviet Union's industrial capacity and 40 percent of its agricultural land. The war claimed at least 27 million lives, left 25 million homeless, and destroyed one-quarter to one-third of Soviet wealth. The evacuation of over 1,500 plants in the face of the German invasion caused a major geographic shift in the Soviet economy, while defense increased to more than half of Soviet gross national product.[7]

At a regional level, more than 600,000 local men and women from the Novosibirsk region departed for the war front, where almost 200,000 of them died, causing a significant decrease in the working-age population.[8] Hundreds of thousands of refugees to the Novosibirsk region joined over 150,000 ethnic deportees, including Poles, Ukrainians, Moldavians, and Volga Germans who arrived at the outset of the war, and 18,000 Kalmyks sent to Novosibirsk in 1944 after the dissolution of their home republic.[9] Central Asian workers were also brought to Novosibirsk during the war to fill the acute labor shortage.[10] These large population transfers literally filled the city with completely new faces over the course of the war.

In spite of the damage and dislocation of the war, many of the most important industrial, scientific, and bureaucratic institutions that would guide development in Novosibirsk during the next four decades were founded between 1941 and 1945. The city was an attractive location for evacuated industry because it was centrally situated, allowing quick initial transport of personnel and equipment and delivery to both western and eastern fronts. About 10 percent of all the industry that was transferred during the German invasion—mostly defense plants—came to the Novosibirsk region, and more than fifty factories relocated to the city of Novosibirsk.[11]

The experience of the Chkalov aircraft factory, one of the largest and most important defense plants in Novosibirsk, gives some idea of the influx of equipment and personnel that occurred in the early months of the war. In its three years of operation before the war, the factory had produced fewer than 1,000 I-16 wooden fighter planes. Attempts to introduce more advanced models fell behind schedule, barely entering production by the outbreak of the war.[12] The preeminent aircraft designer and people's commissar for aviation Alexander Yakovlev, who arrived in Novosibirsk in late 1941, dismissed it as "a recently built aircraft plant, . . . [which] made few machines . . . [and where] production facilities were used very ineffectively."[13]

That changed abruptly. The central authorities decided in 1941 to evacuate

144

to Novosibirsk's six aircraft factories, along with almost 9,000 personnel. Five of these came to Chkalov, including Plant No. 301 from Moscow, which was attached to Yakovlev's design bureau. Between June 1941 and June 1942, the Chkalov factory doubled its territory and tripled its personnel.[14] By 1944, it could produce 5,500 planes in a single year. Overall, the factory sent almost 16,000 fighter planes to the front, most designed by Yakovlev, and was awarded the Order of Lenin in July 1945 for its wartime service, securing a prominent place among the largest and most successful aircraft complexes in the Soviet Union.[15]

An even more dramatic transformation took place at the Kombinat No. 179 factory (later known as Sibselmash), which was originally built in the 1930s to produce agricultural machines. The factory had a slow start. As late as September 1941, the Novosibirsk regional Communist Party secretary Mikhail Kulagin bemoaned the lagging production at the factory, noting that "we have until now continued to speak the language of peacetime. . . . We have not concentrated all of our energies on producing shells."[16] But the evacuation of ten factories in the second half of 1941 brought almost half of all Soviet munitions capacity to No. 179. Even after an administrative reorganization, which transferred much of the evacuated equipment and personnel to new independent factories, No. 179 produced 48 million shells during the war.[17] The wartime expansion also positioned No. 179 for its Cold War role as an important producer of antiaircraft and rocket components.

The evacuation of an assortment of instrument-making, radio, and electronics factories from Moscow and Leningrad created a wholly new branch of industry in Novosibirsk, further adding to the depth of the wartime transformation. Factory No. 69 ("im. Lenina"), evacuated from the Moscow region in October 1941, produced optical equipment for cannons, other artillery, and tanks, becoming the largest Soviet producer of such devices by 1944. No. 644, also from Moscow, developed military projection equipment. No. 208 ("Comintern") from Leningrad produced radio communications and radar equipment. Leningrad's "Svetlana" factory became the basis for the enormous Factory No. 617, which supplied vacuum tubes for military communications, and later for radio factories across the eastern part of the Soviet Union. No. 590 ("Elektrosignal") from Voronezh produced radios and aircraft communications systems.

Novosibirsk's development as a major research center also began during the war. Several of Moscow's leading aircraft research and design institutes relocated their top personnel to Novosibirsk, and their presence promoted the city as an intellectual as well as an industrial center. The Central Aviation Institute (TsAGI), Moscow Technical Aviation Institute (MATI), and the Experimental Flight Institute (LII) all crowded into three floors of Novosibirsk's aviation training academy.[18] The designer Nikolai Polikarpov and his experimental factory No. 51 were housed in a partially constructed automotive factory.[19] The Central Aviation Institute's director, Sergei Chaplygin, served as the first chair of the Novosibirsk Scientists' Committee, which was founded in January 1942. The Soviet Academy of Sciences, which would greatly expand its presence in Novosibirsk in the 1960s, founded its Western Siberian Branch in October 1943 with four divisions, each focused on applied research to support a sector of the regional economy.[20]

Specialists who came to Novosibirsk in the wartime evacuations trained local workers and experts, leaving an educational and cultural legacy along with the industrial infrastructure. For example, although the staff of the Central Aviation Institute returned to Moscow after the war, a Novosibirsk branch, known as SibNIA, was founded in early 1946. In 1949, three research institutes for the development of electronics, radar, and rocketry were established. A number of scientific specialists who came to Novosibirsk with evacuated industry stayed on to become directors of defense plants and research institutes throughout the 1950s and 1960s.

The cultural face of the city also changed. Wartime evacuations had included paintings from the Tretyakov and Hermitage museums, and actors and musicians from Leningrad, bringing Novosibirsk unprecedented cultural opportunities even in the midst of wartime deprivations. In February 1943, for example, a resident in Novosibirsk could choose between an exhibit of Russian Realist art on view at the Novosibirsk State Opera and Ballet Theater, performances by the Pushkin Theater Company from Leningrad and the Jewish Theater Company from the Belorussian Republic, and a concert of the Leningrad Philharmonic.[21] As with the scientists, these artists left a lasting mark on the city, which completed construction of the biggest opera house outside of Moscow and founded the Novosibirsk Philharmonic in the last year of the war.

Alongside the newcomers from the western parts of the country, the war also brought rural migrants to Novosibirsk, definitively shifting the balance between city and countryside in the region. During the war years, the overall rural population decreased by almost 26 percent, and the working-age population by more than 45 percent. If, before the war, there were more than twice as many rural as urban inhabitants in the Novosibirsk region, by 1946, the numbers were almost equal.[22] The area of land under agricultural cultivation fell by one-third between 1941 and 1945, accompanied by a significant decrease in livestock and farm machinery.[23] These rural losses had serious consequences for the postwar period in the region, when the harsh winter of 1946–47 caused poor harvests and food shortages. The famine of 1946–47 in turn also worsened the problem of rural flight, because the hunger was particularly acute in rural areas.

Although the war claimed a disproportionate number of rural men's lives, the greater reason for the demographic shift was mass migration to the cities for industrial work. One worker, recruited as a teenager in 1942 to an ammunition factory in a suburb of Novosibirsk, remembered the dislocation of the moment: "They brought us to the train station. Scared, we stood there, crying. After all, we had never been anywhere outside of our village, Pikhtovka, we had never seen a station or steam engine or a tram."[24] As the city absorbed many of its neighboring rural residents, it spread out geographically, because many evacuated factories were located on the outskirts of existing settlement. Shortages of industrial space and housing also pushed evacuated and newly constructed factories to suburbs like Berdsk, Kupino, and Bolotnoe, all of which were established during the war.[25]

Youth and women dominated the wartime workforce. Whole classes of middle school and high school students in Novosibirsk were removed from their studies and sent to work. The Novosibirsk historian Ivan Savitskii estimates that children under the age of eighteen years accounted for between one-third and one-half of the defense workers in Novosibirsk.[26] A history of the Chkalov factory cites an even higher figure of 70 percent.[27] Children as young as twelve and thirteen came to the factory after several months of training. Those who were too short to reach their equipment stood on makeshift footstools. As it became clear that many of these young new workers could not meet their quotas, their more experienced colleagues set up more than 200 "Stakhanovite schools" to train them. Nevertheless, because of their lack of familiarity with factory work, the young workers' productivity lagged behind the daily quotas, and they were notorious for their violations of workplace disciplinary rules, especially for tardiness.[28] Although most of these young workers left the factory at the end of the war, as late as January 1947, 10 percent of the workers at the Chkalov factory were under the age of eighteen.[29]

Women accounted for more than half the industrial workforce during the war years, and they performed almost 80 percent of the labor on collective farms.[30] Patriotism and the desire to help loved ones fighting at the front was a driving motivation for many of the women who went to work in the war industries. In an interview with the local daily newspaper, a lathe operator, K. Kudriatseva, explained that "at the beginning of the war, the Trud factory received an order for equipment that could only be filled by lathe operators. But there were not enough workers. Then I decided to take the place of my husband, who had left for the front. Starting as a fourth-class turner, within two years I became a sixth-class general lathe operator."[31]

Gender divisions remained, because women worked mainly in light industry and were particularly overrepresented in undesirable rural work. Furthermore, women's possibilities for advancement did not keep pace with their growing numbers, and they rarely were promoted into management positions. The social expectations for women, especially as mothers, held throughout the war, with a renewed emphasis on women's domestic roles beginning in 1944. A July 1944 Central Committee decree called for expanding government aid for mothers and "strengthening protection of motherhood and childhood." In addition to increasing rations for pregnant women, extending pregnancy leave, and constructing new clinics and child care facilities, the decree also established awards for mothers with multiple children. Shortly thereafter, the local newspaper began featuring women (awarded the title of mother-heroine) with more than ten children and stressing their children's contributions to the war. For example, the mother-heroine and city council deputy Sofia Yakovlevna Ignatova had thirteen children; eight of her nine sons had gone to the front, and two had perished.[32]

Novosibirsk ended the war with a great deal of dislocation resulting from huge population migrations, an overtaxed city infrastructure, and uncertainty about the future role of the evacuated defense industries. But because of the patterns of defense industry evacuation, it also emerged as a center of electronics, aviation, and radar technologies crucial to the delivery of nuclear weapons. In short, the wartime developments left Novosibirsk in a position to take advantage of the shifts in defense priorities that occurred in the late 1940s and early 1950s. The political and industrial infrastructure established during the war is key to understanding the rapidity and comprehensiveness with which production for the Cold War was set up in the late 1940s, reversing a brief period of civilian conversion.

Postwar Conversion

The end of the war brought a break in military production of almost three years. Beginning in the second half of 1945, plans in Novosibirsk focused on bringing order to the temporary construction and haphazard development demanded by wartime influxes of population and industry, and converting evacuated industry for the production of consumer goods. Planners foresaw postwar development based on the factories that had been evacuated during the German invasion, but with a decidedly civilian or consumer orientation. The state planning agency's (Gosplan's) proposals, circulated in August 1945, called for the construction of a horizontal planing machine–tool factory and a textile factory by 1947. During the following fifteen or twenty years, there would be major plants for the production of turbines, telephones, automobiles, and gas generators, along with "5–10 alimentary and light factories to process local raw materials and provide food products and consumer products."[33]

By September 1945, the level of military production had fallen to almost a quarter of what it was at the beginning of the year, though civilian production failed to increase significantly. Low rates of production continued through 1946, as conversion efforts were complicated by unclear and contradictory orders from central ministries and high rates of labor turnover. Many plants were not given clear instructions about what their future production would be. Sometimes their future location was not even certain, as officials argued back and forth about whether or not to reevacuate them. In addition, in the extreme conditions of the war, a number of the factories had been located in food and textile factories, government buildings, schools, and needed newly constructed space more suitable for heavy industrial production.[34] High worker turnover, compounded by acute housing shortages, added to these problems. Local officials also experienced difficulty in securing resources from central authorities, who placed first priority on rebuilding the industrial base in the western part of the country.[35]

The experience of Kombinat No. 179 illustrates the extent of the confusion involved in this initial postwar period. In February, its overseeing ministry (the Ministry of Agricultural Machine Building, Minselmash) gave an order for conversion of the plant to produce motors. Regional Party Secretary Kulagin, in a report to Central Committee Secretary Georgii Malenkov, expressed his skepticism of the wisdom of trying to produce a product so alien to the plant's previous mission.[36] In April, Minselmash pulled the order for motors and instead called for the production of agricultural machinery. The third-quarter plan from the ministry reinitiated the order for motors and demanded a four-fold increase in production. The fourth-quarter plan eliminated the order for motors and gave new production targets for tractors.[37] Eventually, the plant became an important producer of agricultural machinery, a role it continued even after it resumed military production at the end of the decade. Although this is an extreme example, many factories experienced multiple changes in production plans from their supervising ministries in the year following the end of the war.

The Chkalov factory spent the second half of 1945 preparing for the production of grain-harvesting machines. But at beginning of 1946, this order was cancelled and primary production reverted to aircraft, including retooling to produce all-metal planes. A consumer goods division, established in April 1946, focused on producing bicycles, but also other metal housewares, from bed frames to spoons.[38] Conversion took a toll on the plant's overall production, as it failed to meet its targets, production levels fell to almost one-fifth of the previous year's, and the workforce declined by one-quarter.[39] More than 3,000 workers left in December 1945 alone.[40] Production levels did not return to their wartime highs until the 1950s. Chkalov's director, Vladimir Lisytsin, complained to ministry officials that not only did conversion affect productivity, because many workers lacked the skills necessary to make bicycles rather than aircraft, but also that it decreased the value of the plant's output.

Irina Bystrova has argued that outward signs of demobilization in the postwar years, such as those outlined above, obscure a more important trend: a restructuring of defense industries toward development and production of new weapons technologies, most notably nuclear weapons and their delivery vehicles.[41] When military production picked up again in 1948, it reflected these changing priorities.

Nuclear weapons, although publicly downplayed, were an important engine for this renewed military production. The reporting on the Hiroshima bombing in the Novosibirsk main daily newspaper, *Sovietskaia Sibir',* was limited to reprinting a short statement by U.S. president Harry Truman, without commentary and buried on the last page.[42] The official response to the July 1946 U.S. atomic bomb test on Bikini Atoll was aggressively dismissive, asserting that the bomb was far less destructive than Americans had been led to believe. November 1947 meetings held at factories to discuss the reestablishment of the Cominform encouraged participants to minimize the power of American atomic weapons. In one typical statement, a worker in Novosibirsk is reported to have said: "We must make each American warmonger understand that our nerves are not weak and we can't be scared with an atomic bomb." And yet, Communist Party officials were concerned that people were not wholly convinced because "they conduct conversations that a war will soon be inevitable, about the danger of the atomic bomb, and so forth."[43]

Only one factory in Novosibirsk was directly involved in nuclear weapons production. In 1948, the construction site for a major new automobile factory in Novosibirsk became a nuclear facility, globally unique in being located within the limits of a major city.[44] However, many more were involved in the push to develop delivery vehicles, including research on and the production of electronics, radar, and rocketry, and Novosibirsk emerged as a major center of this work. The increasing priority placed on electronics work can be seen in the fortunes of the Comintern radar factory. During the war, the factory was evacuated into four separate buildings, including a labor center, facilities of the Novosibirsk Institute of Agriculture, and a movie theater. Construction on a more appropriate permanent home for the factory, ordered in 1946, suffered from repeated delays. Then, in February 1949, the Council of Ministries declared construction of the factory a top government priority. In August, a series of resolutions established research facilities at Comintern and two other related factories, and strengthened regional cooperation in the Siberian electronics sector.

In 1950, the Elektrosignal factory, which had been producing both civilian and military radio equipment, turned its focus entirely to military orders, becoming the top Soviet producer of aircraft communications equipment by 1953. This same period saw the construction of a radio parts factory and two other electronics factories, all of which began production in the mid-1950s. These joined a growing collection of factories in Novosibirsk that designed and produced onboard and ground-based navigation and guidance systems for aircraft and rocketry, devices to detect and scramble enemy radar, radio-controlled explosives for air defense, and military communications technologies. The industry grew so quickly that it soon required a local feeder factory, built in the late 1950s, to outfit Novosibirsk-area electronics factories with specialized equipment.

Rising Cold War tensions, and particularly the outbreak of war in Korea, also brought a surge of new orders to the Chkalov factory. In 1948, Chkalov received an order from the Council of Ministries to begin production by 1949 of MiG-15 fighter jets. The new order required extensive retooling and rapid expansion of the infrastructure and workforce. Production began slowly, with just 144 planes in 1949 and 360 in 1950. Large-scale production of MiG-17s began in 1951. The SibNIA aircraft research facility, which opened in 1946 with only fifty personnel and few resources, also began to receive additional investment after 1948. By the early 1950s, it had emerged as a major center for testing the durability of aircraft parts and assemblies, as well as conducting research into atmospheric turbulence, aircraft stability, and control systems.[45]

These new fields of defense production increasingly required workers with greater skills and technological sophistication, and the lack of such qualified workers was a major handicap on local industry throughout the late 1940s and 1950s. Local party officials tried to address this problem by expanding the technical schooling available locally, with 35,800 young workers receiving training in Novosibirsk oblast during the Fourth Five-Year Plan (1946–50), many of them through defense-plant-sponsored technical schools.[46] By the mid-1950s, Novosibirsk defense factories sponsored technical training schools in aviation, optics, electromechanics, and radio engineering.

Thus, between 1948 and the end of the Korean War, defense production in Novosibirsk was transformed from its wartime configuration to one based on more technologically sophisticated industries and demanding greater levels of worker training and education, mechanization, and specialization of production. There was nothing inevitable about this transformation because planning documents from the immediate postwar period projected a renewed predominance of light industry in the city.[47] But the aircraft, radio, and electronics production facilities and accompanying scientific capability, transferred and developed during the war, put Novosibirsk in a position to receive continued investments.

Defense as Political Currency

In addition to the infrastructure provided by evacuated defense industries during World War II, the war also strengthened ties between Novosibirsk and Moscow, which continued during several decades, from increased interactions between local and central party officials, to the direct control of national ministries over large sectors of local industry. Thousands of workers and scientists continued to come to Novosibirsk, drawn by the industrial and scientific institutions of the defense complex. After 1950, a civilian airport connected Novosibirsk to Moscow, with a daily flight that stopped over in Omsk, Sverdlovsk, and Kazan.[48]

Much, if not most, of the heavy industry in the city was overseen by national ministries and thus remained outside the jurisdiction of the regional party secretary and other local officials. These ministries shared responsibility not only for factory production but also for the housing, child care, schools, and other infrastructure needed by workers at these plants. Each industry and its supervising ministry had its own construction "trusts," which were responsible for both industrial and nonindustrial construction projects, from factories to housing and playgrounds.

Chkalov provides a good example of the growing role of factories, oriented toward national defense production, but also providing basic local services and infrastructure. Like other large plants in Novosibirsk, the Chkalov complex stretched far beyond its production facilities to provide important services for city residents. In 1946, the factory owned more than 100,000 square meters of housing, 8,500 hectares of agricultural land (not including workers' individual garden plots), cultural spaces, day care facilities, and medical institutions, which provided services to the entire neighborhood. The Aviation Ministry's Building Trust No. 7 provided much of the necessary construction at the factory, for both production and social needs.[49] In addition, Chkalov, together with Kombinat No. 179, provided the necessary repairs and resources to rebuild the Novosibirsk system of tram transport after the war.[50] By the 1950s, Chkalov also ran a theater and a cinema.

When infrastructure was insufficient, local leaders explicitly used the presence of these factories to demand additional resources from the central authorities. For example, a February 1946 letter from the city council to Sovnarkom vice chair Vyacheslav Molotov focused on the Kirov neighborhood of the city. Despite the presence of five of the city's major factories, including the enormous Kombinat No. 179, the neighborhood lacked schools, health care, and day care facilities, and most residents were housed in temporary barracks. Streets and sidewalks were not adequately constructed and repaired, and local tram service was insufficient. Therefore, they called on Molotov to put pressure on the overseeing ministries of these plants to invest more in the neighborhood.[51] Such interactions demonstrate the growing local sense of a connection between defense production and the ability to procure basic social goods and services.

The war established defense as a means of justifying demands for the city's infrastructural and social needs. For example, the director of an electronics factory prefaced a request for additional production space and worker housing by pointing out the importance of its unique products to both the Red Army and the naval forces.[52] A representative of the party committee at the Central Aviation Institute warned Kulagin that "history will not forgive the disgrace" of the poor conditions his institute had faced since evacuation.[53]

Postwar letters from local officials to Moscow likewise underlined the importance of Novosibirsk's contributions to the war effort as a rationale for demanding additional investments. Kulagin opened a March 1946 report on the economic situation in Novosibirsk at the Supreme Soviet with a summary of its wartime achievements.[54] As plants shifted to consumer production, Kulagin used this wartime record to justify priority for receiving these goods, as in a June 1946 letter to Gosplan head Nikolai Voznesenskii. After reminding Voznesenskii that "the Chkalov factory became indebted to the workers of this region during the war," Kulagin argued that the first several thousand bicycles produced at the plant should be sold locally. Another, almost identical, letter sought local priority in selling radios from the Elektrosignal plant.[55]

Defense factories also figured prominently in the repeated requests by local officials for expanded access to prison labor.[56] David Holloway has demonstrated the extensive role of the security services, and Lavrentii Beria directly, in the Soviet atomic bomb project.[57] Less well known is the extent of dependence on prison labor outside the nuclear complex, and throughout even open cities like Novosibirsk. In fact, the Novosibirsk historian Ivan Savitskii has argued that the demands of the arms race promoted and prolonged the use of prisoner labor through the mid-1950s, especially in construction work.[58]

About 50,000 prisoners lived in camps in and around Novosibirsk during the war in at least sixteen camps, along with numerous smaller subunits of 20 to 30 prisoners each. The Third Central Siberian Camp, with about 10,000 prisoners, was located just across the railroad tracks north of the Chkalov factory, and its brigades built the factory's aerodrome and runway, as well as working on construction for a new automobile factory nearby.[59] Reliance on prison labor across the Soviet Union increased further in the early Cold War years, as a renewed political and cultural crackdown and a new wave of arrests brought the number of people in prisons, camps, and special settlements to a height of 5.5 million by the time of Stalin's death in 1953.[60]

Numerous requests from officials in Novosibirsk for additional prison labor nevertheless went unanswered. The archival record suggests that petitions involving defense factories were the most likely to be fulfilled by the central authorities. The first significant postwar influx of prisoners to the region occurred in July 1946, when Kulagin wrote to the Ministry of Internal Affairs (MVD, successor to the NKVD), citing a "large discrepancy between plan for industrial and housing construction and the use of the labor of prisoners and prisoners of war at individual sites." He requested an additional 8,000 prisoners for work in seven factories and construction organizations, all related to defense production.[61] Although his request was not completely fulfilled, the prisoner labor force in Novosibirsk increased by almost 3000 between mid-August and the beginning of October. At that point, 11,350 prisoners and almost 5,000 prisoners of war were working in Novosibirsk.[62] These figures may still understate the reliance on prison labor by not including organizations controlled by the MVD. For example, construction organization No. 600, the largest in the region, employing as many as 15,000 prisoners and over 6,000 military personnel, built parts of the Chkalov plant.[63] Branches of the prison camps were established at many of the defense plants, including at Chkalov, No. 179, and several electronics factories. The number of prisoners living and working at such factories would have made them a common sight for Novosibirsk residents in the late 1940s and early 1950s.

In addition to claiming their perceived fair share of social and economic resources, local officials also lobbied for further construction of defense facilities in Novosibirsk, suggesting that even within a centralized command economy, local agitation could influence the location and investment in industry. For example, in March 1946, the Regional Party Committee (Obkom) wrote to Gosplan head Nikolai Voznesenskii arguing that three electronics factories slated for construction around Siberia should all be concentrated in Novosibirsk. To make their case, the committee members cited the existing density of the industry, the concentration of scientific expertise, and the high quality of the workforce.[64] Thus, existing defense facilities were used as a rationale for continued concentration, demonstrating the historical process that gradually turned Novosibirsk into a city dominated by defense industries. The final step in this process brought scientific power to match the city's capacity for defense production, through the founding of the Siberian Division of the Soviet Academy of Sciences.

Scientific Progress, Economic Competition, and the Founding of Akademgorodok

The growing complexity of military technologies in the postwar period prompted the Soviet leadership to expand investment for scientific research, particularly in Siberia. Scientists' livelihoods improved sharply after World War II, including the doubling and tripling of their salaries.[65] A California Institute of Technology rocket scientist, Theodore von Karman, during a trip to the Soviet Union in 1945, noted an emerging "aristocracy of the scientist, the engineer, and the artists."[66] Scientific institutions also expanded rapidly as the annual Soviet science budget increased from 300 million rubles in 1940 to 5.7 billion rubles in 1960.[67] In debates over scientific development and economic restructuring in the Khrushchev period, Novosibirsk emerged as a symbol of the modern Soviet economy—one built on decentralized production and technological sophistication. Central to its growing prominence was the establishment of Akademgorodok, a suburb built for the newly established Siberian Division of the Soviet Academy of Sciences.

Efforts to expand the Academy of Sciences' presence in Siberia date back to a 1931 proposal to establish academy branches in six Siberian and Central Asian cities. This early effort was stymied, however, by a lack of resources and the prevailing trend toward political and economic centralization. Even after the establishment of the Western Siberian Branch in 1944, made possible by the wartime transformation of Novosibirsk, Siberian scientists suffered from a lack of coordination with central Academy of Sciences officials and a shortage of funding. Furthermore, Novosibirsk-based institutes were highly specialized toward applied research aimed at supporting the exploitation of natural resources and industrialization. As a result, geology and biology were heavily overrepresented, while fewer than 1 percent of all Siberian researchers were engaged in physics and mathematics.[68] At the same time, Novosibirsk saw growth in other areas of science, particularly within institutes controlled by defense industries. For example, Novosibirsk-based institutes attached to the radar, electronics, and optics factories grew from dozens of employees in the late 1940s to thousands by the end of the 1950s.[69]

The transformation of Novosibirsk into a top-ranking scientific center in the late 1950s was made possible by the Soviet leadership's desire to improve the quality of technical support provided to the growing collection of defense factories in Siberia and to upgrade production technologies more generally. Beginning in late 1956, the prominent mathematician Mikhail Lavrentiev began to advocate the construction of an interdisciplinary science center in Siberia, staffed with top-quality academics imported from Moscow and Leningrad. Lavrentiev hoped that the concentration of a wide variety of scientific institutes in one place would help to overcome the rigidity of existing Soviet scientific institutions by creating space for high-quality interdisciplinary work. Novosibirsk's position as a city with a solid scientific base, but still on the periphery of the scientific establishment, made it a perfect candidate for his project.[70] In May 1957, the Council of Ministries approved plans for the establishment of Akademgorodok, with Lavrentiev at its head. Khrushchev took a personal interest in Akademgorodok, visiting the site in October 1959 and again in the spring of 1961, which expedited its construction and the recruitment of high-quality scientists.

The immense investment into Akademgorodok was part of an explosion of funding for defense-related research. As weapons systems became more technologically sophisticated, scientists played an increasingly important role in the defense complex, and they were therefore accorded increased privilege within the Soviet system. At the same time, prominent scientific institutions tied themselves more closely to the needs of the Soviet state. Lavrentiev, who was a computer pioneer and member of the Academy of Sciences Presidium, also enjoyed a close relationship with Khrushchev as a part of his informal scientific council of advisers. He was known for his views in favor of applied, pragmatic science, and he played an important role in turning the Academy of Sciences from its traditional role as a bastion of theoretical research to increasing involvement in military research in the 1950s and 1960s. His personal ties to military research began with aerodynamics work for the Central Aviation Institute in the 1930s. In the postwar period, he worked closely with Igor Kurchatov, who ran the Soviet nuclear research program, and he also became a prominent proponent of Akademgorodok. With such sponsors, one historian has noted, the Siberian Branch of the Russian Academy of Sciences "condemned itself from the beginning to friendly ties with the military-industrial complex."[71]

Although closely related to military production, scientific and technological progress also became an end in itself and an important means of demonstrating the success and vitality of the Soviet system. In an arms race where weapons were becoming so deadly as to prohibit their use, symbolism became as important as the military reality, and technological advances took on meaning beyond their military applications.[72] Sputnik and then the lunar missions played huge roles in proving, both domestic and internationally, the technological prowess of the USSR. In a similar way, Akademgorodok was meant to play an important symbolic role as a showcase of Soviet scientific excellence.

Science also had come to be seen as increasingly important to economic prosperity, causing scientific and economic reform to become intertwined. In July 1955, the Central Committee declared that industrial growth depended on "improving production technologies as much as possible, based on electrification, complex mechanization, and automization," a sentiment that was often repeated in official statements in the following years.[73] In addition, technological progress in the military arena was expected to help the Soviet Union redirect resources to domestic needs because Khrushchev, like Eisenhower, hoped that nuclear weapons would allow greater defense at a reduced cost.[74]

It is not an accident that the founding of Akademgorodok coincided with the replacement of the system of national ministries overseeing branches of industry with regional development councils (*sovnarkhozy*) in 1957. Both reforms aimed to focus development in the eastern regions of the country. The first annual report of the Novosibirsk Sovnarkhoz reflects this, explaining the region's natural strengths in heavy industries: the proximity of raw metals; the proximity of the region to consumers in Siberia, the Far East, Kazakhstan, and Central Asia; a strong educational and scientific base; the availability of cheap energy; and transportation networks.[75] Scientific decentralization, through the establishment of the Siberian Division, would bring scientists closer to the areas with natural resources and growing industry, and thus improve the overall performance of the Siberian economy.[76]

Akademogorodok's attempts to contribute to economic growth outside the defense complex were largely ineffective. The Siberian Division's isolation from other branches of science and the economy prevented it from contributing more significantly to the Novosibirsk economy. As Paul Josephson has shown, this failure is due in part to the divergent goals held by political and scientific proponents of Akademgorodok from the outset. Though Khrushchev's aim in supporting the construction of the new science city was to promote cooperation between scientists and local industry, the scientists themselves came to Siberia to escape the stifling atmosphere that dominated institutes in Moscow.[77]

The most notable economic venture in Akademgorodok was Fakel, a scientific-production association founded in 1966 under the auspices of the district Komsomol (the youth wing of the Communist Party). It was made possible by the confluence of a reform slate taking control of the Komsomol and a fleeting interest by Soviet authorities in nontraditional economic ventures. But its existence depended equally on an ability to work within defense-oriented institutes with large, flexible budgets. Through the administrative mechanism of the Komsomol budget, Fakel converted the expertise and materials of these institutes into desirable products that were sold to local industry and other organizations.[78] It began with associates of the Center for Counting Machines creating and selling software, and expanded into eight branches, each corresponding to an institute. By late 1967, it was doing almost 1 million rubles of business, involving over 1,000 students and researchers in Akademgorodok.[79] By 1971, when its profitability drew unfavorable attention from regional party officials, leading to its closure, Fakel's activities accounted for one-quarter of the district party budget.[80]

Meanwhile, the military importance of the scientific research in Akademgorodok created a paradoxical situation for Soviet leadership. Having been created to strengthen Soviet power and operating as a first-class research institution providing high-quality military research, Akademgorodok soon also became a center of political dissent and critique of the Soviet system. The privilege accorded to the scientists' work, compounded by their distance from Moscow and traditional bureaucratic structures, gave those working in Akademgorodok unusual freedom of scientific inquiry and political discussion. Social scientists produced some of the first sociological and economic work that called into question the efficiency of the Soviet economy. Scientists in Akademgorodok were also among the first in the Soviet Union to pay attention to environmental concerns.

Many instances of dissent, noted by Novosibirsk Communist Party authorities, were largely individual acts. In June 1960, a young scientist at the Institute of Inorganic Chemistry suggested in a party-sponsored meeting on Soviet foreign policy that the Soviet government was as much to blame as its U.S. counterpart for the breakdown in relations following the U-2 spy plane incident. He was strongly reprimanded, and the institute's party secretary was replaced.[81] In debates throughout the early 1960s at Novosibirsk State University, students challenged the Communist Party's control over science and the structure of Komsomol organizations, and they criticized both local and national party leaders. Similar public declarations, at odds with official orthodoxy, occurred relatively frequently in the Khrushchev era, particularly in universities.[82]

What set Akademgorodok apart is the ways in which political debate and unconventional views found institutional backing and organized, ongoing forums. As one scientist noted, Akademgorodok was a place where you could say what you thought not only at home but also at work.[83] The prominence of Lavrentiev and other institute directors allowed them to promote an unusually permissive governance structure, including a Communist Party organization that was independent from regional authorities. Communist Party structures in Akademgorodok, especially the Komsomol (using money made by Fakel), provided most of the funding and sponsorship for social clubs, art exhibits, and political discussions that would become controversial by the late 1960s.

One of the main beneficiaries of Fakel's profits was the Pod Integralom social club, which operated from 1963 to 1969 with the backing of the Akademgorodok Presidium. German Beznosov, one of the club's organizers, characterizes its activity as existing in the gray zone between what was allowed and what was forbidden.[84] The club hosted everything from discussions about science and society to readings by prominent poets from Moscow, dances with live music, and an annual beauty pageant.[85] The club's most famous event was a "festival of the bards" in March 1968, in which twenty-four poet-songwriters played to standing-room-only crowds for five days. The Moscow writer Aleksandr Galich infuriated regional authorities with his openly political lyrics, including a "Ballad on Surplus Value" and a song in memory of the writer Boris Pasternak.[86] That same month, forty-six residents of Akademgorodok signed a letter protesting the arrest of several dissidents for publishing transcripts from the trial of the writers Andrei Sinyavsky and Yuli Daniel. This so-called *podpisanty* affair, coinciding with the festival, triggered a crackdown on cultural and political freedoms, signaling both their high point and their end.[87]

Conclusions

By concentrating on the national level, most studies of the military-industrial complex have divorced defense industries from their surroundings. This chapter has demonstrated the analytical advantages that local history can bring to an examination of subjects that have traditionally been the realm of the social sciences and diplomatic historians. Shifting the focus away from national decisionmakers to the dynamics on the ground in Novosibirsk leads to several important conclusions.

First, a local, provincial vantage point reveals the importance of the political, economic, and social institutions developed during World War II for the defense complex that arose during the Cold War, while also making visible the break between these two periods. Wartime developments account for the particular shape and remarkable speed of the Cold War buildup in the late 1940s and early 1950s, but they did not make remilitarization inevitable. The discontinuity of the period from 1945 to 1948, though easy to overlook on a national scale, is readily evident on a local level.

Second, a local vantage point demonstrates how the city's existing military factories became the rationale for the further concentration of defense industries. For example, additional electronics factories were built in the late 1940s on the basis of a few evacuated factories. These factories, in turn, successfully argued that they required scientific research and design bureaus to complete their work effectively. The increasing concentration of scientific capability then made Novosibirsk an attractive option for Academy of Sciences and Central Committee officials looking for a place to open a science center in the 1950s, which brought internationally significant military research to the city.

Third, looking at the buildup of defense industries from a local level allows a more complex reading of cause and effect. Tracing the development of ties between local officials in Novosibirsk and their counterparts in Moscow reveals their multifaceted nature. Defense facilities were not built as a result of simple orders issued from central authorities but through a genuine back and forth, in which local leaders tried to leverage these factories to obtain economic and social resources. Roger Lotchin, in his work on the defense complex in California cities, has underlined the importance of local boosters to the development and location of lucrative defense industries. He insists on the need to "re-examine the military industrial complex from the bottom up in order to understand its sources of support."[88] He argues that the weakness of the conception and theorizing of the military-industrial complex by scholars of the U.S. system is that its focus on collaboration among military, business, and governmental elites at the national level ignores the strenuous attempts by city leaders to attract federal defense dollars.[89]

Extending Lotchin's analysis to politics at the local level (rather than asserting a unitary voice for the city, as he does) further complicates the picture of a military-industrial complex. An examination of the collection of industries, Communist Party leaders, and ministry officials active in and around Novosibirsk shows that the local defense complex was not monolithic.[90] For example, in 1951 as the Chkalov factory was struggling with production of MiG fighter jets, a feud developed between the factory management and an Air Force representative stationed at the plant. Although both parties had an interest in expanding aircraft production, Engineer-Major A. A. Bogun complained that production was of insufficient quality, while the factory director criticized frivolous recalls by the Air Force as interfering with production quotas. Far from providing a united front, they spent considerable energy denouncing each other to Aviation Ministry and party officials.[91]

Finally, nonmilitary forms of competition became increasingly important in maintaining the Soviet government's legitimacy in the context of the Cold War, both at home and abroad. As early as March 1946, Kulagin, in speech to the Supreme Soviet, explicitly linked security and economic success. After promising that production in Novosibirsk would surpass prewar levels by 1950, he underlined that "we must achieve a level of development in all areas which will allow us within the next three five-year plans to reach and surpass [*dognat' i obognat'*] the most industrially advanced capitalist countries. This is the only way to guarantee our country in the face of whatever may come."[92] Increasingly in the 1950s, economics moved to the center of U.S.-Soviet competition, as both countries struggled with the economic burden of high military expenditures while also trying to offer themselves as an attractive model to newly independent states in the developing world.

Cities like Novosibirsk, created and sustained by military industries, bring together two distinct aspects of Cold War competition: the military standoff and accompanying arms race and an intense economic competition between two ideological systems. Both forms of competition depended heavily on scientific and technological development, creating a new elite class of scientists, who on the one hand contributed to Soviet power through military development and more symbolic achievements like the space program but on the other hand could use their new status to criticize government policies. These elites of the defense complex discovered the limits of their freedom in Cold War politics as well—in the crackdown that followed the Soviet invasion of Czechoslovakia in 1968. It would be another twenty years before these boundaries would be challenged again.

To explain the complexity of the relationships between the various parts of this system of military production is not in any way to discount its power or importance. In fact, the defense complex in Novosibirsk became *pervasive,* establishing a system of incentives and understandings of the world that run through the correspondence of local officials. Knowing that the wartime evacuation of defense plants had fundamentally shifted Novosibirsk's importance to national politics, local officials used these industries to appeal for priority in obtaining labor, raw materials, or the approval of new building projects coming out of the war. As large parts of the city's political and economic fortunes became bound up with the production of aircraft, electronics, and rockets, the benefits of these industries extended well beyond those employed in defense factories to whole neighborhoods and even the entire city.

Anita Seth

Notes

1. Richard M. Nixon, *Six Crises* (Garden City, N.Y.: Doubleday, 1962), 274; Harrison Salisbury, *To Moscow—And Beyond* (New York: Harper & Brothers, 1960), 182.

2. Ibid., 193.

3. *Novosibirsk: 100, Istoriko-geograficheskii atlas* (Novosibirsk: Roskartografiia, 1993); L. M. Goriushkin, ed., *Novosibirsk 100 let. Sobytiia, Liudi: 1893–1993* (Novosibirsk: Nauka, 1993).

4. I. M. Savitskii, *Oboronnaia promyshlennost' Novosibirskoi oblasti: opyt' poslevoennogo razvitiya (1946–1963 gg.)* (Novosibirsk: ZAO Olsib, 1996), 76.

5. Presentation by N. V. Propirnyi, assistant head of the Department of Armaments and Communications Supply, Land Forces, "Stenogram from the Conference on the Quality of Communications Equipment, 23–24 September, 1958," Gosudarstvennyi Arkhiv Novosibirskoi Oblasti (hereafter GANO), fond (f.) 1653, opis (op.) 6, delo (d.) 123, list (l., i.e., page), l. 128. Propirnyi included in his assessment other factories in neighboring regions, including Omsk and Irkutsk.

6. For a development of this argument as applied to California cities, see Roger Lotchin, *Fortress California, 1910–1961: From Warfare to Welfare* (New York: Oxford University Press, 1992).

7. Dmitri Volkogonov, *Stalin: Triumph and Tragedy*, ed. and trans. Harold Shukman (London: Wiedenfeld & Nicolson, 1991), 505; R. W. Davies, *Soviet Economic Development from Lenin to Khrushchev* (Cambridge: Cambridge University Press, 1998), 59–67. For a larger discussion of social conditions during the war, see John Barber and Mark Harrison, *The Soviet Home Front, 1941–1945* (New York: Longman, 1991).

8. *Nasha malaia rodina: Khrestomatiya po istorii Novosibirskoi oblasti, 1921–1991* (Novosibirsk: Ekor, 1997), 217. Working-age people decreased from 53.4 to 51.1 percent of the overall population; "Report by Novosibirsk Obkom First Secretary M. V. Kalugin on Labor Shortages," May 1946, Partinyi Arkhiv Novosibirskoi Oblasti (hereafter PANO), f. 4, op. 34, d. 209, ll. 166–82. The city of Novosibirsk is the administrative center of a region (*oblast*) of the same name. Before the war, the region's territory also included the present-day Tomsk and Kemerovo regions.

9. *Nasha malaia rodina*, 216–24.

10. Savitskii, *Oboronnaia promyshlennost'*, 19. Savitskii notes that many of these Central Asian workers were deemed unsuited to industrial work and replaced with deportees, particularly Volga Germans.

11. Ibid., 4.

12. Letter from 3rd Department Head SibVO Major for State Security Mozhin to Obkom Secretary Pugovkin, May 21, 1941, PANO, f. 4, op. 34, d. 122, ll. 163–65.

13. Alexander Yakovlev, *Notes of an Aircraft Designer* (New York: Arno Press, 1972), 144.

14. I. M. Savitskii, "Sozdanie v Novosibirske krupneishego v Sibiri tsentra oboronnoi promyshlennosti v gody velikoi otechestvennoi voiny;" in *Ural i Sibir' v stalinskoi politike,* ed. S. Papkov and K. Teraiama (Novosibirsk: Sibirskii Khronograf, 2000), 194. See also V. N. Shumilov, *Sozdanie oboronnoi promyshlennosti v Novosibirskoi oblasti, 1941–1945 gg.* (Novosibirsk: N.p., 2000).

15. Savitskii, *Oboronnaia promyshelnnost'*, 14.

16. PANO, f. 4, op. 34, d. 118, l. 46.

17. Kulagin speech to the Supreme Soviet, March 2, 1946, PANO, f. 4, op. 34, d.

209, l. 68; *Kuznitsa stepnykh korablei: Istoriia Novosibirskogo proizvodstvennogo obedineniia "Sibselmash"* (Moscow: Mysl', 1983), 58–92.

18. Notice of evacuated factories and departments arrived in Novosibirsk, September 24, 1941, PANO, f. 4, op. 34, d. 114, l. 142.

19. Letter from N. N. Polikarpov to Kulagin, December 13, 1941, PANO, f. 4 op. 34 d. 116, l. 81.

20. *Sovietskaia Sibir'*, February 8, 1949.

21. *Sovietskaia Sibir'*, February 7, 1943.

22. In 1939, there were 1,282,700 rural and 587,300 urban inhabitants in Novosibirsk Oblast. In 1946, the numbers were 1,002,500 and 849,700; "Report from Kulagin to Voznesenskii," June 20, 1946; PANO, f. 4, op. 34, d. 209, ll. 162–65. For a larger discussion about demographic shifts in Western Siberia, see V. A. Isupov, *Gorodskoe naselenie Sibiri: Ot katastrofy k vozrozhdeniyu* (Novosibirsk: Nauka, 1991).

23. "Stenogram from the 15th Session of the Oblispolkom, 26–28 February 1947," GANO, f. 1020, op. 1, d. 655, l. 105; "Report from Kulagin to Voznesenskii."

24. Quoted by S. S. Bukin, *Iskovtsy: Istoriya Novosbirskogo mekhanicheskogo zavoda "Iskra"* (Novosibirsk: Izd. "Gumanitarnye tekhnologii", 2002), 15.

25. *Sovietskaia Sibir'*, December 9, 1945.

26. Savitskii, "Sozdanie," 203.

27. M. L. Talalova, "Vse vyshe, vyshe i vyshe," manuscript provided to author, 8.

28. Shumilov, *Sozdanie oboronnoi promyshlennosti v Novosibirskoi oblasti,* 76.

29. This is from a 1946 report from Lisytsin, director of no. 153, PANO, f. 34, op. 4, d. 245, l. 47.

30. Barber and Harrison, *Soviet Home Front,* 98.

31. *Sovietskaia Sibir'*, January 7, 1945.

32. *Sovietskaya Sibir'*, January 19, 1945, 2.

33. "Plan for Novosibirsk," sent to Novosibirsk Obkom secretary Mikhail Kulagin, August 4, 1945, PANO, f. 4, op. 34, d. 189, l. 243.

34. Letter from Kulagin to Malenkov, 1945, PANO, f. 34, op. 4, d. 204, l. 41.

35. Savitskii, *Oboronnaia promyshlennost',* 22.

36. Letter from Kulagin to Malenkov, 1945, PANO, f. 34 op. 4 d. 204, l. 45.

37. "Report on Operation of Factories of the Ministry of Agricultural Machine Building for 1946," PANO, f. 4 op. 34, d. 228, l. 7.

38. This is from a 1946 report from Lisytsin.

39. Ibid., 9.

40. "Report on the Work of Factories under the Administration of the Department of Aviation Industry during the Great Patriotic War and Postwar Period (until 1 January 1947)," PANO, f. 43, op. 4, d. 228, l. 76.

41. I. V. Bystrova, *Voenno-promyshlennyi kompleks SSSR v gody kholodnoi voiny* (Moscow: Institut Rossiiskoi istorii RAN, 2000), 35. See also Mark Harrison, "New Postwar Branches (1): Rocketry," in *The Soviet Defence-Industry Complex from Stalin to Khrushchev,* ed. John Barber and Mark Harrison (New York: St. Martin's Press, 2000), 118–49.

42. *Sovietskaia Sibir'*, August 8, 1945.

43. "Report from Kulagin to Central Committee Board for Control of Party Organs, Department of Information Head I. I. Pozdniak," November 6, 1947, PANO, f. 4, op. 34, d. 256, ll. 284–88.

44. Savitskii, *Oboronnaia promyshlennost'*, 193. Information is sparse because this nuclear facility, currently known as Khimkonsentrat, is the one factory in Novosibirsk for which information, whether about its historical function or its current waste discharges, is largely still classified and unavailable to the public.

45. Savitskii, *Oboronnaia promyshlennost'*, 80–81, 207–8.

46. *Promyshlennoe razvitie Novosibirskoi oblasti 1946–1965 gg.: Sbornik dokumentov* (Novosibirsk: Novosibirskoe knizhnoe izd-vo, 1991), 18.

47. "Plan for Novosibirsk," sent to Novosibirsk Obkom secretary Mikhail Kulagin, August 4, 1945, PANO, f. 4, op. 34, d. 189, l. 243.

48. *Nasha malaia rodina,* 348.

49. During the war and in the immediate postwar period, the overseeing authority was known as the People's Commissariat for Aviation Industries, and Trust No. 7 as Construction-Design Directorate No. 7 (SMU-7).

50. S. S. Bukin and A. A. Dolgoliuk, "Razvitie gorodskogo passazhirskogo transporta v Novosibirske (1946–1985)," in *Voprosy kraevedeniia Novosibirska* (Novosibirsk: N.p., 1997), 133.

51. Letter from Novosibirsk Gorispol'kom to Sovnarkom Vice-Chair V. M. Molotov, February 26, 1946, PANO, f. 34, op. 4, d. 204, ll. 20–22.

52. Letter from Prozhektornyi zavod director Estrin to Kulagin, December 8, 1941, PANO, f. 4, op. 34, d. 116, l. 59.

53. Letter from V. I. Dushin to Kulagin, November 22, 1941, PANO, f. 4, op. 34, d. 116, l. 53.

54. PANO, f. 34, op. 4, d. 209, ll. 67–68.

55. PANO, f. 34, op. 4, d. 226, l. 23, 109. A copy of the first letter was also addressed to Aleksey Kosygin at the Council of Ministries (f. 34, op. 4, d. 209, l. 158).

56. For a larger account of the development of the Gulag and its important economic role, see Anne Appelbaum, *Gulag: A History* (New York: Doubleday, 2003).

57. David Holloway, *Stalin and the Bomb* (New Haven, Conn.: Yale University Press, 1994).

58. Savitskii, *Oboronnaia promyshlennost'*, 33.

59. Yuri Magalif, "Dalekii vzlet" in *Moi Novosibirsk: Kniga vospominanii,* ed. T. Ivanova (Novosibirsk: N.p., 1999), 152.

60. Davies, *Soviet Economic Development,* 68. The Ministry of Internal Affairs controlled 9 percent of capital investment in 1952, with plans for this to double by 1955; Appelbaum, *Gulag,* 471. Stalin's death in 1953 sharply reduced the reliance on prison labor, although it continued in some areas, e.g., in the defense plants (especially nuclear production sites) overseen by the Ministry of Medium Machine Building.

61. Letter from Kulagin to S. N. Kruglov, July 15, 1946, PANO, f. 4, op. 34, d. 226, ll. 119–21. Telegrams from Chernyshev to Kulagin on June20 and July 18, 1945, show examples of unsuccessful bids for more prisoners; PANO, f. 4, op. 34, d. 194, ll. 283, 304.

62. PANO, f. 4, op. 34, d. 226, ll. 178–80.

63. Savitskii, *Oboronnaia promyshlennost'*, 31.

64. PANO, f. 34, op. 4, d. 204, ll. 36–39.

65. Medvedev, *Soviet Science,* 44.

66. Theodore von Karman, *The Wind and Beyond* (Boston: Little, Brown, 1967), 187–88.

67. E. G. Vodichev, *Put' na vostok: formirovanie i razvitie nauchnogo potentsiala Sibiri* (Novosibirsk: Ekor, 1994), 18.

68. E. T. Artemov, *Formirovanie i razvitie seti nauchnykh ucherezhdenii AN SSSR 1944–1980* (Novosibirsk: 1990).

69. Savitskii, *Oboronnaia promyshlennost'*, 221.

70. Vodichev, *Put' na vostok,* 89.

71. Ibid., 91.

72. E.g., Khrushchev based an enormous amount of international bluster on just four intercontinental ballistic missiles—a confidence that went far beyond their military significance.

73. Quoted by V. N. Vostrikov, *Poslevoennoe vosstanovlenie i protivorechiia etogo perioda 1945–1955 gg.: Lektsiia* (Novosibirsk: N.p., 2002).

74. For a clear statement of this, see Khrushchev's Memo to the CC CPSU Presidium, December 8, 1959, suggesting troop cuts of 1 million to 1.5 million, reprinted in *Vremya: Liudi. Vlast',* by N. S. Khrushchev, vol. 4 (Moscow: Moskovskie Novosti, 1999), 544–51.

75. Explanatory memorandum to the Novosibirsk Sovnarkhoz annual industrial report, 1957, GANO, f. 1653, op. 6, d. 10, ll. 1–2.

76. Vodichev, *Put' na vostok,* chap. 1.

77. Paul Josephson, *New Atlantis Revisited* (Princeton, N.J.: Princeton University Press, 1997), xvi.

78. I. I. Korshever, who was involved in Fakel, has written a short history of the organization: "Ot goroda solntsa k gorody zero," *Nauka v sibiri,* nos. 32–33, August 2001.

79. Report on the scientific-technical, industrial and financial affairs of NPO "Fakel" under the Sovietskii RK VLKSM, January 1968, PANO, f. 4, op. 34, d. 668, ll. 1–17.

80. Korshever, "Ot goroda solntsa k gorody zero," 6.

81. "O rezul'tatakh provedeniia mitingov i sobranii trudiashchikhsia" from Novosibirsk regional secretary Goriachev to the Central Committee, July 4, 1960, PANO, 4-34-535, 68–70.

82. A number of examples, both in Novosibirsk and throughout Siberia, are chronicled by A. G. Borzenkov, *Molodezh' i politika: Vozmozhnosti i predely studencheskoi samodeiatel'nosti na vostoke Rossii (1961–1991 gg.),* 3 vols. (Novosibirsk: Novosibirskii gos. universitet, 2003).

83. Interview with L. S. Truss, June 18, 2003.

84. Interview with G. P. Beznosov, November 18, 2004.

85. *Pressa o kafe-klub "Pod Integralom" (v pomoshch' rukovodeliam molodezhnykh klubov)* (Novosibirsk: VLKSM—Novosibirskii obkom komsomola, Sovetskii raikom komsomola, 1966).

86. PANO, f. 4, op. 34, d. 667, ll. 29–43.

87. Josephson, *New Atlantis Revisited,* 296–304.

88. Lotchin, *Fortress California,* 15.

89. The term *"voenno-promyshlennyi kompleks"* (military-industrial complex) has been widely adopted by scholars of the Soviet defense industries. Many Russian scholars mean simply to denote the collection of bureaucracies, factories, and research institutions engaged in military work. Irina Bystrova is one of the few that attempts to

follow English usage in addressing not just structure but also impact. See Bystrova, *Voenno-promyshlennyi kompleks SSSR,* 8–9; and Irina Bystrova, "Razvitie voenno-promyshlennogo kompleksa," in *SSSR i kholodnaia voina* (Moscow: Mosgosarkhiv, 1995). Others continue to question the use of the term in the Soviet context. John Barber and Mark Harrison prefer the term "defense-industry complex" because it emphasizes that it as a discrete, distinct part of the Soviet economy; Barber and Harrison, *Soviet Defence-Industry Complex,* chap. 1.

90. Other authors have argued for the importance of pulling apart and understanding the complexities of other Soviet institutions. By taking a close view of daily life, Stephen Kotkin and Sheila Fitzpatrick have tried to show the contradictions within Stalinist politics and society as a whole. Stephen Kotkin, *Magnetic Mountain: Stalinism as a Civilization* (Berkeley: University of California Press, 1995); Sheila Fitzpatrick, *Everyday Stalinism: Ordinary Life in Extraordinary Times: Soviet Russia in the 1930s* (New York: Oxford University Press, 1999).

91. Letter from Engineer-Major Bogun to Partkom No 153 Yaroshenko and Obkom Secretary Yakovlev, May 5, 1951, PANO, f. 4, op. 34, d. 391, ll. 6–13; Letter from Bogun to Obkom Secretary I. I. Tur and Nach, PGU Ministry of Aviation A. N. Ter-Markarian, August 15, 1952, PANO, f. 4, op. 34, d. 407, ll. 57–60; Letter from Director of No 153 Smirnov to Bogun, August 29, 1952, PANO, f. 4, op. 34, d. 407, ll. 160–66.

92. Kulagin speech to the Supreme Soviet, March 2, 1946, PANO, f. 4, op. 34, d. 209, ll. 70–71.

Part III. Environmental Costs

7. Project Lamachus: The Cold War Comes to Scotland—The Holy Loch U.S. Nuclear Submarine Base and Its Impact on Scotland, 1959–1974

Alan P. Dobson and Charlie Whitham

In 1961, the Cold War was fraught with danger. Those who believed that the Soviets had destabilized the East-West nuclear balance saw Polaris missiles as a corrective counterweight, and anything that helped their operational efficiency was welcomed. Thus, on March 3, 1961, the *USS Proteus,* a Polaris submarine support ship, arrived at Holy Loch on the west coast of Scotland. It was 573 feet long, it displaced 18,500 tons, and it carried 50 officers and 900 men. A Miss MacPhail, the provost of Dunoon, welcomed the American crew on March 11 and was ceremonially piped aboard. A week later, there was Highland dancing on *Proteus,* and soon the local licensing authority was being pressed to grant a cocktail bar license for one of the town's hostelries.[1] At the time, a cocktail bar in a provincial holiday town like Dunoon, albeit the largest in Argyllshire with close to 10,000 people, was as common as haggis at a New York hamburger stand. Scottish and American culture seemed to be intermingling well, but the development of the base at Holy Loch was to have a more far-reaching impact than a cultural exchange of cocktail lounges and Scottish dancing. By 1992, when the base closed, approximately one-quarter of the population in Dunoon and its immediate environs was American.

As well as *Proteus,* there was a floating drydock to service up to three Polaris submarines at any one time with their sixteen Polaris missiles. *Proteus* carried reserve missiles and had the capacity to store nuclear warheads. British officials would declare themselves "unable either to confirm or deny" that it carried warheads (in fact it always did), but they did confirm that none would be stored ashore.[2] The total of U.S. Navy personnel was likely to be 1,500, accompanied by around 400 families of *Proteus* crewmen, with some 500 children of school age. The only land initially required by the U.S. Navy was a small area at Greenock for naval stores and staff, and parking for a few cars near the Ardnadam jetty on Holy Loch.[3] Later, in May 1962, the U.S. Navy took over the nearby Ardnadam Hotel for recreational purposes for enlisted men and petty officers. It was also used for a PX shop where U.S. servicemen could buy American goods at discount prices. All this was done without any undue fuss, and the attitude of the Scottish Office was very deferential to Westminster. However, when in 1973 the Americans proposed a major expansion of the Holy Loch base, the story was very different. Scottish opposition was marked, and this was indicative of the base's cumulative impact and of changing Scottish sentiments, not so much toward the Americans per se but regarding Westminster and the right of Scots to have a significant say in their own affairs. This chapter is an account, among other things, of how the American presence affected Scotland in this way.

At Camp David, March 21–27, 1960, Prime Minister Harold Macmillan and President Dwight D. Eisenhower agreed on the U.S. sale of Skybolt missiles for Britain's V bomber nuclear deterrent force, and provision of facilities for U.S. nuclear submarines on the West Coast of Scotland. Although it was later claimed that the Scottish Office had been fully consulted and approved, it was a mere formality rather than a serious granting of agreement. The details still had to be worked out, and these proved to be deeply troublesome. The British tried a variety of maneuvers to extract concessions regarding joint control over the use of the U.S. Polaris nuclear missiles and an option to buy Polaris submarines as an independent deterrent for themselves at a knockdown price. In the end, all that they achieved were some rather meaningless public reassurances about Anglo-American consultation on the use of the missiles and an understanding that a future purchase of Polaris by Britain was a possibility.[4] Project Lamachus, the Admiralty code name for the proposed American base at Holy loch, was thus born.

Perhaps more worrying for the immediate future was the fact that the Americans refused to accept absolute liability for any accidents arising from the Polaris base, and the Memorandum of Understanding, which notionally governed the operation of the base, was not finalized until February 1964.[5] So, for nearly three years, there was no agreement on how to deal with accidents and pollution, things that were of direct import to the local Scottish people. Furthermore, even before the memorandum was signed, difficulties had already arisen, and, as we shall see, how London and the Scottish Office dealt with them is instructive.

On November 1, 1960, Macmillan announced the Holy Loch arrangements to the House of Commons. Anticipation that this would "arouse controversy" in Britain was not fulfilled.[6] At his first meeting with the local representatives, Jack Maclay, the minister of state for Scotland, heard little opposition. In fact, some of the authorities were "optimistic" about the situation, and "seemed to be thinking in terms of the tangible benefits to the smaller towns round the Holy Loch which have hitherto been dependent on seasonal tourist trade." Maclay concluded that "no serious local problems are likely to be encountered in the establishment of these facilities."[7] This uncritical stance of the Scottish Office was a common feature of the Holy Loch story. When the Americans briefly raised the possibility of using Scottish drydock facilities in 1961, a note from Edinburgh observed that their interest in "this proposal is, of course, slight since it would not in itself involve any burden on any of the services for which we are directly responsible."[8] They did not like the idea of another center for possible "gorilla" [sic] activities by antinuclear protestors, but the responsibility so far as they were concerned lay with London and political decisions there.[9]

It was repeatedly emphasized, to allay public fears in Britain and to minimize Soviet antagonisms, that Holy Loch was not a U.S. nuclear submarine base.[10] The submarines remained "based" in the United States. Even so, within months of their arrival at Holy Loch, the Americans requested maintenance and drydock facilities; the most likely option for this was the Rosyth Naval Dockyard on the Firth of Forth.[11] If the request had been complied with, it would have completely dispelled the fiction that the submarines were not based in Scotland. But the request was quickly withdrawn. Nevertheless, as things were they made Holy Loch *look* like a *base* and its strategic importance made Scotland, in words used by Winston Churchill in 1951, "the target, and perhaps the bull's eye, of a Soviet attack."[12] Not surprisingly, this cast an air of unease over the population of the Clyde area, which with Glasgow, Britain's second city with over a million inhabitants at its heart, was far from being inconsiderable in size.

Although the government tried to give the impression that Britain would have significant control over the missiles,[13] the extent to which the Americans kept unilateral control was revealed clearly to British and Scottish officials in October 1962 by the Cuban missile crisis and the temporary move of *Proteus* out of Holy Loch. A Scottish official reported that it was agreed that "an operational move, i.e., a move made during war or in active preparation for imminent war (as this was) must be a matter for the Americans themselves; we could not reasonably object to such a move or claim the right to inform local authorities; and we certainly could not set up a local liaison committee on the

Holy Loch pattern. This applies to Proteus herself, to her nuclear-powered submarines and to any other nuclear powered ships which the U.S. Navy may be using in the future."[14]

Throughout the negotiations for the base, Scottish sensibilities had only been nodded to in passing, even when the British prime minister was a Scot! The issue of situating the base in a heavily populated area was raised at one point, and the British suggested the Fort William area as an alternative. But, this was duplicitous on the part of Whitehall. Faslane, on the Clyde, had already been identified as the likely base for a British nuclear submarine base. In any case, once President Eisenhower objected to the Fort William area, the British soon forgot about the "insuperable [Scottish] political problems" that they had identified in mid-June and replaced them with broader priorities in Anglo-American relations. British control or even public knowledge about the movements of U.S. ships was for cosmetic purposes only. In an emergency— the only time that really counted—the British would have no say in the movement or use of the submarines or their support craft. The Clyde Local Liaison Committee (of which more just below) could only liaise when things did not really count and about unimportant matters. If the Liaison Committee ever had the temerity to be assertive, it would soon have discovered what was really going on or, more to the point, it would not. The Westminster government had cut a deal with the United States that would allow U.S. Polaris missiles and their warheads to be stored in Scotland and for up to three Polaris missile carrying submarines to be in Holy Loch at any one time without anything other than a commitment to consult on their use by the Americans, without any control over their use outside the three-mile limit, without a memorandum of understanding having been finalized that would deal with safety and compensation issues, and without any prior discussion with the local authorities or people in the Holy Loch area. Somewhat surprisingly, neither the Scottish Office nor the local authorities in the area seemed at all troubled by this.

U.S. nuclear bases in Britain were commonplace long before Holy Loch and were governed by an understanding reaffirmed by President Harry Truman and Prime Minister Churchill in 1952: "Use of the bases in an emergency would be a matter of joint decision by His Majesty's Government and the United States Government in the light of circumstances prevailing at the time."[15] This still applied in November 1960.[16] However, the Holy Loch base had four novel aspects, which had an impact on the regional life of Scotland in a way that U.S. nuclear bases had not, for example either in East Anglia or the English Midlands. First, it was a naval nuclear base, and that raised novel and difficult control complications. Second, nuclear submarines were small nuclear power stations, which raised new safety issues. Third, Polaris nuclear submarines discharged low-level radioactive waste. And fourth, the main U.S. nuclear deterrent in the United Kingdom was now based in Scotland, and this raised difficulties in the relationship between Westminster, the Scottish Office, and Scotland more generally.

The 1707 Act of Union established Scotland's relationship to the U.K. government at Westminster. However, in 1885, broadening of the franchise and rural unrest over land ownership in the Highlands and Islands resulted in reforms, which created the Scottish Office and the secretary of state for Scotland, who took a seat in the Cabinet. In 1894, the Scottish Grand Committee was formed in the House of Commons to deal with Scottish affairs, and after World War II further standing committees were created to help deal with an expanding workload. The secretary of state for Scotland was sometimes referred to as the Scottish prime minister, but this was misleading because, as one scholar has noted, "he 'speaks for Scotland' in London, [but] he also 'speaks for London' in Scotland."[17] Furthermore, he was not the leader of a Scottish majority party; he was the Scottish spokesperson of the ruling majority party in Westminster. Neither should one make the mistake of thinking that matters falling under the authority of the Scottish Office departments simply mirrored their Westminster counterparts. They did not. For example, both education and agriculture and fisheries were of higher significance in Scotland than in the United Kingdom as a whole, and there were areas where Scotland had considerable discretionary power, such as in its distinctive sphere of criminal law.[18] These differences created tension, but of course, in "financial matters the Treasury [in London] has ultimate control and no Scottish Secretary could pursue a policy which was wholly at variance with that being pursued south of the border, especially on politically sensitive matters."[19] Though this relationship seemed well embedded in 1960, it was soon to change.

Liability and Radioactive Contamination

Having U.S. nuclear submarines based in Scotland raised new issues to do with liability for accidental damage. In the absence of any governing international agreements to which the United States subscribed, the only course of action for the British regarding accidents and the dumping and discharge of radioactive waste, both on the near high seas and within U.K. territorial waters and in Holy Loch itself, was to negotiate with the Americans. Because the British had to do this after agreeing to provide the facility, their hand was not strong.[20] By June 1961, while the British were satisfied that the U.S. Navy general instructions from its *Radiological Controls Manual for Naval Nuclear Propulsion Plants* were "fully acceptable," neither they nor the Memorandum of Understanding between the United States and the United Kingdom on the Holy Loch base governed "discharges of radioactive waste in U.K. territorial and internal waters" or on the high seas. This raised concern about fishing grounds used by British trawlers, and although the U.S. Navy confirmed that it did not discharge waste in known fishing grounds, a British official laconically commented, "If so, the obvious course would appear to be to seek confirmation that the fishing grounds with which we are concerned are regarded by the [U.S. Navy] as known fishing grounds."[21] In the end, these issues had to be dealt with on a case-by-case, navy-to-navy, and government-to-government basis. The more parochial issues that were to arise in the Holy Loch area itself, however, were supposedly to be dealt with in a more formal way through a local liaison committee.

After a serious accident at the Windscale nuclear plant in Cumberland, the Fleck Report in 1957 made recommendations for future monitoring of operations at all nuclear stations.[22] It subsequently became standard practice to have a Local Liaison Committee with terms of reference: "to reassure local opinion on the hazards involved, to convey to the public the significance of any accident and to create administrative machinery for the protection of the population in the unlikely event of a serious accident."[23] It was also standard practice at civilian nuclear power stations to have regular reports confirming radiation safety. Immediately after the announcement of the U.S. base, there was a meeting on November 3 between Royal Navy officials and local authority representatives at Greenock to establish the Local Liaison Committee.[24] It was swiftly formed and consisted of local worthies such as Provost MacPhail, local councilors, the county clerk of Argyllshire, local chief constables, and representatives of the Ministry of Agriculture, Fisheries, and Food (MAFF), the Atomic Energy Authority, and the Scottish Home Department.

The captain in charge of the Clyde Area, a Captain Mayo, was the responsible Royal Navy officer in command who dealt with the committee. It met on November 30. Captain Mayo opened the proceedings, but most of the work was left to Commander K. I. Short of the Admiralty Nuclear Propulsion Safety Office, who considered two hazards. First, there was the possibility of gamma radiation from the submarines. He explained that it was only harmful within a 35-yard radius, but they were allowing for a 200-yard safety margin. "He stressed that the ranges quoted were based on genetic doses, which were *very much less than lethal doses.*"[25] Second, was the danger of release of radioactive iodine gas, but he assured the liaison committee that this "would only be harmful if breathed for 24 hours."[26] The committee also discussed the eventuality of a release of radioactive coolant in the event of a serious collision. Again, Short reassured the committee that this would produce no "danger to the public," though it might be "necessary to ban fishing for a time." In appendix III to the minutes, the impossibility of a nuclear explosion was categorically stated, and it was "emphasised that for nearly all practical purposes a Nuclear Propelled Submarine presents exactly the same problem as a conventional submarine."[27]

The hope that officials could palm off nuclear submarines as presenting the same risks as conventional submarines was not to be fully realized. On December 1, *The Scotsman,* somewhat misquoting Captain Mayo, reported, "It is only prudent to take precautionary steps against the very remote chance of a serious explosion."[28] It should have read "serious accident." The authorities, though irritated, did not feel that it was a sufficiently important issue to complain directly to *The Scotsman.*[29] On December 17, the local paper in Dunoon mentioned the possible danger of radioactive milk because of the way cows rapidly ingest poison from grass contaminated by iodine gas. However, the article continued with the reassuring comment that "most of the milk consumed in Dunoon, however, comes from Bute."[30] There was no indication of the fate of locally produced milk.

Concern about radiation prompted debate in the House of Commons on December 16. The leading spokesperson for the Holy Loch area was the Labour member of Parliament for Greenock, J. Dickson Mabon. Charles Ian Orr-Ewing, the civil lord of the Admiralty, wrote to Mabon on February 9 in an attempt to assuage his fears. Five days later, Mabon published the information in the *Glasgow Herald,* and now the talk was of three kinds of radioactive waste disposal. Previously the talk had been of three types of radioactive pollution—liquid spillage, gamma rays from the hull, and iodine gas clouds—in the context of possible accidents by collisions or whatever. Now the focus was more on the deliberate disposal of radioactive waste: "relatively small quantities of low-activity primary coolant [discharged] directly overboard as the reactor is warmed up before going "critical"; the transfer of solid waste, again of relatively low activity, into sealed containers for ultimate disposal elsewhere; and the release of small amounts of low-activity gas, mainly of an inert nature."[31] The publication of this letter appears to have calmed worries, and certainly the flurry of letters and articles in the local paper soon petered out; but behind the public facade of reassurances, a number of concerns were still being addressed by the government.

Official thought about an accident only seems to have stretched to, "at worst milk restrictions for a short period over at the most a radius of about 5 miles, the destruction of unsealed food and liquid over a half-mile radius, and the evacuation for perhaps 24 hours of those living within a radius of rather less than half a mile."[32] Though this might appear rather complacent, there was continuing concern over monitoring of radiation—something on which Mabon had pressed the government—over dumping of waste at sea, and also over the amount of radioactive effluent to be discharged into Holy Loch. The Royal Navy opposed surveying Holy Loch before the U.S. nuclear submarines arrived, arguing that it was unnecessary and expensive. At a Liaison Committee meeting, Commander Short "refused to accept" monitoring before *Proteus* arrived. It was "absolutely unnecessary." However, as something of a sop to those exercised by this matter, he pointed out that the Department of Health would monitor water supplies as part of their normal duties.[33] Whether Short was concerned to prevent any adverse publicity for both the Americans then and for the Royal Navy in the future, if and when it acquired Polaris submarines, is difficult to say. However, local feeling on the need for monitoring before and after the arrival of nuclear submarines ran high. This was especially pertinent to local fishing, and though there were reassurances that fishing would not be harmed, it had been conceded: "Some controlled discharge of a small amount of radio-active liqued [*sic*] will take place in Holy Loch." There was also concern that "as far as possible that responsibility for any increase in radio-activity in the Firth of Clyde is fairly apportioned" between the nuclear submarines and the civilian Hunterston nuclear power station due to be commissioned in 1963.[34] Notwithstanding Royal Navy opposition, the MAFF Marine Laboratory at Lowestoft was instructed to carry out surveys, which should begin before the arrival of *Proteus*. Nine monitoring points were established, and seaweed and shore sand were monitored quarterly and seabed and mussels half yearly. In looking at the consumption of locally caught fish by three families on the loch, MAFF scientists concluded that "the consumption of these locally caught fish by the families and friends of the fishermen concerned constitutes the most restrictive condition in the Loch from the view of radioactive waste disposal."[35]

Not surprisingly then, when the maximum limit for liquid discharges was considered with the Americans, the British were determined to set a definite maximum. The figure put to the Americans was 6,000 U.S. gallons per month. When the United States responded in a manner that suggested that it had simply received this as information and not as a restrictive limit, the British pressed the point and insisted that any discharge above this figure would require approval of the captain in charge of the Clyde Area. The Americans finally agreed.[36] During the first year of operations, surveys showed that there was no detectable increase in radiation due to the arrival of the submarines, though "in November, i.e., after the Russian [nuclear] test series, total beta activity levels in seaweed were found to have increased [maximum recorded was at sampling station 6, where beta activity in seaweed per gram wet weight rose from 4.6 to 15.1]." The radioactivity in question was identified as that from fallout from the Soviet 58 megaton nuclear test, at that time the largest nuclear explosion ever made. So, for the time being, at least radioactivity pollution from Polaris submarines was not a matter of concern for officials or the public, and effective monitoring was taking place even though the public would not necessarily be made aware of its findings. Unlike the affirmative monitoring of civilian nuclear power plants, it was decided not to issue regular reports confirming that all was well in Holy Loch.[37] Four years later, just such an issue of whether or not to inform the public about developments arose.

The British first detected raised levels of radioactivity that could be attributable to Polaris submarines around Holy Loch in 1963 but suppressed news of the "slight increase," which they thought "might be attributable to the operations of nuclear powered submarines" even when pressed by an inquisitive politician in the Commons.[38] Even so, the Medical Research Council believed that it was prudent to assume that "even the lowest doses of radiation may involve a finite though correspondingly low probability of adverse effect" and that it was unwise for the government to assert that "even a slight increase" in radioactivity involved no risk or no danger.[39] In the summer of 1965, a much more serious situation arose. Though the rise in radioactivity was not considered dangerous by officials, the matter brought fresh discomfort to Anglo-American relations and was potentially damaging for the American base.[40] A routine British survey detected substantially raised levels of radiation in the mud flats of the loch in April, and a joint British-American survey of May through June identified coolant discharge from the submarines' reactor plants as the source. Although the survey found that the radiation levels were still "far below" the annually acceptable human dose, the rise was considered sufficiently "disturbing" by the Foreign Office for it to contemplate the dispatch of a protest to the U.S. State Department. But in the end it opted for an immediate meeting of British and American experts.[41]

The Americans were embarrassed by this revelation, especially because they had agreed in the Memorandum of Understanding (paragraph 5b), released in February 1964, that "no effluent or other waste will be discharged which would cause a measurable increase in the background radio-activity of the environment."[42] The Americans were told to cease discharging effluent into Holy Loch until the matter had been investigated. America's leading authority on nuclear submarines, Vice Admiral Hyman G. Rickover, was quickly dispatched to London with a scientific team to talk with the British. A pioneer of atomic submarines, Rickover was director of the nuclear power division of the U.S. Bureau of Ships. After meeting with Sir Christopher Mayhew, the chief scientific adviser to the British government, on July 17–18, the Americans

177

agreed to take remedial action. They would impose tighter limitations on discharges, carry out more regular safety checks, and install a new filter to reduce the radioactive content of the effluent. However, the Americans were unable to maintain a "complete ban" on direct discharges of radioactive effluent into the loch. Rickover could only agree to avoid direct discharges from his submarines as far as was "operationally feasible," and he signed a personal undertaking to this effect.[43]

Disappointed that they could not achieve a complete ban on discharges, British naval experts nonetheless agreed to American terms.[44] Denis Healey, the British defense secretary, thought the talks with Rickover were "satisfactory" and told Prime Minister Harold Wilson that he was "highly satisfied" with the way the whole affair had been handled. Healey was particularly pleased that the incident had engendered closer collaboration between the British and the Americans on safety issues, something that he thought had been "sadly lacking" since the signing of the Memorandum of Understanding, when all American information on radiation levels came to an abrupt stop.[45] But this did not end the matter. Pressure was now building for a formal announcement about the radiation levels, especially as it was thought that a local newspaper already had the information. The British government had also been quizzed in Parliament about radioactivity in Holy Loch in February 1965. After their reassurances that all was well in February, the government might now be vulnerable to criticism that it had tried to suppress information about radioactivity, a valid accusation given its silence over the 1963 discovery.[46] So in August, the Cabinet decided that it was best to "go public" with the news of the raised radiation levels to avoid embarrassment in the event of a premature leak by the press.[47] The Scottish Office agreed with Westminster: "We cannot say nothing about the recent rise in radioactivity in the Holy Loch." Samples taken on June 14 and 15 showed the increases given in table 7.1.

These figures seem more scary than reassuring, even though the unit of measurement is very small. So it was hardly surprising that the Americans wanted the discovery kept secret. Not only might there be problems with Holy Loch; disclosure might also jeopardize visits of their nuclear submarines elsewhere, especially to Japan and Spain. After a decision made "at the highest level," George Newman, defense counselor of the U.S. Embassy in London, pleaded with the British not to make an announcement, or at least to make a postponement, to give the Americans the chance to make "further representations."[48] The Foreign Office, anxious to "reduce the risk of anti-American publicity," had no objection to a postponement,[49] and in the end it decided not to make a public statement but to deal with questions as they arose after local members of Parliament had been informed.[50] The reaction was muted, and the

Table 7.1. Rise in Radioactivity in the Holy Loch, Scotland, Resulting from the U.S. Nuclear Submarine Base (gamma dose rates, roentgens per hour measured at 0.5 meters)

Station	From	To
10	7.1	47.7
13	8.3	11.0
18	—	524.5
20	4.0	43.9
30	16.4	440.0

Source: DD 9/281, A. K. Steele and J. C. Robson, Holy Loch Monitoring, Scottish Records Office, June 1965.

Dunoon local paper optimistically reported in September that the last two months had seen no further increases in radioactivity.[51] All other U.K. ports and harbors where American nuclear-powered ships had been berthed showed no rise in radiation levels, and by the end of August 1965 submarine operations in Holy Loch were back to normal.[52] A year later, at the end of 1966, MAFF rather unbelievably stopped monitoring Holy Loch for the Ministry of Defence.[53]

During the period from 1965 to 1974, it would appear that there were no further problems at Holy Loch, but the attitude of the authorities is fairly clear from the period 1960 to 1965. In the aftermath of the scare about increased radiation levels in June 1965, MAFF produced a survey to "reassess the degree of public exposure to radiation." It looked at consumption of fish and shellfish from the area and seemed to dismiss concerns on the grounds that little was actually caught or consumed rather than on the grounds that the mussels and fish were safe to eat. Calculations of danger on the basis of information available is extremely difficult, but according to current safety standards, if someone had been consuming about 5.5 ounces of mussels a week over the course of a year they could easily have exceeded the maximum safe intake of radiation. The conclusion to the report hinted that dangers were diminished by the fact that not many people were exposed to the loch for long, which is not a compelling reason for complacency. "Most of the local inhabitants must at some time or other go on the shore for short periods, if only to dump garden refuse, but none of their activities involves them in regularly spending long periods there apart from the boat-hirer of Lazarretto Point and the shipyard workers, although not actually working on the beach, spend many hours in proximity to it."[54] Possibly the most dangerous scenario involved the shipyard workers who spent five days each year removing silt from near the jetty. If that

179

silt had been contaminated to the level of some of the highest readings discovered in June, then they could have been exposed to radiation levels that were even considered to be unsafe at the time.

Perhaps this is all a little harsh on the authorities. Perhaps they did not override the needs of the local Scottish population for the sake of the U.S. Polaris base and good Anglo-American relations, and the need for the British Polaris Base at Faslane. Yet one cannot get away from the lack of transparency, and even if that were justified by fears of a possible distortion of information in the press and among some of the politically extreme among the general public, it is difficult to see how it could be fully excused, especially when combined with what amounts to a blatant attempt to manipulate the Local Liaison Committee. The Clyde Area Local Liaison Committee hardly had a distinguished career, but then that was never the intention. A document from 1957 circulating at the time of the establishment of the committee in 1960 makes this abundantly clear. In November 1957, the chairman of the Atomic Energy Authority sent a document to Prime Minister Macmillan explaining the experience with local liaison committees set up at civilian nuclear power stations in the aftermath of the accident at Windscale:

> Their success [i.e., local liaison committees] and the co-operation of the various local interests depends on their being encouraged to believe that they have a significant measure of autonomy in the matters within their terms of reference. . . . While encouraging a sense of independence and local autonomy, the Authority representatives must ensure that local liaison committees do not undertake independent action publicly which could have embarrassing consequences for other Establishments, for the Authority as a whole or for the Government.[55]

Seen in this context of official thinking, the termination of monitoring in Holy Loch by the MAFF laboratory at Lowestoft at the end of 1966 looks suspiciously like a case of "If you do not know, then you cannot be held responsible or called to account."

The patronizing attitude of "government knows best" and the view that disclosure would panic the general population and only lead to distortions in the press were increasingly difficult to tolerate as the 1960s and 1970s progressed. They were even more difficult to tolerate in a general population that was beginning to awaken to a sense that the government in London was remote and not in Scottish best interests. At the very least, if such attitudes had to be tolerated, it would be better if they were emanating from Edinburgh rather than from London.

Local Reaction and Demonstrations

The first edition of the *Dunoon Observer and Argyllshire Herald* to appear after Macmillan announced the Holy Loch base published three letters from local people. Two were against and one was supportive of the base development. Those against suggested "Unholy Loch" as an appropriate name for the loch and spoke of greedy minds picturing the "roll of dollars the Monster [personified America] will have in both hands." There was mention of radiation dangers and U.S. supermarkets sprouting up to undercut local traders. In fact a self-service store did open in June 1961, but it was a conversion of the Maypole Dairy Company shop that had been trading in Dunoon for over fifty years. The lurid language of a third letter spoke of "Mr. K [Krushchev] and his fellow executioners with their bloody record of bestial savagery," which made the author's sympathies pretty clear.[56] Over the following weeks, there was a flurry of articles and letters in the paper, which was generally critical of the base and the coming of Americans. However, they were badly informed, unimaginative articles. The only pollution danger mentioned had to do with oil, and the November 12 edition referred to "polarized" submarines. However, a rising tide of anger and distress was evident and was carried forward by trade union and religious groups and demonstrations in Glasgow in the middle of November and late December 1960.[57] The latter was the largest in Glasgow since World War II. However, by late February 1961 the flow of articles and letters eased; in the April 29 edition of the local paper, there was nothing about the base. But over the following four years, a pattern emerged that reflected the relationship between the Americans and their hosts.

On the third anniversary of the arrival of *Proteus,* the *Dunoon Observer and Argyllshire Herald* carried four articles on the American presence at Holy Loch. The first reported that three sailors had been charged with not having their car license plate properly illuminated. Minor traffic offenses and driving without insurance became commonplace and prompted one of the local lawyers, who frequently defended the Americans in court, to observe that driving regulations in the United States were somewhat different than in Scotland. He was right. The second article noted that Lieutenant Commander R. Cooper had spoken at the Saint Andrew's Guild. This type of social interaction flourished and was a more positive aspect to the U.S. presence, as were intermarriages between U.S. sailors and local girls, which usually merited front-page coverage. The third article complained of too many taxis and too much traffic congestion, all blamed on the American presence, though presumably the taxi drivers and the local shops and hostelries did not complain about American custom. And the fourth article reported on alcohol-related offenses by Americans. Again, this became commonplace and, though most incidents were fairly trivial, one or two were not. In July 1961, there was one of the few incidents of racial bigotry, with a black sailor being called nigger. The incident involved alcohol and a woman known to both men, and it was nasty, with the African American sailor involved slashing a local man's neck badly; but in court, he was acquitted on a majority verdict. In November 1961, Petty Officer Ronald Cox was stabbed waiting for his girlfriend in broad daylight. A month later, Gerald Austin Grimes was the first U.S. serviceman from Holy Loch to be court-marshaled; the crime was bigamy. The first American from the base to be jailed (a rare occurrence) was Petty Officer First Class Michael Edward Beece, for drunk driving. Tracking forward to February 1968, the record was similar, with articles on four driving offenses and three mildly critical letters about matters to do with the base. In February 1973, there were two articles about driving offenses. In February 1974, along with articles about the theft of an excise license and possession of an inefficient vehicle, a U.S. sailor was charged with possession of cannabis. Possibly the most serious altercation was a small riot in October 1973 involving six sailors who broke twenty shop windows and assaulted a thirteen-year-old girl and a policeman.[58] All this had quite an impact on the small tourist town of Dunoon, and over the years some of the local population tried to blow some issues up out of all proportion.

In October 1963, Dunoon councilor Anne Melville introduced a motion in the Council Chambers to ban all Americans from the town except those living with their families. Melville used such language as a "Town of Shame" because of the activity of prostitutes. Her fellow councilors seemed to take a more relaxed view of things, as no one could be found to second the motion. The following week, the ex-provost of Dunoon, E. F. Wyatt, wrote to the local paper to take Melville to task for the language she had used and the picture of Sodom and Gomorrah she had tried to paint. He acknowledged that there were prostitutes, but their activities were not flagrant or extensive and the police were now attending to two boarding houses of ill repute. On the whole, he asserted, the Americans were decent and so was the town of Dunoon. It had not been corrupted.[59]

Although a few local residents were clearly disturbed by the Americans, not all Americans fell in love with the Scots. In March 1963, a *"Proteus* wife" wrote to the local paper. Her letter was a bitter retort to seven criticisms often leveled against the Americans. "Americans were highly paid." Yes, she replied, they need to be when they were charged £35 a month for rent when locals would be charged £5. "Polaris would get us all blown to bits." Hardly, as it moved out into open water at times such as the October 1962 Cuban missile crisis. "Americans drive big cars." Well, yes, but they pay for them and one of the leading local figures drives a Cadillac. "U.S. sailors were ruining local girls." If they were, it was not always their fault, as parents did not seem to mind allowing thirteen-year-olds to dress in ways indistinguishable from twenty-year-olds. "Americans get duty free goods from the PX shop." This was no different from the privileges British servicemen enjoyed overseas. "Americans were loud." Well, yes, Americans are gregarious, outgoing, and friendly. "Americans do not like us and should go back to America." Her parting shot was: "Thanks, I will. You folks would be treated differently in our country."[60]

Perhaps most remarkable of all, Dunoon seemed little exercised by the dangers of radioactive pollution, though this may have been because people were never made fully aware of them. But even during the 1965 scare, all the local paper had to say was: "Some alarm has been caused in the Holy Loch district by press reports. . . . Although radiation escaping from the submarines had been underestimated, readings were below the danger level, and it was safe to bathe or eat sea food caught in the Loch." It observed that if the rate of pollution had continued for a further two years, then it would have reached danger levels, but all was now well as there had been no increases in radiation levels for the past two months. However, it did note rather ominously that there no longer appeared to be either mussels or seaweed living in the loch!![61]

The base at Holy Loch did not initiate antinuclear protests in Britain; they already had a distinguished history. The National Campaign Against Nuclear Weapons Testing and the Direct Action Committee Against Nuclear War appeared in 1957 and were soon followed by the Campaign for Nuclear Disarmament (CND), founded in 1958 by the Yorkshire dramatist J. B. Priestley and supported by such luminaries as the philosopher Bertrand Russell. Alongside the CND, from 1960 the Committee of One Hundred also tried to put nonviolent mass demonstrations to work to abolish nuclear weapons. Easter 1958 witnessed the first of the Gandhi-inspired marches from London to the Government Weapons Research Establishment at Aldermaston. These marches exceeded anything that happened at Holy Loch. They attracted 10,000 marchers in 1958 and up to 200,000 at the later demonstrations from 1959 to 1963. Demonstrations at Holy Loch peaked at around 2,000, but their impact was proportionately greater than those in London because of the small population in Argyllshire and because of the U.S. base itself. The protests at Holy Loch fed off existing organizational structures and their momentum, but they also contributed something of their own, and they aroused a sense that the Scottish situation was primarily Scotland's concern. They also caused resentment at the influx of protesters from south of the border who were concerned to make their point about universal nuclear disarmament, whereas many of the locally based protesters had more parochial concerns.

On December 3, the *Dunnon Observer and Argyllshire Standard* reported on the first local protest, the Sandbank Petition of 300 signatures organized by Margaret Robertson, which was sent to Prime Minister Macmillan. The local marching season did not get under way until May 1961, when over 2,000 people marched from Kirn to Dunoon. It was organized by the Glasgow District Trades Council, the Glasgow Co-operative Association, and Glasgow City Labour Party. The vanguard was the Arniston Miners' Pipe Band, and the whole affair was orderly and very Scottish—so Scottish in fact that the opening speaker, William Scholes, a former taxi driver from Dunoon, was deeply unhappy about the imminent influx of demonstrators from London and one of their leaders in particular, Pat Arrowsmith: "The best help she can give us in Scotland is by going back to London. We will achieve our object through the democratic machinery of this country, and we will not be influenced by cranks or anyone of that nature."[62] Similar sentiments, but with the added inference that the antinuclear protesters were peculiarly deranged English people, came from the Scottish establishment at Westminster. One of them regaled the prime minister with: "As a fellow Scot, . . . [does] he realise that the local people are perfectly happy with "Proteus" if they could keep away the "beatnik" Englishmen?" Macmillan humorously parried with the comment "there are sometimes Welshmen too." Others called for prosecution of the demonstrators, especially because they were "mainly sassenachs anyway" or "English weirdies."[63]

On Whitsunday, May 21, the sit-down protest at Ardnadam Pier, the canoe and power boat assaults on the *Proteus,* and the arrests that ensued included many people from south of the border. But the first canoeist to reach *Proteus* and temporarily raise the CND pennant was Hamish Gow from Glasgow, clad in "a jersey, grey flannels, and a red knitted skullcap." The local paper clearly thought that the skullcap gave away his political affiliations. The culprits, including Pat Arrowsmith, were brought before the Sheriff's Court in July, and she along with three others refused to pay fines and elected to go to prison instead. An anonymous donor saved them from that fate. Four months later, the CND and the Committee of One Hundred organized another demonstration at Holy Loch. Inclement weather depleted their ranks by half, but the resolute of about a thousand persevered, led by clergymen and "several refreshingly normal-looking raincoats."[64] The *Scottish Daily Express* described them as "labourers, lecturers, artisans, shapely models, and machinists."[65] In all, 351 cases were brought before the local courts, and among them was Pat Arrowsmith's. Pleading guilty and disclosing a previous conviction in July, she was sentenced to three months in jail. As a policewoman led her from the dock, she cried: "Good luck chums." "Immediately there was uproar. The protestors in the public benches cheered so loudly that the water carafe on the court bench shattered."[66] If that seems highly improbable, then so does some of the behavior of the authorities. One of the substitute sheriffs on duty told Mavis Joan Alman: "If I care to go to the extreme it could wreck your career as a student because you would not be admitted to Loughborough College with a conviction for disorderly conduct against you." In fact this was probably just tactless, but well-intentioned, paternalism. The Crown Office in Edinburgh, after looking at how the cases had been handled, concluded that the substitute sheriff in question "appears to have been gentle with the students."[67]

Nevertheless, the strain that the number of cases had put upon the local judiciary was clear, and not everything was well handled. Furthermore, national prominence was given to differences between the English and Scottish judicial systems, because of the harsher penalties meted out by Scottish as opposed to English law. Finally, the case of Arrowsmith rumbled on for weeks. She went on a hunger strike in prison and had to be "force fed," though she did not resist. A psychiatrist interviewed her, but the proceedings came to an abrupt halt when he asked why she was not married. Scottish Office officials subsequently noted his tactlessness.[68]

There were further protests at Holy Loch over the next two years. In January 1962, Women Against the Bomb made their voices heard; and on May 25, 1963, there was another large demonstration by 2,000 people. On that occasion, there were no incidents and no arrests. Thereafter, the demonstration culture went into a steep decline, and Holy Loch, notwithstanding its continuing capacity for wreaking Armageddon, returned to something resembling a peaceful normality.

Expansion in 1973?

In May 1973, the U.S. authorities, worried by the danger of bad publicity from possible rowdy behavior by U.S. servicemen in Dunoon, approached the British government about the possibility of buying 160 acres at the head of the loch to provide more on-base facilities.[69] This came at a most inauspicious time, "especially in the light of current state of Anglo-American relations"; the administrations of President Richard Nixon and Prime Minister Edward Heath did not get on well, and yet the British were dependent on the Americans for future upgrades of their nuclear deterrent.[70] Some thought that a refusal to allow an expansion of the base might prompt the Americans to seize on that as an excuse to pull out from Holy Loch altogether, with consequent damage to Anglo-American nuclear cooperation, whereas a yes would lead to a series of difficulties for the British and the Scots.[71] A government paper, the Nugent Report, had just recommended the move of the weapons-proof and experimental facilities at Shoeburyness in England to Tain in Scotland, and there was fear that this would be controversial in Scotland and that matters would be exacerbated if an extension to the U.S. Holy Loch base were announced simultaneously. The proposed site for the base expansion was also environmentally sensitive and of good agricultural quality. Finally, there were perceived to be political problems in Scotland. Gordon Campbell, secretary of state for Scotland, observed that "the suggestion of any move would start up the opponents of the Holy Loch base, who include the SNP [Scottish National Party] besides left wing elements of the Labour Party. The Americans would be stirring up trouble for themselves."[72]

It was this issue of political problems in Scotland that exercised officials in Edinburgh. After World War II, there was a substantial expansion in the Scottish Office establishment. The Scottish civil service, based largely in Saint Andrew's House in Edinburgh, grew from 2,400 in 1937 to 8,300 in 1970 and to 10,910 in 1981. In addition, there were 68,710 Scottish civil servants working directly for British government departments in 1981.[73] That size and the expertise it nourished had political clout. At the same time that the Scottish political and bureaucratic establishment grew, there were also increasing calls for devolution and independence. The SNP, originally formed in 1934, won an important by-election at Hamilton in November 1967. Soon after that, the discovery of North Sea oil and gas fueled not only industry but also Scottish nationalism. In the October 1974 general election, the SNP won eleven seats at Westminster and took 30.4 percent of the vote in Scotland. In March 1979, there was a referendum on devolution that only narrowly failed.[74] It is against these developing trends that the proposed extension of the Holy Loch base in 1973 needs to be assessed.

Foremost among the potential troublemakers for Westminster was Katherine Gillender of the Scottish Development Office. After Defence Secretary Lord Carrington had broached the difficulties with their request with the U.S. secretary of defense in Washington in August, the Foreign Office in collusion with the Ministry of Defence proceeded to develop an argument that environmental and agricultural problems and sensitivity about implementing the Nugent Report would prevent them from agreeing to the American request at this time.[75] Gillender was angry, for this argument did not include the "united views of Scottish Office Ministers." They placed emphasis on the political problems already articulated by Campbell and had "more or less independently" arrived at these conclusions.[76] Though pleased at "determination with which [the Ministry of Defence] have dealt with the request," there was a point of principle at stake in that the Scottish view had not been made clear in the explanation of the refusal, or at least postponement of the project, handed to the Americans. As Gillender explained, "From the Scottish point of view the tie in with Nugent is a very subsidiary part of the political objections."[77] The Americans renewed their approaches in December 1973, and Secretary of State Campbell again robustly rehearsed the arguments made by Gillender earlier in the year. In mid-1974, the Americans withdrew their request and made do with a modest development on land that they already held.[78]

Conclusion

The manner of the Cold War's arrival in Holy Loch and the safety issues that it raised are revealing of the attitude of the British government and the pro-union Scottish establishment of the time. Scotland, in the form of the Scottish Office and Scottish public opinion, were wholly subservient to the priorities set in Whitehall. And the Scottish Office was largely willingly so. The decisions that were made were those of a highly unitary state, which hardly paid even lip service to Scotland as a political entity. Scottish public opinion was used rather than listened to. The U.S. nuclear submarines arrived with only restricted consultations having been held after the de facto decision on the base had been taken. British control over the use of U.S. Polaris missiles was no different from that over other U.S. land-based weapons, even though Polaris's maneuverability posed serious new difficulties. The U.S. Holy Loch facility thus revived concern and refocused attention on the strategic dangers posed by the presence of U.S. nuclear weapons in Britain. But unlike in the past, when the main U.S. nuclear capability was centered in England's heartlands of the Midlands and East Anglia, it was now in the more sensitive Scottish region, which had authentic and age-old claims to its own national identity well differentiated from England's. By 1973, Scottish Nationalists and those with a strong sense of Scottish identity, which stopped short of calls for Scottish independence, felt irked and aggrieved by the way decisions were made in London about the Holy Loch base.

Evidence of the rather cavalier attitude of the English and pro-union Scottish establishments can be seen in the fact that for three years after the establishment of the base, no firm arrangements existed for compensation for accidents or for pollution. And the final agreement when it came reflected British national rather than local Scottish interests. In 1964, Britain agreed with the American position that large claims for damages should simply be negotiated on a case-by-case basis. This was because Britain did not want to be on the receiving end of a large claim if there were a nuclear accident abroad involving one of its own nuclear vessels. Safeguards for the fishing grounds and in-shore fishing were less than exemplary, and the Liaison Committee was never intended to have power and was for cosmetic purposes only. Government officials were submerged in the cult of secrecy and were unwilling to accept any kind of transparency on the operation of the submarines. There were not even to be reassuring positive confirmations at regular intervals about radiation safety, as there were at civilian nuclear power stations. In 1963 and 1965, the official line on worrying, if not dangerous, radiation pollution was evasive at best and probably misleading at worst. Such effrontery was sadly often matched by local complacency about reports of the disappearance of seaweed and mussels from the loch.

The arrival of Americans at the base transformed the local character of the area. At the most basic level, Argyllshire would not have experienced the American effect at first hand. Without the base, there would have been fewer cocktail bars, fewer large American cars, fewer taxis, fewer prostitutes, fewer minor driving offenses, fewer cases of brawls and drunkenness, fewer intermarriages, more cultural insularity, more economic depression, less political awareness, and less security for the West. The rise in political awareness came with the cost of diminished peace and quiet, as the base became the focus for antinuclear demonstrations. The demonstrations clearly publicized the issue of nuclear dangers and their very local presence in Scotland. In doing so, they helped to raise Scottish self-awareness and the Scottishness of the local anti-nuclear movement raised some difficulties and resentment toward the more national movements such as CND and the Committee of One Hundred, which were seen as particularly English by many in Scotland. The marches and protests mobilized sections of public opinion, and the SNP capitalized on that in its resolute opposition to nuclear weapons in general and to their presence in Scotland in particular. Without Holy Loch, there would have been no demonstrations that raised the issues of Scottish needs for disarmament and Scottish democratic control over its own nuclear destiny in the way that those in Glasgow and at Holy Loch raised them.

In addition to these effects that were largely immediately felt in the local area, there was also a ripple effect that reached out to a broader audience in Scotland. Scottish expressions of concern about developments at Holy Loch and the self-confidence with which they were made in 1973 contrast very starkly with the complacent and passive way that official Scotland received the U.S. Polaris base in 1961. Many things had changed during this time frame, and many of them were completely unconnected with the American nuclear presence at Holy Loch. However, the growing sense of a Scottish identity distinct from the rest of the United Kingdom and requiring more political self-determination than the Scottish Office provided was partly to do with the broad experience of the presence of U.S. nuclear submarines at Holy Loch and what appeared to many to be a rather arrogant and politically inept treatment of Scottish sensibilities both by the pro-union Scottish establishment and the political establishment at Westminster. Rather ironically, the Cold War, while suppressing many traditional national differences for the sake of strategic priorities in a nuclear, perilously bipolar world, also fostered differentiation within one of the key Western Cold War nations: the United Kingdom. By the end of the Cold War, and at least partly because of the Cold War, the United Kingdom was less united and more politically differentiated than it had been when the Iron Curtain descended in 1946.

Notes

1. *Dunoon Observer and Argyllshire Standard,* March 11 and 18, 1961.
2. Scottish Record Office (hereafter SRO), ED 48/1648 Notes for Supplementary Questions [House of Commons], October 31, 1961.
3. Public Record Office (hereafter PRO), Prime Minister's Office (hereafter PREM), 11/2941; U.S. Department of Defense, draft of anticipated press questions and proposed answers, Washington to Foreign Office, tel. 2167, October 29, 1960; U.S. Department of Defense, "Facilities in the Clyde for US Polaris Submarines: Notes for Supplementary Questions," October 31, 1960.
4. For a detailed account of the Skybolt discussions, see Ian Clark, *Nuclear Diplomacy and the Special Relationship* (London: Clarendon Press, 1994); and Richard Neustadt, *Report to JFK: The Skybolt Crisis in Perspective* (Ithaca, N.Y.: Cornell University Press, 1999). For general context, see John Baylis, *Anglo-American Defence Relations 1939–84* (London: Macmillan, 1984); and for a Scottish focus, though rather on the period after the concerns of this chapter, see Malcolm Chalmers and William Walker, *Uncharted Waters: The UK Nuclear Weapons and the Scottish Question* (East Lothian, U.K.: Tuckwell Press, 2001).
5. A copy of the memorandum is in PREM, 11/4741.
6. Ibid., Foreign Office to numerous ambassadors, tel. 378, October 31, 1960.
7. Ibid., Maclay to Macmillan, November 5, 1960. A handwritten remark from Macmillan added "This is very encouraging" (November 7, 1960).
8. SRO, Home and Health Departments (hereafter HH), 56/76, Note by Scottish Departments, draft, April 14, 1961.
9. Ibid.
10. Even though officials emphasized in public that it was not a base, confidential official communications regularly used the term "base," and in what follows "base" and "facility" are used interchangeably. In U.S. Navy official jargon, it was Site 1.
11. SRO, HH, 56/76, P. Mehew, Head of Military Branch II Admiralty, memo, April 12, 1961; Note by Scottish Departments (draft), memo, April 14, 1961; J. H. McGuiness, April 19, 1961, and Mehew to Stephens, April 18, 1961.
12. 484 House of Commons Debates, 632, February 15, 1951.
13. "Draft Universal Answer to Polaris Questions," c. November 1960, PREM, 11/2941.
14. SRO, HH, 56/76, More to Hutchison, November 14, 1962.

15. Harry S. Truman Library, President's Secretaries File, box 115, folder General File, Churchill-Winston meeting with President Truman, January 1952, folder 2.

16. For more detailed treatment of the Churchill-Truman understanding, see Alan P. Dobson, "Informally Special? The Churchill-Truman talks of January 1952 and the State of Anglo-American Relations," *Review of International Studies* 23 (1997): 27–47. For the broader issue of U.S. bases in Britain and on British territories, see Charlie Whitham, *Bitter Rehearsal: British and American Planning for a Post-War West Indies* (Westport, Conn.: Praeger, 2002); Simon Duke, *US Defence Bases in the United Kingdom: A Matter for Joint Decision?* (Basingstoke, U.K.: Macmillan, 1987), and D. A. Walbrecht, "The Machinery of Alliance: Anglo-American Air Power Diplomacy, 1917–1965," Ph.D. thesis, University of East Anglia, 2001.

17. James G. Kellas, *The Scottish Political System* (Cambridge: Cambridge University Press, 1994), 27–28.

18. James Mitchell, "Scotland in the Union, 1945–95: The Changing Nature of the Union State," in *Scotland in the Twentieth Century,* ed. T. M. Devine and R. J. Finlay (Edinburgh: Edinburgh University Press, 1997), 88. Mitchell's view of Scotland in the union is the idea of a union state with distinct Scottish aspects rather than a unitary state. He suggests that Kellas conceptualizes things in terms of a distinct Scottish system, Richard Rose sees a subsystem within the United Kingdom; and Keating and Midwinter identify a complex of networks some of which operate within and others reach out of Scotland. See Kellas, *Scottish Political System;* Richard Rose, *Understanding the United Kingdom* (London: Longmans, 1982); and M. Keating and A. Midwinter, *The Government of Scotland* (Edinburgh: Edinburgh University Press, 1983).

19. Ibid.

20. SRO, HH, 56/76, draft letter to CINCUSNAVEUR; H. T. A. Overton, Foreign Office to Mehew, Admiralty, May 16, 1961.

21. SRO, HH, 56/76, Treasury Solicitor's Office, B. B. Hall to P. Mehew, Admiralty, signed by A. B. Lyons, June 16, 1961.

22. British Government Command Paper 342, 1957.

23. SRO, HH, 56/77, draft to be considered at January 18, 1961, Clyde Area Liaison Committee.

24. *Dunoon Observer and Argyllshire Standard,* November 5, 1960; SRO, HH 56/77 Office of the Flag Office Scotland to Binns, Scottish Home Department, November 18, 1960.

25. SRO, HH, 56/77, Minutes Clyde Local Liaison Committee, Greenock, November 30, 1960, emphasis by underlining in pencil in the original.

26. Ibid.

27. Ibid.

28. *The Scotsman,* December 1, 1960.

29. SRO, HH, 56/77, Mr. Clark, Report, December 1, 1960, on 1st Meeting of Liaison Committee.

30. *Dunoon Observer and Argyllshire Standard,* December 17, 1960.

31. *Glasgow Herald,* February 14, 1961, letter from Orr-Ewing to Mabon.

32. SRO, HH, 56/77, Memo to Elliott-Binns, January 13, 1961.

33. Ibid., memo, January 19, 1961, relating to January 18 meeting of Working Sub-Committee of Liaison Committee, and Elliott-Binns to Mr. Braid, January 19, 1961.

34. Ibid., minute, April 18, 1961, by Mr. Stark.

35. SRO, Scottish Development Department, 9/281, A. Preston, Ministry of Agriculture, Fisheries, and Food, Confidential, January 31, 1961, "Holy Loch: Low-Level Waste Discharges from Nuclear Submarines."
· 36. SRO, HH, 56/76, Mehew Admiralty to Myers, Atomic Energy Authority, January 5, 1962.
37. Ibid., MacLehose to Hume, July 19, 1961.
38. PRO, Foreign Office (hereafter FO), 371/173507 Z3/63, F. H. Mawer (Admiralty) to F. J. Stephens (Ministry of Defence), December 10, 1963. Neither did the ministry inform the Clyde Local Liaison Committee. The documents contain a brief for an official reply to a parliamentary question, in which it is admitted that no "positive admission" that the radioactivity came from the American submarines had yet been received.
39. Ibid., J. R. Brough (Foreign Office) to F. H. Mawer (Admiralty), December 11, 1963.
40. PRO, PREM, 13/129, from "Navy Department Press Release: Holy Loch," August 27, 1965.
41. PRO, FO, 371/184536 Z12/29, G. G. Arthur minutes, June 30, 1965. There is a discussion of the response in various minutes in the same file.
42. PRO, PREM, 11/4741, "Holy Loch: Facilities for United States Polaris Submarines," c. March 1963. This fact was raised by J. A. N. Graham (Permanent Under-Secretary's Department), minutes, May 28, 1965, FO, 371/184536 Z12/28.
43. PRO, PREM, 13/129, Healey minute to Wilson, 30 July 1965.
44. PRO, FO, 371/1845537 Z1/34, mentioned in J. A. N. Graham, minutes, July 30, 1965.
45. Ibid.
46. Ibid.
47. PRO, PREM, 13/129, Gore-Booth memorandum to Henry Hardman, August 17, 1965. Local MPs would be told privately beforehand, as would the Clyde Local Liaison Committee.
48. PRO, PREM, 13/129, quoted in Gore-Booth memorandum to Henry Hardman, August 17, 1965.
49. PRO, FO, 371/184537 Z12/35, the idea of a postponement had already been broached in G. G. Arthur minutes, August 3, 1965.
50. Ibid., Z12/42; see G. G. Arthur minutes, August 19, 1965. For the text of the release that was not sent, see "Navy Department Press Release: Holy Loch," August 27, 1965, PREM, 13/129.
51. *Dunoon Observer and Argyllshire Standard,* September 4, 1965.
52. PRO, FO, 371/184537 Z12/45; see "Responses to Queries on Holy Loch," August 26, 1965.
53. SRO, Scottish Development Department, 9/281, Preston to Birse, January 25, 1967.
54. Ibid., Ministry of Agriculture, Fisheries, and Food, Holy Loch Habits Survey, C. Hewett, July 1965.
55. SRO, HH, 56/77, Admiralty Paper, Local Liaison Committee, undated, no signature, referring to Nuclear Warships Safety Committee, NWSC/P18, United Kingdom Atomic Energy Authority Experience with Local Committees, Chairman of Atomic Energy Authority to Macmillan, November 1957.

56. *Dunoon Observer and Argyllshire Standard,* November 5, 1960.

57. Ibid., November 1960 to April 1961. Not all religious bodies were against the base. The February 14, 1961, *Glasgow Herald* carried a story about the Church of Scotland reporting in favor of the base to restore effective deterrence.

58. *Glasgow Herald,* February 8, 1964, July 22, 1961, November 4, 1961, December 9, 1961, March 10, 1962, June 30, 1962, February 3, 1968, February 3, 1973, February 9 1974, October 20, 1973.

59. Ibid., October 12 and 19, 1963.

60. Ibid., March 16, 1963.

61. Ibid., September 4, 1965. Just how accurate that observation was is debatable. Certainly by the late 1970s and early 1980s, after Polaris had been superseded by Poseidon, and later by Trident, eyewitnesses recall fishing in the loch. It is also true that very toxic antifouling paint, used then but banned now, was highly poisonous to sea life.

62. *Glasgow Herald,* May 20, 1961.

63. Hansard Oral Answers, June 1, 1961, col. 420; also see Hansard, May 10, 1961.

64. *Dunoon Observer and Argyllshire Herald,* September 23, 1961.

65. *Scottish Daily Express,* September 19, 1961.

66. Ibid.

67. *The Guardian,* September 19, 1961; HH, 60/821 Crown Office Minute, Mr. Ogilvie, October 19, 1961.

68. SRO, HH, 60/822, History of Imprisonment of Miss P. Arrowsmith, November 30, 1961, HM Prison Greenock, September–November 1961.

69. SRO, Scottish Development Department, 12/3246, longhand comment by Gillender on a cutting from *Glasgow Herald,* December 24, 1973.

70. Ibid., draft note, September 19, 1973, Lord Carrington, secretary of state for defence.

71. Ibid., Scottish Development Department to Colin Davenport, Ministry of Defence, July 9, 1973.

72. Ibid., Marshall to Spence, August 22, 1973, quoting Campbell, secretary of state for Scotland.

73. Iain G. C. Hutchison, "Government," in *Scotland in the Twentieth Century,* ed. Devine and Finlay.

74. In fact, of a 62.8 percent turnout, 51.6 percent were in favor of devolution, but under the terms of the referendum, at least 40 percent of the entire electorate was required to vote in favor for devolution to proceed; and in the event, despite the majority of votes cast in flavor, it only amounted to 32.9 percent of the total electorate and so the proposal for devolution fell.

75. Ibid., undated draft letter from Jackson to John Reed Jr., political/military attaché at the U.S. Embassy in reply to the U.S. proposal of May 29 to extend the Holy Loch facilities.

76. Ibid., Gillender, longhand note, October 3, 1973,and Gillender to Miller, Ministry of Defence, October 4, 1973.

77. Ibid.

78. Ibid., Goulding to Jackson, December 17, 1973, and December 18, 1974, Background Note to Scottish Development Department.

8. Landscape Change in Central Europe and Stalin's Postwar Strategy, 1945–1949

Arvid Nelson

The origins of the Cold War remain contentious despite John Lewis Gaddis's revelations and analysis drawn from once secret Soviet archives in his recent book *We Now Know: Rethinking Cold War History*.[1] There are other sources for estimating Soviet intentions in the period 1945–49, sources held secret with equal force, that complement the wealth of documents from which Gaddis drew, on Eastern European farm and forest landscapes' structure, resilience, and populations. Their qualities and dynamics reveal secrets once hidden in Soviet archives, offering leading indicators of the emerging Cold War in 1945–49. Joseph Stalin's "war on the countryside"—waged through land reform and reparations, policies that took precedence over his other policies— laid bare his opportunism and political design.[2] A reduction of rural community and ecological structures lay at the core of his hegemonic strategy to crush U.S. and British influence throughout Europe. We can read the early signs of Stalin's intent and design in unambiguous ecological data and in the narratives of rural communities today, just as British and American policymakers and the German people did in 1945–49.

Origins and Early Steps

Land reform, Stalin's first political initiative in the Soviet zone, prepared Germany for Soviet rule as the key plank of his "parliamentary road to democracy." His formal goals were clear: liquidation of the Soviets' traditional foes in the countryside, the "backward peasant" and rural landowners and aristoc-

Figure 8.1. Emergence of the German Nation, 1937–1990

BALTIC SEA

TO
SOVIETS

Tilsit

Köningsberg (Kaliningrad)

Stolp
(Słupsk)

Danzig
(Gdańsk)

Elbing (Elbląg)

EAST PRUSSIA

TO POLAND

Köslin
(Koszalin)

Marienburg
(Malbork)

Allenstein
(Olsztyn)

Vistula

EASTERN
POMERANIA

Bromberg
(Bydgoszcz)

Narev

Bug

NEW
MARK

Warthe

Vistula

POLAND

Warsaw

Landsberg
(Gorzów Wlkp)

Posen (Poznań)

Piliza

Grünberg
(Ostrów Wlkp)

TO
POLAND

Breslau
(Wrocław)

Warthe

Neiße

Oder

S I L E S I A

Oppeln
(Opole)

Vistula

Krakow

Königgrätz

GALICIA

Prague

Elbe

CZECHOSLOVAKIA

Moldau

Map Area

racy. Land reform, at first a program that enjoyed broad-based popular support, also brought great pressure to bear on the British and Americans to enact a similar program in their zones as well as to adopt central control with a strong Soviet voice. Land reform also created chaos and shortages throughout Germany, which Soviet propaganda exploited. In contrast, reparations for industrial and forest products were manifestly harsh and unpopular, even if accepted as just compensation for the Soviets' grievous war losses. Yet both lay at the core of Soviet policy: to destroy rural communities and ecosystems, to foment the chaos and deprivation that favored central planning, and to seize resources and land that otherwise might fall to the West. Everyone anticipated prompt reunification in the immediate postwar period, and Stalin wanted to prepare his dominions to maximize Soviet advantage and power when that happened.

But reunification and a peace treaty did not follow promptly after the war ended in May 1945, and British and American cautious hope for a postwar partnership with the Soviet Union soon faded. Western leaders' growing distrust of the Soviets in the last months of 1945 flowed from land reform's and reparations' direct threat to their interests. Stalin's "war on the countryside" also fueled popular outrage in Britain and America at the severe deprivation that it caused throughout Germany. This distrust blossomed into open hostility by September 1946, when U.S. secretary of state James Byrnes made his seminal statement of U.S. policy at Stuttgart, declaring America's determination to protect western German independence and even to recover Germany's eastern provinces lost across the Oder-Neiße line to Stalin's "border adjustments." Not only would U.S. forces remain indefinitely in Europe, but the United States also explicitly challenged the legitimacy of postwar borders and Stalin's assertion in April 1945 that "everyone imposes his own system as far as his armies can reach."[3] Ultimately, the Soviet eastern European empire foundered in 1989 over the regimes' lack of legitimacy, artificial borders, and human rights abuses—all enduring features of the entropic initial conditions set with Soviet land reform and reparations (figure 8.1).

The destruction of Soviet-zone rural communities—the integrated whole of humans, ecosystems, and society that define them—came first on Stalin's agenda and presaged a comparable reduction and radical simplification of structure and population throughout the Soviet zone. Yet collateral damage from Stalin's "war on the countryside" inadvertently denied Stalin his ultimate prize: U.S. withdrawal from Europe and Soviet hegemony. It alerted Western policymakers to Soviet intentions and made manifest to the British and American peoples the destructiveness and violence behind Stalin's policies.

Secrecy surrounded the terror that accompanied land reform and reparations; the Soviets and the eastern German communist leadership insisted until

1989 that "fascist looting" and British and American ("imperialist") war damage caused the massive levels of forest damage, hunger, and poor farm production first acknowledged in the mid-1950s. Yet Soviet-zone farms and forests emerged from the war relatively unscathed not only by battle damage but also by Nazi predation.[4] German farmers, despite wartime shortages, continued to feed the German people at the same level as the British population until the end of the war, yielding daily rations of about 2,500 calories. Albert Speer, the Nazi production minister, made "an independent decision of his own that the war was lost and the next year's crop should be protected," shifting nitrogen stocks from explosives to fertilizer production in the last months of the war.[5]

Forestry enjoyed a comparable reprieve from the otherwise relentless demands of the National Socialist war economy. The Nazis' war timber harvest only exceeded annual growth, one measure of sustained yield, "by not more than thirty percent," leading a surprised U.S. forester to remark in 1948 that the German forest was "not badly overcut."[6] Nazi forest and farm policy remained "green" throughout the war, despite Joseph Goebbels' mesmerizing cry for "total war" in his February 18, 1943, speech at Berlin's Sportpalast.[7]

Environmentalism suffused Nazi ideology. The Nazis also managed the farms and forests in their conquered eastern lands ecologically, taking great care to conserve and protect the natural landscape.[8] Even Reichsführer Heinrich Himmler, the head of the SS and Gestapo and warden of the death camps—and an agronomist by training—preached environmentalism in his late-war decree "On the Treatment of Land in the Eastern Territories": "The peasant of our racial stock has always worked steadily to increase the natural powers of the soil, plants, and wildlife, and to conserve the balance of the whole of nature. If, therefore, the new *Lebensräume* [living spaces in eastern Europe and the Soviet Union] are to become a homeland for our settlers, we must steadfastly manage the landscape as a close-to-nature organism. It is the critical base for fortifying the German *Völk*."[9] Himmler's sentiments flowed directly from radical ecologistic writings of the post—World War I period, a romantic view of nature shared by others in the Nazi hierarchy such as Field and Reich Marshall Hermann Hermann Göring (1893–1946), boss of the Four-Year Plan and Reich master forester and hunter.[10] National Socialist farm and forest management never strayed far from ecological principles, even as the Holocaust raged and the German nation faced destruction.[11]

So at the war's end in mid-1945, German farms and forests were in good condition and the rural communities healthy, even considering the grievous war losses every family felt. Yet by 1948, the Soviet-zone forest neared collapse, blighted by "huge clear-cuts of unimaginable size, with depressed stocking and thin, poorly tended stands."[12] One-third of the state forest was high graded, its battered stands stripped of all valuable timber and "without a forestry future." Food riots and near famine stalked all of Germany. Eastern Germany's farm and forest landscapes faced imminent ecological and economic collapse, the direct result of Stalin's land reform and reparations.

Stalin imposed land reform, his first political initiative in the Soviet zone of occupation, for political and ideological ends over the timid objections of his "Ulbricht Group" of German communist suzerains. No one in the postwar environment of grave shortages and population crisis welcomed land reform. Walter Ulbricht, the leader of the German Communists in their Moscow exile and future East German Communist Party boss, noted that the Communists and Social Democrats wanted order and work for the people, not radical land reform or collectivization.[13] As Norman Naimark observed, "Virtually every agricultural expert agreed that breaking up the large estates would hurt rather than help productivity. Expropriating the Junkers and their agents meant destroying the basic economic unit of agricultural production"—one that had evolved in concert with the dry climate and poor soils of the North German Plain over centuries.[14] But Stalin prized land reform's political benefits. Land reform's end products of chaos and mass deprivation throughout Germany only added to land reform's class warfare appeal.

Stalin's diktat forced land reform on the German Communist Party leadership (Wilhelm Pieck, Walter Ulbricht, Gustav Sobottka, and Anton Ackermann, the German Communist Party's leading theorist) at two Kremlin meetings on June 4, 1945.[15] Stalin angrily listened to Ackermann's concern that land reform would lead to hunger and hurt the party. Ackermann meekly advised: "The Party comrades do not recommend an immediate introduction of land reform just yet."[16] They met again at midnight with Stalin and senior Soviet officials Molotov, Malenkov, and Kaganovitch. Furious with the Germans for their caution, Stalin lashed out, demanding immediate land reform and "liquidation of the Junker class."[17]

When Ackermann returned to Berlin, he carried a draft land reform law in Russian for translation into German, publication, and action.[18] Ulbricht, upon his own return from Moscow, now declared that Soviet communism was his model and the "highest form of democracy," declaring; "What we (the communists) do must appear democratic, so long as we keep everything in our own hands!"—Stalin's "parliamentary road to democracy."[19] Soviet experience, Erich Honecker, future East German party boss, proudly declared later, particularly Stalin's forced collectivization and breaking of the kulaks' power (1929–33), was of "overwhelming significance."[20] Ideological and administrative forms mattered: The peasant and worker classes must be one to fulfill Vladimir Lenin's "Alliance Doctrine," the Bündnisdoktrin.[21] So even medium-size farms of between 100 and 500 hectares had to come under land reform's knife. With Stalin's impetus and the Soviet model to guide them, the German Communist Party leadership prepared the Soviet land reform campaign.

One week after the German Communist Party leadership took its instructions from Stalin, it published the party's demand for the "liquidation of the large estates of the Junkers, dukes and princes, and the expropriation of their entire property and land."[22] Seven days later, Wilhelm Pieck announced the Communist Party's land reform program under the slogan "Junkerland in Bauernhand!"—"Junker Land into the Peasants' Hands!"[23] Land reform was a key weapon to win the allegiance of rural voters, who were traditionally hostile to communism. Perhaps because of Marx and Engels' well-known disdain for "backward peasants" and the "idiocy of rural life," as well as farmers' visceral dislike of socialism, the party's position was "particularly precarious in the agricultural economy and rural society."[24] Land reform was key to the "parliamentary road to democracy."

Three months passed as the party leadership prepared the land reform and marshaled support from the bloc parties, particularly the Social Democrats. Pieck finally announced the full land reform program on September 4, 1945. The first directive stated: "Land reform must liquidate the feudal Junker large estates and bring an end to Junker and large estate owner rule in the villages which has always been a bastion of reaction and fascism in our land and a main source of aggression and wars of conquest against other peoples."[25] Identical directives for the other four states were complete by September 10, 1945, calling for expropriation without compensation of all farms over 100 hectares. The bloc parties (Christian Democrats, Social Democrats, and Liberals) issued a joint declaration of support on September 13, 1945, reflecting land reform's broad-based appeal. Only the Liberal Party chairman, Waldemar Koch, and the conservative (CDU) leaders Andreas Hermes and Walther Schreiber, criticized the failure to compensate landowners or warned of looming collectivization.[26] Ulbricht quickly dismissed them from their leadership positions, recalling later, "The workers struck them down and they had to flee to the power regime of monopoly capital and estate owners [West Germany]."[27] Hermes was a "fascist" because of his criticism of land reform's brutality; yet the Nazis had condemned Hermes to death for his role as a member of the Karl Goerdeler (1884–1945) circle in the July 20th plot against Hitler. Only the end of the war had spared Hermes from execution.

Soviet propaganda claimed land would be seized only from Nazis and war criminals, or from Junkers and absentee landlords. Yet war criminals and Nazis only owned 4.3 percent of all farm and forestland in eastern Germany. Expropriation, as an East German forest historian noted in the 1970s, had "very little to do with who was a Nazi and who was not."[28] A senior land reform official in Thuringia reported; "The only way to escape being labeled as a war criminal or Nazi is to have been in a concentration camp or a Hitler prison—those who protest against the madness, in today's food crisis, of experimentation with soil and land are arrested."[29] Political enemies—Social Democrats, Christian youth leaders, conservatives, and apolitical forest scientists and agronomists—were labeled Nazis if they tried to keep the land reform democratic and focused on strengthening the rural economy rather than on advancing the Communist Party's political interests.

If Nazis and war criminals were not land reform's targets, then neither were the farm and forest owners of the eastern German squirearchy, the totemic Junkers. Yet Junkers made up less than 30 percent of land reform victims, and farms and forests in the Soviet zone were very different in size and character from the large, often near-bankrupt estates of East Prussia lost to Poland and the Soviet Union behind the Oder-Neiße line. Despite the rhetoric, 90 percent of expropriated farms were less than 500 hectares, a moderate size given northern German ecological conditions.[30] The average farm expropriated was 200 hectares, an efficient size given the region's dry, sandy soils—hardly the mammoth estates ruled by autocratic, absentee landlords pilloried in the Soviet-zone press. Only 66 farms in the Soviet zone were larger than 1,000 hectares.[31] There were, in fact, few Junkers in the Soviet zone after Soviet ethnic cleansing and seizure of the core of Prussia; Stalin had already broken Junker power months before land reform, taking 2.4 million hectares of farmland and forestland east of the Oder-Neiße line—11,000 estates over 100 hectares—months before the Soviet land reform. "Junker land into Soviet and Polish hands!" was a more accurate slogan than "Junker land into peasants' hands!"

The Land Reform Commission's regulations and procedures promised "the most democratic principles." Land reform victims, even though their farms and forest were seized without payment, would be treated fairly and humanely.[32] Yet land reform "functionaries" arbitrarily drove families off their land and out of their homes, underscoring the "class antagonism" Marxist-Leninists felt for farm and forest owners.[33] Popular opposition surged as Red Army soldiers brutalized the rural population and Communist Party functionaries flouted land reform regulations. Evictions, as Naimark commented, "were not infrequently accompanied by rampages by Soviet soldiers, first when they entered the local agricultural regions in April and May 1945, then again in September 1945 when the Soviets took the initiative—along with German authorities—in carrying out far-reaching land reforms."[34] This meant terrorizing and imprisoning landowners who defended their farms and forest —and the liquidation of traditional ecological and social structures in the countryside.

High-ranking land reform administrators and local Communists joined with officials from village to state level to protest land reform's brutality, some resigning in frustration.[35] The Soviets arrested the most effective protesters, such as Thuringia's vice president, Max Kolter, condemned them to former Nazi concentration camps, or murdered them. Anton Hilbert, an idealistic socialist who came from western Germany to support agrarian reform in the Soviet zone, witnessed crimes similar to the Nazis' Krystallnacht pogrom against German Jews in November 1938, "so that one could almost believe they were conceived in the same brain."[36] Hans Schlange-Schöningen, the former commissioner for Eastern relief (the *Osthilfe*) and chief of British-zone farm and forest administration, visited Hilbert in Thuringia in May 1946 to observe Soviet land reform first hand. He wrote: "A new style of Nazi power rules in communist clothing. It's not a question of land reform but liquidation of the intelligentsia, just as in Russia. In two years' time, today's Russian-zone showcase will be a land of absolute hunger." Indeed, soon after land reform, the Soviet-zone population did soon suffer near starvation.[37]

Land reform expropriations moved quickly. By the end of November 1945, the Soviets had expropriated without compensation over one-third of the Soviet zone's agricultural and forestland, 3.3 million hectares.[38] The party leadership kept over 1 million hectares as *Volkseigenengüter,* or "the people's own estates," distributing the balance to farm workers, industrial workers, refugees, "land-poor peasants," tenant farmers, and unemployed urban workers to make a new class loyal to the party. When the foreign ministers of the Four Powers met on April 14, 1947, to discuss joint land reform policy, the Western Allies found to their dismay that the Soviet-zone land reform was already a year and a half old and irreversible.[39]

Traditional land reform might have made sense, if only to absorb refugees fleeing Stalin's ethnic cleansing, or for equity, or to rationalize food production at a time of spiraling food shortages and surging populations of refugees and displaced persons. Yet Soviet land reform, as anticipated, crippled food production. The near-famine conditions following land reform hit western Germany as hard as they did the Soviet zone. In Stalin's plan to dominate postwar Europe, no branch of German society was as critical to win over as the traditionally hostile rural landscape, the power base of Marxism-Leninism's archetypal foes: the large landowner and backward peasant. Fritz Lange, a member of the German Communist Party Control Commission, recalled: "Land reform for us was above all a political problem, the need to destroy the

201

strongest underpinnings of reaction: the estates and the manors."[40] The Soviets would never "secure the fruits of victory," a German frontier pushed 525 miles west of the Soviet Union's 1938 borders and hegemony in central Europe, until they liquidated the Junker bogeyman and replaced him with a rural proletariat loyal to the party and the working class.

The party's emphasis on political goals deeply disappointed the idealistic young socialist Anton Hilbert, who was drawn to Thuringia by the promise of agrarian reform: "Are we not conscious that the elimination of larger farms must eventually be reversed through imposition of pure socialist economic forms? Land reform's rationale is purely political and has nothing to do with factual arguments."[41] The party's political goal was control of the hostile countryside and collectivization, voluntarily if possible. Get the administrative forms and ownership correct, the orthodox Marxist-Leninist cadres were thinking, and success would follow. Ultimate collectivization was never in doubt, for ideological as well as political reasons.

Land reform was the perfect strategy to expand party membership beyond its traditional urban base into the countryside.[42] It recalled traditional themes of German political life and would "anchor" small farmers, Lenin's favored class, to the party.[43] The party allowed in its first, rare, free election to win popular support through calling upon land reform's broad-based appeal. Voters chose 52,000 delegates to the Land Reform Commission to oversee land reform legislation and protect citizens' rights.[44] Over half the delegates were independents: land reform's "target," in Ulbricht's words, for conversion to communism.[45] This strategy worked well at first; following land reform, party membership in rural Mecklenburg soared from 3,200 in July 1945, about as many as before the war, to 19,500 in October 1945, three months after Pieck announced the land reform at a Peasants' Assembly. Party membership swelled to 32,000 by August 1946 despite the near-famine conditions land reform had created. Pieck, East Germany's first president, commented: "I want to emphasize that land reform created a great number of supporters in the villages, 300,000 to 400,000 people. The Soviet Occupying Power and the Party of the Working Class gave German peasants their land, a good preparation for the alliance of workers and peasants [the Bündnisdoktrin]. It's also good for German-Soviet friendship, since 300,000 to 400,000 of our supporters got their farm land from us."[46] In a later telephone conversation with the Russian adviser to the Soviet commander in chief, Pieck noted land reform's importance to "neutralizing the bourgeois parties" and asked the Soviets to hurry up the division of the forest to shore up peasant loyalty to the Soviet Union and the Communist Party.[47] The party leadership, except perhaps Ackermann, had moved beyond their early concern for the people's welfare to appreciate how land reform's chaos and shortages hobbled western Germany by halting normal food shipments to western Germany and shored up their own precarious political power.[48]

The Soviets and German land reform functionaries doled out small allotments averaging 7 to 8 hectares, which were too small for survival on the light soils of the North German Plain—in the words of a new peasant, "too large to die on and too small to live on."[49] Newly enfranchised owners were expected to join socialist cooperatives once, inevitably, the impossibility of independent management on their pitifully small allotments became clear to them.[50] New peasants paid roughly 200–290 marks per hectare for their land ($430 in current value), based on the price of one to 1.5 tons of rye, or one year's harvest.[51] Later East German historians qualified this price as a recovery of overhead and transfer costs: to legitimize final forced collectivization in April 1960 (the "Socialist Spring in the Countryside") and to defend against potential future claims to actual ownership. Title and property rights were murky. The new land reform farms were classified as personal property and inheritable. Yet the farms were classified as "work property" and could not be sold, leased, mortgaged, or pledged as security. The only transfer permitted, apart from inheritance, was a return to the land account, the *Bodenfonds*.[52] The new peasants' farms and forest had neither the quality of a capital asset nor of personal property. But nor were they yet the people's property, *Volkseigenengüter.* Collectivization *loomed* to correct this. In the meantime, farms—and particularly the forest—were thrown into a punishing commons.

Most new peasants got only bare land without barns, tractors, and machinery, much less seed, fertilizer, fuel, or loans for spring planting. Only 16,000 of the 209,000 new peasants got houses, and only 58,000 had even primitive living quarters; the rest suffered in unheated stables and outbuildings.[53] The new peasants were not only inexperienced but often strangers in their districts resented by old farmers. "New peasants," worried Schwerin's vice president, were "cast into an hostile social environment without any economic foundation."[54] Older experienced farmers, who normally helped their neighbors, shunned the new peasants whose very presence cast the aroma of expropriation. From the first postwar days, Norman Naimark commented, "collectivization was on everyone's mind."[55] Any farm expropriation naturally worried farmers, as did the party's class warfare rhetoric and demonizing of modest farmers as "kulaks." Land reform had already deeply disturbed the balance of the Soviet zone's rural communities. New and old farmers alike read *Kolkhoz,* socialist farm collective, in the chaos.

As agricultural and forest experts predicted, farm production crashed with the fall 1945 harvest. Farmers brought in the 1945 harvest short and with great difficulty. Grain and sugar beet yields plummeted 30 percent, and potato production slid 22 percent in 1946, the first full year after land reform.[56] Within a year of land reform, the Soviet-zone population suffered from near famine. The damage endured; East Germany was the only European country still rationing food in 1954, even though the population had fallen markedly since 1945.[57] Food shortages and episodic rationing lasted until May 1958, and meat and butter rationing returned in 1961. This region, which once had a food surplus, was forced to import potatoes and sugar beets from Poland in the 1960s, much to Soviet premier Nikita Khrushchev's chagrin.[58] Even so, East Germany's constant regime of fixed prices, central control over the food supply, and persistent shortages were food rationing in all but name. The East German people were never truly free of rationing until the Berlin Wall fell in November 1989.

Work on land reform plots stalled as new peasants and farmers shunned the socialist collectives, streaming into traditional forest cooperatives or quitting their farms and fleeing west, a harbinger of the population flight, the *Republikflucht,* which would drain the East German Republic, threaten the state's collapse, and lead to building of the Berlin Wall in August 1961.[59] With collectivization always on their minds, few farmers either bothered or knew enough to prepare their fields for winter sowings of oil seed or winter wheat.[60] There were no fall cover crops to enrich the soil, and there would be no spring harvest. Worse lay in store, as Soviet soldiers spread throughout the countryside; free of Western observation, they requisitioned food, seized equipment, and drove off the few surviving farm animals.[61] Reparations withdrawals and requisitions for support of Soviet troops independent of land reform made the hunger crisis far worse in all four zones.

Farm and forest owners fled headlong to the West in reaction to Soviet control and harassment. By mid-1947, 1,166 new peasants in Brandenburg had abandoned their farms and forest. Two and a half years later, more than 22 percent of land reform farmers had fled to western Germany to escape the inflexible delivery quotas and their heavy debt to the state.[62] By 1950, the state had taken back 20 percent of the new farms. A further 30 percent of all land reform recipients, 60,000 farmers, abandoned their farms by March 1952.[63] Fear of collectivization and "a fundamental distrust of the party" drove abandonment, as a secret internal report advised the East German State Planning Commission in 1958.[64]

As new peasants fled their meager plots, communist farm administrators by mid-1946 began commandeering established farmers' carefully husbanded seed, fertilizer, and fuel, and expropriating draft animals, plows, and harrows, to give to the new peasants and halt their headlong flight to the Western Allies' zones.[65] Such seizures penalized the most efficient and experienced farmers at the expense of the Soviet zone's food supply. Yet, despite pressure to collectivize, reparations withdrawals, and party requisitions of their assets and labor, old farmers and traditional cooperatives thrived even as the socialist collectives struggled. This political embarrassment quickened the communists' resolve to push forward collectivization, yet they reluctantly abandoned Stalin's "parliamentary road to socialism." In late 1947, the Social Democratic Party's news service reported: "Now that the land reform project is widely acknowledged as collapsed, old established farmers must ever more follow the same path as new peasants—*Kolchoz*! [socialist collective]. That's the prospect for farmers" (emphasis in original).[66] Memories of Stalin's forced collectivization between 1929 and 1933, and the murder of millions of Ukrainian peasants, must have heightened eastern German farmers' anxiety; every successful independent farmer in the Soviet zone had to fear that someday the Communist Party might brand him or her as kulak or Junker, no matter how modest their farm or birth.

Food shortages brought land reform's discontent from the countryside to the city. As Carl J. Friedrich and Henry Kissinger observed, "Perhaps no single other factor contributed so much to the Soviet-zone population's discontent with the régime as this failure to provide adequate food."[67] The party leadership fed East Berlin during the Berlin Crisis of 1948–49 only by requisitioning food from the countryside, reducing even the rich Magdeburg Börde farm region with its fertile loess soils to hard rationing and bread shortages.[68] A British correspondent reported: "The raiding and robbing of the fields for food is a regular occurrence. Some of the resources of the district are being directed to maintaining the supplies the Russians are sending to Berlin. Resentment is rising. It expressed itself at the weekend in a strike of the workers of the Schäffers and Budenberg machine works as a protest against the lack of meat and fats. Thirty arrests are stated to have been made. The Russians are searching the baggage of all travelers to Berlin and confiscating food and other goods."[69]

The Soviet zone's farm economy fell into a wasteland after the first, meager postwar harvest of 1945–46. People living in this once-productive farmland now faced near starvation.[70] At first, Western observers did not see the significance of the Soviet destruction of eastern German farm and forest communities, perhaps blinded by the twin shibboleths of the "Junker" and "Prussia." American correspondents touring the Soviet-zone countryside in late 1945 under the close scrutiny of Soviet chaperones witnessed "much doubt and complaint," although the new peasants they saw did seem content.[71] But this contentment did not survive the first harvest year, and Marxism-Leninism did not catch on in the countryside. British and American journals suddenly filled in mid-1947 with stories of food riots in the Soviet zone; of arrests of farmers and young men and women, usually leaders of socialist and conservative political and Christian youth groups; of police dogs driving gleaners from early-winter stubble fields; and of guards shooting children scavenging for fuel for their families' stoves in rail yard coalbunkers. By the end of the first postwar winter of hardship, shortages, and Soviet reparations, most farmers, both new and old, were increasingly critical of the Communist Party.[72] Only the most active party cadres and followers felt loyalty to the party—probably not more than 10 percent of the total population.[73] The strategy of using land reform to win the rural population over to the party might have worked if the new farms had been supported, and if the new peasants had, in fact, owned the farms.

As with reparations, land reform's effect on the forested landscape was disproportionately harsher than on the farm landscape. The party had seized all former Reich forests even before land reform, taking 1.6 million hectares of the best-quality and best-stocked forestland by September 1945.[74] Soviet land reform expropriations then brought a further 1 million hectares of forest, bringing a third of all forestland under the party's control. The party leadership distributed to new peasants less than half the forest expropriated in average parcels of 1 hectare, an even more unsustainable structure than farmland, holding onto more forest proportionally than they did of farmland. Paradoxically (for a land reform program), this cut private forest ownership from 45 to 32 percent.[75] The party controlled over two-thirds of the Soviet zone's forest by April 1946, while farm ownership remained perched between the commons and the collective. This control was essential to deliver the almost limitless volumes of wood required for Soviet timber reparations quotas, demands constrained only by the capacity of forced labor and impressed peasants to cut and haul the unprecedented volumes harvested.

Kurt Mantel, a leading West German forest historian and policy scholar, warned of the historical dangers of land reform for forestry: destruction of forest structure, irretrievable loss of forest, and abandonment.[76] Forest destruction followed the *Osthilfe* land reforms of the early-1930s, when a district forester warned that "the many different forms of forest ownership must be preserved, principally forms of private ownership, and all available resources and planning must be directed to prevent partitioning of forests."[77] A Soviet-zone land reform administrator also cited land reform's threat to forestry: "Of particular importance, forests must be removed from expropriation. Divided peasant forests have always been the problem child of rational forest economics, and forests also have broader ecological functions which small forest management harms. Peasants came together in the previous centuries in private forest cooperatives in recognition that small peasant forest holdings can't be managed correctly." The private forest cooperatives traditional in Germany, however, competed with the Communist Party's own socialist collectives, and competed too well, drawing in many new peasants and smaller farmers as the socialist collectives languished.

Central European foresters and ecologists generally recognize 100 hectares as the absolute lower boundary for forest management—the Soviets created small land reform forest allotments of one to 1.5 hectares intentionally, to force farmers, who typically held much of the private forest as a complement to their farm fields, into socialist collectives.[78] The authors of the authoritative Social Democratic survey of Soviet-zone forest management reported: "None of the small farmers could have survived on the small parcels [of forest] they were given."[79] Hans Lemmel, the successor to Alfred Möller (the most influential forest ecologist of the twentieth century and founder of the *Dauerwald,* "permanent forest," school of silviculture) at the Forest Research Institute at Eberswalde, forecast land reform's failure and ultimate collectivization: "It remains to be seen how long the artificial, mostly too small, capital poor and especially extremely poorly equipped new landowners can survive or the consequences the reform will have for the people's food supply."[80] New forest owners were typically inexperienced. They stripped their allotments of valuable timber, leaving only worthless trees and inferior phenotypes behind after destructive waves of high grading: razing and then abandoning their forestland. They fell upon the forest for fuel, food, and cash, prodded by their insecure sense of ownership, shortages, and hunger following land reform.

The party campaigned from the start to force farmers into socialist collectives.[81] Yet land reform began as a fiction of popular will. Indeed, all properties of private farmland and forestland over 100 hectares in size were seized and partially distributed to "land-poor peasants," refugees, and the unemployed. The party's strategy followed Stalin's "parliamentary road to democracy": to allow a brief period during which new peasants would first learn loyalty to the party, then realize that they could not survive on their own without the party's help, and finally, voluntarily, enter socialist collectives and mutate into Marxism-Leninism's iconic workers. Social Democratic forest scientists concluded: "The granting of land reform forests deceived the peasants into believing that the party would support the new peasants." Propaganda promised technical training to overcome the "backwardness of peasant life" through education "in the greatest school of all, the socialist collective," while the party leadership withheld extension help and credit to steer farmers into the socialist collectives.[82] Yet the party forbade foresters to instruct the peasants in management, just as Soviet "experts" set over German foresters forbade foresters to stop peasant destruction of forests for firewood, or cutting wood to sell in the thriving black market along the East-West zonal borders.[83]

Angry at the new peasants' refusal to accept voluntary collectivization, the party leadership intensified its struggle against "enemy elements sabotaging land reform." In a five-hour speech to senior party cadres on April 14, 1948, Ulbricht, the Soviet-zone party boss, demanded that farm production increase to "industrial levels," foreshadowing the Industrial Production Methods of the 1970s and 1980s and the remaking of farm and forest as "factories on the land."[84] At the September 1948 Party Conference, Ulbricht introduced his "New Course," demanding intensified "class warfare tactics" in the country-side and faster collectivization of private farm and forestland while ominously branding reluctant farmers as "rich peasants and kulaks."[85]

The party raised the delivery quotas of larger farmers even above those set for comparable farmers in Russia to drive them into socialist collectives languishing from the lack of experienced farmers.[86] These quotas meant to break farmers holding more than 20 hectares, particularly farmers holding between 50 and 100 hectares, who were suddenly anathematized as *Großbauern*" or kulaks. Delivery failures against the harsh quotas meant losing one's land or arrest and being sentenced to prison.[87] Because the party could not distinguish between "saboteurs and profiteers" and honest farmers, the party punished uniformly for short deliveries.[88] Fear of collectivization, arrest, and the concentration camps led farmers to advertise in newspapers for seed and produce to fill their quotas.[89] And it fueled desertion and flight to the west, deepening the historic population deficit east of the Elbe River and ultimately threatening the survival of the East German state.

The party also reversed forest enclosure, reopening the forest to livestock grazing, fallen wood gathering, and litter raking, artifacts of the medieval low forest and a major cause of forest decline.[90] The withdrawal of forest guards made the effects of the illegal cutting for firewood, poaching, and grazing of livestock even worse.[91] Thus no one could expect peasants to follow sound management practices. Dire need drove refugees, new peasants, and small farmers to exploit their forests to survive.[92] Once land reform smashed apart the large forest management units, the small, isolated allotments degenerated into an unregulated commons, which the new owners despoiled. Peasants and farmers also reasonably feared imminent collectivization, so they took their value while they could.[93] As a result, most of the forestland doled out in the Soviet land reform was under "socialist management," either in state forests or in socialist collectives by 1949, or high graded by new peasant owners with Soviet encouragement.[94]

Consequences and Later Developments

Land reform created a socialist tabula rasa in the countryside. As the Soviets expropriated farm and forest, they systematically destroyed property registers, maps, and estate records, liquidating the institutional memory of traditional rural society under a decree "providing for the complete destruction of all records of previous land ownership."[95] The editors of *Neues Deutschland,* the party's official organ, reported in August 1946: "Old land registers, titles deeds, and other documents of those large Junker estates that land reform divided up were recently destroyed as the last evidence of the power of the old feudal overlords. The unencumbered transfer of the large Junker estates to new peasants has now ushered in a new age."[96] As surveyors ran transects for the new, fractured farm and forest landscape, they obliterated existing boundary markers, cultural symbols that had sparked the German conservation movement a century before. Tractors tore apart hedgerows dividing ancient fields while axes felled allées of pleached linden and poplar trees. The destruction of legal and cultural records made land reform irreversible in the event of German reunification, which many assumed was imminent; it also cleared the landscape for simple, flat social and ecological structures that conformed to Marxist-Leninist precepts.

The Soviets destroyed architecture, landscape, and memorials to liquidate memory, custom, and culture. They leveled more than 10,000 old manor houses, barns, and stables in 1947 as "symbols of a feudal age."[97] The party forbade new peasants to share management within traditional cooperatives, or to join cooperatively on the foundations of the former estate, perhaps with the former owner as manager. The party leadership ruled: "Any attempt at collective or communal management is sabotage of land reform!"[98] Not only the physical structure of traditional architecture was abhorrent to the Soviet and German communists, but the idea of traditional cooperatives competing with socialist collectives—competing all too successfully—was more than infuriating; it was "sabotage."

And they were right. The party leadership could not permit the form of the old estates to survive, nor could they allow the rhythms and patterns of the old landscape and communities to endure. The traditional cooperatives in which many smaller farmers sought shelter not only subverted Lenin's Bündnispolitik but also looked suspiciously like old wine in new bottles. So a thriving Thuringian cooperative was told abruptly in the spring of 1946 so that its members would get no seed, a stratagem to force them into the socialist collectives.[99] The Communists would not allow any challenge to their political power or permit the cooperatives' success to thwart the destruction of their class enemies. Land reform's goal was the reordering of rural communities—

people, economy, and ecosystems—to fit Marxist-Leninist norms, not efficiency or equity.

Human rights abuses infused the Soviet and German Communist campaign to impose collectivization through intimidation and denial. The party branded farmers who resisted collectivization as "reactionary peasants," enemies of progress hobbled by a feudal attachment to "non-democratic, old production relations."[100] In the fall of 1945, a Soviet judge sent a new peasant and party member charged with "sabotage of land reform" to three years' imprisonment in a former Nazi concentration camp.[101] Special Soviet courts condemned seventeen- and eighteen-year-old sons of recalcitrant farmers to forced labor camps in the Soviet Union or to concentration camps for "political reeducation," often on the pretext that the boys were former Hitler Youth.[102]

The Berlin newspaper *Telegraf* reported the party's harassment of farmers in Kreis Niederbarnim who had petitioned local administrators to stop the conscription for forced labor, most often to harvest timber to fill Soviet reparations quotas: "A young man, known in the district as a good communist, told the Party officials boldly, 'I'll decide who comes on my land [*auf meinem Grund und Boden*].' The mayor retorted, '*Mein Lieber,* you [using the intimate, and in this context condescending, "*du*" form] are only a *Kolchose*. We decide what you must do and what is permitted. You have your fields to farm, and you will plant and harvest what we tell you to."[103] Ownership may have been murky in September 1945, but by 1946 the conundrum was resolved: the party countryside.

Edwin Hörnle, the first head of the Soviet zone's Department of Agriculture and Forestry and president of the German Central Organization for Agriculture and Forestry, made a secret report to the Soviet military government at the end of 1946 on land reform problems. He cited pervasive crisis: the failure to plan systematically for settlement and support of new farmers, the small, non-sustainable size of land reform farms, and the "incorrect" partitioning of forest-land. As he reported, Red Army and Communist Party functionaries ignored the land reform statutes and regulations, laws mandating that the democratically elected Land Reform Commission oversee land reform, the impartial division of expropriated farm inventories and equipment, and humane treatment and fair notification to expropriated farmers. Land reform functionaries also regularly seized farms under the official low water mark of 100 hectares, one of a long list of charges.[104] Soviet officials did not dispute Hörnle's grim record. They instead ordered an immediate halt to further discussion, warning Hörnle to silence and forbidding public discussion.

British and American early occupation and food policies had destructive consequences hardly distinguishable from the Soviet land reform. Western

Germans also suffered near famine and disease worse than in the notorious years after World War I—due not only to the Soviet denial of the food promised at Potsdam in return for reparations but also to the constraints imposed by U.S. policy directive JCS 1067.[105] This directive's authors sought to support farm production while limiting Germany to tractor and fertilizer production levels below 1932 and forbidding farm machinery, seed, or fertilizer imports. Nor could Germany export surpluses, all to reduce Germany to its post—Versailles Treaty, relatively primitive, condition, and its people to a grim, "middle-European" standard of living—"pastoralizing" the German economy.[106] Early postwar U.S. policymakers wanted to drive the western Germans back almost to the Pleistocene Era, while, in contrast, Soviet land reform was radically materialistic, designed to recreate farms and forest as "factories on the land." Yet the result of Soviet and U.S. policies were the same: near starvation. However, the U.S. authors of JCS 1067 anticipated that imports of surplus Soviet-zone food would support civilians in the American zone in exchange for Soviet reparations withdrawals from western Germany. So the Americans' shortsighted policies seem more misguided than malevolent (figure 8.2).

The radical and destructive qualities of Soviet land reform and the Soviet persecution of farmers, together with the near collapse of the western German food supply with the halt of normal shipments from the Soviet zone to the west, posed a direct threat to Allied interests and alerted Western policymakers to the looming Soviet threat to their security. Faced with growing U.S. popular concern at the suffering in Germany and the growing threat from a Soviet Union eager to take advantage of the crisis in the British and American zones, President Harry Truman sent seventy-three-year-old former president Herbert Hoover to survey Europe's food needs and report on the emerging humanitarian catastrophe in the Western zones in the wake of JCS 1067 and Soviet pressure. Hoover was a brilliant choice: a man of exceptional integrity, competence, and experience in international relief work as head of the Committee for Relief in Belgium after World War I and of the American Relief Administration (1921–23), where he organized relief for Europe and the Soviet Union with equal success. General Lucius Clay—who effectively ran the U.S. zone as General Dwight D. Eisenhower's deputy military governor until he assumed the full title and command of U.S. forces in Europe on March 15, 1947—recalled Hoover's pivotal role: "Hoover came back with the recommendations that we supply food for Western Europe, including West Germany, and Mr. Truman backed him completely. If it hadn't been for this, we would have had mass starvation."[107] And conditions were ripe for a Soviet advance into Western Europe.

Hoover reported in February 1947 that German conditions were "the worst

Figure 8.2. Allied Occupation Zones, 1945

modern civilization has seen, the [people living at the] lowest level known in a 100 years of human history."[108] The western German population was near starvation, and its disease and mortality data were below levels in the developing world. The German people despaired, and many British and American policymakers saw that the chaos and near famine in their zones fueled Soviet propaganda and demands for central planning: a direct Soviet role in the western German economy and polities. Hoover carried the core of the Republican Party with him in his campaign for massive American aid to halt the deepening humanitarian crisis in western Germany, paving the way for bipartisan aid and for Secretary of State George C. Marshall's call for U.S. support for European reconstruction, including for Germany, in his Marshall Plan address at Harvard University on June 5, 1947.[109]

Yet despite land reform's direct contribution to hunger in the West, Communist propagandists used the example of Soviet-zone land reform to court Western opinion and attack the British and Americans. When the British military government was forced to reduce rations in July 1946 (a consequence of Soviet stoppages of food shipments to the West), the Communist Party press attacked the British as "*Volksfremde*" ("enemies of the people"), asserting that the "starvation of the Germans is a deliberate Anglo-American policy."[110] Western administrators and politicians, meanwhile, struggled to sustain near-starvation diets in their zones without the resources that should have flowed from surplus food production in the Soviet zone or been paid for by German exports. The editors of *Neues Deutschland* stated late in 1946 that only through Soviet-style land reform and "socialist production relations" could the Western population be fed: "The hunger crisis in the West is due principally to the fact that, with the exception of the German Communist Party, western German parties, politicians and bureaucrats have failed to demand the thoroughgoing measures [Soviet land reform] we have here in the East. The Western press admits that the care of the peoples' daily bread remains in the hands of the bourgeoisie—more precisely said, in the hands of Junkers, corrupt markets, Nazi farm administrators, and reactionary bureaucrats. The security of the workers' daily bread is in the first instance a *political* question" (emphasis in original).[111] The Soviets could not permit a unified Germany within its 1937 borders as long as independent farm and forestland persisted in the Western zones; they demanded an ecological and economic revolution in the western German countryside matching the destruction in the Soviet zone—and the liquidation of the Communist Party's political enemies in the western German countryside. Furthermore, Germany would recover the Oder-Neiße territories only "when in all Germany, West and East, internal political conditions are unmistakably democratic, antifascist, and anti-chauvinist"—that is, when Germany was unified under Soviet control.[112]

One of the "reactionary bureaucrats" whom Soviet propaganda targeted was Hans Schlange-Schöningen (1886–1960), former commissioner for the *Osthilfe* in the late Weimar era. The Nazis had attacked him as an "agrarian Bolshevist" for breaking up bankrupt large estates and distributing land to poor farmers and the urban unemployed; radical conservative and Nazi opposition to the *Osthilfe* had sparked the fall of the Heinrich Brüning government, the last democratically elected government before Hitler.[113] Schlange-Schöningen survived the war and Nazi prisons to become a key farm reformer and critic of Soviet-zone land reform, aided by his impeccable anti-Nazi credentials. His appeal to the people of the Soviet zone and his demand for an independent, mixed farm economy in the Soviet zone threatened the party's legitimacy. So *Neues Deutschland*'s editors attacked him with broadsides such as "Schlange-Schöningen Must Go!" deploying rhetoric similar to the Nazis' and militarists'. No longer an "agrarian Bolshevist," Schlange-Schöningen now emerged in the Soviet-zone press as an "agrarian-monopolist."[114]

Soviet reparations, although naked in their purpose and lacking the democratic aura that land reform enjoyed at first, worked in concert with land reform to smash rural social, political, and ecological structures. Farm reparations were as onerous as industrial reparations. Yet, as in land reform, the Communist Party singled out the forest landscape for disproportionate damage. Part of this is due to timber's near-cash, hard currency status in a global market particularly short in forest products. The most damaging form of reparations is cash reparations, a lesson learned from the Versailles Treaty; timber reparations were undoubtedly the most lucrative reparations the Soviets seized, as well as most damaging to the forest.

The Allies agreed at Potsdam to consider Soviet reparations demands of $10 billion ($100 billion in 2002 terms), allocating fixed, noncash assets from each zone. But the Potsdam limits to reparations, never formally ratified, were irrelevant to Soviet withdrawals, which were "as severe as could be devised and tolerated" and more than gross investment in the economy between 1945 and 1954.[115] The British and Americans recalled the disastrous consequences of the Versailles Treaty's cash reparations of 132 billion gold marks ($34 billion in 1947 value) and insisted that reparations be limited to fixed assets and made "short and sharp." Although the three principal Allies (Russia, Britain, and the United States) agreed at Yalta to bring Germany down to a "middle-European standard for some time," echoing the Morgenthau Plan and the goals of JCS 1067, the Americans and British argued that the Allies could not risk the political chaos that followed Versailles' punitive cash reparations.[116]

The Western Allies feared that cash reparations, such as timber reparations (the form Molotov and Stalin favored) not only would slow global economic recovery by suffocating the German economy but would also create suffering and economic hardship that could only favor the Communists. The Soviets ignored British and American cautions and Potsdam's limits, as they did with the Potsdam agreements about coordinating land reform and forest management. The Soviets did not see a difference between cash and fixed asset reparations, except that cash reparations were far more valuable and efficient than shipping German plants and factories to the Soviet Union—much better to take the goods, not the plant and equipment.[117] And the chaos that followed in the trail of the Red Army reparations teams roving across western Germany could only advance Soviet political influence and popular demand for central planning.

Cash reparations, also known as "reparations from current production," were the Soviets' preferred form of reparations. Most of the fixed asset reparations taken—factories, machinery and machine tools, locomotives and tractors, railroad rails—were often wasted, abandoned to rust in vast yards along the Urals. The Soviets also took many thousands of German civilians to the Gulag after the war, as well as holding onto at least 890,000 former German prisoners of war in Soviet forced labor camps, a portion of the 2 to 3 million German prisoners of war who were unaccounted for in May 1945—slavery in all but name, but also a vicious form of cash reparations.[118] Yet no material form of cash reparations was as valuable to the Soviets as German timber, sold into a surging global market of rising prices and accounted for in low, 1939 fixed-mark prices. And, best of all, buyers (mostly British merchants) paid in U.S. dollars, as agreed at Potsdam. Forest reparations combined the worst features of fixed asset and cash reparations, stripping production out of the local economy without payment and slashing capital asset values, because timber is both real property as well as a critical raw material.[119]

The Soviet focus on reparations withdrawals, and their indifference to hunger in their zone, puzzled Western leaders. The London *Times*'s Berlin correspondent marveled at the central role reparations played in Soviet policy and the opportunism that harmed Soviet long-term strategic interests: "The only discernable policy of the Soviet occupation—namely, that the Russian zone should be exploited for Russia's benefit, regardless of German interests and of what on a longer view might have seemed to be Russian interests also—has been carried farther than had been thought probable or profitable."[120] Bruno Gleitze also marked the opportunism in Soviet policy: "Any policy seemed correct (to the Soviets) as long as it revived the German economy and made possible the withdrawal of reparations."[121] Stalin designed reparations to compensate the Soviet Union for its grievous war losses, to pay for reconstruction in the Soviet Union, and to reduce Germany's "war potential," but mostly to advance Soviet power at the British and Americans' expense. Yet in the final analysis, the material benefits of reparations were swamped by the counterreaction his harsh policies sparked in his former Allies and the German people.

Timber markets, and markets all basic commodities, exploded in the postwar economic environment of released demand and shortages. The global economy until early 1948 was desperately short of everything, but particularly short of basic raw materials—food, coal, steel, and timber. Population problems and perceptions of uncontrolled population growth fueled a Malthusian gloom as demand seemed to grow faster than food production. After food, basic raw materials were in greatest demand. Timber was next to brown coal and scrap metal in importance, and the Soviets "took everything from the forest that could be turned into hard currency or other value" to sell on international markets, mostly in the West.[122] Europe desperately needed pit props to rebuild coal mines and railroad ties ("sleepers") to mend the broken rail lines.[123] The economy needed timbers, planks, and beams to rebuild bridges, workshops, farmsteads, and homes. Pressure on the forests was far heavier in the postwar years than it ever had been under the Nazis, but particularly in the French and Soviet zones, where reparations withdrawals were most severe.

Reparations demands crowded out all other tasks in the countryside. Red Army teams spread out, taking food for support of Soviet troops or for shipment to the Soviet Union along with anything of value that could be moved: machinery, tractors, livestock, and farmers' personal possessions, as well as timber. Soviet requisitions of farm livestock cut the Soviet-zone horse and cattle population between 65 and 70 percent. Sheep counts fell 40 percent and pigs 20 percent, and only because they were not as easily driven as cattle and horses.[124] Soviet reparations officers impressed farmers to cut timber for reparations, taking them from providing food for the increasingly famished population. Hörnle complained, "The worst aspect of the shortage of work horses is that all horses are completely overworked skidding wood."[125] Timber reparations, and the massive task of cutting and hauling the unprecedented volumes needed to fill Soviet reparations quotas, consumed most of the available sources of rural labor, material, and planning. Soviet military officials were so nervous about short deliveries that they overharvested to ensure the complete fulfillment of their quotas. They even delivered high-quality veneer logs to fill low-grade timber reparations quotas rather than fail to meet their targets.[126] Between 1947 and 1952, the Soviets even broke down German houses, taking more than 3 million cubic meters of first-quality timber.[127]

Red Army officers charged with filling timber expropriations were in no doubt as to Soviet priorities. When timber reparations deliveries faltered in the first six months of 1948, the Soviet military administration issued an edict holding key Soviet officers personally responsible. Reparations, the edict declared, had the "top priority" of all Soviet policy in Germany. Timber reparations yielded the maximum cash value of all withdrawals, and the Soviets would not be denied.[128]

The Soviets cut down over thirteen years of growth as reparations in the four years between 1945 and 1949, and they continued their withdrawals until reparations formally ended in 1954.[129] An East German forester in 1965 looked back on the waste and damage, describing Soviet harvests as "reaching shocking dimensions."[130] Although industrial reparations claimed more than 25 percent of total eastern German production, timber reparations took almost 100 percent of the eastern German postwar harvest—most of the 44 million cubic meters officially harvested between 1945 and 1953.[131] And these harvests came from forest muscle and sinew—its best-quality, oldest timber and capital—destroying stand structure and forest health. The Soviets also failed to replant their clear-cuts, the most basic charge of plantation forestry, turning productive forestland into a wasteland. Never in European history has any ecosystem seen levels of destruction and purposeful waste like those that defined Soviet reparations harvests.

The Soviets kept the catastrophic results of their reparations harvests a state secret until reparations ended in 1954, another feature of Soviet policy that alienated Western opinion.[132] The Soviets banned Western observers and refused to conduct joint forest surveys or share data, as had been agreed at Potsdam.[133] They laid the cause of the ecological catastrophe revealed with the first forest inventories in the early 1950s at the feet of "fascist looting" and "capitalist production relations." Soviet reparations policy flowed from Stalin's opportunism—better to take everything possible now, before a peace treaty was signed and the opportunity lost, and to cover up the economic and ecological catastrophes that followed in its wake. As the editors of *Die Neue Zeitung* pointed out in 1949, "The eastern zone's most fearfully guarded secrets are the mortality data—only reparations come close in secrecy."[134] Gleitze marked the years of Soviet reparations from 1945 to 1954 as the "period of improvisation and covering up."[135] The Soviets ordered eastern German foresters to hide the intensity and scale of the reparations harvests and to deny plummeting growth and health data to their Western colleagues while learning as much as possible about Western forest conditions. The Soviets never published an accounting of the massive timber volumes they harvested. The perfunctory forest inventories the Soviets did supply the Allies were useless, so "primitive and incompetently manned as to be unacceptable." Social Democratic forestry experts concluded: "One glance at Soviet forest inventories and practice shows at once that everything is intentional camouflage—a wordy paper swindle."[136] However, the inherently adversarial stance of Soviet foreign policy, which underlay Soviet reparations, was as impossible to disguise as were the vast gaps in forest structure or the endless columns of rail wagons carrying timber to Baltic yards for delivery to Western buyers.

The Soviet failure to replant the vast clear-cuts was even more destructive than the years of growth they ripped out, unprecedented though these volumes were for European forestry. The area of unplanted clear-cuts in the Soviet zone almost doubled between 1945 and 1949, a staggering economic loss to the eastern German economy that persisted into the late 1960s as foresters struggled to clear the huge overhang of unplanted forest from Soviet reparations.[137] This deficit linked the destructive force of reparations with the chaos left in the wake of land reform: "Efforts to replant these clear-cuts have been so ineffective that it will take one hundred years to clear away the damage. All the Soviet zone power's policies, particularly land reform, end up with the disappearance of the forest into the machinery and schemes of the monopolistic command economy."[138] Forest stocking in 1948, a critical measure of the capital invested in standing timber, plunged 33 per cent from 1933 levels.[139] Reparations harvests claimed the older, more valuable trees, leaving many stands overlit (i.e., the most valuable trees were torn out, leaving great gaps in the canopy that let sunlight in on the forest floor) and stagnant. East Germany struggled well into the 1960s to eliminate the huge overhang of unplanted forest inherited from Soviet occupation.[140] The German people knew, viscerally, that what the Soviets were doing in the forested landscape prefigured Stalin's' design for their society: leveled diversity, flattened and reduced structures, high levels of uncertainty, and shortages.

From the British and American perspectives, land reform's and reparations' effects demonstrated equally the Soviet Union's opportunism and its disregard for its treaty obligations. General Clay recalled how the Soviet failure to ship food to the West (land reform and Soviet requisitions took care of that) scuttled the Allies' overall reparations agreements, and with it the wartime alliance and chances for a peace treaty:

> I learned that [taking a strong stand against the Soviets] from the way they were removing equipment, without any kind of accounting, from East Germany where they were in occupation, and still putting in their claims for reparations from West Germany. They were not abiding by the general rules that all of this would be done by the Reparations Commission, representing all of the countries that had suffered damage from Germany. This was the beginning of my concern. We tried very hard to get East-West trade going. The initial effort was to get a common utilization of the food sup-

plies, because East Germany was a surplus food production area. When we couldn't get any food out of East Germany, it was quite obvious that there was nothing else to divide. I mean that we would have been foolish to open up trade in the things that they wanted when we couldn't get out of them the food that we had to have. We couldn't get any willingness on their part to share in the food production of East Germany. I think this was another one of the fundamentals which led us to believe that we couldn't possibly get together.[141]

Ernest Bevin, the British foreign secretary, reported to the House of Commons on May 16, 1947, on the domestic political threat Soviet land reform and reparations posed to Western leaders:

The Prime Minister and myself never for a moment imagined that they [Soviet reparations] would involve the imposition of added taxation on the British people. The Soviet Government had taken from their own zone reparations from current production ["cash" reparations such as timber and food]. They had consistently refused to give any information about those unauthorized removals which, with removals of capital equipment and the effect of Soviet cartels of German enterprises, amounted in value to well over $7 billion. Yet at the same time the taxpayers in Britain and America had to find money to keep Germany from starvation. Since the end of the war the United Kingdom's contribution to the reestablishment of German economy had been over £200 million [$806 million; almost $6 billion in 2002 terms].[142]

Bevin later restated his anger at the Soviets' parasitical reparations policy: "We would not and could not agree to the principle of reparations from current production which involved Great Britain and the British people, and other Allies, in virtually paying reparations to another ally. (Opposition cheers.)"

The editors of the London *Times,* looking forward to the Council of Foreign Ministers' Moscow meeting in April 1947, echoed Bevin's impatience: "The Soviets scheme to use Germany as a channel through which Allied assistance would flow to her benefit."[143] Carl J. Friedrich and Henry Kissinger agreed: "At the end of the Second World War, it was the manifest desire of the Soviet Union to employ reparations from Germany as a device to siphon resources from the United States."[144] Soviet reparations' destructive force and hostility led to an early break with the Western Allies, sooner than the Soviet Union wanted.[145]

The traditional agricultural wealth and food surpluses east of the Elbe River had vanished into the chaos of land reform and Soviet reparations. Even if the Soviets had wanted to honor their Potsdam commitments to deliver food to western Germany, land reform and reparations made it impossible. Reports of forced labor camps, of the arrest of the Communists' political enemies and their imprisonment in former Nazi concentration camps, of near famine and food riots, and of the suffering of former German prisoners of war in Soviet camps, bolstered by harsh Soviet propaganda and reparations, united emerging Western opinion against the Soviets.[146]

Conclusions

Stalin's "war on the countryside" resolved a core problem for Western leaders who had to mobilize Western public opinion despite years of wartime propaganda that painted the Red Army and Soviet people as heroic, and sweetened Stalin as "Uncle Joe." General Clay reflected; "How, overnight, could we turn around and convince people that they [the Soviets] were a threat to our national security? It was a very difficult thing to do. If the Russians hadn't taken the steps they did, I don't know that we would have done it at all. If they had been more subtle they might indeed have gained Western Europe before we realized what was happening."[147] Thanks to Stalin's opportunism and indifference to the starvation of civilians in all four zones, and his near destruction of east Elbian farms and forests, Western leaders and the public grasped the imminent Soviet threat.

The recovery of global food supplies and shipping capacity in 1948 brought relief to the near-destitute peoples of the Western zones, and to the British and American taxpayers who had to make up the food deficits from the Soviet zone. The western German economy could not be rebuilt until the British and Americans merged their zones (May 29, 1947), relaxed central controls, and introduced a liberal market economy.[148] Why, however, was the German population patient until liberal economic policies, all with long lead times, bore fruit, and why did they accept intolerable conditions long after the end of the war? The answers certainly included the profound general depression and the burden of shared guilt for the Holocaust and the war, but also their fear of the Soviet danger revealed in Stalin's ethnic cleansing and theft of Germany's eastern provinces, in Soviet predatory reparations policies and abuses of human rights, and Stalin's war against nature. These turned German opinion against the Soviets, giving the British and Americans time to correct the short-sighted policies of Eisenhower and of the authors of JCS 1067.

If land reform signaled Stalin's designs for hegemony, and reparations showed his opportunism, then his forcing of Marxist-Leninist norms on the Soviet-zone farm and forest landscapes revealed the central importance of ideology to Soviet and East German leaders. Marxism-Leninism was the principal source of Soviet and German Communists' legitimacy, and particularly crucial once memories of the Terror faded and the central planners managed to alleviate the worst shortages. Land reform and collectivization asserted the Communist Party's control but also forged an alliance between worker and peasant, erasing the distinction between rural and industrial labor, a key plank of Lenin's Bündnisdoktrin. Hörnle, as head of the Soviet zone's Department of Agriculture and Forestry, clearly laid out the two-stage process of Communist land reform: "Land reform has changed the village's social structure. Now the socialist collectives will change the village's spiritual structure."[149] Liquidating large landowners through class warfare changed the social structure of villages; the spiritual structure would change when the peasants entered socialist collectives, voluntarily liquidating themselves as the peasant class to become rural analogues of industrial workers and thus advance in the Marxist-Leninist class structure. For ideology was the very foundation for East German elites, as Adam Ulam observed: "for the societal *solidarity* and for the *legitimacy* of their rule" (emphasis in original).[150]

Soviet farm and forest policies, key elements of Stalin's "war on the countryside," halted the equilibration of central Germany's population, ecosystems, and economy to their geographic and global economic environments, locking the landscape and population into a downward spiral that did not stop until the dissolution of the East German Republic in November 1989. The economic and ecological adjustments long under way in the German landscape in 1932 and the gradual equilibration of Soviet-zone farms into medium-sized, flexible units were suddenly reversed with land reform, reparations, and the imposition of Marxist-Leninist "economic science." The monotonal rural community of worker and peasant, industrial collectives, and forest-as-factory—and low productivity and decline—became telltale signs of the East German state's entropic trajectory and ultimate dissolution.[151] The Soviet remaking of the rural communities was near perfect: an economic, ecological, and social revolution that will endure for generations, despite eastern Germany's recovery of democracy, liberal markets, and ecological farm and forest management. Since reunification in 1990, no other aspect of Soviet or East German communist policy has endured or continued to have an influence more powerfully the modern, united German state than Stalin's "war on the countryside."[152] Today's depressed rural population, inefficient collective farms, and stagnant forest are fixed *pentimenti* of Soviet land reform and reparations and of Stalin's opportunism.

Although the Communist Party leadership tried for more than forty years to recover productivity in the rural economy following land reform and reparations, the natural landscape never escaped the original burdens of Soviet occupation or the imposition of Marxist-Leninist ideology. The five new states of the former East German Republic may never recover the complex social structures of diverse communities lost to Soviet land reform and reparations. Land reform succeeded as did no other Communist initiative, emerging after 1989 as the only significant structural holdover from the East German state. In an odd shifting of roles, Chancellor Helmut Kohl's Conservative government ratified Soviet land reform expropriations without compensation, ignoring the example of eastern German Christian Democrats in 1945, who had asked for equity and compensation for expropriated landowners. Kohl had joined with the postwar Marxist-Leninists against their now shared enemy, the "Junker class."

Western policymakers in the immediate postwar period and the East German people read the signs of the East German Republic's entropic path in Stalin's "war on the countryside." Although most Western policymakers and analysts came to ignore telltales in the rural landscape, seeing the East German state as strong, disciplined, and permanent, the East German people read their existential peril directly in forest death. They joined after the 1970s in the "church-environmental" movement, first to study environmental and forest destruction, and then in the 1980s to resist and then overthrow the party leadership weeks after Honecker and Gorbachev celebrated the Republic's fortieth anniversary in October 1989. The Berlin Wall fell in November 1989 with even greater speed than with which it went up in August 1961.

How will history judge East Germany's forty-year span? Stefan Heym, the East German writer and intellectual, commented wanly in a television interview at the Palace of the Republic after the stunning Christian Democratic victory in the October 14, 1990, elections returned Chancellor Kohl's conservative government to power: "There will be no more East Germany. It will be but a footnote in world history."[153] More and more, the postwar division of Germany, which once seemed so absolute, appears to have been temporary, even a footnote, as Heym mourned. But Stalin's reduction of complex central German ecosystems and communities does survive in full force, despite Heym's complaint. Forest decline and the destruction of East Germany's diverse and flexible rural economy begun in 1945 at Stalin's command, and the damage the Communist Party's forty-year reign of control and fear wreaked on the eastern German people's psyches, not political ideas and structures, are the East German Republic's legacies. Polluted rivers, dying forests, and exhausted, nitrate-poisoned agricultural commons are lethal political remnants of authoritarian irrationalism, outward and visible signs of the twisted idealism and arrogance suffusing the "First Workers' and Peasants' State on German Soil."

Notes

1. John Lewis Gaddis, *We Now Know: Rethinking Cold War History* (New York: Oxford University Press, 1997). Gaddis draws a realist picture of complex causality, a narrative which fortifies the postrevisionist school's estimation of the central importance of Stalin's opportunism and the Soviets' hegemonic aims in Central Europe.

2. This was after Germany's potential security threat to the Soviet Union had been satisfactorily eradicated.

3. This is Stalin in conversation with Milovan Djilas. Milovan Djilas, *Conversations with Stalin* (New York: Harcourt, Brace & World, 1962).

4. These reports are G. D. Kitchingnam, "The 1945 Census of Woodlands in the British Zone of Germany," *Empire Forestry Review* 26, no. 2 (1947): 224–27; G. B. Ryle, "Germany: Military Government, C.C.G., North German Timber Control (NGTC)," *Empire Forestry Review* 26, no. 2 (1947): 212–23; E. H. B. Boulton, "The Forests of Germany: What They Can Supply on Reparations Account for the U. K.," *Timber Trade Journal* 173 (1945): 7–8; A. C. Cline, "A Brief View of Forest Conditions in Europe," *Journal of Forestry* 43 (1945): 627–28; Joseph C. Kircher, "The Forests of the U.S. Zone of Germany," *Journal of Forestry* 45, no. 4 (1947): 249–52; and Office of the [U.S.] Military Government for Germany, *Special Report of the Military Governor: The German Forest Resource Survey* 17 (October 1, 1948).

5. The daily ration given here fell to 2,000 calories from 2,500 calories during most of the war. Werner Klatt, "Food and Farming in Germany: I. Food and Nutrition," *International Affairs* 26, no. 1 (January 1950): 45, 47. Also see United States Strategic Bombing Survey, "The Attack on German Cities," in *Final Reports of the United States Strategic Bombing Survey, 1945–1947* (Washington, D.C.: U.S. Government Printing Office, 1947), and "Summary Report," 10, 14, and chap. 7, "Civilian Supply, Food Supply," 132.

6. Office of the [U.S.] Military Government for Germany, *Special Report of the Military Governor,* 7. In 1945, the volume of wood in the forest was down only 10 percent from 1930 levels, leading the Food and Agriculture Organization (FAO) to comment: "German forests were well husbanded throughout the war years and now are in excellent condition. It is safe to say that not more than the increment of the next two to five years has been cut, and in northern Europe the growing stocks remain practically unimpaired." FAO, *Forestry and Forest Products: World Situation, 1937–1946* (Stockholm: Stockholms Bokindustri Aktiebolag, 1946), 9, 15. A U.S. forester who toured Soviet-zone forests reported that war damage was limited to 2 to 3 percent and that "the forests are in an excellent state."Joseph C. Kircher, "The Forests of the U.S. Zone of Germany," *Journal of Forestry* 45, no. 4 (1947): 249–52. Also see S. H. Spurr, "Post-War Forestry in Western Europe. Part II," *Journal of Forestry* 51, no. 6 (1953): 415–21. Stephen Spurr, a young forest ecologist and future dean of the Yale School of Forestry, observed that "the visitor cannot but be impressed with the overall good condition of the German forest." Coming from Scotland, where perhaps 70 percent of the

merchantable forest was clear-cut during the war, the small acreage of clear-cut areas in Germany seems insignificant.

7. Joseph Goebbels, "Nun, Volk steh auf, und Sturm brich los! Rede im Berliner Sportpalast," *Der steile aufstieg; reden und aufsätze aus den jahren 1942/43* (München: F. Eher nachfolger, 1944).

8. Peter Staudenmaier, "Fascist Ideology: The 'Green Wing' of the Nazi Party and Its Historical Antecedents," in *Ecofascism: Lessons from the German Experience,* ed. Janet Biehl and Peter Staudenmaier (Edinburgh: AK Press, 1995), 16; G. B. Ryle, "Forestry in Western Germany, 1948," Forestry 22, no. 2 (1948): 158; E. Reichenstein, "Entwicklung von Vorrat und Zuwachs in den vier Besatzungszonen Deutschland seit 1945," *Weltholzwirtschaft* 1, nos. 7/8 (1949); E. Reichenstein, "Die forstwirtschaftliche Lage Deutschland vor und nach dem 2. Weltkrieg," *Forstarchiv* 21, nos. 1–3 (1950): 30. Ryle expected to find that the National Socialists had "looted and thoroughly and scientifically exploited" the forests of central and eastern Europe. National Socialist forestry was if anything anodyne and constructive in its emphasis on smaller dimension lumber, particularly the younger pine age classes for mine timbers and railroad ties and the younger spruce age classes for pulp. "Durchführung kriegswirtschaftlicher Maßnahmen in der Forst- und Holzwirtschaft," *Der Deutsche Forstwirt* 21, nos. 76/77 (September 22, 1939): 909; Früchtenicht, "Leistungssteigerung im Walde," *Der Deutsche Forstwirt* 22, nos. 69/70 (1940). Früchtenicht reflected the continued importance of ecological considerations again later as the end of the war approached. Michael Charles Kaser, "Interwar Policy: The War Reconstruction," in *The Economic History of Eastern Europe, 1919–1975,* ed. Michael Charles Kaser and Edward Albert Radice (Oxford: Oxford University Press, 1986), 411, 413; Von Dieterich, "Der Ausbau der Forstwirtschaft," *Forstliche Wochenschau Silva,* 1941. Von Dieterich showed that National Socialist forestry in the conquered lands remained ecological even as the Holocaust gathered momentum and military crises cascaded. See also Heinrich Rubner, *Deutsche Forstgeschichte, 1933–1945: Forstwissenschaft, Jagd und Umwelt im NS-Staat* (St. Katharinen: Scriptae Mercaturae Verlag, 1985), 173; Karl Hasel, "Forstbeamte im NSStaat am Beispiel des ehemaligen Landes Baden," *Schriftenreihe, Landesforstverwaltung und Forstwirtschaft Baden-Württemberg* 62 (1985): 197; and Michael L. Wolf, "The History of German Game Management," *Forest History* 14, no. 3 (October 1970): 16.

9. Heinrich Himmler is quoted by Staudenmaier, "Fascist Ideology," 16; also see Heinz Haushofer, *Ideengeschichte der Agrarwirtschaft und Agrarpolitik im deutschen Sprachgebiet,* vol. 2 (Munich, 1985), 107.

10. Göring enacted Europe's most enlightened wildlife and forestry laws, was a follower of Alfred Möller's radical ecologistic *Dauerwald* philosophy of natural regeneration and abolition of clear cutting, and was a committed environmentalist. Foresters acted with his imprimatur; as late as 1944, Alfred Heger, a future senior East German forester, still vigorously promoted close-to-nature forest management throughout the Nazi empire despite looming defeat—and despite Göring's pivotal role in the war economy, which otherwise suggested unlimited harvests of timber invaluable to the Nazi war effort. A. Heger, "Aufbau und Leistung von naturnahen Wäldern im Osten und ihre forstwirtschaftliche Behandlung," *Forstwissenschaftliches Centralblatt* 1 (1944): 34–35.

11. Karl Hasel, "Forstbeamte im NS-Staat am Beispiel des ehemaligen Landes

Baden," *Schriftenreihe, Landesforstverwaltung und Forstwirtschaft Baden-Württemberg* 62 (1985): 128; FAO, *Forestry and Forest Products,* 18. The Nazi forest minister, Alpers, did extend the Second Four-Year Plan's 150 percent of growth harvests from state forests to private and communal forests. Nevertheless, these targets were rarely met.

12. Kurt Hueck, "Aktuelle Aufgaben der Forstwirtschaft," speech by dean of Forstfakultät Eberswalde at Agricultural Science Congress, Berlin, February 4, 1947, *Forst- und Holzwirtschaft* 1, no. 1 (1 April 1947): 6. Hueck was the first postwar dean at the Institute for Forest Sciences in Eberswalde. Stephen Haden-Guest, John Wright, and Eileen M. Teclaff, *A World Geography of Forest Resources* (New York: Ronald Press, 1956), 285. Sopade (Executive Committee, Social Democratic Party, Germany),"Die Forstwirtschaft in der Sowjetzone," in *Denkschriften, Sopadeinformationsdienst* (Bonn: Vorstand der Sozialdemokratischen Partei Deutschlands, 1955), 29.

13. Jochen Laufer, "'Genossen, wie ist das Gesamtbild?' Ackermann, Ulbricht und Sobottka in Moskau im Juni 1945," *Deutschland Archiv* 29, no. 3 (May–June 1996): 355.

14. Norman M. Naimark, *The Russians in Germany: A History of the Soviet Zone of Occupation, 1945–1949* (Cambridge, Mass.: Belknap Press of Harvard University Press, 1995), 144–45.

15. H.-G. Merz, "Bodenreform in der SBZ: Ein Bericht aus dem Jahre 1946," *Deutschland Archiv* 11, no. 24 (1991): 1159.

16. Carl J. Friedrich and Henry Kissinger, eds., *The Soviet Zone of Germany,* HRAF-34 Harvard-1, section 1 (New Haven, Conn.: Bechtle, 1956), 384. Ackermann was responsible for the "special German way toward socialism," which fell out of favor after the Tito crisis in the spring of 1948. Ulbricht later "purged Ackermann for his 'conciliatory attitude' following the June 1953 workers' revolt."

17. Wolfgang Zank, "Als Stalin Demokratie befahl," *Die Zeit,* June 23, 1995; Ekkehard Schwartz, "Die demokratische Bodenreform, der Beginn grundlegender Veränderungen der Waldeigentums und der Forstwirtschaft im Gebiet der Deutschen Demokratischen Republik," *Sozialistische Forstwirtschaft* 20, no. 10 (1970): 290.

18. Wolfgang Leonhard, director of the Party School, was responsible for drafting the first land reform legislation and edicts. Wolfgang Leonhard, *Die Revolution Entlässt Ihre Kinder* (Cologne: Kiepenheuer & Witsch, 1955). This is also cited by Merz, "Bodenreform in der SBZ," 1162.

19. Wolfgang Leonhard, "Es muß demokratisch aussehen," *Die Zeit,* May 7, 1965, cited by Mark Kramer, "The Soviet Union and the Founding of the German Democratic Republic: 50 Years Later—A Review," *Europe-Asia Studies* 51, no. 6 (September 1999): 1093; Wolfgang Leonhard, "Iron Curtain: Episode 2," Interview, October 4, 1998, National Security Archive, http://www.gwu.edu/~nsarchiv/coldwar/interviews/episode-2/leonhard2.html; Leonhard, *Die Revolution Entlässt Ihre Kinder,* 348–58, 389–90. Leonhard reported: "The next task first was of course the local administration, then the Berlin administration, and everything changed on the 4th of June. On the 4th of June 1945 suddenly Ulbricht disappeared, and you didn't know where and what. Only years later we heard that he went to Moscow and in Moscow on the same day was invited to the Soviet Politburo and Stalin personally. And Stalin gave him a new order. The order was immediately set up the Communist Party. Immediately set up a Communist Party and help to create a Social Democratic Party, a Catholic Party and a

Liberal Party and set up then an anti-fascist Democratic United Front, and also fulfill this summer already, make all the preparations, maybe autumn, land reform. The confiscation of the feudal landowners and the division of the land in the hands of the peasants. So Ulbricht was there, Ackermann, much more intelligent, more capable, he wrote the program. You needed a programmatic statement. And on the 9th of May '45, the group returned and literally in a few hours we got a newspaper, I was one of the three to prepare the first issue of the Party newspaper, and immediately everything was prepared for constituting the Communist Party. And on the 10th you had the famous Marshal Zhukov order stating that anti-fascist democratic parties are permitted, and literally six hours later the radio announced that the Communist Party is the first one organizing. And so after the organization of the Communist Party we had to go in all the different districts and make foundation conferences, of the future Communist Party. And I was at that time very optimistic because in the official statement it was said the Communist Party has no intention to introduce the Soviet system of the Soviet Union in Germany. No intention whatsoever. And the Communist Party is in favor of a parliamentary democratic republic with all rights and freedoms for the population. And I must admit, sadly but true, I believed it. I believed that, and I was really hoping that an anti-fascist democratic period would start in Germany. This was the biggest mistake of my life, to believe that. And I can only say I was not the only one. There were millions of other people who also believed that." In addition, Communists were installed as heads of education and the police in each district. Ulbricht stated: "It is crystal clear: It must appear democratic, but we must have all the strings in our hands."

20. Erich Honecker, "Bündnis war, ist und bleibt Eckpfeiler unserer Politik," *Neues Deutschland,* September 6–7, 1975. This is also discussed by Naimark, *Russians in Germany,* 155, 163. Lenin's (1870–1924) agricultural policy of 1917–28 was also valued by the party leadership for its "overwhelming significance." In 1917, the Bolsheviks purged the largest landowners, the *pomeshchiki,* a class very roughly similar to the Junkers, yet they allowed large farmers, the kulaks (similar to the German *Großbauern*), to remain to supply food to the cities during Lenin's New Economic Program until Lenin's death in 1924. See Edgar Tümmler, Konrad Merkel, and Georg Blohm, *Die Agrarpolitik im Mitteldeutschland und ihre Auswirkung auf Produktion und Verbrauch landwirtschaftliche Erzeugnisse* (Berlin: Duncker & Humblot, 1969); Theo Stammen, "Zur Verfassungsentwicklung," in *DDR: Das politische, wirtschaftliche und soziale System,* 4th edition, ed. Heinz Rausch and Theo Stammen (Munich: Verlag C. H. Beck, 1978), 196; Karl Willy Hardach, *The Political Economy of Germany in the Twentieth Century* (Berkeley: University of California Press, 1980), 119; and Hans Herbert Götz, "Als der Klassenkampf in der DDR began: Die Bodenreform vor 40 Jahren," *Frankfurter Allgemeine Zeitung,* September 6, 1985.

21. This was at the Second World Congress of Comintern, July 19–August 7, 1920. For more on the *Bündnidoktrin,* and the influence of Lenin's economic theories on land reform, see Arnd Bauerkamper, "'Loyale Kader'? Neue Eliten und die SED-Gesellschaftspolitik auf dem Lande von 1945 bis zu den fruhen 1960 er Jahren," *Archiv für Sozialgeschichte* 39 (1999): 270, 273.

22. The demand was published on June 11, 1945. Ekkehard Schwartz, "Die demokratische Bodenreform, der Beginn grundlegender Veränderungen der Waldeigentums und der Forstwirtschaft im Gebiet der Deutschen Demokratischen Republik," *Sozialistische Forstwirtschaft* 20, no. 10 (1970): 290; Joachim Piskol, "'Junkerland in

Bauernhand': Wie deutsche Antifaschisten die demokratische Bodenreform 1945 vorbereiteten," *Neues Deutschland,* August 24, 1985.

23. Erich Honecker, "Bündnis war, ist und bleibt Eckpfeiler unserer Politik," *Neues Deutschland,* September 6–7, 1975. This is also discussed by Naimark, *Russians in Germany,* 163, and Ernst Goldenbaum, "Demokratische Bodenreform hat unseren Bauern eine gesicherte Zukunft eröffnet," *Neues Deutschland,* August 28, 1975. In German, the *"Liquidierung des Großgrundbesitzes."* The first edition of the communist *Deutscher Volkszeitung* formally set out the Communist Party's platform on June 13, 1945, including land reform and the "liquidation of large estates." See Zank, "Als Stalin Demokratie befahl"; and Piskol, "'Junkerland in Bauernhand.'"

24. Bauerkamper, "'Loyale Kader'?" 265–98. Arnd Bauerkamper, "Zwangsmodernisierung und Krisenzyklen: Die Bodenreform und Kollektivierung in Brandenburg 1945–1960/61," *Geschichte und Gesellschaft: Zeitschrift für Historische Sozialwissenschaft* 25, no. 4 (1999): 556–88.

25. Hans Lemmel, "Der deutsche Wald in der Bodenreform," *Allgemeine Forst- und Jagdzeitung* 125, no. 3 (1954): 89. The *Provinzalverordnung über die Bodenreform,* issued September 3, 1945, for Saxony-Anhalt, was essentially in the same form as Pieck's September 4, 1945, announcement at a pro forma peasants' assembly in Kyritz.

26. The Christian Democrats alone asked, in vain, for compensation for landowners. Piskol, "'Junkerland in Bauernhand.'"

27. Walter Ulbricht, "Die demokratisches Bodenreform—ein rühmreiches Blatt in den deutschen Geschichte," *Einheit* 10 (1955): 849.

28. Ekkehard Schwartz, "Die demokratische Bodenreform, der Beginn grundlegender Veränderungen der Waldeigentums und der Forstwirtschaft im Gebiet der Deutschen Demokratischen Republik," *Sozialistische Forstwirtschaft* 20, no. 10 (1970): 291. Naimark, *Russians in Germany,* 156.

29. Anton Hilbert, "Denkschrift über die ostdeutschen Bodenreform" Gräflich Douglas' sches Archiv Schloß Langenstein (1946) (Anm. 18), cited by Merz, "Bodenreform in der SBZ," 1167.

30. Klaus Peter Krause, "Begriffsbewirrungen über die 'Bodenreform' zwischen 1945 und 1949," *Frankfurter Allgemeine Zeitung,* September 2, 1994. Only sixty-six expropriated farms in the Soviet zone were larger than 1,000 hectares.

31. S. Duschek, "Wirtschaftspolitische Betrachtungen des deutschen Großgrundbesitzes," *Zeitschrift für Weltforstwirtschaft* 2 (1935): 477. Statistisches Bundesamt, "Bevölkerung und Wirtschaft, 1872–1972" (1973): 152; 200 hectares was also the upper end of the size class toward which eastern German farms were equilibrating in the interwar period. The increase in parcels of 20–100 hectares (*Großbauerlichen Betriebe*) was greatest in East Prussia and Pomerania, the core of agrarian Prussia. See Krause, "Begriffsbewirrungen über die 'Bodenreform' zwischen 1945 und 1949."

32. Edwin Hörnle, "Ein Jahr nach der Bodenreform, Materialzussamenstellung für einen Bericht an die Sowjetische Militäradministration," December 9, 1946, Archives of the DDR Agricultural Ministry, quoted by Ulrich Kluge, historian at the Technische Universität Dresden (the TUD) in a letter to the editor, *Frankfurter Allgemeine Zeitung,* September 13, 1994; Wolfgang Hassel, "'Junkerland in Bauernhand' war damals die Kampflosung. Dokumente des Staatsarchivs Magdeburg über die Bodenreform," *Neues Deutschland,* October 27, 1984. The land reform laws gave the elected Land Re-

form Commission authority to monitor the land reform processes and responsibility to notify farmers to be expropriated well in advance of any action, to treat expropriated farmers humanely, and to divide expropriated farm inventories and equipment fairly. The expropriation of farms under 100 hectares in area was prohibited, but done where "class enemies"—former local government officials and political opponents of the German communists—owned farmland and forestland of any area.

33. Hassel, "'Junkerland in Bauernhand.'" Also see Gerhard Grüneberg, "30 Jahre Marxistisch-Leninistische Agrarpolitik—30 Jahre Bündnis der Arbeiterklasse mit den Bauern," *Neues Deutschland,* August 9, 1975. Gerhard Grüneberg, Erich Honecker's deputy in building the Berlin Wall in 1961 and hard-line minister of agriculture and forestry in the 1970s, declared: "Implementation and securing of the democratic land reform took hard class warfare. The presence of our Soviet class brothers in the uniform of the Red Army prevented counterreaction from escalating to open violence." Grüneberg, who was a champion of Industrial Production Methods for farming and forestry, promoted land reform as a spontaneous "anti-imperialist, democratic agrarian revolution, the largest and most comprehensive mass action, a victorious revolution in German history undertaken by the collective action of the workers and peasants. It was wholly carried out by the workers themselves."

34. Naimark, *Russians in Germany,* 85–86.
35. Hilbert, "Denkschrift über die ostdeutschen Bodenreform."
36. Ibid. Soon after Kolter's arrest, he "died under mysterious circumstances."
37. *Wirtschaft und Arbeit* (Essen), May 17, 1947, cited by Sopade, "Die Agrarsituation in der Ostzone," June 1948, 17.
38. H. O.Spielke, G. Breithaupt, H. Bruggel, and H. Stand, *Ökonomik der sozialistischen Forstwirtschaft* (Berlin: VEB Deutsche Landwirtschaftsverlag, 1964).
39. Hans Lemmel, "Der deutsche Wald in der Bodenreform," *Allgemeine Forst- und Jagdzeitung* 125, no. 3 (1954): 102; Ralf Neubauer, "Rückkehr der Junker?" *Die Zeit,* September 9, 1994.
40. Norman M. Naimark cites SAPMO-BA, ZPA, NL 277/4 (Zaisser), b. 214, in Naimark, *Russians in Germany,* 144.
41. Hilbert, "Denkschrift über die ostdeutschen Bodenreform." Hilbert was a land reform administrator in Thuringia from the fall of 1945 throughout the spring of 1946.
42. Bauerkamper, "'Loyale Kader'?" 273.
43. Ibid., 270.
44. The October 20, 1946, *Landtag* elections were the last free elections in the Soviet zone. The official "Socialist Unity Party" won only 47.5 percent of the votes despite pressure and intimidation. Stefan Creuzberger, "The Soviet Military Administration and East German Elections, Autumn 1946, *Australian Journal of Politics & History* 45, no. 1 (March 1999): 89–98.
45. Walter Ulbricht, *Zur Geschichte der neuesten Zeit,* vol. 1 (Berlin, 1955); 57 percent were independents. Naimark, *Russians in Germany,* 156, also discusses the Socialist Unity Party's (SED's) political motivations in land reform, in particular their competition with the CDU for the support of former Nazi farmers. Sopade, "Die Forstwirtschaft in der Sowjetzone," 8. Erich Honecker declared on land reform's fortieth anniversary in 1985: "The democratic land reform accomplished what generations of peasants had dreamed of and fought for since the day of Thomas Münzer. The days of castles and crofts are over forever. Junker land came into the peasants' hands!"

Honecker repeated the themes of traditional German political discourse as late as the mid-1980s, of equity in rural society and of breaking up concentrations of ownership, even though all East German agriculture had long been reconsolidated on a larger and more inefficient scale than ever seen before. Götz, "Als der Klassenkampf in der DDR begann."

46. Wilhelm Pieck, in a speech given at the end of August 1947 before the Second Party Congress; undated speech manuscript quoted in *Wilhelm Pieck: Aufzeichnungen zur Deutschland Politik 1945–1953,* ed. Rolf Badstübner and Wilfried Loth (Berlin: Akademie Verlag, 1994).

47. Wilhelm Pieck, notes on telephone conversation with V. S. Semenov, October 4, 1946, ZPA NL 36/734, 213–15, cited in *Wilhelm Pieck,* ed. Badstübner and Loth, 83.

48. The Soviet zone historically produced reliable food surpluses, despite the relative poverty of its soils and dry climate. Soviet land reform so damaged the farm economy that the Soviets could not deliver food to the west as decided at the Potsdam Conference (July 17–August 2, 1945) as a part of the general agreement on reparations.

49. Horst Kohl, ed., *Ökonomische Geographie der Deutschen Demokratischen Republik,* 3rd ed. (Leipzig: VEB Hermann Haack, 1976), 354; Konrad Merkel, *Die Agrarwirtschaft in Mitteldeutschland: 'Sozialialisierung' und Produktionsergebnisse* (Bonn: Bundesmininsterium für gesamtdeutsche Fragen, 1963); Gerhard Seidel, Kurt Meiner, Bruno Rausch, and Alfonso Thoms, *Die Landwirtschaft in der Deutsche Demokratische Republik* (Leipzig: VEB Editions, 1962); Bundesministerium für gesamtdeutsche Fragen, *SBZ von A–Z,* 1st ed. (Bonn: Deutscher Bundesverlag, 1953); Gerd Friedrich et al., *Die Volkswirtschaft der DDR,* Akademie für Gesellschaftswissenschaften beim ZK der SED (Berlin: Verlag die Wirtschaft, 1979); Werner Klatt, "Food and Farming in Germany: II. Farming and Land Reform," *International Affairs* 26, no. 2 (April 1950): 202; Naimark, *Russians in Germany,* 157; Neubauer, "Rückkehr der Junker?"

50. Ekkehard Schwartz, "Die demokratische Bodenreform, der Beginn grundlegender Veränderungen der Waldeigentums und der Forstwirtschaft im Gebiet der Deutschen Demokratischen Republik," *Sozialistische Forstwirtschaft* 20, no. 10 (1970): 289–93.

51. Ten percent of the price was due by the end of 1945, and the balance in goods, services, or cash within ten to twenty years. Seidel et al., *Die Landwirtschaft in der Deutsche Demokratische Republik,* 29.

52. The Soviet land reform regulations were similar to conditions in National Socialist agricultural policy and to the Nazi Farm Inheritance law.See Friedrich et al., *Die Volkswirtschaft der DDR,* 156; Seidel et al., *Die Landwirtschaft in der Deutsche Demokratische Republik,* 31; Bauerkamper, "'Loyale Kader'?" 275; and Panorama DDR, *Agriculture in the German Democratic Republic: Some Information about the Life and Work of the Cooperative Farmers* (Berlin: Panorama DDR, 1979).

53. Dorothea Faber, "Entwicklung und Lage der Wohnungswirtschaft in der sowjetischen Besatzungszone, 1945–1953," *Wirtschaftsarchiv* 8, no. 17 (5 September 1953): 5943.

54. Hörnle, "Ein Jahr nach der Bodenreform." Schwerin's vice-president was Herr Möller.

55. Naimark, *Russians in Germany,* 162–63.

56. *Wirtschaft und Arbeit,* May 17, 1947. The Soviet-zone 1946 harvests as a per-

centage of 1938, 1944, and 1940–44 yields were as follows: Harvests of maize: 1938, 56.8; 1944, 69.1; 1940–44, 63.5. Harvests of potatoes: 1938, 66.3; 1944, 82.6; 1940–44, 74.6. Harvests of sugar beets: 1938, 56.2; 1944, 67.4; 1940–44, 69.5. Harvests of mustard seed: 1938, 23.4; 1944, 44.6; 1940–44, 41.0.

57. Naimark, *Russians in Germany,* 161; Heinz Kuhrig, "Demokratische Bodenreform legte den Grundstein für stetig steigende Agrarproduktion," *Neues Deutschland,* August 21, 1975; Wolfgang Zank, "'Junkerland in Bauernhand!' 3.3 millionen Hektar Land wurden 1945–49 während der Bodenreform in der Sowjetzone beschlagnahmt," *Die Zeit,* October 12, 1990.

58. See Friedrich and Kissinger, *Soviet Zone of Germany,* 466. Also see Economic Commission for Europe, *Economic Survey of Europe in 1954* (Geneva: Economic Commission for Europe, 1955), 49: "The per capita consumption of meat, meat products, and milk remained well below pre-war levels as late as the second half of 1953."

59. Naimark, *Russians in Germany,* 155. The communists deeply distrusted the traditional cooperatives, the "Raffeisen cooperatives," named after a nineteenth-century agrarian policy innovator.

60. Hilbert, "Denkschrift über die ostdeutschen Bodenreform."

61. Klatt, "Food and Farming in Germany: II. Farming and Land Reform," 195.

62. Götz, "Als der Klassenkampf in der DDR begann." Erwin Kienitz, *Denkschrift über forstwirtschaftlichsorganisatorischen Reformen, insbesondere des Bauernwäldes der Deutschen Demokratischen Republik: Eine Beitrag zur sozialistischen Umgestaltung der Forstwirtschaft* (Tharandt: Institut für Forstliche Wirtschaftslehre, 1958), also reflected the great practical difficulties facing small farmers and forest owners in the 1940s and 1950s.

63. Bauerkamper, "'Loyale Kader'?" 284. Naimark, *Russians in Germany,* 155: "Some 10,000 new peasants, according to Soviet reports, abandoned the land altogether. In the worst case, Mecklenburg, nearly 20 percent of the new peasants left their settlements between 1945 and 1949."

64. Kienitz, *Denkschrift über forstwirtschaftlichsorganisatorischen Reformen, insbesondere des Bauernwäldes der Deutschen Demokratischen Republik.*

65. Hilbert, "Denkschrift über die ostdeutschen Bodenreform."

66. Sopade, "Farmers in Saxony," August 1947, 5. Reporting on farming in Saxony; Sopade, October 1947, 21.

67. Friedrich and Kissinger, *Soviet Zone of Germany,* 3.

68. Diplomatic Correspondent, "Dearth of Food in Soviet Zone: Demonstrations and Arrests—Stocks Reduced by Requisitioning for Berlin," *The Times,* August 4, 1948; Diplomatic Correspondent, "Western Powers and the Moscow Talks: Dearth of Food," *The Times,* August 11, 1948.

69. Diplomatic Correspondent, "Western Powers and the Moscow Talks."

70. *Wirtschaft und Arbeit,* May 17, 1947.

71. "Life in the Soviet Zone," *The Times,* December 27, 1945.

72. Kienitz, *Denkschrift über forstwirtschaftlichsorganisatorischen Reformen, insbesondere des Bauernwäldes der Deutschen Demokratischen Republik.* Kienitz reported in depth to the party leadership in 1958 on the growing alienation of the rural population.

73. Friedrich and Kissinger, *Soviet Zone of Germany,* 237.

74. Schwartz, "Die demokratische Bodenreform," 292; Reichenstein, "Die forst-

wirtschaftliche Lage Deutschland." In contrast, the British and American zonal governments handed management of former Reich forest, only 30 percent of the Western zone's forest area, back to the individual states, the *Länder*. Both Soviet- and Western-zone governments, however, abolished forestry's separate ministry and brought forestry back within the Agriculture Ministry's suzerainty, a reversal of National Socialist reforms that signaled the importance of production and cash flow over capital asset growth and close-to-nature forest management throughout Germany.

75. W. Schindler, "30 Jahre staatliche Forstwirtschaftsbetriebe—30 Jahre sozialistische Entwicklung in der Forstwirtschaft: Staatliche Forstwirtschaftsbetrieb Löbau, Löbau, D.D.R.," *Sozialistische Forstwirtschaft* 32, no. 11 (1982): 321–23; Spielke et al., *Ökonomik der sozialistischen Forstwirtschaft,* 60. The party distributed 500,000 hectares of forestland to new peasants. Also see J. Säglitz, "Die Forstwirtschaft in Ostdeutschland—Stand, Probleme, Ziele," *Forstarchiv* 61, no. 6 (November–December 1990): 226. The party kept 56 percent (585,000 hectares) of farmland and forestland expropriated under land reform. The forest and personal property of 12,000 forest owners were "dissolved and divided without compensation," declared the authors of the October 7, 1949 Constitution. Tümmler, Merkel, and Blohm, *Die Agrarpolitik im Mitteldeutschland,* 26; Lemmel, "Der deutsche Wald in der Bodenreform," 139. Privately owned land over 100 hectares provided 76 percent of *Bodenfonds.* Land was taken from 8,000 forest owners of more than 100 hectares and 4,200 owners of less than 100 hectares; the provision of the 1949 Constitution was article 24, section 5. By January 1, 1950, 1,050,000 hectares of forest had been taken, and 31 percent of *Bodenfonds;* 76 percent was former private forest, 21 percent was former state and local, and 3 percent was *Körperschaft* forest. Privately owned land over 100 hectares provided 76 percent of *Bodenfonds.*

76. Kurt Mantel, "Forstgeschichte," in *Stand und Ergebnisse der forstlichen Forschung seit 1945,* ed. Schriftenreihe des AID (Land- und Hauswirtschaftlicher Auswertungs und Informationsdienst) (Bad Godesberg, 1952), 144–53.

77. [No first name] Hämmerle, "Das Osthilfegesetz und seine Auswirkungen auf die Forstwirtschaft," *Der Deutsche Forstwirt* 14 (1932): 119.

78. Lemmel, "Der deutsche Wald in der Bodenreform," 107.

79. Sopade, "Die Forstwirtschaft in der Sowjetzone," 4, 10.

80. Lemmel, "Der deutsche Wald in der Bodenreform," 3.

81. Schwartz, "Die demokratische Bodenreform."

82. *Wirtschaft und Arbeit,* May 17, 1947.

83. Bundesministerium für gesamtdeutsche Fragen, *SBZ von A–Z,* 48.

84. Wilma Merkel and Stephanie Wahl, *Das geplünderte Deutschland: Die wirtschaftliche Entwicklung im östlichen Teil Deutschlands von 1949–1989,* 2nd ed. (Bonn: Instituts für Wirtschaft und Gesellschaft, 1991), 29; Mike Dennis, *German Democratic Republic: Politics, Economics and Society* (London: Pinter, 1991), 23. Ulbricht made his speech to the party's Hochschule élites.

85. Merkel and Wahl, *Das geplünderte Deutschland,* 29. Ulbricht made his speech at the September 16, 1948, Party Conference.

86. *Wirtschaft und Arbeit,* May 17, 1947. "Large farmers" meant independent farmers with 20 to 100 hectares.

87. Hörnle, "Ein Jahr nach der Bodenreform," 15; Sopade, "KZs in der Ostzone," August 1947, 66.

88. Paul Merker, editorial, *Neues Deutschland,* December 19, 1946.

89. *Wirtschaft und Arbeit,* May 17, 1947. The party formally allowed peasants to sell surplus produce on the free market "after fulfillment of their delivery obligations," but the party increased quotas once they were met, constantly absorbing surpluses and killing farmers' incentives to produce more food.

90. Sopade,"Die Forstwirtschaft in der Sowjetzone," 29.

91. Ibid.

92. Ibid., 10.

93. Erwin Kienitz, *Denkschrift über forstwirtschaftlichsorganisatorischen Reformen, insbesondere des Bauernwäldes der Deutschen Demokratischen Republik.* Farmers' fear of collectivization permeates this confidential study of farmers' attitudes in the mid-1950s.

94. Sopade,"Die Forstwirtschaft in der Sowjetzone," 8, 9, 10.

95. Beate Ruhm von Oppen, *Documents on Germany under Occupation, 1945–1954* (London: Oxford University Press, 1955), 148; Schwartz, "Die demokratische Bodenreform."

96. Von Oppen, *Documents on Germany under Occupation,* 148.

97. Friedrich and Kissinger, *Soviet Zone of Germany,* 445.

98. Zank, "'Junkerland in Bauernhand!'"

99. *Wirtschaft und Arbeit,* May 17, 1947.

100. "Bauern sichern die Ernährung: Antifascisten aufs Dorf," *Neues Deutschland,* June 1, 1946.

101. This was the Mühleberg concentration camp.

102. Sopade, "KZs in der Ostzone," *Querschnitt durch Politik und Wirtschaft* #5, August 1947, 77.

103. Telegraf, "Bloß ein Kolchose" *Telegraf* (Berlin), October 8, 1947, cited by Sopade, "Landwirtschaft in der Ostzone," in *Querschnitt durch Politik und Wirtschaft* (Hannover: Vorstand der Sozialdemokratischen Partei, 1948), 40. Managers of the collectives continued to commandeer farmers' labor to help harvest wood for reparations into the early 1950s. The efficiency of using farm labor to help with forestry operations pleased management but was a constant source of irritation to farmers and local managers operating within the narrow constraints of the plan. See also Edwin Hörnle, *Volksstimme* (Chemnitz), July 3, 1947, cited by Sopade, "Landwirtschaft in der Ostzone," in *Querschnitt durch Politik und Wirtschaft* (Hannover: Vorstand der Sozialdemokratischen Partei, 1947), 9.

104. Hörnle, "Ein Jahr nach der Bodenreform," 15.

105. Michael L. Hoffman, "The Harvest in Europe Is Hunger Once More," *New York Times,* September 21, 1947. Hoffman quotes the head of the FAO, John Boyd Orr: "Next winter and spring many in Europe will be worse fed than they were during the war." See also U.S. Department of State, "Directive to Commander-in-Chief of United States Forces of Occupation Regarding the Military Government of Germany; April 1945 (JCS 1067)," paragraphs 16, 18, in *Foreign Relations of the United States,* ed. U.S. Department of State (Washington, D.C.: U.S. Government Printing Office, 1945), vol. 3, "European Advisory Commission; Austria; Germany," 484, http://usa.usembassy .de/etexts/ga3-450426.pdf.

106. U.S. Department of State, "Directive to Commander-in-Chief of United States Forces of Occupation Regarding the Military Government of Germany; April 1945

(JCS 1067)," paragraphs 21–22, 27. JCS 1067 prescribed for the U.S.-zone commanders, even as it slashed German production of farm machinery and particularly fertilizer: "27. You will require the Germans to use all means at their disposal to maximize agricultural output and to establish as rapidly as possible effective machinery for the collection and distribution of agricultural output. 28. You will direct the German authorities to utilize large-landed estates and public lands in a manner which will facilitate the accommodation and settlement of Germans and others or increase agricultural output."

107. Richard D. McKinzie, ed., "Oral History Interview with Lucius D. Clay," New York, July 16, 1974, Harry S. Truman Library, Independence, Mo., 1979, http://www.trumanlibrary.org/oralhist/clayl.htm. General Clay commented on problems with JCS 1067, and how U.S. commanders circumvented it: "JCS-1067 would have been extremely difficult to operate under. If you followed it literally you couldn't have done anything to restore the German economy. If you couldn't restore the German economy, you could never hope to get paid for the food that they had to have. By virtue of these sort of things, it was modified constantly; not officially, but by allowing this deviation and that deviation, et cetera. We began to slowly wipe out JCS-1067. When we were ordered to put in a currency reform this was in direct contravention of a provision of JCS-1067 that prohibited us from doing anything to improve the German economy. It was an unworkable policy and it wasn't changed just without any discussion or anything by those of us who were in Germany. It was done by gradual changes in its provision and changes of cablegrams, conferences, and so on."

108. Herbert Hoover, "Text of Hoover Mission's Findings on the Food Requirements of Germany," *New York Times,* February 28, 1947.

109. President Harry S. Truman signed the European Recovery Program into law on April 3, 1948.

110. This is from *Neues Deutschland*'s (July 28, 1946) editors' comments on an *Hamburger Volkszeitung* (July 17, 1946) article on British-zone ration-level reductions. Despite the great agricultural and fisheries wealth of the British zone, reported the *Neues Deutschland* writer, "hunger is turning into starvation." Intentional starvation was a frequent charge against the British and American in *Neues Deutschland;* Our Own Correspondent, "£40,750,000 Spent on Western Zone," *The Times,* May 26, 1947.

111. "Nur Demokratie kann die Hungerkrise im Westen überwinden," *Neues Deutschland,* November 26, 1946.

112. "Die SED zur Grenzfrage," *Neues Deutschland,* September 19, 1946; "Nur Demokratie kann die Hungerkrise im Westen überwinden"; Max Fechner, "Klarheit in der Ostfrage!" *Neues Deutschland,* September 14, 1946.

113. General Kurt von Schleicher (1882–1934), an army major general and political intriguer, manipulated Germany's aging president, Paul von Hindenburg (1847–1934), into dismissing Chancellor Heinrich Brüning (1885–1970) on May 30, 1932, ending the Weimar Republic. Six months later, on January 30, 1933, Hitler outmaneuvered and seized the chancellorship from von Schleicher in the Nazi *Machtergreifung.* S.S. assassins murdered von Schleicher on January 30, 1934, the "Night of the Long Knives."

114. *Neues Deutschland* filled in the years between 1945 and 1947 with attacks on Schlange-Schöningen's polices, on his aristocratic heritage, and on his protection of

Arvid Nelson

"Junker interests." The following are typical: "Herr Schlange will den Spuren ver-
wischen," *Neues Deutschland,* October 24, 1946; "Nur Demokratie kann die Hungerkrise im Westen überwinden," *Neues Deutschland,* November 26, 1946; "Schlange-
Schöningen muß gehen!" *Neues Deutschland,* November 30, 1946; "Der Weg
Schlange-Schöningen: Zweierlei Maß für Umsiedler," *Neues Deutschland,* December
29, 1946.

115. Wolfgang F. Stolper and Karl W. Roskamp, *The Structure of the East German
Economy* (Cambridge, Mass.: Harvard University Press, 1960), 5; Stephen F. Frowen,
"The Economy of the German Democratic Republic," in *Honecker's Germany,* ed.
David Childs (Boston: Allen and Unwin, 1985), 36; Jörg Roesler, "The Rise and Fall
of the Planned Economy in the German Democratic Republic, 1945–1989," *German
History* 9, no. 1 (February 1991): 46; Merkel and Wahl, *Das geplünderte Deutschland,*
16; Bundesminister für innerdeutsche Beziehungen, ed., *D.D.R.-Handbuch,* vol. 2, *M–
Z* (Cologne: Bundesminister für innerdeutsche Beziehungen, 1985), table 1, "Reparations and Other Expenses in the Soviet Zone and East Germany between 1945 and
1953." Estimates of total reparations cost through 1953 run between DM66 billion
($119 billion in 2002) and DM120 billion ($216 billion in 2002), overwhelming for an
economy with a 1950 gross industrial product of only DM75 billion.

116. Diplomatic Correspondent, "Fixing the German Reparation," *The Times,* June
19, 1945.

117. The Soviet joint-stock companies, *Sowjetische Aktiengesellschaften* (SAGs),
were formed on October 30, 1945, through the Soviet military government's (SMAD)
Orders 124 and 126 of October 31, 1945. The Soviets took more than one-quarter of
German industrial production for export to the Soviet Union. On the SAGs, also see
note 128 below.

118. Vyacheslav Mikhaylovich Molotov, quoted in the *Sozialdemokratische Pres-
sedienst* (Hannover), August 21, 1947.

119. Roland Barth, interview by author, Eberswalde, March 20, 1991. Roland
Barth, East Germany's senior forest statistician, estimated that the cut for reparations
and fuelwood was as high as 25 million cubic meters each year.

120. Berlin Correspondent, "In the Russian Zone," *The Times,* September 25, 1947.

121. Bruno Gleitze, "Zielsetzung und Mittel der sowjetzonalen Wirtschaftspolitik
bis zur gegenwärtigen Krisensituation," speech to the Working Group of German
Economists Research Institute; cited in Sopade, *Die sowjetzonale Wirtschaftspolitik,*
no. 937, September 1953, 41.

122. "Report on Reparations," *Telegraf* (Berlin), March 7, 1949, cited by Sopade,
Raubbau an den Ostzonen-Wäldern (Hannover: Vorstand der Sozialdemokratischen
Partei, 1949), 10; Sopade,"Die Forstwirtschaft in der Sowjetzone," 15.

123. A senior German forester reported in 1949: "Delivery of pit props to the pits
and mines continues to be forestry's critical economic task." Julius Speer, "Die Forstwirtschaft im Wirtschaftsgeschehen des Jahres 1948," *Allgemeine Forstzeitschrift* 4,
no. 1 (5 January 1949): 1.

124. Klatt, "Food and Farming in Germany: II. Farming and Land Reform," 195.

125. Hörnle, *Volksstimme,* 9.

126. Sopade,"Die Forstwirtschaft in der Sowjetzone," 15.

127. Ibid., 2.

234

128. Edward R. Morrow, "Reparations Lag in East Germany: Russian Officials Are Warned to Let Nothing Interfere with Deliveries to Soviet," *New York Times,* October 17, 1948. Also see the undated speech by a senior official of the Soviet zone, possibly Colonel Sergei Tulpanov, between the end of August and the beginning of September 1947, ZPA NL 3 6/734 Bl 347–3 62, quoted in *Wilhelm Pieck,* ed. Badstübner and Loth, 162. An unidentified senior official of the Soviet zone, again possibly Tulpanov, declared in an internal memorandum that reparations withdrawals were the Soviets' primary policy in Germany, followed by the creation of Soviet joint-stock companies, the notorious *Sowj etische Aktiengesellschaften,* or SAGs, which ran eastern German factories to produce exclusively for the Soviet economy. "Without resolution of these two issues [reparations and the SAGs]," the author concluded, "there can be no democratization of eastern Germany. But how can we explain to the German worker the significance of the SAGs?"

129. Reichenstein, "Die forstwirtschaftliche Lage Deutschland"; Bundesministerium für gesamtdeutsche Fragen, *SBZ von A–Z,* 48.

130. G. Schröder, "Zu einigen Problemen der Forstwissenschaft und -praxis in Prozeß der wissenschaftlichtechnischen Revolution," *Sozialistische Forstwirtschaft* 15, no. 11 (1965): 323.

131. Fuelwood harvests, which equaled reparations' harvests in intensity, are not included in official harvest figures.

132. Sopade, "Die Forstwirtschaft in der Sowjetzone," 26.

133. C. Wiebecke, Zum Stand der deutschen Forststatistik," *Forstarchiv* 26, no. 1 (15 January 1955): 1, 2; G. Hildebrandt, "Die Forsteinrichtung in der D.D.R. 1950 bis 1965: Ein Beitrag zur jüngeren deutschen Forsteinrichtungsgeschichte aus Anlaß des 80. Geburtstages von Albert Richter in Eberswalde," *Allgemeine Forst- und Jagdzeitung* 160, no. 6 (1989): 123; H. Eberts, "Forstwirtschaft in Ost und West," *Holz-Zentralblatt* (1949): 942. Eberts perplexedly commented on Soviet refusal to release ownership data or share other data necessary for planning. Potsdam forest management was to be carried out by the Quadripartite Forestry Subcommittee of the Quadripartite Directorate of Economics. As a palliative to Western requests for information, the Soviets commissioned the superficial *Waldfondserhebung* forest inventory followed by the unsatisfactory 1949 *Forsterhebung* and 1952 inventories.

134. "Report on Soviet Zone Mortality," *Die Neue Zeitung* (Berlin), March 13, 1949, cited in Sopade, *Querschnitt durch Politik und Wirtschaft* (Hannover: Vorstand der Sozialdemokratischen Partei, 1949), 44.

135. Gleitze, "Zielsetzung und Mittel der sowjetzonalen Wirtschaftspolitik bis zur gegenwärtigen Krisensituation," 41.

136. Sopade, "Die Forstwirtschaft in der Sowjetzone," 11.

137. Reichenstein, "Die forstwirtschaftliche Lage Deutschland"; Statisches Amt für die sowjetischen Zone, cited in Sopade, "Die Forstwirtschaft in der Sowjetzone," 26; "Report on Forestry in Eastern Germany," *Darmstädter Echo,* January 20, 1949. The total area of bare clear-cuts in 1950 was 400,000 hectares. Unplanted clear-cuts meant an annual loss to the Soviet zone's economy of DM90 million from forgone growth alone, roughly $21 million, or almost $170 million in annual lost production in 2002 value.

138. Sopade, "Die Forstwirtschaft in der Sowjetzone," 10. Another expert observed,

"The damage is so severe that it won't be overcome in a man's lifetime." "Waldraub-bau-Holzexport," *Neuer Vorwärts* (Hannover), January 8, 1949, cited by Sopade, *Raubbau an den Ostzonen-Wäldern,* 16.

139. Stocking fell to 78 square meters per hectare, well below normal stocking levels of 120 square meters per hectare. Forest stocking in 1948 was one-third below the 1933 level of 113 square meters per hectare. The Soviet zone's 1946 informal inventory showed a stocking density of 96.81 Vorratsfestmeter (cubic meters) per hectare and an unplanted area of only 2 percent calculated on an area of only 2.6 million hectares. "Working Paper," Forstprojektierung Potsdam, Archives, Handwritten and undated, said to be 1949.

140. 1948/49 Clearcut and Unplanted Forest Area, Four Zones, Reichenstein, "Die forstwirtschaftliche Lage Deutschland."

141. McKinzie, "Oral History Interview."

142. Our Special Correspondent, "Mr. Bevin Backs American Plan for Germany," *The Times,* May 16, 1947; "No Surrender in Berlin: Mr. Bevin's Review—Ernest Bevin's 30 June 1948 Speech to Commons," *The Times,* July 1, 1948.

143. Board of Editors, "Opportunity in Moscow" (lead article), *The Times,* April 7, 1947.

144. Friedrich and Kissinger, *Soviet Zone of Germany.*

145. Günther Bischoff, "History: Introduction," in *The German Economy, 1945– 1947: Charles P. Kindleberger's Letters from the Field,* ed. Charles Poor Kindleberger (Westport, Conn.: Meckler, 1989), xiv. Twenty-five percent of total Soviet reparations of $10 billion (a figure also under debate) would come from the Western zones. In return, the British and American zonal economies would get 15 percent of the value of Soviet withdrawals in food from the Soviet zone.

146. Hoover, "Text of Hoover Mission's Findings"; Tania Long, "German War Prisoners Present Complex Issue; 3,680,000 Still Held," *New York Times,* March 9, 1947; "Captives of Soviets Found in Hunger," *New York Times,* October 1, 1947; Heinz Rusalle, "Buchenwald Concentration Camp," *Echo der Woche,* January 23, 1948, cited by Kathleen McLaughlin, "Buchenwald Held a Camp of Misery," *New York Times,* January 25, 1948; Edwin L. James, "Concentration Camps are Made an Issue by the U.S.," *The New York Times,* March 28, 1948; C. L. Sulzberger, "Soviet Forced Labor Held Economic Asset in Study," *New York Times,* June 30, 1948; Our Own Correspondent, "Dearth of Food in the Soviet Zone," *The Times,* August 5, 1948; Kathleen McLaughlin, "German Food Lack in East Zone Told," *New York Times,* October 28, 1949; "Captive of Soviets Held Starving," *New York Times,* November 25, 1948; Kathleen McLaughlin, "Hope Dwindles in Germany for the Return of 1,000,000 Missing, Mostly in Russia," December 22, 1948; "U.S. Accuses Soviets of Breach of Faith," *New York Times,* January 5, 1949; "80,000 Camp Deaths Cited," *New York Times,* March 27, 1949.

147. McKinzie, "Oral History Interview."

148. They launched a thoroughgoing currency reform, introducing the deutsche mark on June 20, 1948, accepted Ludwig Erhard's announcement a few days later ending price controls, and lowered tax rates, all central to the German *Wirtschaftswunder* and German recovery. Full recovery, however, did not come until the Allies brought Germany into the Marshall Plan, the European Recovery Program (1948–52). Walter W. Heller, "The Role of Fiscal-Monetary Policy in German Economic Recovery,"

American Economic Review, Papers and Proceedings of the Sixty-second Annual Meeting of the American Economic Association 40, no. 2 (May 1950): 531 (http://links.jstor.org/sici?sici=0002-8282%28 1 95005%2940%3A2%3C53 1%3ATROFPI %3E2.0.CO% 3B2-6); "Tax and Monetary Reform in Occupied Germany," *National Tax Journal* 2, no. 3 (1949): 215; Daniel Yergin and Joseph Stanislaw, *The Commanding Heights: The Battle between Government and the Marketplace That Is Remaking the Modern World* (New York: Simon & Schuster, 1998), 35–36. David R. Henderson, "German Economic 'Miracle,'" *The Concise Encyclopedia of Economics* (http://www.econlib.org/library/Enc/GermanEconomicMiracle.html).

149. Edwin Hörnle, "Wie kann die deutschen Landwirtschaft ihre Aufgabe erfüllen?" *Neues Deutschland,* May 16, 1946.

150. Adam Bruno Ulam, *Unfinished Revolution: An Essay on the Sources of Influence of Marxism and Communism* (New York: Random House, 1960); Thomas Arthur Baylis, "Economic Reform as Ideology: East Germany's New Economic System," *Comparative Politics* 3, no. 2 (January 1971): 212.

151. See Charles Maier, *Dissolution: The Crisis of Communism and the End of East Germany* (Princeton, N.J.: Princeton University Press, 1997), for the best history of the fall of East Germany, the only Soviet bloc state to disappear without a trace.

152. The Unification Treaty of October 3, 1990, avoided either reversing or affirming Soviet land reform. The treaty left land reform's fate to the new, all-German parliament, which legalized Soviet land reform expropriations in Article 142 of Germany's new Constitution.

153. Timothy Garton Ash, "East Germany: The Solution," *New York Review of Books,* April 26, 1990, 14; Tony Judt, "New Germany, Old NATO," *New York Review of Books,* May 29, 1997, n. 12. As Judt comments, although more than half of the East German people voted for the conservative CDU coalition in the March 18, 1990, elections, the first free, all-German election since 1932, that East German "intellectuals were slower to notice. Three weeks after the fall of the Wall, Christa Wolf, Stefan Heym, and other leading figures of the East German literary scene published an appeal 'For Our Country,' in which they beseeched their fellow East Germans to save the socialist German state. Bärbel Bohley, a leader of New Forum, deplored the 'premature' elections—the voters were not 'ready,' she averred. Many months later, she was still bemoaning the outcome—in her own self-revealing words, 'We wanted justice and we got the Rechtsstaat.' Little wonder that New Forum won just over 2 percent of the vote in the GDR's first and last free election."

9. Nuclear Country: The Militarization of the U.S. Northern Plains, 1954–1975

Catherine McNicol Stock

In the darkest days of the Great Depression, Franklin Delano Roosevelt dispatched a respected journalist, Lorena Hickok, to survey conditions in some of the hardest hit areas of the United States. Her first stops were in North Dakota and South Dakota. There, she visited children sharing a single set of clothing, families with nothing to eat but flour and lard, and towns on the verge of depopulation. When she reported back to New Deal administrator Harry Hopkins, she compared Pierre, South Dakota's capital, to the only other place on Earth that she imagined was as remote and as impoverished as the northern Great Plains: "This is the Siberia of the United States," she said. "A more hopeless place I never saw."[1]

Within thirty years of Hickok's correspondence, the connection between the northern plains of the United States and the Siberian region of the USSR would change from convenient metaphor to concrete reality. In the 1950s, the northern plains became home to three Air Force bases that were critical to air defense in the Cold War: Ellsworth Air Force Base (AFB) in Rapid City, South Dakota, and Minot AFB and Grand Forks AFB in North Dakota. These air bases housed three of the nation's 137 Strategic Air Command bomber wings, and, through the use of new computerized radar equipment, formed an "interceptor shield" across the nation's northern border. In the early 1960s, the Air Force also identified the plains states as superior locations for land-based intercontinental ballistic missiles (ICBMs). By 1975, more than 1,000 underground nuclear missile "silos" dotted the northern plains. Some of these missiles were programmed to hit targets in Siberia, where Soviet SS-17, SS-18, and SS-19 ICBMs were stored. As the journalist Ian Frazier wrote in 1989,

"Today the Great Plains are more than linked to Russia. They are also, in a sense, aimed at it." Of course, Soviet Siberia was also aimed at the Great Plains. "Somewhere in Russia, in an underground silo in western Siberia along the Trans-Siberia Railroad, a missile knows about this exact piece of nowhere prairie."[2] However remote either region may have seemed, they were not "in the middle of nowhere." They were instead in "the middle of a thousand nuclear bullseyes."[3]

Land-based nuclear missiles were beyond most scientists' imaginations as recently as 1945. In the immediate post war period, military strategists considered long-range bombers like the B-29, launched from bases in Europe and Asia, to be the most important element of nuclear defense. Vannever Bush, a wartime scientific director, derided the very idea of the ICBM:

> [Some] people . . . have been talking about a 3,000-mile, high-angle rocket, shot from one continent to another, carrying an atomic bomb, and so directed as to be a precise weapon, which could land exactly on a certain target, such as a city. I say, technically, I don't think anybody in the world knows how to do such a thing, and I feel confident it will not be done for a very long period of time to come.[4]

Nevertheless, swiftly accelerating tensions between the superpowers following the 1949 announcement that the USSR had detonated its own atomic weapon led scientists in the United States and (Americans believed) the USSR to work feverishly to create just such a weapon.[5] The first generation of American ICBMs, the Atlas system, was in place by 1959. Atlas missiles were deployed from 1959 to 1968, at eight sites on the central plains, and one each in Washington, California, and New York. The second generation, the Titan missiles, followed in 1962. These were also housed in rural parts of the American West, at bases in Texas, Oklahoma, New Mexico, Kansas, Arkansas, and elsewhere, until 1987.

Both early ICBM systems had significant technical shortcomings. The Atlas missiles were cumbersome and slow to launch; it took technicians many hours to raise the missiles from their horizontal resting position to their vertical launching position. The Atlas was also positioned above ground—fully exposed to enemy attack. Though the Titan could be launched from a concrete silo carved into the ground, its liquid fuel could not be stored for long periods in the missile. Thus even the Titan had to be fueled before it could be launched. Though the first two generations of American ICBMs were better than Bush had expected, they were still far from perfect.

The development of the "Minuteman" missile resolved these technical problems and determined Dakotans' nuclear future. By 1961, American scientists had discovered how to use solid rocket fuel in nuclear missiles so they could be prefueled and later launched at a minute's notice. Likewise, scientists improved the design of the storage silos. President John F. Kennedy called these missiles his "ace in the hole" during the Cuban missile crisis and, afterward, he authorized the construction of hundreds of Minutemen to supplement and then replace the older weapons.[6] In 1965, the government introduced the Minuteman II, which boasted improved range and accuracy. By 1967, Minuteman I and II missiles occupied 15,000 square miles of land on the northern and central plains at AFBs in the Dakotas, Nebraska, Wyoming, Montana, eastern Colorado, and Missouri. Finally, in 1971, the military introduced the Minuteman III—59.9 feet long, 79,000 pounds, with a 6,000-mile range, two or three nuclear warheads, and a price tag of $7 million. This time the northern plains received the largest number of weapons of any region, with 300 missiles going to North Dakota alone.[7]

Military officials chose to house the Minuteman missiles on the northern plains for both technical and strategic reasons. First, they knew that the relatively arid climate suited the dynamics of the new solid rocket fuel better than more humid climates where the fuel absorbed water vapor from the air. As Frazier explains, "The easiest way to wreck a nuclear missile would be to keep it in a damp basement."[8] Officials also preferred the northern plains because they lay closer to targets in the USSR, if the missiles flew over the Arctic Circle. Last, they selected the northern plains because they perceived the region to be remote, lightly populated, and containing expansive air space. As the technical sergeant and historian for the Space Warfare Center in Colorado, James Mesco, explains, "It was best to place the missile sites as deep in the country as you could. It allowed for a longer reaction time to ensure that, yes, the threat is there and we can retaliate because we have the time before the first sites might be hit to launch back."[9]

Developments in global military strategy quickly transformed the plains from the primary storehouse of nuclear weapons to the primary target of nuclear destruction. Recognizing that nuclear war would bring catastrophic damage, federal officials in the United States worried first about how to win a nuclear war, then about how to survive one, and finally about how to deter one altogether. An early attempt at increasing "survivability" was expressed in Secretary of State Robert S. McNamara's "no cities" doctrine. Under this proposal, both sides would pledge to target only military and other strategic sites in the countryside, should nuclear conflict begin.[10] The destruction of densely populated urban centers, he reasoned, was too horrific to condone. By the late 1960s, mutual assured destruction (MAD) replaced "no cities" as deterrence replaced survivability. Nuclear arms were better used to make war too terrible to contemplate, strategists on both sides of the Iron Curtain reasoned, rather than as tactical weapons. Still, the missile silos and surrounding communities remained safe from a direct attack until scientists improved the guidance systems on the ICBMs so that they could target individual military installation facilities. At that moment—in the early 1970s—the mutual destruction of the American and Siberian countrysides was assured.

MAD required constant nuclear proliferation on both sides to remain effective. As a result, the entire Great Plains region eventually became a new kind of nuclear zone. By the late 1970s, Congress was considering a fourth missile system—the MX, or "Peacekeeper," missile—which contained ten nuclear warheads and would be continuously transported on railroad cars across the plains countryside. Meanwhile, U.S. senators and representatives from the region endorsed the construction of an anti—ballistic missile system (ABM), the precursor of the Ronald Reagan administration's "Star Wars" proposal. Along with ICBMs, the region played host to uranium mining sites, toxic waste transportation systems, and nuclear reactor sites. According to a map titled "Deadly Nuclear Radiation Hazards, USA," in case of "extreme nuclear crisis," huge portions of both North Dakota and South Dakota were considered to be total "evacuation zones."[11]

As Valerie Kuletz has said of the Four Corners region of the American Southwest, by the 1970s the northern plains had become the object of federal "deterritorialization"—a process in which one section of the country bears the burden of risk for the nation at a whole.[12] Like the indigenous people of the Four Corners, the people of the Dakotas proved unable to beat back this threat from Washington. Indeed, many of them never tried, preferring to welcome the economic advantages of integration into the permanent military economy and to minimize its inherent risks. But the story of how the people of the plains experienced the military state is worth telling even if the outcome, in hindsight, seemed predetermined. All over the world, the postwar years brought new encounters between powerful states and rural peoples. Unlike the people of the Dakotas, most rural people around the globe were people of color with troubled colonial pasts and uncertain postcolonial futures. Some of their stories are told in this book. In those places—Angola, East Timor—and many others—Laos, India, Vietnam, Afghanistan—rural people believed they could negotiate a benefit from militarization for themselves, while maintaining control over local decisionmaking, culture, and tradition. Dakotans believed that, too—after all, they had successfully negotiated with the modern state in the 1930s when they had worked with and through the democratic structures of the New Deal. But whether they were new players on the global stage or hard-

241

ened veterans, many rural people ultimately found their lands decimated, customs annihilated, and villages depopulated in the name of the Cold War imperative. Widely untold, the story of the encounter between the global military superstate and rural peoples is one of the most important chapters in Cold War history.

Background: Dakotans and the Federal Government

In the late 1990s, in accordance with the Strategic Arms Reduction Treaty (START), the United States began to deactivate and destroy its Minuteman II and many of its Minuteman III ICBMs. Journalists rushed to the areas around Grand Forks, Minot, and Rapid City to interview local men and women about their role in the Cold War. Some Dakotans reacted with pride that "their missiles" had deterred nuclear conflict. They imagined that the Dakotas were "where the Cold War was won."[13] A state historian even boasted that "North Dakota would have been No. 3 as far as nuclear powerhouses go if we had seceded from the union."[14] A North Dakota boy who had grown up to become a technical sergeant at South Dakota's Ellsworth Air Force base said, "We did our jobs. . . . We did our jobs well. The Cold War is over. And we never had to use these. That's deterrence." A fifteen-year-old whose town lay near fourteen missiles put it simply, "Well, we didn't get blown up, did we?"[15]

But others, like the farmer Russell Lorenz, whose property had adjoined a "military reservation," were more ambivalent about the role they had played in the Cold War and the potential sacrifice that their region had been asked to make. In the case of an actual nuclear war, Lorenz said, "our missiles would survive, but we wouldn't."[16] Tim Pavek, a missileer who had grown up around Rapid City, recalled "laying in bed as a child hearing the rumble of B-52 bombers. I lay awake wondering whether we'd brought about the nuclear strike that would destroy us all."[17] On the nearby Pine Ridge reservation, Lakota men and women had similar fears, and they also wondered whether the bombers were "purposefully flying too close to their homes, rattling windows and knocking dishes from shelves."[18] A North Dakota newspaper editor remarked that even the most conservative farmers in his area felt "uneasy about what they see out there, . . . the massiveness of it."[19] Some folks simply hoped that once the Cold War was over, things in the Dakotas would return to normal. As the mayor of Luverne, North Dakota, put it when the silo in his town was destroyed, "Perhaps now we can get back to being North Dakotans again."[20]

If the people of the plains had been both proud and relieved when the IBCMs were deactivated, how had they felt when the bases had originally been built and the missiles initially deployed? Throughout the first half of the twentieth century, the people of Dakotas were far better known for their distrust of the federal government and for their ardent isolationism than for anything resembling acceptance of centralized or militarized authority. What, if anything, had changed their perspective? We know remarkably little about this period, the early and middle years of the Cold War. In fact, much of the scholarly history of the Dakotas ends just as the nuclear history of the region begins.[21] Likewise, few studies of the Cold War highlight the experiences of individual communities or regions in the global conflict.[22] To the contrary, most major syntheses focus on the power of the modern state to bring individual localities under the single rubric of militarization. According to Michael Sherry, for example, "militarization reshaped every realm of American life—politics and foreign policy, economics and technology, culture and social realms—making America a profoundly different nation."[23] Just the detonation of the atomic bomb, he argues, had made people feel that "history . . . had been sundered, humankind had begun a new era."[24]

To be sure, militarization significantly and permanently altered the economy, culture, and society of the Dakotas. Yet, however powerful the state, the men and women of North Dakota and South Dakota still viewed the Cold War through a prism of their own cultural values, histories, and economic and political needs. Far from creating a "profoundly different" culture or believing that their own history had been "sundered," Dakotans used and adapted their traditional antistatist, isolationist, and agrarian values to negotiate and evaluate their new role in international affairs. Even so, they discovered that the systems and structures of the military state were quite different from those of the welfare state they had encountered a generation before. Some differences were so striking that they made the possibility of simply "becoming North Dakotans again" seem rather remote indeed.

The Military State Comes to the Northern Plains

The people of the northern plains encountered the military state of the postwar period armed with the collective memories of nearly one hundred years of complex interactions with and attitudes about the federal government. As new western historians have reminded us for more than a decade, Frederick Jackson Turner's notion that pioneers went out and "conquered" the plains without the assistance of the government was nationalist mythmaking of the highest order. Instead, the American West as a whole served, in Richard White's words, as a "kindergarten for the American state."[25] Surveying, counting, assessing, exploring, commanding, and possessing—each of these state-mandated activities made the West "legible" long before most parts of the East were.[26]

On the northern plains, the Homestead Act, Morrill Act, Timber Culture Act, and dozens of other pieces of legislation made land, infrastructure, and services available to Euro-American settlers. Even the military state was in a sense "born and raised in the West."[27] On the northern plains, the U.S. Army made Euro-American settlement possible by building forts, forcibly removing indigenous peoples, confiscating their "surplus" lands, and murdering resisters.

As the Cold War began, adults in the Dakotas remembered most vividly their encounter with the centralized policies and programs of Roosevelt's New Deal. As Lorena Hickok reported, drought and depression combined to bring environmental and economic ruin to the northern plains in the 1930s. Year after year, wind blew the soil away and sun seared through what little crop remained. Per capita income was less than 47 percent of the national average—less than $150 dollars a year in 1932. By 1940 nearly 150,000 people had left the Dakotas, most of them never to return.[28] Many more would have moved away had not the New Deal spent over 400 million dollars on programs like the Agriculture Adjustment Act (AAA), Works Progress Administration (WPA), and the Civilian Conservation Corps (CCC). All across the plains, federally funded electrical service, courthouses, sidewalks, wildlife refuges, municipal swimming pools, schools, and roads permanently changed the landscape and improved rural standards of rural living. For the first time since statehood, a majority of voters in both states chose a Democratic presidential candidate in both 1932 and 1936.

But the Great Depression was a struggle for people on the plains in more ways than one. However omnipresent the federal government had always been and however omnipotent it may have seemed in the 1930s, the people of the Dakotas nevertheless considered themselves to be independent, self-reliant farmers and townspeople in the best tradition of Jeffersonian agrarianism. This made accepting the help of the government particularly hard. For instance, Grace Martin Highley, a welfare inspector for the town of Edgemont, South Dakota, in those years, saw the same story repeated again and again. Proud and independent men and women struggled mightily against accepting relief before finally giving in. "I think men face up to reality and do what they can to survive," Highley ultimately concluded. "And I think that people compromise. I think [they] attach to something that comes somewhere near their ideal, but in reality [they] reach out and take what [they] can if [they] need it."[29] The entire decade was a struggle—"an ideological struggle" against dependence.[30]

Even when people compromised, as Highley said, they did not always like it. Dakotans worried that government programs were filled with "shovel-leaners" who would forget the value of honest labor. They also bemoaned the red tape that made it hard and sometimes even impossible to receive benefits.

Last, they wondered why Washington's "army of bureaucrats" felt they knew the "farming business" better than local folks did. After all, no farmer would suggest, as the New Dealers did, that production should be reduced to bring down prices when people throughout the country were starving.[31] As a result, Dakotans continued to resist the policies of the Roosevelt administration, even as they cashed the checks that came from its programs. In 1932, the Farmers Holiday Association went on strike for higher prices; in 1933, officials with the Farmers' Union testified before Congress that their plan for the agricultural economy was far better than the one developed by Roosevelt's "Brains Trust." In 1933 and 1934, North Dakota's governor, "Wild Bill" Langer, put an embargo on the shipment of wheat and the foreclosure of property. Ordinary farmers learned the ways of everyday resistance as they found ways to undermine the very programs in which they participated. It was well known among "cooperators" in the AAA, for example, that farmers could alter their records to make their average yields look higher than they were, and thus be approved for larger production quotas.[32] Townspeople occupied themselves with recreating and reenacting the pioneer heritage of the state through sculpture, literature, architecture, and a myriad of fiftieth-anniversary celebrations, all of which inherently denied the centrality of the federal government in the region's development.

Compromise, which left local people in power and local values and culture by and large intact, was possible due to the fundamental respect for agrarianism embedded in the New Deal. Roosevelt's secretary of agriculture, Henry Wallace, though he might not have been a "real farmer" by Dakota's standards, certainly was one by Washington standards; and, as a versatile politician, he helped ease the tension between urban and agrarian interests in the administration. With his input, the New Deal planners organized many agricultural programs on a county basis, with county boards comprising local farmers making recommendations on acreage to put under production. Presumably, then, these same local board members sometimes turned a blind eye to a friend or neighbor's imaginative record keeping. Indeed, as the historian Michael Grant has recently noted, the New Deal sought to help Dakotans stay on their lands rather than remove them or convince them to give up on dry-land farming. Though a few radicals within the New Deal believed that farming west of the 100th parallel had been a mistake and should not be continued, Roosevelt himself knew policies that mocked the nation's frontier heritage would be political suicide.[33] Independent-minded rural folks were hard enough to keep under the New Deal's umbrella. Indeed, most Dakotans' allegiance to the Democrats was short-lived. By 1940, the majority were voting Republican again.

Ongoing mistrust of federal power also shaped Dakotans' responses to many aspects of foreign policy, which had begun to take center stage by the late 1930s. Fear of centralization, for example, fueled Dakotans' campaign against American intervention in World War II. World War I had exacted a terrible cost on the plains in both human and political terms. Many socialist and pacifist groups, leaders of the Nonpartisan League, as well as ethnic Germans and German-Russians had initially campaigned against the war and then been bitterly persecuted following American entry into the conflict. In the 1930s, Dakotans joined with the Minnesota-born aviator Charles Lindbergh in the America First Committee, a fiercely isolationist organization committed to keeping Americans out of foreign wars. Even closer to home, an enthusiastic group of North Dakotans began to plan for an International Peace Garden to remind people "never again to see a world drenched in blood."[34] At its inauguration in 1932, speakers remarked that "the world is not going to the dogs. . . . It is trying to save itself . . . and to discard forever guns and forts and things which pertain to hellish war and to a period of human barbarism."[35] Life was hard enough and the federal government was powerful enough already on the plains; its residents were typically not eager to seek out new troubles abroad.

On the national stage, North Dakota senator Gerald Nye investigated the role that munitions manufacturers played in the Woodrow Wilson administration's decision to enter World War I. Like many of his constituents, Nye suspected that Americans boys had been sent to the war not as much for honor as for profit (and eastern profit at that). He concluded that "giant fortunes [were] carved by men and corporations out of war while millions died."[36] When Nye heard about the attack on Pearl Harbor, he did not express shock. Rather, he expressed his most deeply held fear: "This is just what the British wanted," he exclaimed. "Roosevelt has manipulated us into war."[37]

Like most Americans, Dakotans generally abandoned their isolationist views during the war, which they came to see as both necessary and just. By 1945, 58,000 North Dakotans had served in the nation's armed forces. Moreover, North Dakota families spent a higher percentage of their income on war bonds than families did in any other state. They turned angrily against their leading isolationist senator. In his reelection campaign in 1944, Nye was bitterly attacked for having been "un-American and a friend of Hitler."[38] In the end, he carried only eleven counties in the state and lost his seat to the Republican John Moses. Politicians from outside the area were quick to use Dakotans' isolationist heritage to their advantage as well. During a tour of the Red River flood of 1950, President Harry Truman made a point of reminding men and women in Fargo that a "rebirth of isolationism could bring on war."

He then criticized the Republican Congress for failing to support his cuts in the wheat tariff, saying that the economic isolationists of 1950 were no different from the "yes-but boys" of 1936.[39] Once more, Dakotans were left between the sentiments of home and the politics imposed from Washington.

In the immediate aftermath of the war, Dakotans still sounded more like hawks than doves and more like internationalists than isolationists. One 1948 poll revealed that a large majority of North Dakotans supported the Marshall Plan for the rehabilitation of Europe.[40] Likewise, when the Soviets announced the successful detonation of an atom bomb, the editors at both the *Bismarck Tribune* and the *Fargo Forum* reminded their readers that "missile work deserves priority."[41] Moreover, writers who supported a massive rearmament campaign reiterated the "lessons of Munich," arguing that "appeasement will not stop a tyrant" and that "the men in the Kremlin" had learned their lessons from Hitler."[42] "It's later than we think" worried a cartoon character in the *Fargo Forum*.[43] Last, local editors boasted that the Midwest would play a big part in the job of rearming. A visitor to a defense industry plant reported with pride what great defense workers farm boys made "probably because of all that hard work on the farm."[44] The geographic realities of global warfare would require a disbursement of important defense industries to the "remote areas of the countryside," a description tailor made for the isolated and sparsely populated Dakotas.[45]

In the late 1940s, Dakotans took leading roles in the national effort to root out communists at home. Members of the Farmers Union and the Farmers Holiday Association pushed political radicals from leadership positions until the latter no longer existed and the former became, in the historian William Pratt's words, "more of a business-oriented pressure group, not the radical organization it had been."[46] The University of South Dakota also purged radical faculty from its ranks. The notorious anticommunist, Joseph McCarthy, even had a counterpart from the Dakotas, Karl Mundt. Born in Humboldt, South Dakota, in 1900 and first elected to Congress in 1939, Mundt was an unrelenting anti-communist throughout his thirty-two years as a representative and senator in Washington, contributing directly to the enactment of the International Security Act of 1950. In 1947, Mundt was the first congressman to call for the registration of communists and members of front organizations.[47] In one attack, he declared that "for eighteen years [the country] had been run by New Dealers, Fair Dealers, Misdealers and Hiss dealers who have shuttled back and forth between Freedom and Red Fascism like a pendulum on a cuckoo clock."[48] When a young rival, George McGovern, dared to challenge Mundt for his seat, Mundt accused McGovern of socialist leanings in his academic work as a graduate student at Northwestern. Mundt won handily. McGovern went on, years later, to win a Senate seat in South Dakota, but he never dared to run against Mundt again.[49]

A closer inspection of Dakotans' support for rearmament, intervention, and anticommunism, however, reveals important continuities between the isolationism, antistatism, and agrarian producerism of the Depression years and hawkish rhetoric of the early Cold War. In 1938, Dakotans wrote into an essay contest sponsored by the *Dakota Farmer* on what Americanism meant to them. Intriguingly, five of the six winners identified Americanism with "freedom" and "liberty"—in contrast specifically to an authoritarian state. J. H. Boese defined Americanism as "something that grants every individual and every family the right to put himself on his own feet, independent and self-directing."[50] Mrs. L. A. Philbrook agreed: "Americanism is every honest man striving to solve his own problems, . . . keeping us from communism, Nazism and fascism and all other isms. Except Americanism.[51] Edgar Syverud wrote, "Americanism admits of no superior, overlord, kind, or dictator."[52] Thus the ability to be independent small producers was keenly tied to life in a country without a totalitarian government. The "real Revolution" in the world, the *Bismarck Tribune* agreed in 1951, occurred when governments allowed for freedom from the government itself.[53]

Just as communists outside the United States threatened self-reliant individualism and agrarian producerism, so did communists at home. Speaking at the Mandan Elks Club in 1950, Senator Bill Langer made the connection between populist antistatism and populist anticommunism explicit. Communists (like the New Deal "brains trust" of the past) were "highly educated. They obtained their education in the United States and wormed their way into the highest councils of government. Then trusted by the president and holding the most important government positions, they have been found working toward the destruction of our nation." What was, in Langer's view, the best antidote to the insidious communism of an educated elite? "The people [must] exercise their franchise and not let small percentages of the population run the nation."[54] Anna Corbin from Livona, North Dakota, agreed. She wrote, "It seems to me that our government is only by a few, in place of by and for the people."[55] On a visit to Bismarck in 1950, Vice President Alben Barkley reassured the audience that a government free of communists would become "the servant and agent of the people, the only agent on which the people can rely and depend."[56]

But could the people of the Dakotas rely and depend on their government? In the early Cold War period, they were no more convinced that they could than they had ever been before. Familiar complaints of excess spending, waste, and overtaxation filled the news on an almost daily basis. Small business owners complained that they were so overregulated they could not compete, and that income taxes made it impossible to get ahead. Indeed, by 1950 local editors were arguing that "getting the government's fiscal house in order on the domestic front" was equally as important as "strengthening our defense."[57] Even with crops fetching relatively high prices, farm programs did not escape the critical eye of Dakotans. When a local official, Robert Geissler, was named to head a federal agricultural agency, community leaders rejoiced that there would finally be an administrator with practical knowledge of the area and its people. Previously, they complained, "federal farm programs [had] been taken away from the farmer and run from the top down."[58]

With the onset of the Korean War, even the military was not immune from the postwar antistatist critique, which grew more insistent as the 1950s progressed. Editors of the region's major newspaper officially supported the war effort. But they—and their readers—were still highly suspicious of how the military operated. Like the government as a whole, Dakotans worried that the military was inefficient and top heavy, while the individual solider was underpaid and sometimes cheated of the benefits he was promised.[59] Some Dakotans worried about changing the draft age to eighteen; others complained that information from the military was so heavily censored as to be essentially useless. North Dakotan politicians expressed these views particularly provocatively when they debated the state senate's concurrent resolution to support the "conscription of wealth as well as manpower when this nation's security is imperiled."[60] Though all fifty-five lawmakers supported the resolution, twenty-five voted to delete language that equated the army with a dictatorship. Supporters argued that "the army is a virtual dictatorship because they tell you when you can get up, what you can eat, and when, what you can and can't do . . . and that a man hauled before a court martial is guilty until he is proved innocent." Detractors suggested that "the federal government is doing a pretty good job now of preventing anyone from amassing wealth and that discipline in the army shouldn't be confused with a dictatorship."[61] The resolution carried no practical weight, but as a statement of the region's ongoing antistatism and anticorporatism, it is an invaluable tool for historians.

By the election of 1956, isolationism was back in full force on the northern plains. One poll showed that in January 1956, a majority of the state's citizens opposed foreign aid. Likewise, they were utterly against forging a new alliance with Chiang Kai-shek and going to war over Formosa. According to the historian Elwyn Robinson, at their state convention in 1956, the Republicans called the Democrats the "war party and Usher Burdick promised that there would be no more killing if Eisenhower were re-elected."[62] Senator Langer said, "The issue is: Shall we have more carloads of coffins?" Even the most internationalist of the region's senators, the Republican Milton Young, said that he opposed shipping "our sons to the slaughter fields of Europe and Asia."[63] In November, Eisenhower carried both North Dakota and South Dakota easily. He embodied both respect for the military's mission in World War II and concern for the future of an ever-growing bureaucratic war machine. Under his leadership, they hoped, the world could be safe for independent men and women to go about their daily tasks without constantly fearing war in a distant land.

The relationship between people of the plains and the federal government became a great deal more complicated in 1956 than Dakotans anticipated. Beginning that year, the war machine—or at least a tiny part of it—took up residence in their communities. When the Air Force came to the northern plains looking for land on which build military bases, Dakotans believed they could reap the economic benefits of militarization while maintaining local control over basic decisionmaking processes and long-term social consequences. In short order, they would find that much more than geopolitical boundaries had shifted since 1936. Negotiation and compromise with the new state—the national security state—would prove harder than many Dakotans imagined.

Local Competition for Air Force Bases

North Dakotans and South Dakotans were hardly the only men and women in the postwar American West to experience the ascendancy of federal defense spending or the consequences of militarization. In fact, World War II and the Cold War permanently transformed the American West. First seen as an "outdoor laboratory"[64]—an appropriate location for secret experimental activities—the West later became "the nation's military bastion."[65] In the late twentieth century, it also became home to protest groups whose members voiced their concern about the impact of uranium mining, nuclear testing, and toxic dumping on the environment and public health. Even on the remote northern plains, by the 1980s some residents had had enough. Along with a grassroots peace organization called the Red River Valley Peaceworkers, North Dakotans nurtured a nuclear freeze movement and passed a nuclear freeze referendum by a large margin.[66]

The American military was born and raised on the frontier and, some say, owes a debt, both in its organizational style and its experience with total war, to its frontier heritage.[67] Nevertheless, the exponential increase in military spending that began in World War II made any previous association between the military and the West obsolete. Between 1945 and 1965, for example, the federal government spent 62 percent of its budget, or $776 billion, on defense.

At least one-third of that or $250 billion went to western states, where only 16 percent of the nation's population resided.[68] The construction of research complexes, mining and manufacturing facilities, military bases, experiment stations, and weapons sites created a federal landscape and a federalized economy in every western state. In Utah in 1965, one-third of personal income depended on defense spending.[69] Throughout the region, U.S. senators and representatives were frequently elected on promises to deliver large defense contracts to their states and just as frequently were sent packing if they failed to deliver the goods.

But few westerners were aware of the risks that rapid militarization and nuclearization entailed. It took many decades to realize that the federal government had changed from a relatively transparent and magnanimous welfare state to a national security state—a "state within a state"—whose administrators did not always reveal the plans, procedures, or risks associated with new projects. Thus, when Senator Ed Johnson of Colorado went to Washington to lobby for his constituents and win one of the Cold War's biggest prizes, the Rocky Flats nuclear facility, he truly believed he was acting in their best interests. A native Coloradoan and a rancher, he considered himself a "self-sufficient individualist, a man who carved a homestead out of wilderness after overcoming tuberculosis."[70] He understood that at Rocky Flats workers would mill plutonium from Hanford, Washington, into weapons components that would then be shipped to the Pantex facility outside Amarillo, Texas, for construction into warheads.[71] What he did not know was how dangerous that activity would be, and that the government would ultimately act in its own rather than the public's best interest. By the end of the Cold War, the Rocky Flats facility had helped to manufacture 70,000 nuclear bombs. On Sunday May 11, 1969, however, a small fire very nearly grew out of control and threatened to contaminate the region as badly as the accident at Chernobyl, USSR. The national security state's "thick walls" of secrecy prevented Coloradans from knowing the full extent of the danger for more than twenty years.[72] In southern Colorado, a real disaster befell the people of the Four Corners region, who were exposed to uranium mining and nuclear testing. By the 1970s, their rates of cancer were so high that one government official suggested the area be designated a "zone of national sacrifice."[73]

Like other westerners, Dakotans hoped that securing large defense contracts would permanently aid their region's economy, priming the pump just as the New Deal had, but for what seemed an even "higher" purpose—national security. Both the construction of air bases and, later, the installation of Minuteman missiles involved large expenditures of federal funds. When it began, one Air Force general called the Minuteman program "the largest military development program ever undertaken by this nation in peacetime."[74] The government would spend billions of dollars on the missiles, employ hundreds of thousands of workers, and subcontract with more than 2,000 companies.[75] Such an engine of economic growth was impossible to resist. It was impossible for most Dakotans to see then that federal defense spending would not sustain prosperity indefinitely or that "other types of spending might have produced greater benefits for society or a greater multiplier effect in the economy."[76] Likewise, North Dakotans could have never known the potential risks they were undertaking. In fact, communities on the northern plains may have been even more fervent in their desire to acquire federal defense dollars than their counterparts in the Far West because they came to the game relatively late. Between 1946 and 1960, the defense department budget became increasingly regionally specific, with huge expenditures in northeastern states like New York and Connecticut, and ever-growing expenditures in Texas, Washington, and California, creating what sociologist Ann Markusen calls the new "gunbelt."[77] By the mid-1950s, the Great Plains was fast becoming the permanent war economy's flyover zone. Dakotans hoped that with the bases, their time to cash in on the Cold War had finally arrived.

At the beginning, it seemed obvious which communities in North Dakota would get the air bases, the B-52 bomber wings, and the subsequent ICBM facilities: Fargo and Bismarck. Both were mentioned by name in the Military Construction Bill of 1953. Both had municipal airports that could be expanded and sufficient population (38,000 and 18,000 respectively) to provide support services, housing, and educational facilities for incoming personnel. And both local chambers of commerce had reassured the Air Force of the enthusiasm and cooperation of the citizenry. After the Air Force performed initial surveys of the areas in November 1953, both the *Fargo Forum* and the *Bismarck Tribune* announced that their cities were definitely going to get a base.[78] To everyone's surprise, however, a second site survey conducted in the spring of 1954 determined that neither airport could be adequately converted to military use after all. Hector Field in Fargo sat too close to the urban area, and the terrain surrounding Municipal Airport in Bismarck was "unfavorable to expansion." What would work better, the engineers reported, would be to find a "virgin site" in the Fargo and Bismarck "areas."[79]

From this moment, competition among the communities near Fargo and Bismarck became fierce. The prize was enormous: Air Force officials had informed leaders in Fargo that 850 men would be stationed at each of two new bases in North Dakota with an annual payroll in excess of $2.7 million. Moreover, they expected to create significant infrastructure improvements.[80] And yet federal largesse would not come for free. As the Air Force legislative liaison, General Joe Kelly, wrote to North Dakota Senator Milton Young, "The Air Force has an obligation to the taxpayers of the nation to develop its base structure with a minimum expenditure of federal funds."[81] Thus an important criterion for selection was "community support" and "economy of development." In other words, municipalities willing to put up funds to defray real estate costs would get particularly serious consideration. Soon Bismarck voters agreed to raise $150,000 for land, Minot approved $50,000, and Valley City allocated $62,500. Grand Forks and Jamestown offered land for free. Only the Fargo Chamber of Commerce refused to pass a comparable resolution.[82]

Mayor Oscar Lunseth of Grand Forks and his friend, Chamber of Commerce president Henry Hansen, were particularly aggressive in their campaign to attract the Air Force. The chamber sent a representative to the original survey site in Fargo when military officials first visited. The next day Hansen sent a letter complete with a careful map of "four or five sections of very level, quite useless alkali land" west of the city that could be used for the base, should the Air Force decide against Fargo. He also purported that land appraisers had decided "this morning . . . that none of this land would be appraised for more than $25 an acre."[83] Better yet, the mayor and chamber promised to raise $65,000 for the purchase of a different plot of land, if necessary. In a letter of solicitation to the Lence and Englund Construction Firm, Lunseth began with a reminder: "By making these contributions, we are doing our part in the defense of our country." Then he got to the more "practical and materialistic side to this new project"—that economic growth in the area will benefit all concerned:[84]

> All of the proposed buildings will directly affect those of us in the building business and, of course, will stimulate all types of business in and around Grand Forks. Your firm is well represented here, and you have become part of the community. I trust that you will be able to contribute to this fund and share with us not only the costs but much of the benefits which will certainly accrue in the months to come.[85]

According to the historian Rich Nolan, the only thing that the leaders of Grand Forks did not do—although the leaders of Fargo, Bismarck, Jamestown, Minot, Devils Lake, and Valley City did—was send a delegation to Washington in June when the final decisions were being made.[86]

The June 17 announcement that Grand Forks and Minot had been awarded the bases set off a firestorm of criticism from the original towns whose residents felt they had been promised the bases. Leaders in Bismarck and Fargo complained that the Air Force had not followed proper procedures, particularly

253

when they only gave a vague explanation of their reasons. All they knew was that the deciding factors were "operational suitability, community support, and economical development of the site."[87] More than one leader demanded that Senator Milton Young get to the bottom of the controversy, cut through the military's secrecy, and get some answers. Of particular importance was the question of whether Minot could be considered to be in the "area" of Bismarck and Grand Forks to be in the "area" of Fargo, because both cities were more than 50 miles away from the original sites. On this issue, the military brass made quick work, explaining that those cities were in a "defense circle" set by the positioning of the new computerized radar systems. Moreover, because Minot and Grand Forks were north of Fargo and Bismarck, they would actually be better positioned to intercept Soviet bombers flying over the Arctic Circle.[88] The lesson of the past—that Dakotans might be working with the federal government—seemed no longer to be true. In this case, the federal government had the final say; indeed, it had the only say.

But people in the Dakotas, long suspicious of federal power, also wanted Young to find out the extent to which land donations had made the difference and why the reasons for the decision had been so secretive. In testimony before the Senate Appropriations Committee in late July 1954, Colonel Mauck claimed that, even if no land payments had been promised, the same sites would have been selected because "strategic" reasons had always been of primary importance. Yet there were still good reasons not to discuss the matter fully. As South Dakota senator Francis H. Case admitted in 1954, "We cannot submit to the Senate all the considerations we studied,"[89] implying that for reasons of national security, the military would keep its deliberations secret. Another reason for the secrecy, not surprisingly, was to prevent land speculation in the areas that had been chosen and to keep land prices as low as possible.[90]

Dakotans had not expected the Air Force to change its mind, to play one community against another, or to refuse in the end to explain itself fully. But once Young submitted his report to them, they at least thought the entire, frustrating, bewildering experience was over. And yet one more chapter had just begun, a chapter that this time made some families in Grand Forks wonder what they had gotten themselves into after all. On December 7, 1954, only a few months after awarding the base to the city of Grand Forks, the military announced that it had changed its mind about the suitability of the "alkali flats." It preferred a section of farmland further west of the city near the townships of Mekinock and Emerado. Unfortunately, that land was under cultivation and considered very productive by its owners. Hardly alkaline, the farms collectively produced $162,400 in 1953, would produce over $2 million in the next ten years, and included two large turkey farms.[91]

Within a few days, more than twenty families had signed a petition requesting that the military reconsider its decision to use the Mekinock location and had hired a lawyer, Richard King of Grand Forks, to file suit on their behalf if necessary. And, of course, they had contacted their senators. Both Young and Langer were sympathetic to the landowners' argument. Young also told the landowners that he "was trying his best to persuade the Air Force to build on the poorer land."[92] But it did not take long before Young knew he was dealing with a power greater than himself. In a January letter to King, he wrote:

> If the decision goes against us, which I certainly hope it doesn't, I doubt that it would be of any use to try to stop it by action of Congressional Committees. It may be a difficult thing to stop, because Congress wants to get these bases in operation as soon as possible.[93]

To make matters worse, the community leaders of Grand Forks, who had already invested so much time and energy to acquire the base, publicly criticized the landowners for being unwilling to "make a sacrifice" for their communities. Then they began a campaign to raise funds to help the Air Force acquire land on the new site. On December 30, the publisher of the *Grand Forks Herald,* M. M. Oppegard, sent a telegram to Young, minimizing the number of the landowners and implicitly threatening Young. "King represents only four or five affected farmers and one or two of them since said no objection. This area trusts there will be no protests entered by you that would jeopardize the base project."[94] Young asserted his neutrality and claimed he was only fulfilling his duty to all his constituents. One more editorial appeared in the March 6 issue of the *Herald,* calling on the landowners to give up their struggle for the greater good of the city and the nation at large.

In the end, several of the landowners rejected all offers from the government for the purchase of their land and forced the Air Force to condemn it through its "quick take" procedure. The landowners had to accept the appraised value of their land or proceed to a jury trial. Eight landowners, owning between 37 and 960 acres of land, took their cases to trial. In April 1958, two years after their land had been condemned, they received a settlement of $334,640, which was $92,350 above the appraised value. All the landowners lost their farms, and some left farming altogether. The price per acre they received averaged $150, which Richard King estimated years later was well below the price the land would have fetched in the following years of good harvest and strong real estate prices.[95] According to King, the landowners remained bitter for years.

This pattern of government secrecy, deception, and intrusion continued in the selection of locations for the ICBMs. The development of ICBMs in the

United States began in 1954, just as the locations for the bases on the northern plains were being selected. Though funding was spotty at first, the use of a Soviet ICBM to launch the Sputnik orbiter and Soviet boasts that they were turning out missiles "like sausages" guaranteed a twenty-fold increase in the budget to close the "missile gap."[96] The initial research that led up to the Minuteman, a solid rocket fuel missile capable of being mass produced, was done under the code name "Weapons System Q." The project was deemed so critical to national security that even the initials of the command in charge—the Western Development Division—were classified above top secret.[97] When the first Minuteman was tested at Cape Canaveral in early 1961, the sleek new rocket immediately made its predecessors obsolete. Rather than "a fat man getting out of an easy chair," as an observer described the launching of the Titan and Atlas missiles, the Minuteman "shot up like a skyrocket," and twenty-five minutes later, it splashed down in the Atlantic Ocean 4,600 miles away—exactly as planned. "'Brother, there goes the missile gap," an engineer commented.[98]

But where would the Minuteman missiles themselves go? Initially the military considered using a single huge "missile farm" equipped with 1,500 ICBMs, but "for reasons of economy," it decided to organize six missile "wings" that in turn were divided into three or four "squadrons" of fifty missiles. Within each squadron were five "flights" with a single, manned launch control facility and ten missiles. Each "flight" was separated from the others by several miles, so no single attack could directly strike more than one facility. Though the Air Force briefly considered putting missile wings on the southern plains, soil conditions and flight plan locations made the northern plains their final choice.[99]

Like the bases, many Dakotans considered the Minuteman missiles to be a fine prize of the Cold War economy. Local leaders anticipated that the government would spend millions on construction and then create a permanent flow of funds to support personnel, equipment, and supplies over time. Indeed, it was estimated that more than 4,000 construction workers would be paid more than $2.5 million a month in each missile field. Boeing, the major general contractor, was expecting to make $250,000 in local purchases each month as well.[100] Begun just months after the terrifying events of the Cuban missile crisis, construction continued at a fevered pace: six or seven days a week, three shifts a day, and twelve months a year.[101] Other construction sites and services were needed to support the project, including trailer parks for visiting engineers, new housing for missile personnel, upgraded electrical service, and new road construction in the area of the missile fields.[102] Dakotans knew that this massive influx of federal spending was likely to prop up the sagging economies of the communities that "won" the missile sites. But along with economic motivations, people supported the missile projects because they believed that the safety of the United States was at stake in ways it had not before. After the Cuban missile crisis, most Americans—Dakotans included—were convinced that the Soviets were bent on world domination.

As he did with the bomber and fighter bases, Senator Young placed himself squarely at the center of the drama over missile site location. He acted as a spokesman for the Air Force on all matters concerning the missiles and announced any new developments to the press through his office. He unequivocally supported housing as many of the missile wings in North Dakota as possible and, as a member of the Senate Appropriations Committee, scrutinized every detail of the process. In December 1961, for example, he announced that he had convinced the Army Corps of Engineers to change gravel specifications so that the gravel available in the Grand Forks area would be suitable for the project and the military would not have to pay extra to truck it there. This decision, he announced in the *Grand Forks Herald,* "has almost assured construction of a Minuteman missile complex around Grand Forks Air Force Base."[103] Today, Senator Young's hometown, tiny LaMoure, North Dakota, honors his important contributions and "political clout" with a bronze plaque placed in front of an actual Minuteman II missile—the tallest structure in town.[104]

As it turned out, however, neither Senator Young nor anyone one else in North Dakota, for that matter, had any significant influence over the decision to place two missile wings in the state. All six wings were built near preexisting Air Force bases on the northern or central plains: the first at Malmstrom AFB in Montana, and then one each at Whitman AFB in Kansas, Warren AFB in Wyoming, Ellsworth AFB in South Dakota, and Minot and Grand Forks AFBs in North Dakota. This made practical sense: Though missileers would live and work in the launch control facilities of their flights when they were on duty, they would rejoin family and colleagues on the bases when they were off duty (and they were more frequently "off" than "on"). Moreover, bases could house much of the support equipment that maintaining the missiles required.

It was likely decided early on, then, that the ICBMs would be located in groups around preexisting Air Force bases. In a 2003 interview with Nathan Johnson of North Dakota State University, William Guy, governor at the time of the missile installation, remembered that neither he nor Young had had any influence on the missile site selection process. For example, though he had "close relations" with President Kennedy, it made no difference because the missile selection process was, as Guy put it, "above the president."[105] The decision was up to the military, plain and simple. Even Young acknowledged the military's ultimate authority when it was convenient. In response to a letter from a constituent, Mrs. Peter Peterson, who feared the presence of the silos and asked Young to be sure that no more were placed in North Dakota, he responded that missile location "was entirely a Defense Department decision."[106]

Mrs. Peterson was not the only North Dakotan who complained about the headaches of construction and, more important, the unforeseen consequences of nuclearization. Contractors brought in enormous quantities of materials and thousands of workers to build so many silos and launch facilities so quickly. The *Grand Forks Herald* estimated that "a road eight feet wide and three inches think could be laid from Grand Forks to Williston with the concrete used in construction the missile complex." Likewise, enough steel was used to "manufacture 40,000 automobiles."[107] Three hundred forty miles of roads had to be graveled and upgraded to handle the heavy equipment used in construction and to service the silos.

A project of this magnitude inevitably disrupted many individuals' lives for a short period. But letters written to Young also reveal chronic, ongoing disruptions that the military had not corrected or would not correct. One set of letters, for example, concerned road conditions. Although roads were meant to be upgraded for the use of heavy equipment, some North Dakotans saw local roads used and, consequently, damaged, without repair. Mr. and Mrs. Nels Peterson of Petersburg, for example, lived within two miles of a missile site and gravel trucks used many roads in their township. They wrote that they "had understood they [the government] would replace what gravel they drove off. But so far nothing has been done."[108] Several other families had problems with water drainage. In 1965, the Air Force dug a huge ditch on George Johannsen's farm in Parshall, North Dakota, which was across the road from a missile site. The trouble was that, by 1967, they still had not filled it in. The ensuing water on Johannsen's land made it impossible for him to cultivate 15 acres of corn. To add insult to injury, wild oats went to seed on the same acreage, costing him $75 to spray. The Air Force turned down his request for compensation for these damages.[109] Sometimes the road and drainage problems blamed on the military were related. In a personal letter written in 1969 to his colleague from South Dakota, Karl Mundt, Young admitted that there were "some water problems with these Minuteman sites about three years ago due to faulty grading."[110] Though Young assured several constituents that the Air Force provided funds for extra road repair, the problems remained unsolved. Melvin Jensrud wrote as late as 1970 that "I can get no satisfaction as to who will fix these roads. . . . These missile trucks use all of our roads not only the designated ones. Can you help us with monies and designating who is responsible so they can quit passing the buck?"[111]

Along with concerns about property damage, Dakotans wrote Young about their concerns regarding nuclearization in general. A few, like Mrs. Peter Petersen, simply wrote to express outrage at the very presence of missile silos. A couple from Salem, Oregon, who had been raised in North Dakota, told Young that on a recent trip home they had been "surprised and saddened to see so many explosive depots (Minute Men Missiles) buried all along. Our relatives and friends living there do not want them. We, too, think this is all a big waste of money."[112] Other constituents wrote with questions. A farm woman, Mrs. Robert Lefevre, wanted to know if it would still be safe to eat fruit and vegetables from the garden after the spring rains. A schoolteacher, Dennis Carter, wanted information about how people would know when it was safe to come out of their fallout shelters after a nuclear attack.[113] The government's secrecy again reinforced Dakotans' traditional suspicion of federal power. Harley Steffen of Garrison, North Dakota, wanted to know why the missiles were only replaced at midnight and whether the water that drained from the silos onto his property might contaminate his crops. In a side comment to Mundt about Steffen's observations, Young remarked that "you get all kinds of weird stories about these missiles, usually from a small minority of people."[114]

If only a "small minority" expressed their fears or condemned the government's irresponsibility—admitting that anything shrouded in so much secrecy and mystery must be dangerous in some way—a much larger group responded when the government displayed actual incompetence. On August 14, 1968, congressional representatives, many members of the press, military brass, and local men and women gathered near Michigan, North Dakota, for a test firing of a Minuteman II. The "missile fizzled" and the launch failed—just as it had on October 19, 1966, and October 29, 1966. The initial response of the *Grand Forks Herald*—a longtime supporter of the military in the area—was to worry that this setback might delay production of the Minuteman III missiles that were headed for the state. But its editors nevertheless reminded the government of the promise implicit in nuclearization:

> North Dakota has accepted its roles as the nuclear stronghold of the free world's defense arsenal without complaint. But it would like to be reassured that there is good reason for any risk in the deposit of so much nuclear destruction in its prairies may entail.[115]

The *Devils Lake Journal* gave much the same message in many fewer words, asking "Is this Protection?"[116] In a letter to his senator, Lawrence

Woehl of Carrington was even more direct: "Well, with three tries I'm convinced that [Defense Secretary] Mr. McNamara sold the nation an Edsel for
defending the nation. . . . They may be able to sell [their] slop to somebody
else but not to me and a lot of thinking people."[117] "Thinking people" were
those in the Dakotas, by Woehls's definition, who after a decade of living with
the bases and the bombs that accompanied them still would not naively trust
the government and its many outside experts. "Slop," he well knew, was rot-
ted food and spoiled milk that passed for dinner in the hog barn. By 1968,
Dakotans smelled something rotten, and were not afraid to say so, even after
all those years.

Consequences and Conclusions

The broadest consequences of militarization were changing social and cultural
trends that began with demographic shifts and were often accompanied by conflict and controversy. World War II had encouraged the mass migration of
workers, particularly from the South, to industrial cities in the North and West.
Men and women left the Dakotas in these years for new "gunbelt" jobs in California and the Pacific Northwest. But in the late 1950s and 1960s, the trend
reversed somewhat when new faces also came to the Dakotas, bringing with
them a measure of the social change that other regions had been experiencing
for a decade or more. Most significant, construction workers and military personnel did not always match the highly uniform racial and ethnic background
of the people of the plains. Today, Dakotans often remember these new friends
and neighbors fondly because they brought new foods, accents, and cultural
traditions to their communities. For example, one woman from a tiny town
north of Grand Forks remembered that the children of the construction workers were the only new friends that she and her siblings had made in years.[118]
But the historical record also reminds us that other Dakotans were not so happy
about the onset of social change. For example, when J. M. Cranor of Salinas,
Kansas, wrote Mayor Lunseth of Grand Forks to reassure him about the kinds
of people who might move to town when the Air Force base was completed,
he assumed that Mayor Lunseth was concerned about social change. After all,
he too had been very concerned about the impact that nearby Schilling AFB
would have on his community. But his worries were eased when he met the
"very high type intelligent and industrious personnel serving in the Air Force
today."[119]

The boomtowns that sprang up around federally funded programs in the
Dakotas were the first places where workers from other regions of the country lived. The longtime NBC News anchor Tom Brokaw spent much of his

childhood and adolescence living in Pickston, South Dakota, where his father was a construction worker at the Fort Randall Dam project on the Missouri River. Pickston was an instant boomtown filled with "a constantly evolving workforce" from many states.[120] Workers from the South introduced local children like Tom to hush puppies, okra, butter beans, and collard greens at church suppers. "Some of my friends from the South had a taste for fried squirrel. My mother drew the line at that culinary adventure." [121] But Brokaw was aware of class as well as regional differences among the migrants. Many of them, he recalled, "had a difficult past" and "were happy to arrive and get a fresh start or at least put their troubles on hold during the run of prosperity."[122] For example, one friend's mother had "several children with different last names and the relationship with her current husband was problematic." One day she revealed to Tom's mother that she always kept $800 in her purse in case her husband suddenly left her. Only then did he fully appreciate "the difference between [my friend's] family life and my own."[123] Even so, Brokaw admitted that his experience with diversity was limited until he left South Dakota for California. When it came right down to it, Pickston was still "the quintessential white-bread Christian community."[124]

More significant diversity—ethnic, religious, and especially racial—awaited the communities that were awarded the Air Force bases and missile sites. Desegregation of the armed services was a top priority of early Cold War civil rights leaders like A. Philip Randolph. Through the end of World War II, all branches of the military had maintained segregated units for African American servicemen, and opportunities for advancement had been severely limited. In the Army, for example, only nineteen of more than fifty technical training schools were open to black servicemen. Moreover, the Army historically had maintained a 10 percent limit on the number of African American recruits they accepted into the service. Though the Army remained resistant to change, the Air Force was in the forefront of desegregation efforts. When Harry Truman issued Executive Order 9981 in 1948, declaring "equality of treatment and opportunity for all persons in the armed services" to be a policy of the president, the Air Force already had plans for full integration of their forces by the end of that year.[125] According to E. W. Kenworthy, the executive secretary of the Presidential Committee on Equality of Treatment and Opportunity in the Armed Services, by February of 1950, 25,891 blacks were serving in the Air Force, 71 percent in fully integrated units.[126] The war in Korea hastened the process of desegregation. Casualties were so high in many units, commanders reported, that it was simply deemed an "inefficient use of manpower" to put newly trained African American troops in segregated units rather than where they were needed as replacements. As a result, far more African American soldiers and airmen served in Korea than had served in World War II. Thirteen percent of all U.S. troops on the Korean Peninsula were black, anticipating the day when members of racial minority groups would be significantly overrepresented in fighting forces representing the United States.[127] Perhaps due to the new opportunities open to them, more black servicemen than ever chose to make the military a career after the Korean conflict ended.

Dakotans would have noticed shifting trends like these. In 1930, there were so few African Americans in North Dakota that the census did not bother to give the exact number. In 1950, there were still fewer than 1,000. Yet changes were coming—that much men and women could read in their papers and see on the evening news. At 6 p.m. on February 27, 1950, on the *CBS Evening News,* for example, Eric Sevareid reported on the efforts to integrate the armed services. He described black and white airmen living in "completely integrated" facilities, "sleeping, studying, working, eating, side by side, with whites," and even making use of the same swimming pools and servicemen's clubs. Such "excellent news," Sevareid concluded, "is a kind of quiet social revolution . . . that in time will have an incalculable effect upon the civilian population."[128]

Not all Dakotans believed that the "complete integration" of their communities was "excellent news." The only experience they had with a large minority group—Native Americans—was mediated through its own system of de jure segregation on reservations. Whites saw Indians as distinctly different from themselves, and few would have considered them as equals. Full integration with them, or any other nonwhite group, was difficult for some Dakotans even to imagine. Indeed, as some people remember it today, the fact that militarization would bring African Americans to the region was a tacit concern during negotiations with the Air Force in 1954. It may have even been the reason why Fargo alone of the bidding municipalities refused to provide low-cost land for the base.[129] In the end, city leaders in Fargo may not have wanted the base—and its airmen—after all.

Dakotans' concerns with integration were expressed in a variety of ways. Sometimes, for example, they used racially coded language in place of explicit references to diversity. In 1956, for example, the superintendent of the Public School System in Grand Forks alerted others in the municipal government to the "social problems that will have to be faced in this area and community in connection with the new Air Base."[130] But their objections to and anxieties about racial integration did not stay encoded all the time. At meetings of the Base-Community Council in 1958, Mayor Lunseth and officials from the Air Force explicitly addressed what they called the "colored problem." First, they discussed the "colored problem" in the area of housing. At one meeting, Air Force officials reported that airmen were being assigned to the base at the rate of two and three families per day and that the base was not ready to house them all. By June 1959, 3,000 men would be assigned to the base, but only 744 housing unit would be completed. Assuming that two-thirds of airmen were married, they would still need 1,256 rental units in and around the city of Grand Forks. Half of those would be for "lower grade airmen, who could not afford to pay more than $75 per month for rent."[131] In response, local builders agreed to meet to discuss the construction of additional low-cost housing.

More vexing, however, was the "matter of [housing] colored personnel." As reported by Amos Martin, secretary of the Base-Community Council, in the minutes of that evening's meeting, Sergeant Burt explained that "[we] had several married colored personnel being assigned to the Base in the near future and . . . there may be a problem in finding permanent housing for these people."[132] Married servicemen were by practice not housed on the base but in homes or apartments in the larger community. There is no record of anyone on the Base-Community Council asking why finding housing for African American families in local neighborhoods might cause a problem—that much everyone understood without saying. But there is also no record of anyone at the meeting proposing a concrete plan to solve the problem. Instead, they put off the discussion until the Grand Forks Ministerial Group could be in attendance, highlighting the presumption that integration would pose a moral or spiritual crisis for the community.

Thousands of military men, some of them "colored," many of them single, and all of them looking for something to do when off-duty, presented related problems for the community. As expected, many African Americans had come to North Dakota as part of the Air Force. (By 2000, there were close to 4,000 African Americans in the state, 58 percent of whom lived in either Grand Forks or Ward counties, the two counties with bases. The base populations themselves that year were around 10 percent black.[133]) In November 1958, an African American serviceman had been refused service at a local bar and had complained to his commanding officer.[134] Assumed to be an isolated incident, the matter was handled privately with the bar owner. A year later, in December 1959, however, Commander Leon Lewis wrote Lunseth about his airmen's inappropriate use of time off duty. "Specifically I am becoming increasingly concerned over my teenage Airmen and their off duty actions, mainly as to their proclivity toward using various establishments as hangouts to the detriment of the respective managements."[135] Whether some of these Airmen were African American, Lewis did not say. But he did suggest that the problems with

Airmen just "hanging out" in local bars could be solved if members of the community would open, operate, and at least partially fund a "place for social relaxation" for noncommissioned military men in downtown Grand Forks.

In 1960, the Base-Community Council agreed to look into the possibility of building a United Service Organizations (USO) center in Grand Forks, first by sending a representative to investigate the USO center in Rapid City, South Dakota, a city of similar size with a large Air Force base nearby. They discovered that Rapid City's club was partially funded and fully operated by the national USO organization. It was a popular place, to say the least, hosting 8,000 servicemen each year, 200 on an average night, and between 300 and 400 for special events.[136] Unfortunately, the national USO did not have the funds to operate a facility in Grand Forks. Even so, Commander Lewis hoped that some group in the community would take on the project, possibly by using a preexisting facility in town.[137] "The teenage problem has been somewhat reduced," he reported encouragingly, "as they have been eliminating some sub-standard airmen who have been prone to getting into trouble." Moreover, he suggested that a local facility could operate its club on a limited schedule: 4 p.m. to 11:30 p.m. and possibly only five to six nights a week.[138] However "limited" this undertaking seemed to Commander Lewis, its consequences escaped none of the civilians involved. Without ever saying no to him, they resolutely backed off the idea. First, the local YWCA refused to operate the center. Then the local veterans organizations argued that their facilities were already booked several nights a week year around. Next, the civilian members of the Base-Community Council questioned the expenditure of $10,000 in municipal funds for a military facility.[139] Finally, the matter was dropped.

Whether it was because of the presence of African Americans or unruly teenagers, or perhaps the threat of prostitution, there was not going to be a servicemen's club in downtown Grand Forks. West of town, north of town, on the alkali flats, out near the old turkey farms—that was where militarization was supposed to be, and so long as the people of Grand Forks had any say in the matter at all, that as where it was going to stay. Like communism, Dakotans believed that militarism was best when it was contained in a single part of town, a single sphere of influence. Of course, Dakotans coveted the economic benefits of militarization—consumer spending in town, and new construction, roads, and schools. But just as they had not wanted the experts of the New Deal telling them what to do, they did not want these new experts—the ones who only told part of the story, kept the rest a secret, and then changed their minds anyway—looking into their business or changing their way of life.

And yet, in the long run, militarization was directly connected to every major postwar economic and social trend that would change the lives of men and women in the Dakotas profoundly. One of them was the continuing decline of the rural economy. For all the risks they accepted by putting themselves at the center of the nuclear bull's-eye, the direct, long-term economic benefits of militarization for the men and women of the Dakotas were surprisingly few. During construction phase, for example, the government hired no local firms as major contractors. Many of the laborers were temporary workers, too, taking their paychecks and future productivity home with them. Likewise, neither the missiles nor any of their parts were manufactured, repaired, or upgraded in the two states. No ongoing research or development projects were located there. Moreover, the product of the military's work did not produce goods that benefited the states' economies. As James Clayton put it, "Even though those doing military research [or operating missile silos] use their pay to function as consumers, the product of their working time . . . does not like civilian products become an input for further production."[140]

Although it is true that militarization created jobs on the plains, those jobs were not of long-lasting value to local people or institutions. Thousands of military personnel were stationed on the plains, of course, but most of them came for a short tour of duty, paid vehicle taxes to their home states, bought much of what they needed at the base stores, and went back to wherever they were from—often as quickly as possible. Even the jobs made available to local civilians on the base were not of long-lasting value but were mostly low-paid blue- and pink-collar administrative support positions. Eventually some Dakotans would recognize and articulate the difference between the liberal state that had provided funds for the people's welfare and the military state that provided funds for facilities that could kill them. But it would take time and two decades more of tiresome secrecy, hypocrisy, and deception before some Dakotans would tell their U.S. representatives that the economic benefits of militarization simply were not worth their cost. Arguing in 1988 against supporting a fourth missile system for the plains—this time one that would run continuously along a track and put everyone along its route at risk—Red River Valley Peaceworkers member Marcia Molaner put it plainly: "It's the MX, not the WPA."[141]

Even if the direct impact of militarization on the local economy was not as great as some had hoped, the broad power of the military state in an emerging global economy had an enormous—but largely negative—impact on the state and its future. When the government chose not to establish research, development, or manufacturing on the plains, it tacitly encouraged a continuing drain of residents to urban areas outside the state. These places—Seattle, Oakland, Denver, Los Angeles—were the real winners of the Cold War economic competition. Between 1950 and 2000, the state of North Dakota barely held its ground in total population, while the rest of the country nearly doubled in size. And within the state, rural counties—many of those with missile sites—decreased in size dramatically. Cavalier County, northwest of Grand Forks, had 11,840 people in 1950; today it boasts a mere 4,831. Depopulation accelerated in the 1990s, with several rural counties losing more than 20 percent of their population. More and more, rural areas were repositories for equipment and waste, not places for expansion and growth. The exception, ironically, was Fargo, which has grown rapidly since the establishment of a regional Federal Reserve Bank. In 2001, the first million-dollar home was sold in a golf course development along the Red River. The "loser" in the military sweepstakes of the Cold War era, Fargo alone may be able to participate fully in the new global economy of our time.

The rest of North Dakota has suffered from militarization as much or more than it ever gained. This is due in large part because the spending priorities of the military state in the 1960s and 1970s contributed to huge federal deficits, which in turn drove interest rates sky-high and hundreds of thousands of farmers out of business. When in the early 1970s Secretary of Agriculture Earl Butz told small farmers to "get bigger, get better, or get out," he issued not a threat but a death knell for many of the small communities on the northern plains. After all, when one farmer got bigger, the rest did have to get out. Within a single generation, farms that had been tilled by one family for a century were auctioned off by banks or purchased by ever-growing corporate farms. At the turn of the century, a few Dakota counties had slipped under 1,000 in population and had so few people per square mile that they would have been considered beyond the "frontier line" in the famous census of 1890.[142] Thus, when the ICBMs were taken from their holes and destroyed, few people were left to tell the tale.

Just as they initially welcome today's corporate giant, Wal-Mart, to their communities, rural people welcomed the military because they believed in its promise of long-term economic benefits: jobs, improvements, and a place of importance on the national map. As time went on and ICBMs joined the Air Force bases, growing feelings of trepidation were reinforced by the secrecy with which the national security state operated. Even so, most Dakotans assumed that the benefits they accrued from the military's presence far outweighed the risks it imposed. Within a decade—because of these very changes it brought about—few Dakotans outside the emerging peace movement could imagine living without the military. When the ICBMs were destroyed, the governor of North Dakota asked for $475 million in aid to cover lost spending in the economy. In 1997, when the government considered closing Grand Forks AFB, the city of Grand Fork paid $100,000 to try to save it. But by then city officials did not trust themselves to do the work. Instead they paid $79,000 to Katak Rock, a consulting firm based in Washington, to help the city best present its case. The balance went to a former ambassador under Jimmy Carter who had helped negotiate an arms reduction treaty. The people best qualified to tell the government what was truly important to the people of North Dakota, it seemed, were not North Dakotans at all.

The men and women of the northern plains faced the prospect of militarization armed with the traditions of local control, suspicion of federal power, and trust in democratic processes. They were surprised to discover that the new state—the national security state—operated with much more secrecy, authority, and centralization than the New Deal had a generation before. Still, the people of the plains expected a fair deal—fair payment for their land, repairs of their roads and fields, nuclear weapons that actually worked, and control over their own social and cultural affairs. Much of what came instead was unforeseeable and irrevocable. Like most rural people in the world, the people of the Dakotas were valued for their empty lands and cheap labor much more than for their traditions of independence, self-reliance, and democracy. In most cases, even their histories have been lost, small drops in the rising tide of superpower domination.

Notes

1. Hickock is quoted by Richard Lowitt and Maureen Beasely, eds., *One Third of a Nation: Lorena Hickok Reports on the Great Depression* (Urbana: University of Illinois Press, 1981), 82.

2. Ian Frazier, *Great Plains* (New York: Farrar, Straus & Giroux, 1989), 199, 203.

3. Nicholas Meyer, dir., *The Day After* (New York: ABC Circle Films, 1983).

4. This is as quoted by Samuel Day, ed., *Nuclear Heartland: A Guide to the One Thousand Missile Silos of the United States* (Madison, Wis.: Progressive Foundation, 1988), 12.

5. According to John Lewis Gaddis, recent research reveals that the Soviets were not as far ahead in missile technology in the 1950s as the Americans thought; but they rapidly caught up in the 1960s and 1970s. By prolonging the arms race, Gaddis suggests, nuclear weapons "exchanged destructiveness for duration" and thus kept the Cold War going longer than it otherwise would have. See John Lewis Gaddis, *We Now Know: Rethinking Cold War History* (New York: Oxford University Press, 1997), 240, 291–92.

6. John F. Power, "The New Look, Air Power, and North Dakota," *North Dakota Quarterly* 35, no. 1 (1967): 1–14.

7. Information on the Minuteman missiles can be found at http://www.defense daily.com/progprof/usaf/LGM-30-Minuteman-III. See also http://www.CNN.com/ coldwar/experience/the bomb; and in Day, *Nuclear Heartland,* 14–16.

8. Frazier, *Great Plains,* 60.

9. "Blast Ends Cold War in Plains,' *Daily Southtown,* October 5, 2000, available at http://www.dailysouthtown.com.

10. For a complete text of McNamara's speech, see http://www.cnn.com/coldwar.

11. See David Pepper and Alan Jenkins, eds., *The Geography of Peace and War* (New York: Blackwell, 1985), 152; and "Deadly Nuclear Radiation Hazards, USA" map, 84.

12. Valerie Kuletz, *The Tainted Desert: Environmental and Social Ruin in the American West* (New York: Routledge, 1998).

13. See http://www.cnn.coldwar/experience/thebomb/html; and http://www.missilers.af.mil.

14. "Blast Ends Cold War in Plains, *Daily Southtown,* October 5, 2000, available at http://www.dailysouthtown.com.

15. Ibid.

16. "Blast Ends Cold War in Plains."

17. "Proposed Missile Museum causes Controversy," *Morning Edition,* National Public Radio, July 27, 1999.

18. Personal communication by Delphine Red Shirt to the author, September 19, 2000.

19. Transcript, "North Dakota Media Focus Interview: Issues of Peace," Center for Peace Studies, University of North Dakota, 7.

20. "Blast Ends Cold War in Plains."

21. Catherine McNicol Stock, *Main Street in Crisis: The Great Depression and the Old Middle Class on the Northern Plains* (Chapel Hill: University of North Carolina Press, 1992); Elwyn Robinson, *The History of North Dakota* (Lincoln: University of Nebraska Press, 1982; orig. pub. 1966).

22. A bountiful literature exists on the Cold War and its impact on American culture as a whole. See Michael Sherry, *In the Shadow of War: The United States since the 1930s* (New Haven, Conn.: Yale University Press, 1995); Paul Boyer, *By the Bomb's Early Light: American Thought and Culture at the Dawn of the Atomic Age* (New York: Pantheon, 1985); and Allan M. Winkler, *Life under a Cloud: American Anxiety about the Atom* (New York: Oxford University Press, 1993). Many fewer studies look at the Cold War's impact on a particular community or region; exceptions include Richard M. Fried, *The Russians Are Coming! The Russians are Coming! Pageantry and Patriotism in Cold War America* (New York: Oxford University Press, 1998); Len Ackland, *Rocky Flats and the Nuclear West* (Albuquerque: University of New Mexico Press, 1999); and Kuletz, *Tainted Desert.*

23. Sherry, *In the Shadow of War,* x.

24. Ibid., 119.

25. Richard White, *"It's Your Misfortune and None of My Own": A New History of the American West* (Norman: University of Oklahoma Press, 1991), 57–59.

26. James Scott, *Seeing Like a State: How Certain Schemes to Improve the Human Condition Have Failed* (New Haven, Conn.: Yale University Press, 1998), 2–3, *passim.*

27. Paul Andrew Hutton, ed., *Soldier's West: Biographies from the Military Frontier* (Lincoln: University of Nebraska Press, 1989), 1–8. See also Louis M. McDermott, "The Primary Role of the Military on the Dakota Frontier," *South Dakota History* 2, no. 1 (1971): 1–22.

28. Stock, *Main Street in Crisis*, 18.

29. This is as quoted by Stock, *Main Street in Crisis*, 86.

30. This is as quoted by Stock, *Main Street in Crisis*, 86.

31. Stock, *Main Street in Crisis*, 133–41.

32. Ibid., 142–46.

33. Michael Johnston Grant, *Down and Out on the Family Farm* (Lincoln: University of Nebraska Press, 2002), 169–71. In *Dust Bowl: The Southern Plains in the 1930s* (New York: Oxford University Press, 1979), Donald Worster argues that political considerations kept Roosevelt from making any substantive change in farming to salvage the environment.

34. See http://www.peacegarden.com/history/speeches/19311224.html.

35. Ibid.

36. This is as quoted by David A. Horowitz, *Beyond Left and Right: Insurgency and the Establishment* (Urbana: University of Illinois Press, 1997), 166. On the history of pacifism and the resistance to conscription, see Gordon Isenminger, "Hunhuskers, Red Cross Roosters, and Uncle Sam Whiskers: The McIntosh County German-Russians in World War I," *Heritage Review* 27, no. 4 (1997): 11–20.

37. This is as quoted by Stock, *Main Street in Crisis*, 212.

38. This is as quoted by Robinson, *History of North Dakota*, 438.

39. *Fargo Forum*, May 14, 1950.

40. Robinson, *History of North Dakota*, 469.

41. *Bismarck Tribune*, January 15, 1951.

42. *Bismarck Tribune*, February 1, 1951.

43. *Fargo Forum*, August 30, 1950.

44. *Grand Forks Herald*, March 9, 1951.

45. Ibid.

46. William C. Pratt, "Glenn J. Talbott, the Farmers Union, and American Liberalism after World War II," *North Dakota History* 55, no. 1 (1988): 3–13.

47. Alton R. Lee, "'New Dealers, Fair Dealers, Misdealers, and Hiss Dealers': Karl Mundt and the Internal Security Act of 1950," *South Dakota History* 10, no. 4 (1980): 277–90.

48. This is as quoted by Sherry, *In the Shadow of War*, 175.

49. Robert Sam Anson, *McGovern: A Biography* (New York: Holt, Rinehart & Winston, 1972), 92–98. Anson quotes McGovern as saying, "I don't know how he [Mundt] felt about me, but I knew I hated his guts" (93). McGovern won his Senate seat by beating former governor Joe Foss by less than one hundred votes.

50. *Dakota Farmer*, July 16, 1938.

51. *Dakota Farmer*, May 7. 1938.

52. Ibid.

53. *Bismarck Tribune*, February 21, 1951.

54. *Fargo Forum*, May 21, 1950.

55. *Bismarck Tribune*, March 29, 1951.

56. *Fargo Forum*, June 13, 1950.

57. *Fargo Forum*, July 29, 1950; *Fargo Forum*, September 30, 1950.

58. *Bismarck Tribune*, April 3, 1951.

59. *Fargo Forum*, August 20, 1950; *Bismarck Tribune*, March, 13, 51.

60. *Bismarck Tribune* January 30, 1951

61. Ibid.

62. Robinson, *History of North Dakota,* 470.

63. This is as quoted by Robinson, *History of North Dakota,* 470.

64. Kuletz, *Tainted Desert,* 38.

65. Gerald B. Nash, *The Federal Landscape: An Economic History of the Twentieth-Century West* (Tucson: University of Arizona Press, 1991).

66. The history of the Red River Valley Peaceworkers is carefully collected in "Red River Valley Peace Workers, Record, 1981–1989," collection 1202, Orin G. Libby Collection, Elwyn Robinson Department of Special Collection, Chester Fritz Library, University of North Dakota. Its inventory is also available at http://www.und.nodak .edu/dept/library/collections/og1202.html.

67. Paul Andrew Hutton, ed., *Soldier's West: Biographies from the Military Frontier* (Lincoln: University of Nebraska Press, 1989), 1–8.

68. Nash, *Federal Landscape,* 96, 98–99.

69. Ibid., 95. See also Roger Bolton, *Defense Purchases and Regional Growth* (Washington, D.C.: Brookings Institution Press, 1966).

70. Len Ackland, *Making a Real Killing: Rocky Flats and the Nuclear West* (Albuquerque: University of New Mexico Press, 2002), 29.

71. Bruce William Hevly and John M. Findlay, *The Atomic West* (Seattle: University of Washington Press, 1998), 6.

72. Ackland, *Making a Real Killing,* 158–59.

73. Kuletz, *Tainted Desert,* 7–8.

74. General Bernard A. Schriver, as quoted by Rocky Mountain Region, National Park Service, *Minuteman Missile Sites: Management Alternatives, Environmental Assessment* (Denver: National Park Service, 1995), 14.

75. Rocky Mountain Region, National Park Service, *Minuteman Missile Sites,* 14.

76. Louis Galambos and Joseph Pratt, *The Rise of the Corporate Commonwealth,* as quoted by Sherry, *In the Shadow of War,* 141.

77. Ann Markusen, Peter Hall, Scott Campbell, and Sabina Deitrick, *The Rise of the Gunbelt: The Military Remappping of Industrial America* (New York: Oxford University Press, 1991).

78. Rich Nolan, "Grand Forks Air Force Base: The Beginning," Grand Forks Air Force Base, 1988, 8.

79. Nolan, "Grand Forks Air Force Base," 8.

80. Ibid.

81. General Joe Kelly to Milton Young, as quoted by Nolan, "Grand Forks Air Force Base," 11.

82. Nolan, "Grand Forks Air Force Base," 8.

83. Oscar Lunseth Papers (hereafter OL Papers), box 7, file 1, Orin G. Libby Manuscript Collection, Chester Fritz Library, University of North Dakota, as quoted in "Nuclear Weapons of Grand Forks: An Interpretive Catalog," by James McKenzie, in *Peace Issues* (Grand Forks: University of North Dakota Center for Peace Studies, 1986), 2.

84. Ibid.

85. This is as quoted by Day, *Nuclear Heartland,* 16.

86. Nolan, "Grand Forks Air Base," 11.

87. General Joe Kelly to Milton Young, as quoted by Nolan, "Grand Forks Air Base," 12.

88. Nolan, "Grand Forks Air Base," 12–13.

89. This is as quoted by Nolan, "Grand Forks Air Force Base,"15.

90. Nolan, "Grand Forks Air Force Base,"19.

91. Nolan, "Grand Forks Air Force Base,"20

92. Milton Young to Gordon Thompson, January 24, 1955, as quoted by Nolan, "Grand Forks Air Force Base," 21.

93. Milton Young to Richard King, January 28, 1955, as quoted by Nolan, "Grand Forks Air Force Base," 22.

94. This is as quoted by McKenzie, "Nuclear Weapons of Grand Forks," 2.

95. Nolan, "Grand Forks Air Force Base," 25.

96. "Minuteman Special Resource Study" (http://www.nps.gov/archive/mimi/history/srs/history.html), 28.

97. Ibid., 26.

98. Ibid., 32.

99. Ibid., 33.

100. *Grand Forks Herald,* September 12, 1962, 22.

101. Minuteman Special Resource Study," 34.

102. Nathan A. Johnson, "The Economic Impact of North Dakota's Minuteman Missile Silos," paper presented at Northern Great Plains History Conference, Fargo, October 2003, 5–6.

103. This is as quoted by Johnson, "Economic Impact of North Dakota's Minuteman Missile Silos," 2–3.

104. Ibid., 3.

105. Ibid., 3.

106. Milton Young to Mrs. Peter Peterson, September 13, 1961, Milton Young Papers (hereafter MY Papers), box 315, file 11.

107. *Grand Forks Herald,* 12 September 1962, 22.

108. Mr. And Mrs. Nels Peterson to Milton Young, February 16, 1967, MY Papers, box 342, file 14 , Orin G. Libby Manuscript Collection, Chester Fritz Library, University of North Dakota.

109. George Johanssen to Milton Young, February 15, 1967, MY Papers, box 342, file 14.

110. Milton Young to Karl Mundt, n.d., MY Papers, box 341, file 14.

111. Melvin Jensrud to Milton Young, May 23, 1970, MY Papers, box 342, file 14.

112. Mr. And Mrs. E. L. Johnson to Milton Young, June 28, 1969, MY Papers, box 342, file 13.

113. Mrs. Robert Lefevre to Milton Young, March 28, 1962, MY Papers, box 169, file 1; Dennis Carter to Milton Young, November 21, 1962, MY Papers, box 169, file 2.

114. This is as quoted in Karl Mundt to Milton Young, April 1, 1969; Milton Young to Karl Mundt, April 2, 1969, MY Papers, box 342, file 13.

115. "The Missile Flop," *Grand Forks Herald,* August 16, 1968, n.p., MY Papers, box 342, file 14.

116. "Is This Protection?" *Devils Lake Journal,* August 15, 1968, n.p., MY Papers, box 342, file 14.

117. Lawrence Woehl to Milton Young, August 16, 1968, MY Papers, box 342, file 14.

118. Anonymous audience respondent to author, Northern Great Plains History Conference, Grand Forks, October 2001.

119. J. M. Cranor to Oscar Lunseth, n.d., OL Papers, box 7, file 1, 2.

120. Tom Brokaw, *A Long Way from Home: Growing Up in the American Heartland* (New York: Random House, 2002), 90.

121. Brokaw, *Long Way from Home*, 81.

122. Ibid., 87.

123. Ibid., 88.

124. Ibid., 81.

125. See http://www.trumanlibrary.org/whistlestop/study_collections/desegragation/large/desegragation.html.

126. E. W. Kenworthy to Eric Sevareid, CBS News, February 24, 1950, as found at http://www.trumanlibrary.org/whistlestop/study_collections/desegragation/large/1950/daf123-1.html.

127. According to the historian Michael Lee Lanning, 195,000 African American soldiers made up 4.4 percent of active-duty U.S. troops in World War II, and 13 percent of all troops in Korea. They made up 10.6 percent of troops in Vietnam and 24.5 percent of troops in the Persian Gulf War. Michael Lee Lanning, "The African American Soldier," http://www.bjmjr.com/aamh/html.

128. Transcript, Eric Sevareid, CBS News, February 27, 1950, 6 p.m., as reproduced at http://www.trumanlibrary.org/whistlestop/study_collections/desegragation/large/1950/daf123-1.html.

129. William Young to the author, personal interview, September 30, 2004.

130. Elroy H. Schroeder to Oscar Lunseth, June 8, 1956, OL Papers, box 7, file 1.

131. "Minutes of the Housing and Commercial Services Sub-Committee of the Base Community Council," May 28, 1958, OL Papers, box 7, file 1, 1.

132. Ibid., 2.

133. See http://factfinder.census.gov/servlet/BasicFactsTable/Dec_2000_PL-U_GCTPL_ST7&_geo_id=04000U538.

134. Major Ross Conti and Amos Martin to Base Community Council, November 5, 1958, OL Papers, box 7, file 1.

135. Leon G. Lewis to Oscar Lunseth, November 12, 1959, OL Papers, box 7, file 1.

136. Minutes of the Base-Community Council of the Grand Forks Air Force Base, March 24, 1960, OL Papers, box 7, file 1, 1–2.

137. Minutes of the Base-Community Council of the Grand Forks Air Force Base, March 10, 1960, OL Papers, box 7, file 1, 1.

138. Ibid.

139. Ibid.

140. James L. Clayton, ed., *The Economic Impact of the Cold War* (New York: Harcourt, Brace & World, 1970), 84.

141. "Peaceworker: The Newsletter of the Red River Valley Peace Workers," August 14, 1988.

142. Timothy Egan, "As Others Abandon Plains, Indians and Bison Come Back," *New York Times,* May 27, 2001.

Part IV. Superpower Games

10. "At Least in Those Days We Had Enough to Eat": Colonialism, Independence, and the Cold War in Catumbela, Angola, 1974–1977

Jeremy Ball

Between 1974 and 1977, the Sociedade Agrícola do Cassequel, Angola's most technologically advanced and profitable sugar plantation, located in Catumbela with over 5,000 employees, went from being an important asset in the financial and industrial empire of Portugal's Espírito Santo family to a state-owned symbol of the promises and failures of independent Angola's Marxist-Leninist economic plan. The story of Cassequel's decline, set within the tumultuous years of revolution and civil war, are paradigmatic of the local effects of the Cold War in Angola. For the Angolans who had relied on Cassequel for their livelihoods, this change meant unemployment and subsistence agriculture. In interviews conducted nearly thirty years after these events, former workers all told of their excitement and anticipation for a future without colonialism. The most common grievance against colonialism and Cassequel in particular was low wages. A more subtle and yet universally shared complaint was best summed up by Faustino Alfredo, who had worked for Cassequel as a relatively well paid nurse: "Colonialism was humiliation."[1] Workers, however, also spoke well of Cassequel. They described with pride the size and efficiency of the company, just as they equated plantation life, for all its difficulties, with elements of better times lost. One interviewee summed it up when he said, "At least in those days we had enough to eat."[2] The memories of those difficult times are no less complex than the geopolitical realities in which Cassequel, Angola, and the Portuguese Empire were enmeshed in those years (figure 10.1).

Figure 10.1. Map of Angola

Key

BIE recruitment province

BAILUNDO recruitment district

Quipelo recruitment city/village

Source: Cartography by Chase Langford

In the short period between April 25, 1974, and May 1976, Angolans achieved a contested independence from colonial rule, war engulfed the country, U.S. and Soviet aid fueled the fire, South African troops invaded from the south, Cuban troops arrived in a mass airlift to stop the South African invasion, and roughly a quarter million people, including most of the colony's skilled technicians and business owners, left in the largest civilian airlift in history. The Soviet-backed Popular Movement for the Liberation of Angola (Movimento Popular de Libertação de Angola, MPLA) confiscated nearly all the country's private industry, with the important exception of oil, and declared itself the only legal political party. At Cassequel, an inexperienced workers' committee committed to the remaking of society along socialist lines but with little practical experience running a complex industrial enterprise, took over management.

A part of the explanation for why Angola's transition to independence deteriorated into a fratricidal war is the fact that two revolutions were under way: one in Portugal, the other in Angola. The Armed Forces Movement that overthrew Marcelo Caetano in Portugal ushered in a period of profound change in Portuguese society. The country struggled to implement democracy after almost fifty years of dictatorship, instigated talks to end the wars in Africa, and restructured its economic system through reforms in land ownership and the nationalization of all banks headquartered in Portugal.[3] These revolutionary changes at home, in addition to exhaustion from conducting colonial wars on three fronts, explain Portugal's failure to ensure a peaceful handover in Angola. "The major Portuguese Government objective in Angola is to get out," the U.S. National Security Council noted, "with honor if possible, but in any case to get out."[4]

Meanwhile, Portugal had made no plans, even after thirteen years of war, to prepare Angolans for independence. In fact, the conditions for independence in 1974 were disastrous. Not only did the Portuguese not have the will to ensure a peaceful transition, but three nationalist movements also vied for power, claiming sole legitimacy and denying the right of any other political party to participate in government.

The primary explanation for the war, however, rests with the intervention undertaken by Cold War rivals: the United States, apartheid South Africa, and Zaire on one side, and the Soviet Union, Yugolsalvia, and Cuba on the other. Each of these foreign actors had its own specific reasons for intervening. For the United States, Angola represented a test case for resisting Soviet expansion after the humiliating defeat in Vietnam. For the Soviets and Yugoslavians, Angola offered an opportunity to be seen in the developing world as a champion against Western imperialism. For Cuba, Angola offered the possibility of expanding the peoples' revolution of which it saw itself as the vanguard. For South Africa and Zaire, a communist Angola threatened the status quo in southern Africa. Cold War politics acted as the major catalyst in the decision of each country to intervene in what was essentially a domestic dispute among rival nationalist movements.

Caught somewhere in the midst of this chaotic and deteriorating situation were the Portuguese owners and the Angolan employees of the Sociedade Agrícola do Cassequel. The events of the years 1974–77 transformed Cassequel and the people whose lives revolved around it. Decisions made by foreign powers and their Angolan clients rewarded extremism and destroyed the fragile middle ground of compromise. As we shall see below, their story is a prime example of the local effects of Cold War diplomacy, because when superpower rivalry came to Catumbela, lives would never again be the same.

Background: Labor Conditions before 1974

To understand the Cold War story of Catumbela's workers and residents, one must begin well before the rise of superpower tensions. Angola has the dubious distinction of having been a major source for the Atlantic slave trade. Slavery and forced labor did not, however, end with abolition in the late nineteenth century. Portuguese officials participated in a slave trade to the cocoa-producing islands of São Tomé and Príncipe in the Gulf of Guinea as late as 1908, and forced labor continued as a reality for Angolans until the 1950s. In 1930 Portugal (along with France and Belgium) refused to ratify the Forced Labor Convention of 1930, as officials from Lisbon argued that Portuguese legislation (which allowed for forced labor) "better serves our needs."[5] As a result of international and domestic pressure, Portugal ratified the Forced Labor Convention only in 1959, literally on the eve of independence for most of Africa.

Forced labor had therefore been a reality at Cassequel for much of its history. Company administrators requested workers from colonial officials, known as *chefes de posto,* in the interior. These *chefes de posto* then demanded from the local African chiefs a particular number of men to become contract workers, known as *contratados,* who were then delivered to individual employers such as Cassequel for periods ranging from six to twenty-four months. *Contratados* could not legally break their "contract." The only way for a *contratado* to terminate his contract—*contratados* were all male—was to run away from Cassequel, though this dangerous decision carried important economic consequences. A runaway—a *fugido* in company statistics—forfeited the bulk of his earned salary because this could only be collected from the *chefe de posto* responsible for "recruitment" at the end of the contract. Despite these substantial risks, hundreds of forced laborers ran away from Cassequel every year until the late 1950s. Rates of desertion were higher among men "recruited" in administrative posts within 100 kilometers from the plantation.[6] Surely, then, life at Cassequel, for the workers at least, was no picnic.

Forced labor at Cassequel was phased out during the 1950s as a result of pressures from Portuguese officials, increasing competition for African laborers, and the resulting scarcity of labor in Angola. A 1955 letter from the president of Cassequel's board of directors, Manuel Espírito Santo, to the plantation's administration in Angola, spelled out the new policy:

> The labor problem is without a doubt of maximum importance for our business. . . . The most desirable solution to the labor problem would be a voluntary workforce, not only at present, but principally in the future given the native labor policy that the governor-general of the province [Angola] plans to follow.[7]

The end of forced labor and improved labor conditions aimed at attracting voluntary workers led to slightly higher salaries, a new hospital, and better health care. Further, incentives, such as clothes, were distributed to workers who completed a longer contract, and the abolition of corporal punishment as a means of disciplining workers improved the work experience of Cassequel's roughly five thousand African employees.

Still, by 1960 an end to forced labor within the context of continued Portuguese colonial rule seemed too little, too late to many if not most Angolans. The scars of colonial oppression, perceived so often as national humiliation, were simply too deep to be healed by new clothes or higher wages. The slide into civil war and UN intervention in neighboring Congo in 1960 fueled Portuguese determination to buck the trend of African independence and convinced Angolan nationalists that the forces of imperialism and neocolonialism would stop at nothing to hold on to control over Africa's resources. Meanwhile, Cassequel distributed weapons to its Portuguese employees, who made nightly patrols of the plantation's perimeters. These patrols continued after the beginning of the nationalist revolt in northern Angola in March 1961.

It was in the context of revolt in Angola and movements for independence across Africa that the International Labor Organization (ILO) decided to investigate charges made against Portugal under the terms of the Forced Labor Convention, which Portugal had signed in 1959. A three-member mission visited Cassequel in December 1961 and reported that the unskilled workers at Cassequel "gave the impression of being intimidated."[8] The ILO commission went on to criticize Portugal for a status quo in Angola marked by "social and cultural backwardness in which for many people freedom and compulsion are

Figure 10.2. *Chinguar Guia* (Work Gang) Banner Held by
Recruited Workers at the Cassequel Sugar Plantation Celebrating the
Completion of a Contract

Source: Cassequel Archive.

equally impalpable."[9] The ILO's assessment of conditions at Cassequel must
be understood against the backdrop of an aggressive campaign by the government of Portugal to promote the idea of *lusotropicalismo,* which opined that
Portuguese colonialism was inherently different than the British and French
versions of colonial rule because the Portuguese did not practice a color bar,
and further because Portuguese men willingly intermarried with native women,
whether in Africa, Brazil, or Asia.[10]

The web of power relations at Cassequel must have been in ILO commis-
sioners' minds when they viewed photographs displayed proudly by the plantation's administrators showing a recent celebration marking the completion
of contracts for recruited workers. Recruited workers lived and worked in
guias, or work gangs, based on the administrative district at which they were
recruited. For example, the Chinguar *guia* banner (figure 10.2) proclaims,
"Long live our employer Cassequel; Long live all our bosses; long live St.
Peter hospital; my homeland is Angola; Angola is a part of Portugal, hence I

am from Portugal; my fatherland is Portugal; long live President Tomáz [of Portugal]."

The date on the banner, May 5, 1961, is significant because the nationalist revolt in northern Angola began in March 1961. Thus, we may interpret the banner as a reaction to African nationalism from Cassequel's Portuguese administrators. In January 1962, Manuel Espírito Santo, head of the board of directors of both the Espírito Santo Bank and Cassequel, reflected on the previous year to shareholders:

> For all of us Portuguese, 1961 was a year of suffering and sacrifice that will be engraved in the memories of those who lived through it and remembered in our history as a year of great trial, which we confronted with serenity and a firm determination to defend the principles of Western civilization.[11]

In the context of increasing pressure on Portugal to decolonize and in response to Prime Minister Antonio Salazar's insistence that the "overseas provinces" [including Angola] made up an integral part of Portugal, Cassequel's board of directors implemented a series of reforms, including the abolition of forced labor, an end to corporal punishment, and improved housing and health care for workers. The reforms aimed to defuse international criticism of Portuguese colonial rule and to secure a voluntary workforce. They were, in this sense, made with one eye on the international scene, another fixed firmly closer to home. As a result of these reforms, by 1970, according to a subsequent ILO investigation, contract labor in Angola did not involve coercion.[12]

The reforms did not, however, address one of the most common complaints among Cassequel's African workers: low wages. Between 1965 and 1974, for example, a "non-specialized" worker—a category that included 5,715 out of 5,983 workers in 1965—earned a monthly salary of between 225 and 400 escudos, roughly $8 to $15, plus a food allowance and housing.[13] Skilled employees such as Faustino Alfredo, who worked as a nurse at Cassequel's Saint Peter hospital, earned over 1000 escudos, or $37, per month, which was considered a decent wage, though still only 40 percent of the lowest paid Portuguese employee.[14] But skilled African employees were a small minority, roughly 4 percent of the workforce.

Throughout the 1960s, the Portuguese armed forces contained the nationalist war to Angola's sparsely populated eastern districts. Due to this relative calm and the lack of forceful Western criticism of Portuguese colonialism as a result of Cold War calculations, many among the Portuguese elite believed that it was possible to hold on to Angola. Among the most important of these Cold War calculations were Portugal's role in the North Atlantic Treaty Organization and the U.S. air base in the Portuguese Azores. Among the staunchest supporters of continued Portuguese rule in Angola were the owners of the largest financial-industrial conglomerates in Portugal, including the Espírito Santo family. In 1969 the Companhia União Fabril (CUF), which controlled more than 100 businesses worth one-tenth of the capital of all existing Portuguese firms, hired the U.S.-based Hudson Institute to conduct a survey of Angola's prospects for development. CUF held extensive Angolan investments in banking, mining, and construction. The Hudson Institute recommended to CUF, and later at a conference in Portugal attended by Manuel Espírito Santo, a "go for broke" strategy of massive investment:

> This choice is to push development of Angola at high speed on all fronts with the objective being to make Angola the model African state in terms of industry, social development, employment, education and bi-racial or multi-racial harmony. This choice is a bet on the validity of the work done since 1961 and the relationships of the racial communities throughout the history of Angola. The basis for such a choice is current fact (i.e. no war, no hunger, no hostility) when compared to other African states. In this case Portugal states that premature withdrawal is irresponsible as it is a way of turning people over to control by small cliques. Instead a new plan focusing on all aspects of Angola to make a modern 20th century state with education and opportunity for all and minimum standards of living would be announced having as its objective the provision of Western European standards as soon as possible and programming a referendum in the year 2000 for future political development of Angola. Angola is sufficiently rich in human and natural resources to undertake such a program.[15]

In the early 1970s, the Espírito Santo family made substantial investments in Angola, including the creation in 1973 of the Inter Unido Bank with the First National City Bank of New York (City Bank). Large investments by Portugal's leading conglomerates reflected the conviction among Portugal's ruling elite that it would be possible to hold on to Angola in spite of the nationalist war for independence. This hope was not quixotic. As long as the dictatorship held firm, and Portugal continued to work with the National Party government of South Africa and Ian Smith's illegal regime in Rhodesia, white hegemony in Southern Africa appeared strong. In addition, the Portuguese elite could count on acquiescence from leading Western powers concerned about keeping southern Africa, and its minerals, away from the Soviets.

Revolution

The peaceful revolution begun on April 25, 1974, which toppled Marcelo Caetano and over forty years of dictatorship in Portugal, led to Cassequel's first labor strikes in June and August 1974. Cassequel's workers, including a few Portuguese employees, elected a workers' committee (*comité de trabalhadores*) to represent their collective interests in talks with management. After those negotiations failed to secure a rise in salary, the workers' committee collaborated with the hitherto white and *mestiço* Lobito Employees Union of Commerce and Industry to organize the workers. The vast majority of Cassequel workers subsequently walked off their jobs and demanded higher salaries. This was a first in Cassequel's sixty-year history. Never before had African workers protested or openly challenged company policies, even during thirteen years of nationalist war against colonialism. Taking a hard-line response, Cassequel's administration refused to raise salaries, arguing that without a raise in the fixed government price paid for Cassequel sugar, the company could not afford higher salaries. The workers maintained solidarity, and at one point during the strike they surrounded the company offices and refused to allow the director out of the offices. He managed eventually to extricate himself, but only after agreeing to raise salaries. Meanwhile, Cassequel lobbied the new revolutionary government in Lisbon for a raise in the set price of sugar.

The Portuguese revolution opened a floodgate of pent-up anger and frustration against colonialism during a period of heightened Cold War tension. Union literature of the period reflects a growing sense of strength, as well as an increasingly anticapitalist, anti-imperialist sentiment. For example, in a public statement dated June 22, 1974, the Lobito Employees Union of Commerce and Industry called on Cassequel workers to maintain unity and wait for instructions from their union, in order "to prosecute our fight and defeat one of the principle methods of Capitalist repression: hunger."[16] The company agreed to raise base monthly salaries to 3,500 escudos—approximately a tenfold increase.[17] For workers, this drastic jump in salary validated collective action and the promises of socialism. For the bottom line of the company, however, the tenfold jump in salaries, added to weeks of lost production, translated into substantial financial losses in 1974, even with a rise in the price of sugar.[18] The August strike caused a deficit of 19 million escudos, or roughly $700,000, for the company, about the same amount as its reported profits in 1973.[19]

The 1974 strike invigorated the burgeoning union movement and gave workers a taste of their own strength in a rapidly changing situation. Initially, workers demanded modest gains such as the right to strike, a forty-hour week, and a minimum wage.[20] During 1975, anticapitalist and anti-imperialist rhetoric escalated as the political situation deteriorated. Imperialism and capitalism became—along with colonialism—the enemies of "the People."

It is here, then, in 1975 that the story of Cassequel becomes fundamentally a Cold War tale. In January 1975, Portugal signed the historic Alvor agreement with the three Angolan nationalist movements—the Soviet-backed MPLA, the U.S.-backed National Front for the Liberation of Angola (Frente Nacional de Libertação de Angola, FNLA), and the South African—backed National Union for the Total Independence of Angola (A União Nacional para a Independência Total de Angola, UNITA)—to establish a transitional government made up of the three nationalist movements and the Portuguese, which would govern until November 11, 1975, when Portugal would hand over power to the Angolans. Within six weeks of the agreement, however, the FNLA attacked MPLA troops in northern Angola and the situation quickly deteriorated into a renewed state of war, with the Portuguese wringing their hands and the transitional government defunct. The FNLA's aggressive posture reflected its military advantage as a result of substantial financial and logistical support from the Zairean leader Mobutu Sese Seko. The FNLA figured that if it could capture Luanda, then it would be in the strongest position to take over political power on November 11, Independence Day. As the violence escalated, the FNLA and MPLA engaged in a "discourse of exclusion," which denied any legitimacy to the other nationalist movement, or indeed to any political movement except their own.[21] Another contributory factor to the escalating violence was that neither superpower acted to ensure the Alvor agreement, and, in fact, additional foreign military funding began almost immediately.

In January 1975, the MPLA and FNLA were both actively soliciting funds from their international supporters. The United States acted first, a week after the signing of the Alvor agreement, when the Forty Committee, the top-level review board that passes on covert operations abroad, approved a $300,000 program of covert support for the FNLA leader, Holden Roberto.[22] The MPLA leaders were meanwhile soliciting funds from Yugoslavia, the USSR, and Cuba. Specifically, the MPLA requested $100,000 to cover the cost of shipping its major arsenal from Dar es Salaam to Angola.[23] Soviet and Cuban aid would not, however, begin until July, and it was Yugoslavia that stepped forward to provide the requested $100,000.

Meanwhile, the workers' movement equated the end of colonial rule and imperialist domination as the harbingers of a more just workers' state.[24] The MPLA in particular encouraged workers to discuss their problems, to know their rights, and not to tolerate "criminal exploitation" at the hands of the capitalists and imperialists in Angola. In its official newspaper, *Vitória Certa* (Certain Victory), the MPLA labeled the increasingly ineffectual Transitional Government, of which it was a member, as imperialist.[25] When business owners threatened closures due to increasing labor costs, the MPLA labeled the threats "reactionary manipulation."[26]

At Cassequel and in the adjacent town of Catumbela, the sporadic violence between supporters of the three nationalist movements disrupted the 1974–75 sugar harvest as Portuguese technicians and management began a mass exodus. To further confuse the situation, the government of Portugal issued a warrant for the arrest of the president of Cassequel's board of directors, António Espírito Santo, who then fled Angola for South Africa with the help of Jonas Savimbi, leader of UNITA, rather than face extradition to Portugal, where his family was being charged for collusion with the Salazar and Caetano regimes. António Espírito Santo negotiated the wage increases with workers in August 1974 and was trying desperately to establish a modus operandi with the nationalist movements to hold on to his family's Angolan investments. In March 1975, as fighting escalated, the Espírito Santos decided to support Jonas Savimbi's UNITA. The decision reflected the fact that UNITA was the most probusiness nationalist movement. According to António Espírito Santo's younger brother, "UNITA was the most noncommunist party in Angola, and our hope was that they would allow the private companies to continue."[27] In April 1975, for example, when the transitional government nationalized Angola's private banks, UNITA issued the following statement: "We wish to take an unequivocal stand; UNITA does not support the nationalization because in addition to creating stagnation in our economy; . . . it creates fear on the part of investors and encourages and facilitates capital flight."[28] Statements such as this one delighted UNITA's supporters among Angola's business leaders, as well as among its South African, and soon to be American, supporters.

In March 1975, Victor Ribeiro—an Angolan-born *mestiço* (a person of mixed European and African heritage), MPLA supporter, engineer in Cassequel's sugar factory, and member of Cassequel's workers' committee—assumed the position of plantation director. In March 1975, Ribeiro represented the modus operandi with independent Angola being attempted by the Espírito Santos. With António Espírito Santo in South Africa, Ribeiro attempted to run the plantation, in spite of heightened tension and sporadic fighting among supporters of the MPLA and UNITA. Company employees carried membership cards for both nationalist movements in case of roadblocks. Both the MPLA and UNITA armed civilians and fought for control of Catumbela. Meanwhile, Cassequel's administrators admonished workers to keep working because "everything will be good after independence."[29] In response to this promise, the MPLA declared:

> This is a huge lie. . . . The Angolan people are interested in insti-
> tuting in our country a Democratic Popular Regime under the con-
> trol of the working class, aligned with the peasants and all other ex-
> ploited classes of our people. On the other hand, other Angolans
> are interested in instituting a fascist regime that will terminate all
> the democratic victories already won by the People. These are the
> ones who protect the bosses and threaten the workers and the An-
> golan people. These bandits ought to be unmasked. The fight will
> only be finished when exploitation ends and the People achieve
> economic and political power. But in order for us to achieve eco-
> nomic and political power, we have to pull down the State of Ex-
> ploiters and construct a State of the People.[30]

As a result of such nationalist propaganda, workers "did not," according to a former worker, Daniel Sowende Fiqueiredo, "want to work any longer; they thought that independence would provide everything for free."[31] Another former worker, Germano Castrioto, said that workers just wanted "to do nothing and drink *quimbombo,*" a kind of locally brewed palm wine.[32] Labor productivity plummeted at Cassequel and across Angola. As the American consul explained, productivity simply was not on the minds of most Angolans during this period of upheaval: "For the African workers the end of colonialism signifies above all else the welcome demise of the white foreman's efforts to push the production pace."[33]

Amid the heightened rhetoric and ongoing battles for control of Catumebla, Cassequel found it nearly impossible to recruit workers in the UNITA-controlled interior highlands because of the general uncertainty and violence.[34] Workers were split between support for the MPLA and UNITA. In Catumbela, it was UNITA's union, SINDACO, that commanded the loyalty of most workers in 1975. Support for UNITA also stemmed from ethnic identification. A former UNITA soldier, Sousa Jamba, explained this: "As Ovimbundu, . . . we believed that this was the only movement that would assert our position in the country and save us from *mestiço* [MPLA] domination."[35] As supporters of UNITA and the MPLA competed for the loyalty of Cassequel's workers, the Portuguese government, which by July 1975 controlled little more than Angola's main cities, announced plans to evacuate 250,000 people by air, including nearly all the country's skilled workforce and most business owners.[36] In this vacuum of authority and increasing uncertainty, battles between the nationalist movements continued.

Instability also fueled ideological rhetoric. As late as May 1975, MPLA president Agostinho Neto told the American consul in Luanda that he was not a Marxist and preferred to call himself "a Progressive who takes a pragmatic approach to problems."[37] Neto also explained that "the MPLA is not so anti-American that it cannot see and adapt to reality," and that that the MPLA "wants relations with the United States and will cooperate as long as Angola's sovereignty and its right to make decisions based on its perceptions of its national interests are respected."[38]

In July, the major escalation from foreign supporters began in the context of the dissolution of the transitional government and an escalation of violence and of violent rhetoric. On July 17, the Gerald Ford administration approved a Central Intelligence Agency Action Plan, dubbed iafeature, to increase aid to the FNLA and to begin funding UNITA. On July 18, President Ford authorized the disbursement of $6 million, followed by another $8 million on July 27 and $10.7 million on August 20.[39] U.S. secretary of state Henry Kissinger explained the U.S. decision to intervene:

> Leaving the field to Soviet military operations would doom us to irrelevance in the upheavals in Southern Africa looming on the horizon and probably in other regions as well. The issue, in short, was not the intrinsic importance of Angola but the implications for Soviet foreign policy and long-term East-West relations.[40]

That same month, South Africa began covertly supplying UNITA with weapons.[41] The South African decision to supply UNITA stemmed from UNITA leader Jonas Savimbi's solicitations for help to fight the MPLA and South African fears that an MPLA government in Luanda would provide succor to the South West Peoples' Organization, which was fighting the South African occupation of Namibia. Nathaniel Davis, U.S. assistant secretary of state for African affairs, reported in July that Savimbi "was soliciting arms everywhere."[42]

Cuban intervention began in earnest just as the Forty Committee approved covert funds. On July 25, Cuban representatives arrived in Angola with $100,000 and plans to begin sending in Cuban military instructors. The first Soviet weapons began arriving in August. Still, at a meeting with Cuban representative Raúl Díaz Argüelles on August 11, 1975, MPLA president Agostinho Neto complained about the paucity of support for the MPLA from the socialist countries, especially in comparison with Mobutu's support for the FNLA.[43]

By August 1975, the Revolutionary Council running Portugal recognized that Angola was operating without a government, and "ineffectiveness, incompetence, and corruption" marked what government still existed.[44] A week later, the MPLA took effective control of the Catumbela area, and work at

Cassequel ground to a standstill. According to Catarina Rodrigues Silva, a secretary at Cassequel, Ribeiro, the former engineer and workers' committee member, entered Catumbela "on an MPLA tank."[45] Whether or not Ribeiro actually rode into town on a tank is impossible to determine, though perhaps this is beside the point; the memory represents the impression that Ribeiro decided to work with the MPLA against his former employers.

Meanwhile, as noted, work at Cassequel ground to a near standstill. This was due in part to a scarcity of specie with which to pay workers. In April 1975, private banks in Portugal were nationalized. In Angola, the ownership of private banks was transferred to the Transitional Angolan Government. In August, the Ministry of Finance imposed strict restrictions on bank account withdrawals to avert the run on banks that had begun at several locations, including Lobito, near Cassequel. Thus, money was tightly rationed, and most of Cassequel's administrators, including accountants, had left the country or were busy making arrangements to leave.

War and Independence

From August, the military situation continued to escalate as foreign aid and military trainers arrived in Angola. In October, however, the situation changed dramatically. On October 14, a South African military column, code named Zulu, invaded from the south. The invasion sparked the second, more intense stage of the Angola war. Zulu was composed of more than 1,000 black Angolans and a smaller number of white South African troops. The Angolan troops included FNLA guerrillas and soldiers who had fought with the Portuguese during the war for independence.[46] The aim of Zulu was to take Luanda and turn it over to what by this point in the war had become the FNLA-UNITA alliance. Zulu moved quickly, taking Catumbela on November 1, and continuing up the coast toward Luanda.

It was in response to this invasion that Cuba launched Operation Carlota to stop the South Africans. Carlota included a 652-man battalion of the elite Special Forces of the Ministry of the Interior, flown to Luanda on November 7. A larger artillery regiment consisting of 1,253 men traveled by sea and arrived in Angola between November 27 and December 1. Castro acted without the consent of Moscow and only informed the Soviets after the fact.[47] The Cuban soldiers stopped the South African–FNLA–UNITA advance. On the eve of independence, the South African–FNLA–UNITA forces controlled about two-thirds of the country, including Catumbela, but the Cuban-MPLA forces held the capital.

On November 11, amid civil war, the Portuguese high commissioner lowered the Portuguese flag and left Angola without transferring power to a nationalist administration. The MPLA, which controlled Luanda, proclaimed "a people's republic" and was immediately recognized by the Eastern Bloc and socialist countries, but not Portugal. The FNLA and UNITA announced the formation of a "national revolutionary council" based in their central highlands stronghold. The war continued throughout November and December. The South Africa–FNLA–UNITA alliance increasingly lost ground as the Cubans built up their forces.

The final blow to the South Africa–FNLA–UNITA alliance came on December 19, 1975, when the U.S. Senate passed the Tunney Amendment, banning *any* use of funds for Angola.[48] This meant the end of the U.S. covert program in Angola. The Tunney Amendment reflected Americans' unwillingness, after Vietnam, to become embroiled in another war, in a part of the world most viewed as peripheral to U.S. interests. The Tunney Amendment also reflected Congress's determination to exercise its consitutional war-making authority. After the passage of the Tunney Amendment, the Soviet airlift of weapons and supplies accelerated. On December 30, South Africa decided to withdraw Zulu. The last South African troops left Angolan territory on March 27, 1976. The main reason for this abrupt South African decision was the withdrawal of U.S. support. President Ford blamed the Senate for jeapordizing America's position in the world: "This abdication of responsibility by a majority of the Senate will have the gravest consequences for the long-term position of the United States and for international order in general."[49]

Remaking Angolan Society

The MPLA victory in February and March 1976 cleared the way for the remaking of Angolan society along socialist lines. The South African invasion and the decisive aid supplied by Cuba and the USSR moved the MPLA to adopt a Soviet-style system. On Independence Day, Agostinho Neto declared that "the organs of the state will be under the supreme guidance of the MPLA and the primacy of the movement's strucures over those of the state will be ensured."[50] The MPLA declared itself the only legal representative of the Angolan people, and it guaranteed democracy through participation in its "peoples' power" movement.[51] In fact, the institutions of the MPLA and the government became one in the same. According to article 31 of the 1975 Constitution, "The President of the Popular Republic of Angola is the President of the MPLA."[52] This new order allowed no room for dissenters. The FNLA and

UNITA were declared "traitors" of the Angolan people and became enemies of the MPLA's self-proclaimed "true cause," against which opposition had no legitimate place.[53]

At Cassequel, the remaining workers greeted independence with high expectations and great enthusiasm. Germano Adelino Castrioto, a former cane cutter, remembered the days following independence: "At first it was sweet, it was good, because we still had many things that colonialism left behind; later, it came to an end."[54] According to Sócrates Dáskalos—governor of Benguela Province during the Transitional Government and then again after the MPLA took control of the province from the South Africa–FNLA–UNITA alliance in February—the MPLA victory emboldened the most radical *empelistas* (MPLA stalwarts) to demand the confiscation of anything "that smelled of profit or privilege."[55] On May 8, the MPLA confiscated Cassequel. The legislation provided four justifications for the confiscation: (1) Sugar production was strategic for the national economy, (2) the company employed over 4,000 workers, (3) the administration of the company abandoned the country and cooperated with the "reactionary conspiracy" led by the FNLA and UNITA, and (4) the company had a monopoly on the nation's sugar production.[56] This confiscation also reflected the fact that the Espírito Santos fought on the losing side of the war.

The confiscated Cassequel fell under the authority of the Ministry for Industry and Energy, which set up a National Commission for Restructuring the Sugar Industry, made up of MPLA party officials and several Cuban advisers. The National Commission even changed Cassequel's name to Primeiro de Maio (The First of May) in honor of International Workers' Day and asked Victor Ribeiro to remain as director. Ribeiro worked with MPLA-aligned union representatives to discuss policy- and work-related issues. The local union (*comissão sindical*) replaced the former worker committees after May 1976 as the primary structure through which workers could voice their concerns and discuss issues.[57] In addition, the local MPLA party cell (Comité de Acção) also participated in local issues, including the day-to-day operations of Cassequel / Primeiro de Maio. The most ideological members of the union and the MPLA party cell demanded that the administration be "sanitized" of the remaining Portuguese engineers. Ribeiro managed to safeguard the jobs of these engineers, but he agreed to reduce their salaries by 50 percent. He recognized that these engineers operated the sugar mill and that without their expertise the machinery would eventually cease to function. Because they were receiving half their former salaries during a period of high inflation, however, and in a period of overt ideological strife, the engineers decided almost to a man to leave Angola. Concurrent with the sanitizing of "colonialists," the National Commission for Restructuring the Sugar Industry sent two-dozen Cubans to help the Angolans now running the sugar-processing equipment. Cold War battles thus continued to influence and alter life on the plantation even after the formal close of hostilities.

Daily life in Catumbela became more difficult throughout 1976. Diminishing stocks of staple foods, as a result of the deterioration of networks of distribution and the absence of a reliable currency, led to increasingly expensive food prices and negated the wage gains workers achieved in 1974. The results were practically catastrophic. Generally, Cassequel workers and their families were unable to obtain either consumer goods formerly bought in Portuguese-owned stores in Catumbela or food formerly supplied by farmers in the interior.

Facing these challenges, the revolutionary regime declared 1976 the Year of National Reconstruction. Initially, workers hopeful for a better life in the future welcomed the structural changes and contributed their labor in spite of the erratic payment of salaries and high inflation. In this context, more and more workers stole sugarcane and company equipment; others converted parts of the plantation into subsistence garden plots.[58] According to the provincial governor, the source of the problem was policies made by the National Commission for Restructuring the Sugar Industry: "During that period (1976–77), Cuban cooperation could not be criticized without running the risk of being accused as a counterrevolutionary, and in the sugar industry the Cuban presence was numerous."[59] He even charged that the Cubans wanted to see the Angolan sugar industry fail so that Cuba could sell sugar to Angola.[60] Geopolitics continued, therefore, to play havoc with daily life in Catumbela.

The changes at Cassequel had significant effects not only for the plantation's owners but also, perhaps not surprisingly, for its workers as well. By the end of 1976, which the MPLA, again, had declared "the Year of National Reconstruction," workers at Cassequel harvested less than 40 percent of the 1973 crop. In spite of proud declarations at the Second National Conference of Angolan Workers in December 1976 celebrating the Angolan peoples' victory over "American imperialism," "Maoists," "racist South Africans," and "certain African government who have sold out to imperialism," 1976 proved a difficult year for the workers and their families who depended on Cassequel.[61] Still, Angolans continued to hope that socialism would, as the national workers' union promised, "assure Angola a full independence, social progress, happiness, and well-being for all."[62]

Declining sugar production, the theft of company property, and worker unhappiness over high inflation and the erratic payment of salaries brought Lopo do Nascimento, one of the most prominent MPLA leaders, to Cassequel in 1977. He urged workers to produce for the good of the revolution because "increased production advances the revolution."[63] He also praised Cuban comrades supplying decisive aid in the sugar industry.[64] President Neto also urged the workers to produce.[65] In spite of encouraging words and revolutionary propaganda, the workers who stayed on the plantation increasingly turned to subsistence plots to feed themselves. Without sufficient numbers of engineers and mechanics, equipment deteriorated. According to stories told to the author in 2001 in Lisbon, Cuban officials even took Cassequel's tractors as payment for previous and ongoing debts, thus further adding to the slowdown in production.

In 1977, Fidel Castro reported to the East German leader, Erich Honecker, that the Angolan sugar plantations were back in production and that "things are going well in Angola. They achieved good progress in their first year of independence."[66] In the same year, Ribeiro resigned in protest to directives from the National Commission for Restructuring the Sugar Industry.[67] In spite of Castro's report, production at Cassequel continued to decline until the government shut the plantation down completely in the mid-1980s.

Conclusion

Cassequel's demise resulted from a combination of the MPLA's hard-line ideology of economic transformation, the disillusionment and departure of the plantation's skilled technicians and management, the unstable economic climate in Angola, and mismanagement by the National Commission for Restructuring the Sugar Industry.

Fueling the MPLA's hard-line policies was the intervention in Angola by Cold War foes. Rather than supporting the forces of moderation and compromise—including members of all three liberation movements, the business community, and even the Portuguese military acting in its capacity as guarantor of the transition to independence—the United States, the Soviet Union, Cuba, South Africa, Zaire, and Yugoslavia empowered the extreme ideologues of each movement and destroyed the chances for a negotiated settlement. Each foreign power intervened for its own self-interest. One striking component of these interventions is the disregard for the best interests of the Angolan people. As Kissinger wrote, "The issue, in short, was not the intrinsic importance of Angola."[68]

For Cassequel, the consequences of the Cold War intervention in Angola have been devastating. The hard-line, socialist, Soviet-aligned policies of the MPLA produced a few early benefits for workers, such as higher wages, but ultimately the vilification of the former owners and skilled technicians resulted in lower production and the eventual closure of the plantation. In 2001, tens of thousands of Angolans grew subsistence agriculture on the former sugar plantation, managing to eke out a living as best they could. Social services, such as health care, were virtually nonexistent, and many remembered the last decade of the colonial era as a period of relative abundance.

Notes

1. Interview with Faustino Alfredo, Catumbela, July 5, 2001.
2. Interview with Reinaldo Pereira Machado, Gama, Angola, July 17, 2001.
3. See Kenneth Maxwell, *The Making of Portuguese Democracy* (Cambridge: Cambridge University Press, 1995), esp. chaps. 6 and 7.
4. National Security Council Interdepartmental Group for Africa, "Response to NSSM 224: United States Policy toward Angola," June 13, 1975, 20, enclosed in Nathaniel Davis to the Assistant to the President for National Security Affairs, June 16, 1975, National Security Agency. Quoted by Piero Gleijeses, *Conflicting Missions: Havana, Washington and Africa, 1959–1976* (Chapel Hill: University of North Carolina Press, 2002), 258.
5. "Confidential letter to the Conselho Superior das Colonias, Sobre o Relatorio de 17 de Junho da Presidencia da Delegacao Portuguesa a Sessao da Conferencia Internacional do Trabalho," Gabinete do Ministro, Sala 6, Maço 2878, Arquivo Histórico Ultramarino, 6.
6. For more information about forced labor and runaways at Cassequel, see Jeremy Ball, "'The Colossal Lie': The Sociedade Agrícola do Cassequel and Portuguese Colonial Labor Policy in Angola, 1899–197," Ph.D. dissertation, University of California, Los Angeles, 2003, 154–77.
7. "Letter from Manuel Espírito Santo to Administration in Africa," March 10, 1955, *Cartas Recebidas, 1950–1955,* Arquivo do Cassequel.
8. International Labor Office, *Official Bulletin* 45, no. 2, supplement II (April 1962): 29.
9. Ibid., 245.
10. For a vigorous critique of *lusotropicalismo* in Angola, see Gerald Bender, *Angola under the Portuguese: The Myth and the Reality* (Berkeley: University of California Press, 1978).
11. "Discurso de Manuel Ribeiro Espírito Santo e Silva," *Jornal do Comércio,* January 26, 1962.
12. "Report by Pierre Juvigny, Representative of the Director-General of the International Labor Office, on Direct Contact with the Government of Portugal Regarding the Implementation of the Abolition of Forced Labour Convention, 1957 (No. 105)," in *International Labor Conference,* no. 56, ed. International Labor Office (Geneva: International Labor Office, 1971), 7.
13. Sociedade Agrícola do Cassequel, *Relatório 1965,* Sociedade Agrícola do Cassequel Archive, p. 22.
14. Ball, "'Colossal Lie,'" 167.
15. Hudson Institute, *Angola: Some Views of Deveopment Prospects,* Volume 1 (New York: Hudson Institute, 1969), 83.
16. Sindicato dos Empregados do Comércio e da Industria do Lobito, "Intersindi-

cal Comunicado No. 12," A-T/S, I-13, Centro de Informação e Documentação Amíl-car Cabral, Lisbon.

17. Sociedade Agrícola do Cassequel, *Relatório do Conselho de Administração*, 1974, Arquivo do Cassequel, Angola.

18. Ibid.

19. Ibid.

20. UNITA, "Camaradas Vigilancia contra as Manobras Reaccionárias," May 1975, A-T/S, I-24, Centro de Informação e Documentação Amílcar Cabral.

21. For a incisive analysis of the "discourse of exclusion," see Jean Michel Mabeko Tali, *Dissidências e poder de estado: O MPLA perante si próprio (1962–1977)* (Luanda: Colecção Ensaio, 2001).

22. Nathaniel Davis, "The Angolan Decision of 1975: A Personal Memoir," *Foreign Affairs* 57 (Fall 1978): 109–23.

23. Gleijeses, *Conflicting Missions*, 250.

24. Ibid.

25. See, e.g., "A Luta dos Trabalhadores contra o Imperialismo," *Vitória Certa*, July 12, 1975.

26. Ibid.

27. Interview with José Manuel Pinheiro Espírito Santo, Lisbon, August 30, 2002.

28. "American Consul Luanda to Secretary of State," April 1975, document no. 1975Luanda00342, 2. Freedom of Information Request, November 21, 2001.

29. "A Luta dos Trabalhadores contra o Imperialismo."

30. Ibid.

31. Interview with Daniel Sowende Fiqueiredo, Catumbela, July 4, 2001.

32. Interview with Germano Castrioto, Catumbela, July 16, 2001.

33. "American Consul Luanda to Secretary of State."

34. Ovimbundu workers refused to migrate to northern Angola as well in 1975 as a result of threats of violence. "American Consul Luanda to Secretary of State."

35. Sousa Jamba, "The Idea of Angola," *Times Literary Supplement*, June 8, 2001, 12.

36. Clara Viana, "Uma Ponte Aéreo," *O Público*, no. 277, July 2, 1995, 20–31.

37. "American Consule Luanda to SecState Washington," May 1975, case no. 2002001, 3. Freedom of Information Act Request, November 21, 2001.

38. Ibid.

39. Gleijeses, *Conflicting Missions*, 293.

40. Henry Kissinger, *Years of Renewal* (New York: Simon & Schuster, 1999), 810.

41. Ibid., 294.

42. Davis, "Angolan Decision of 1975," 111. Davis resigned in protest to President Ford's decision to provide covert assistance to the FNLA and UNITA on July 18, 1975.

43. "Raúl Díaz Argüelles to the Armed Forces minister Raúl Castro, 11 August 1975," Cold War International History Project, http://cwihp.si.edu.

44. Conselho da Revolução, "Reunião Extraordinária," August 5, 1975, 2975.031/ im.2-im.4, Arquivo Mário Soares, Lisbon.

45. Interview with Catarina Rodrigues Silva, Lisbon, August 29, 2002.

46. Gleijeses, *Conflicting Missions*, 301.

47. Ibid., 307.

48. Kissinger, *Years of Renewal*, 832. In June 1976, the Clark Amendment made the

Tunney Amendment permanent (until it was in turn repealed by the Ronald Reagan administration in 1985).

49. President Gerald Ford quoted by Kissinger, *Years of Renewal,* 832.

50. Quoted in Lisbon radio, November 11, 1975. Tony Hodges, *Angola from Afro-Stalinism to Petro-Diamond Capitalism* (Oxford: James Currey, 2001), 45.

51. "Lei Constitucional da República Popular de Angola," articles 2 and 3, *Diário da República* 1, no. 1 (November 11, 1975); reprinted in *Angola História Constitucional,* by Adérito Correia and Bornito de Sousa (Coimbra: Livraria Almedina, 1996).

52. "Lei Constitucional da República Popular de Angola," article 31, *Diário da República,* 1, no. 1 (November 11, 1975).

53. For the idea of a "true cause," see Frederick Cooper, *Decolonization and African Society: The Labor Question in French and British Africa* (Cambridge: Cambridge University Press, 1996), 7.

54. Interview with Germano Adelino Castrioto, Catumbela, July 11, 2001.

55. Sócrates Dáskalos, *Um Testemunho para a História de Angola do Huambo ao Huambo* (Lisbon: Vega, 2000), 186.

56. Law no. 3/76, March 3, 1976, *Diário da República* 1, no. 52.

57. Basil Davidson, "Towards a New Angola," *People's Power in Mozambique, Angola and Guinea-Bissau,* no. 9 (July–September 1977): 10.

58. Interview with Germano Adelino Castrioto, Catumbela, July 11, 2000.

59. Dáskalos, *Um Testemunho para a História de Angola,* 210–11.

60. Ibid., 211.

61. UNITA, "Declaração da II Conferência Nacional dos Trabalhadores Angolanos," Luanda, Dezembro 1976, "MPLA" file, A-T/S, 1-33, Centro de Informação e Documentação Amílcar Cabral.

62. Ibid.

63. "Lembrou o Cda. Lopo do Nascimento aos trabalhadores já conscientes da Açucareira," *Jornal de Angola,* January 27, 1977.

64. Ibid.

65. Interview with Germano Adelino Castrioto, Catumbela, July 11, 2000.

66. "Fidel Castro's 1977 Southern Africa Tour: A Report to Honecker," National Security Archive, available at http://www.nsarchive.org.

67. Dáskalos, *Um Testemunho para a História de Angola,* 211.

68. Kissinger, *Years of Renewal,* 810.

11. Cold War and Colonialism: The Case of East Timor

Luís Nuno Rodrigues

We understand the problem you have and the intentions you have.

—President Gerald Ford to President Suharto, December 6, 1975

"**M**any years ago a small crocodile lived in a swamp in a far away place. He dreamed of becoming a big crocodile but as food was scarce, he became weak and grew sadder and sadder." These are the opening words of the most famous legend on the creation of East Timor, but they are also appropriate to symbolize the history of that territory in the second half of the twentieth century. During these decades, the life and the fate of the people of East Timor were above all determined by the actions and the interests of other nations. The major context in which these actions and interests should be integrated is, obviously, the Cold War. The East Timorese, it could be argued, were one of the major victims of Cold War considerations and "realpolitik" practices. After three military invasions during World War II, East Timor was left under Portuguese colonial rule until its invasion and occupation by Indonesian forces, in December 1975, causing more than one hundred thousand deaths in the years that followed.

This chapter focuses on the situation in East Timor between World War II and 1975. First, it analyzes how Portugal received the approval of the United States and other Western powers to maintain its colonial empire, including East Timor, in the final years of World War II and in the early years of the Cold War. Second, it shows how the Cold War context, in which the Portuguese revolution of 1974 and the process of decolonization occurred, made Western leaders—and American policymakers in particular—believe that the best political solution for the future of East Timor was its integration in its "giant" neighbor

Indonesia, instead of a process of self-determination and, eventually, independence. Third, it tries to evaluate the local impact of all these events with special attention to the fate of thousands of East Timorese people.

World War II and the Early Cold War

The former Portuguese colony of East Timor was the eastern half of the island of Timor, the other half being Indonesian territory since the independence of that country, in 1949. This scarcely populated Portuguese colony had resisted Dutch annexation in the seventeenth century and remained in Portuguese hands until 1975. By that time, East Timor had around 670,000 inhabitants, in an area of about 7,400 square miles. It was the poorest of the Portuguese colonies, with most of the population engaged in agricultural activities and with more than 80 percent illiteracy.[1]

During World War II, East Timor had been invaded three times. There was a first preemptive occupation by Allied troops in December 1941. Japan had desired this territory for its strategic position in the Pacific, and a few months earlier, the neutral Portuguese government had signed an agreement with Japan providing for the establishment of regular flights between Timor and Japan. This agreement provoked strong reactions from the Allies, and the British began to consider the possibility of occupying the territory. After Japan entered the war, the situation became more urgent. The British War and Foreign offices decided on December 11 that the occupation of East Timor was essential and that there was no time to wait for a formal agreement with the Portuguese government. On December 17, a small force of 350 Australian and Dutch troops occupied East Timor.

A few months later, in February 1942, there was a second invasion of East Timor, this time by the Japanese. By the end of the war, the territory was finally liberated by Allied forces and restored to Portuguese sovereignty. When the Japanese left the territory, in 1945, Timor was devastated, and approximately 50,000 Timorese had lost their lives as a result of the Japanese occupation either in combat or in concentration camps. Dili, the capital of East Timor, and other towns had been "burned out," and the crops had been "destroyed."[2]

Timor was the only territory of the large Portuguese colonial empire in which Portuguese sovereignty was seriously challenged. However, the Portuguese government, led by Antonio Salazar, was able to convince the Allies to support the continuation of the territory under Portuguese sovereignty, even with Australian opposition.

The United States was strongly interested in the establishment of a base in the Azores, and Portugal wanted to participate in the "liberation of East Timor," to ensure that the colony would remain in Portuguese hands. In February 1944, the American ambassador in Lisbon, Charles Norweb, met with Salazar and mentioned that Portuguese participation in the liberation of its own colony "was naturally not unconnected with action in the matter of authorizing construction of a second airfield [in the Azores] for American use, since in our opinion this constituted the greatest single contribution Portugal could make to liberation of Timor."[3] Therefore, in late 1944, Portugal, which had been neutral throughout the war, negotiated an agreement with the United States whereby the territory of East Timor would be restored to Portuguese sovereignty in exchange for certain air and naval facilities granted by the Portuguese government to the United States on the islands of Azores.

The formal agreement between the two countries was signed on November 28, 1944; the United States accepted the participation of Portugal in operations in the Pacific "as may be conducted eventually to expel the Japanese from Portuguese Timor in order that that territory may be restored to full Portuguese sovereignty." Portuguese participation would be materialized through the "concession to the government of the United States of facilities for the construction, use, and control of an air base on the Island of Santa Maria, for the purpose of facilitating the movement of American forces to the theater of war in the Pacific."[4]

For the next three decades, East Timor would remain a Portuguese colony. Salazar was able to assure the support of the generality of the Western powers not only for his regime but also for the maintenance of the colonial empire. Due to the strategic importance of the Azores islands and the bases the United States maintained there, Portugal was also admitted as a founding member of the North Atlantic Treaty Organization (NATO), even though it had a non-democratic regime. The emergence of the Cold War in the second half of the 1940s gave the rationale for the alignment of the United States with Salazar's Portugal. As George Kennan put it in 1950: "It is better to have a strong regime in power than a liberal government if it is indulgent and relaxed and penetrated by Communists."[5]

Except for a brief period during the John F. Kennedy administration, the United States never seriously challenged Portuguese colonialism—and therefore its presence in East Timor. Even then, in the early 1960s, the United States was more concerned with the fate of the large African territories of Angola and Mozambique—and with the colonial wars that the Portuguese were fighting in those territories—than with East Timor. A paper prepared by the Department of State in early 1962 defined the situation in East Timor as "the colonial problem in its most difficult form." The United States traditionally based its policy toward colonial areas in a "strong element of principle" that included "self-determination, self-government and independence and peaceful change." However, in some situations, these principles had "little relevance," because "the remaining colonial powers have made little or no effort to prepare the colonial peoples for self-determination and independence." This was the case of East Timor: "Both we and the Portuguese would have to recognize that self-determination for Portuguese Timor is meaningless for the indefinite future." In East Timor, there was "little or no sense of national or territorial identity," and the Portuguese had pursued "a policy designed to isolate the population from the outside world." In the case of the dissolution of the Portuguese colonial empire, East Timor "would hardly exist as an independent entity" and "realistically, it had only one possible future—as a part of Indonesia."[6]

Portuguese Decolonization

After the Revolution of April 1974, Portugal went through a complex period of transition to democracy. Until November 1975, several factions disputed the leadership of the country, with five different governments from May 1974 to September 1975. It was during this volatile period that Europe's last overseas empire was dismantled. Portuguese decolonization was regulated by the so-called Decolonization Decree of July 27, 1974, which recognized the right of self-determination and independence for all former colonies, including East Timor. One week later, the Portuguese government delivered an official memorandum to the United Nations secretary-general, Kurt Waldheim, reaffirming its "obligations" regarding the UN Charter and recognizing the "right of self-determination and independence regarding all the territories under its administration."[7] This declaration was followed by the official recognition of the independence of Guinea-Bissau in September 1974. The following year, three more colonies also gained their independence—Mozambique, in June; Cape Verde and São Tomé and Príncipe, in July; and Angola, in November.

East Timor became almost a "forgotten cause," receiving little attention from Portugal and the international community in general. Portugal allowed the formation of political parties in the territory, but only in May 1975 did the Portuguese government present a program for an "orderly" and "phased" withdrawal from the territory. The program called for the creation of a "transitory government" and a "consultative assembly" by October 1975. These organs would prepare for general elections, to be held in 1976.[8]

The plan, however, was disrupted in August 1975 when the more conservative East Timorese political parties launched a coup in an attempt to seize power from the Portuguese and prevent the rise of the left-wing, pro-independence Frente Revolucionária do Timor Leste Independente (Fretilin). Among these parties were the União Democrática Timorense (UDT), founded in May 1974, and the Associação Popular Democrática de Timor (apodeti), which advocated the integration of East Timor with Indonesia. Fretilin, however, was able to gain popular support and military ascendancy over the other parties. Defending the immediate independence of the territory, Fretilin was then defined by the U.S. government as an "extreme left and anti-Indonesian" movement, while the other more "moderate" parties were considered "pro-Indonesian."[9]

Portugal was unable to restore law and order in East Timor, above all due to the political instability it was experiencing at home in the months following the Revolution. The Portuguese garrison and the government officials left the island by the end of August 1975. In the words of Robert Oakley, a State Department official, Portugal left East Timor "without having in any way prepared the people of their half of the island to take over and run the place." Moreover, the Portuguese military, with "left-wing sympathies," apparently "turned over most of their arms to the Fretilin group."[10]

In October 1975, UDT and apodeti merged into the so-called Anti-Communist Movement (MAC), now based on Indonesian territory. Meanwhile, as the Civil War continued, Fretilin was able to assure "effective control of most of East Timor," setting up a "transitional administration." The Indonesian government promptly complained that Fretilin was attacking "Indonesian Timor border villages" and Indonesian foreign minister Adam Malik issued a statement accusing East Timor of becoming "a base for communist subversion."[11] After several months of Civil War, on November 28, 1975, Fretilin unilaterally declared the independence of the territory under the title the "Democratic Republic of East Timor." The move was criticized in Lisbon, but the new Fretilin regime was recognized, among others, by China, Vietnam, and Angola. MAC reacted immediately, declaring that East Timor should become a part of Indonesia.[12]

Indonesian Intervention

The Indonesian government, which had been carefully watching the developments in East Timor, became concerned with the idea of a left-leaning independent East Timor, fearing, above all, that its "backwardness" and "lack of economic viability" would open it to Chinese influence, which could eventually spread to Indonesia. In the opinion of James Dunn, a former Australian consul in Dili who was in Timor in the second half of 1975, the Indonesians had tried since the beginning to "subvert the decolonization process" by supporting and financing the political parties that were "pro-integration," especially APODETI. These efforts, Dunn later recalled, began in late 1974 "after reports that Indonesian leaders had decided that an independent East Timor was a solution to the territory's future that Indonesia could not accept."[13]

As early as September 6, 1974, President Suharto of Indonesia had already emphasized to the Australian prime minister his concern that "decolonization in Portuguese Timor should not upset either Indonesian or regional security." Moreover, there was "a big danger that communist countries—China or the Soviet Union—might gain the opportunity to intervene."[14] The following month, Indonesia launched a "destabilization campaign," called Operasi Komodo, "broadcasting anti-Communist messages into the territory" and infiltrating the more moderate political parties. In early 1975, this operation was transformed into a "military operation," with the "training of APODETI supporters in West Timor."[15]

On July 5, 1975, Suharto visited the United States. The Indonesian president met with U.S. president Gerald Ford and secretary of state Henry Kissinger at Camp David and discussed the situation in East Timor. According to Suharto, there were three different paths for the future of the Timorese: "independence, staying with Portugal, or to join Indonesia." In Suharto's opinion, independence would be "hardly viable" for such a small territory "with no resources." Staying with Portugal was also a difficult choice, for it would be "a big burden with Portugal so far away." Therefore, Suharto declared to "the only way is to integrate Indonesia." Indonesia did not want to "insert itself into Timor self-determination," but it had to take into account that "those who want independence are those who are Communist-influenced" and "those wanting Indonesian integration are being subject to heavy pressure by those who are almost Communists."[16]

Three months later, in October 1975, the first Indonesian military attack on East Timor took place. About 3,200 Indonesian troops crossed the border and attacked several villages. Five Australian journalists were killed. In late November, as mentioned above, Fretilin declared the independence of East Timor. Facing increasing instability in the territory, the Indonesian government prepared the invasion. Following the declaration of independence, Indonesian foreign minister Malik, visited Atambua, in West Timor, and told "the pro-Indonesian Timorese troops" that the situation in East Timor had already gone "beyond diplomacy" and could be resolved "only in the battlefield."[17] The following week, Malik called in ambassadors, "both Eastern and Western," including "the Soviet and American envoys," to "explain the Indonesian position on Portuguese Timor." According to the *New York Times,* during these conversations "definite plans for an invasion were not . . . disclosed to any of these ambassadors."[18]

Nevertheless, on December 7, 1975, the Indonesians decided to move forward with the annexation of East Timor and to invade the territory with a large military force. In the words of the Indonesian government, the security of its own country was jeopardized by the Civil War that was going on in East Timor. Moreover, the decision to invade was made "in response to requests by the two factions opposed to Fretilin—the Timorese Democratic Union and the Popular Democratic Association for the Integration of Portuguese Timor into Indonesia."[19]

Dunn described the Indonesian attacks as "a brutal operation, marked by the wanton slaughter of possibly between 50,000 and 100,000 Timorese, by extensive looting and by other excesses such as rape and torture." In his testimony before the House of Representatives, Dunn considered that the story of East Timor "unfolds a grim tragedy, the rape of a people who, because of their long virtual isolation from the world at large, were vulnerable and unprepared." This story was an example of a "cynical and cruel disregard for basic human rights" committed by Indonesia, the "perpetrator of the abuse," with the complicity of "other powers who appear to have rated appeasement of Indonesia as their paramount consideration."[20]

The United States, Indonesia, and East Timor

The last words of Dunn's testimony were an implicit reference to the role played by the United States throughout this process. To understand the American policy in the case of East Timor, it is important to have in mind the general context of the Cold War and the increasing economic and strategic importance of the Indonesian archipelago for the United States. These islands, extending from the Malay Peninsula to Australia, guarded the western shore of the Strait of Malacca. In the mid-1970s, this strait afforded "the most direct access for the United States' Pacific fleet to the Indian Ocean," where, according to the *New York Times,* "Soviet Naval activity has been reported increasing." Indonesia was also an important source of oil and, in terms of production, "the ninth-ranking of the 13 member nations of the Organization of the Petroleum Exporting Countries."[21]

American policymakers in the mid-1970s saw Indonesia as the "largest and most important noncommunist Southeast Asian state." In a memorandum prepared for President Ford, Kissinger noted that Indonesia was not only "the fifth most populous nation in the world," with "more than three times the size of any other Southeast Asian country" but that its geographic location and resources also were of "major strategic importance in the region." It controlled "the sea passages between the Pacific and the Indian oceans," and its own oil fields provided a "small but increasing part" of the American oil imports, just like its other natural resources, such as rubber, tin, and other tropical products.[22]

Indonesia, under President Suharto, was also seen as a reliable ally by the Ford administration. As Kissinger pointed out, Indonesia had positioned itself in a "somewhat unique diplomatic position as an anti-Communist but non-aligned country" and also as a country capable of "carrying on a dialogue with both radical third world states and the West while cautiously pursuing policies generally compatible with the latter." Its relations with the Soviet Union were "correct but wary," with the Indonesian government receiving only a "small quantity" of aid from the Soviets. Suharto's regime, however, remained "innately suspicious of Soviet intentions." Toward China, the position of the Indonesians was even more careful. The Indonesian government has remained very "cautious about establishing relations with Peking" and believed that China had been behind an attempted communist coup that took place in Indonesia in 1965. Therefore, Indonesian officials were "highly skeptical" of the Chinese assurances of "non-interference in the internal affairs of its neighbors."[23]

The Nixon and Ford administrations tried to improve relations between the United States and Indonesia and to move them away from a "donor-client relationship" and from "preoccupation with aid issues" into a more comprehensive relation that stressed "a broader sharing of interests and views."[24] Nevertheless, the two major issues in this bilateral relation were those of military assistance and economic aid. In July 1975, Ford personally guaranteed to Suharto that Washington would continue with the existing assistance program to Indonesia and, moreover, that it was ready to "make available some military equipment items" to help Indonesia. Specifically, Ford mentioned "four naval vessels, . . . some tanks, aircraft such as C-47, and four C-123 transports." The two countries also agreed to create a "joint commission" to discuss the military needs of Indonesia and further American help. Suharto stressed that "the most important need is not in the military field but in the economic area." Ford promised "more credits and grants."[25]

During subsequent conversations with an Indonesian military mission, in September 1975, the United States agreed to provide $30 million in grants and $12.5 million in credit for "helicopters, ships, communication and radar equipment." In terms of economic aid, after the meeting at Camp David, the White House proposed to Congress "an additional $20 million in loans for Indonesia, bringing the total proposed U.S. assistance package to $85 million for [fiscal year] 1976," which, in the words of Kissinger, corresponded to "the biggest single increase we have proposed this year for any Asian country."[26]

As the events unfolded in East Timor, the U.S. government became concerned with the possibility of an Indonesian military invasion of the territory. The Indonesian forces would certainly use American military equipment in the operation, and this was the major cause of concern for the administration. The utilization of American military equipment by Indonesia would represent a clear violation of the existing agreements between the two countries, which "limited use of U.S.-furnished equipment to internal security and legitimate self-defense." Moreover, these agreements "precluded furnishing new items of assistance while any substantial violation continued."[27] Therefore, the Ford administration took several steps both in Washington and in Jakarta, in the fall of 1975, "to counsel caution in the Timor situation," to indicate its "concern over the possible use of U.S.-supplied military equipment," and also to remind the Indonesian authorities of "the appropriate provisions of our bilateral military assistance agreements in this regard."[28]

By August, it was clear to the U.S. administration that Indonesia was already "mobilizing some forces very quietly" and that the Indonesians "will not let a hostile group—that is to say a Communist-dominated group—take over" in East Timor. In a staff meeting of the State Department, on August 12, 1975, the officer responsible for the East Asian affairs, Philip Habib, said that if the Indonesians took any action, this was "a situation in which we should just do nothing." Kissinger added that it was "quite clear that the Indonesians are going to take over the island sooner or later," a move that would represent the "disappearance of a vestige of colonialism" in Southeast Asia.[29]

The following month, in early December 1975, President Ford visited Indonesia. In a conversation that took place on December 6, the day before the invasion of East Timor, Suharto briefed Ford and Kissinger on his plans for the former Portuguese colony. According to the *New York Times,* Ford urged Suharto "to exhibit continued restraint from direct involvement in the civil war in the Portuguese part of Timor."[30] But the Indonesian leader pointed out that the political situation in East Timor, following the end of Portuguese rule, was increasing the "instability" in Southeast Asia. Therefore, the Indonesian government had already decided what it should do "to establish peace and order for the present and the future in the interest of the security of the area and Indonesia." President Ford replied that his administration "will understand and will not press . . . on the issue." The United States, said Ford, will not oppose to the invasion because it understood "the problem you have and the intentions you have." In the course of this conversation, Kissinger added that the use of

American military equipment could "create problems" and suggested that he and President Ford would be able to influence the reaction in America "if whatever happens, happens after we return."[31]

To fully understand American acquiescence with the Indonesian plans for the invasion of East Timor, one must recall the regional importance of Indonesia in the global context of the Cold War in the mid-1970s, as already mentioned above. The United States, in the words of Kissinger some twenty years later, considered Indonesia as "the key, a key country in Southeast Asia" and, therefore, the Americans "were not looking for trouble with Indonesia" on the question of East Timor.[32] Reflecting on the importance of a good relationship between the United States and Indonesia, David Kenney, country officer for Indonesia in the Department of State in the early years of the Jimmy Carter administration, declared in the House of Representatives that American military and economic assistance to that country served "a great many purposes." Among them, he pointed out "regional stability, support for an independent Indonesia, help for a country that has been very friendly to us, efforts generally to keep that area peaceful." Then he asked: "Should we be allowing this situation in Timor to be affecting all of our policy goals in Southeast Asia?"[33] The historian Brad Simpson has recently pointed to another important factor in analyzing the behavior of the United States and other Western countries: the belief that an "independent East Timor" would not only "produce regional instability" but was also "too small and too primitive to merit self-determination."[34]

Conversely, the Ford administration was worried about the recent fall of the noncommunist regimes in South Vietnam and Cambodia, in April 1975, and the possible "domino effect" in the whole region. The United States wanted to prove that, despite the events in Vietnam and Cambodia, it remained "firmly committed and interested in Southeast Asia," as Ford told Suharto during their July 1975 meeting at Camp David.[35] Justifying his visit to Indonesia in early December, Ford would also declare to a delegation of Republican congressmen that "it was important to go there in the aftermath of Vietnam to show we were still an Asian power." Ford was also visibly "impressed" with Suharto, who was "trying to keep the country together and maintain a viable government and uphold the cause of anti-communism there."[36]

Ford clearly expressed these thoughts on the very same day of the Indonesian invasion of East Timor, in a speech made at the University of Hawaii, where he announced the so-called Pacific Doctrine. The United States, the president declared, still had a "very vital stake in Asia and a responsibility to take a leading part in lessening tensions, preventing hostilities." The American "commercial involvement" in Asia was expanding, and the "center of political power in the United States" had definitely "shifted westward." Therefore, the first premise of the new Pacific Doctrine was that American strength was "basic to any stable balance of power in the Pacific." To achieve that goal, the United States needed to support the "preservation of the sovereignty and the independence" of its "Asian friends." Among them, Indonesia played a special role. It was "a nation of 140 million people, . . . one of our important new friends," and "a major country in that area of the world."[37]

As the historian Walter LaFeber has put it, Ford's doctrine acknowledged that the power of the United States was now "much less than it had been a generation earlier" and that it needed "help from partners in Indonesia, Japan, and the Philippines." According to LaFeber, this had been "one reason why Nixon and Ford said nothing after Philippine ruler Ferdinand Marcos imposed a corrupt martial-law regime on his people in 1972."[38] It was also the major reason why the United States closed its eyes to the Indonesia invasion of East Timor in December 1975.

Washington policymakers believed that the United States could not allow the development of a focus of instability in Southeast Asia, which an independent and pro-Soviet or pro-Chinese East Timor would certainly be. There is no proof that the Soviets or the Chinese were considering any move on East Timor, but the U.S. administration had its eye on another former Portuguese colony—Angola—where the Soviet Union and Cuba were supporting one of the factions involved in the Civil War. According to former secretary of state Kissinger, the United States should "make it clear that Angola sets no precedent" and that "this type of action will not be tolerated elsewhere."[39]

A few days after the invasion, the *New York Times* condemned the action of the Indonesian government. An editorial published on December 13 considered that "by any definition," Indonesia was "guilty of naked aggression in its military seizure of Portuguese Timor." Nevertheless, there was "provocation in the unilateral declaration of independence last month by the leftist Revolutionary Front for an independent East Timor, known as Fretilin, which had seemed to be winning the civil war handily against pro-Indonesian forces until Jakarta began to intervene." The Portuguese administration had also demonstrated "its own utter inability to restore order by fleeing in August to the nearby island of Atauro, leaving a power vacuum that Fretilin promptly filled." In the end, the "real losers" were the Timoreses, "whose interests and desires have been ignored by all parties to this deplorable affair."[40]

The Impact of the Invasion
What was the impact of the Indonesian military operation on the lives of the East Timorese people? The final report of the Commission for Reception,

Truth, and Reconciliation in Timor-Leste (CAVR), from late 2005, concluded that there were between 100,000 and 200,000 deaths during the period of Indonesian military occupation, from 1975 to 1999. The CAVR reports that "many people died from hunger and illness in excess of the peacetime baseline for these causes of death." According to these findings, "the overwhelming number of these deaths occurred in the years 1977–78," and during the "large-scale Indonesian military attacks in the interior and later in Indonesian detention camps and resettlement areas where food and medical care were grossly insufficient."[41] Scholars like Benedict Anderson, a specialist on Indonesian nationalism, mentioned the "vast scale of the violence deployed, the use of aerial bombardments, the napalming of villages, the systematic herding of people into resettlement centres leading to the terrible starvation famines of 1977–80."[42]

The memories of the Timorese people still echo with the violence that followed the Indonesian invasion. Eugenia Martins, for instance, recalls escaping with her mother, brother, and six sisters to the mountains: "During our long and tiring flee, we were pursued by bullets, mortars and bombs from the invaders, who had planned a land and air offensive, night and day."[43] Benjamim Martins also recalled that when the Indonesian forces invaded the village of Bobonaro, he had been able to see "all the attacks, how they burnt all the villages, the fields, all the plantations, how they killed all the animals, how they captured and murdered a great part of the civilians. They destroyed everything we had." During the first three months, "we were unable to stay in the same place for more than one day. We had to face long and arduous walks and on the way, we met other people from other villages that had also been invaded. We formed a long column of refugees without the notion where to go."[44]

Normally, Indonesian troops "advanced in groups," recalls a former Fretilin commander, adding that they "organized into long lines, burning corps and villages behind them." These advances were accompanied by "naval and aerial bombardment." A Timorese refugee, testifying on the U.S. Senate, remembered the bombings in the villages outside Indonesian control. According to his testimony, it was necessary "to leave the villages in the daytime to hide from aeroplanes that would drop the bombs." Therefore, "in the mornings at first light we would move back into the hills leaving behind the old and the sick who could run no more." Another refugee also alluded to the bombardments of Timorese villages, saying that "sometimes the bombardment is every hour; . . . at other times it is non-stop from morning to night and other times it is continued for days." Most of the victims, another refugee recalled, were "women, children and old people, . . . people who couldn't run for cover."[45]

The atrocities continued the following years. The former Australian consul in Dili, James Dunn, who was mentioned above, visited Portugal in January 1977. He met with several of the 1,500 Timorese refugees there. According to the testimonies of these refugees, who had spent some time in East Timor after the invasion, "many of the Indonesian troops killed indiscriminately from the beginning of their attack on Dili. However, several prominent Timorese said that the killing in mountain areas was far more extensive than it was in Dili. In the mountain areas, they claimed, whole villages were wiped out as Indonesian troops advanced into the interior." Another Timorese refugee told him that "when the Indonesian troops captured Remexio and Aileu, all of the Timorese in the village, except children under the age of three, were shot" because they were allegedly "infected with the seeds of Fretilin."[46]

Paulino Gama, a former commander of the Fretilin, recalls that from 1975 until 1978, the "majority of the surviving" East Timorese went to the bush and to the mountains, trying to receive protection from the movement. But again, they could not escape "all manner of barbarism at Indonesian hands, ranging from bombing raids to massacre of whole communities and individual rapers and murders." The late 1970s, as mentioned above, were the years of the "terrible famine," as Gama pointed out, "graphically portrayed in the pictures of emaciated men, women, and children published in various . . . newspapers and magazines, for example, the *Sidney Morning Herald* and the *Financial Times,* of London."[47]

Politically, the Indonesian government and MAC also moved rapidly. The events of December 8, 1975, had been announced by Jakarta radio as the "liberation" of East Timor by the "people's resistance spearheaded by the apodeti, UDT," and other smaller movements, "supported by Indonesian volunteers." Accordingly, a few days after the invasion, MAC named Arnaldo Araújo of apodeti as the leader of the new "Provisional Government of East Timor." In early January 1976, Araújo "presided over a ceremony on Ataúro Island lowering the Portuguese flag and raising the red and white flag of Indonesia." A few days later, he declared in Baucau that "the future of East Timor lay with Indonesia," adding that "since it was clear that the people of East Timor wanted integration with Indonesia, it was not necessary to hold a plebiscite." Foreign Minister Malik visited Dili, and he also declared that "since the Provisional Government of East Timor had invited Indonesia to declare its sovereignty over the territory, there was no longer any need for an election to decide the future of East Timor." Indonesia would formally incorporate East Timor on July 12, 1976, evoking a petition signed by thirty representatives of the East Timorese as an act of self-determination.[48] Resistance to Indonesian occupation, however, continued throughout the years. In May 1976, the Supreme Council of Resistance, a political and military structure created by Fretilin, met in Soibada. The council created what has been described as a "basis for an organized resistance." Among the topics debated were "changes in military strategy," "the tightening of political organization," and "increasing food production." Fretilin divided East Timor into six different sectors, each one with a regional commander and also a "regional secretary," responsible for organization. The movement was preparing itself for more than twenty-five years of resistance.[49]

The international impact of the invasion was relatively small. On December 7, 1975, Portugal informed the United Nations of the invasion, declaring that "in the present circumstances, Portugal is unable to restore peace in Timor" and urging a meeting of the Security Council.[50] On December 12, 1975, the General Assembly approved Resolution 3485, calling for the respect for the right of self-determination in East Timor. The Security Council also approved Resolution 384, on December 22, 1975, calling upon all states "to respect the right of the people of East Timor to self-determination" and requesting the UN secretary-general to send a "special representative" to East Timor for an assessment of the situation and to "establish contact with all interested parties in order to insure the implementation of the resolution."[51]

In the United States, the Committee on International Relations of the House of Representatives initiated hearings on the issue of East Timor, trying to establish the exact role of the United States in this process. As Representative Donald Fraser put it, "If large-scale killing did occur, the subcommittee will want to explore why the United States as well as other members of the international community remain silent." Was this silence "out of ignorance or deliberate intent?" The committee also wanted to evaluate the exact role of American military equipment in the invasion and to establish "how the United States can assist in resolving the situation in a manner to protect the rights of the people of East Timor." During these hearings, the Carter administration maintained that the allegations of "widespread atrocities by Indonesian troops in Timor" in late 1975 and early 1976 were "greatly exaggerated."[52] Therefore, the administration would continue "to treat the developments in Timor as basically an internal matter under the jurisdiction of the government of Indonesia." David Kenney, the country officer for Indonesia in the Department of State mentioned above, stated that the people in East Timor were "relatively happy" with their condition, "given the circumstances and alternatives available to them." The East Timorese had decided "their best interest lies at this time, in incorporation with Indonesia."[53]

Nevertheless, after the invasion, the U.S. administration became aware that the Indonesian forces had used American military equipment. The Indonesian paratroops that descended on Dili were transported by American Hercules

C-130 airplanes. As Robert Oakley, from the Department of State, recognized later, there were also "U.S.-origin arms used by some of the units that went into East Timor." The American government decided to suspend "the provision of additional security assistance to Indonesia although military equipment already in the pipeline continued to be delivered." This was the result of a direct order from the State Department to the Defense Security Assistance Agency, in late December 1975, to place a "hold on issuance of all new letter of offer, MAP (Mutual Assistance Program) orders, invitational travel orders, to Indonesians." In the eyes of the Department of State, there was a "possible conflict between what the Indonesians had done in East Timor that involved the use of U.S.-origin equipment and the provisions of the Foreign Assistance Act." Nevertheless, the U.S. Congress authorized military assistance for Indonesia for fiscal years 1976 and 1977. An amendment to this "authorizing legislation" that would have eliminated the assistance was debated and rejected by the House of Representatives. Therefore, the administration "believed it appropriate to reinstate security assistance" to Indonesia in June 1976.[54]

Following these events, the government of Indonesia issued direct invitations to members of Congress to visit the territory. Representative Helen Meyner, from New Jersey, was one of them. The visit—twenty-three hours spent in East Timor—was prepared by the Indonesian government, which refused "requests by subcommittee staff to meet privately with East Timorese individuals, or proposals that we bring an independent interpreter." As Helen Meyner put it in her report, it was clear that the Indonesian government "would consider efforts to tamper with or question its arrangements as an ungracious response by guests of the Indonesia Government." These "restrictions on the trip" made it difficult to reach "firm conclusions" on the question of "whether the Timorese have freely chosen integration with Indonesia" and the question of "alleged atrocities by Indonesian or Fretilin forces." Nevertheless, the delegation "received the impression that the Timorese people were satisfied with Indonesian integration." Moreover, there was "no indication of ongoing repression; quite the contrary, the people appeared free and uninhibited." Answering to questions on the possibility of a referendum on East Timor, Meyner declared that "the people of East Timor feel they are part of Indonesia, so why go in there and stir things up again?"[55]

As mentioned above, these declarations were clearly ignoring the local developments and the local impact of the Indonesian invasion. In 1976 there were already reports of "a scene of oppression and wanton killing." A report from the Catholic Church suggested that "in the year since the invasion as many as 60,000 Timorese might have lost their lives."[56] The following year, Indonesian foreign minister Malik also admitted that "50,000 people or perhaps

80,000 might have been killed during the war in Timor." These numbers led recently some authors to use the word "genocide" to characterize what happened in East Timor in the years that followed the Indonesian invasion. Ben Kiernan, director of the Genocide Studies Program at Yale University, concluded, with data available in 2003, that the cases of Cambodia and East Timor were "proportionately comparable," with each tragedy taking "the lives of over one-fifth of the population."[57]

Political repression continued throughout the 1980s, but only in 1991 did the infamous "Santa Cruz massacre" alert world public opinion to the situation in the territory. The process that followed is well known and goes beyond the scope of this chapter. Nevertheless, the people of East Timor were finally given a chance to determine their own future. A referendum was held on August 30, 1999, and an overwhelming majority of 78 percent voted for independence. East Timor would became an independent republic on May 20, 2002.

Notes

1. The most recent synthesis on the Portuguese colonial empire in the twentieth century is Valentim Alexandre, "The Colonial Empire," in *Contemporary Portugal: Politics, Society and Culture,* ed. António Costa Pinto (Boulder, Colo.: Social Science Monographs, 2003), 63–84.

2. A. H. de Oliveira Marques, *History of Portugal* (New York: Columbia University Press, 1976), 234.

3. U.S. Department of State, ed., *Foreign Relations of the United States, 1944,* vol. 4 (Washington, D.C.: U.S. Government Printing Office, 1966), 14.

4. *United States Treaties and Other International Agreements* (Washington, D.C.: U.S. Government Printing Office, 1951), vol. 2, part 2, 2124–32.

5. David F. Schmitz, *Thank God They're on Our Side: The United States and Right-Wing Dictatorships, 1921–1965* (Chapel Hill: University of North Carolina Press, 1999), 149.

6. "Indonesia and Portuguese Timor," memorandum prepared by Robert Johnson, February 4, 1963, National Archives, Central Foreign Policy Files, box 4022, 1963.

7. *Os 25 Anos da "Questão de Timor Leste" no Parlamento Português,* vol. 1 (Lisbon: Assembleia da República, 2000), 33.

8. U.S. Congress, *Human Rights in East Timor and the Question of the Use of U.S. Equipment by the Indonesian Armed Forces,* Hearing before the Subcommittees on International Organizations and on Asian and Pacific Affairs of the Committee on International Relations, House of Representatives, Ninety-Fifth Congress, First Session, March 23, 1977 (Washington, D.C.: U.S. Government Printing Office, 1977), 5.

9. Ibid., 6.

10. Ibid., 7.

11. Robert Lawless, "The Indonesian Takeover of East Timor," *Asian Survey* 16, no. 10 (October 1976): 953.

12. Sarah Niner, "A Long Journey of Resistance: The Origins and Struggle of

CNRT," in *Bitter Flowers, Sweet Flowers: East Timor, Indonesia and the World Community* (Lanham, Md.: Rowman & Littlefield, 2001), 18.

13. U.S. Congress, *Human Rights in East Timor,* 30.

14. "Record of Meeting between the Prime-Minister and President Soeharto," September 6, 1974. National Archives of Australia, http://naa12.naa.gov.au/scripts/Imagine .asp.

15. Niner, "Long Journey of Resistance," 18.

16. "Memorandum of Conversation between Presidents Ford and Suharto, 5 July 1975," Gerald R. Ford Library, National Security Adviser Memoranda of Conversations, box 13, July 5, 1975, http://www.gwu.edu/~nsarchiv/NSAEBB/NSAEBB62/ doc1.pdf.

17. *New York Times,* December 5, 1975.

18. Ibid., December 7, 1975.

19. Ibid., December 8, 1975.

20. U.S. Congress, *Human Rights in East Timor,* 30–31.

21. *New York Times,* December 6, 1975, 12.

22. "Your Visit to Indonesia," memorandum to President Ford from Henry Kissinger, c. November 21, 1975, National Archives, record group 59, Department of State Records, box 227, available at http://www.gwu.edu/~nsarchiv.

23. "Your Visit to Indonesia."

24. Ibid.

25. "Memorandum of Conversation between Presidents Ford and Suharto, 5 July 1975."

26. "Your Visit to Indonesia."

27. This was the legal opinion of George H. Aldrich, deputy legal adviser of the Department of State. See U.S. Congress, *Human Rights in East Timor,* 46.

28. U.S. Congress, *Human Rights in East Timor,* 5.

29. "The Secretary's 8:00 a.m. Staff Meeting, Tuesday, August 12, 1975," National Archives, record group 59, Department of State Records, transcripts of staff meetings of Secretary of State Henry Kissinger, 1973–77, box 8, available at http://www.gwu .edu/~nsarchiv.

30. *New York Times,* December 6, 1975.

31. "Embassy Jakarta Telegram 1579 to Secretary of State, 6 December 1975," Gerald R. Ford Library, Kissinger-Scowcroft Temporary Parallel File, box A3, available at at http://www.gwu.edu/~nsarchiv.

32. Remarks by Henry Kissinger after a speech presenting his book *Diplomacy,* at Park Central Hotel, New York, July 11, 1995, http://etan.org/news/kissinger/ask.htm.

33. U.S. Congress, *Human Rights in East Timor,* 19.

34. Brad Simpson, "'Illegally and Beautifully': The United States, the Indonesian Invasion of East Timor and the International Community, 1974–76," *Cold War History* 5, no. 3 (August 2005): 282.

35. "Memorandum of Conversation between Presidents Ford and Suharto, 5 July 1975."

36. "Memorandum of Conversation between President Ford and Republican Congressional Leadership," December 10, 1975, Gerald R. Ford Library, National Security Adviser, Memoranda of Conversations, box 17, http://128.83.78.237/library/document/ memcons/751210a.htm.

37. "Address of President Gerald R. Ford at the University of Hawaii," http://www
.ford.utexas.edu/library/speeches/750716/16.htm.

38. Walter LaFeber, *The American Age: United States Foreign Policy at Home and Abroad* (New York: W. W. Norton, 1994), 670–71.

39. This is as quoted by Raymond L. Garthoff, *Détente and Confrontation: American-Soviet Relations from Nixon to Reagan* (Washington D.C.: Brookings Institution Press, 1994), 580.

40. *New York Times,* December 13, 1975.

41. This is as quoted by Jeff Kingston, "East Timor's Search for Justice and Reconciliation," January 22, 2006, http://www.ictj.org/en/news/coverage/article/790
.html.

42. Benedict Anderson, "Imagining East Timor," *Lusotopie,* 2001, 235 (originally written in 1992).

43. Benjamim Hopffer Martins and Maria de Lurdes Bessa, *Once Upon a Time . . .* (Lisbon: Youth Action for Peace, 1998), 106.

44. Ibid., 42–43.

45. John G. Taylor, *Indonesia's Forgotten War* (London: Zed Books, 1991), 87.

46. U.S. Congress, *Human Rights in East Timor,* excerpts from 5–14.

47. Paulino Gama, "The War in the Hills, 1975–85: A Fretilin Commander Remembers," in *East Timor at the Crossroads: The Forging of a Nation,* ed. Peter Carey and G. Carter Bentley (Honolulu: University of Hawaii Press, 1995), 99–100.

48. Lawless, "Indonesian Takeover," 953–54, 949.

49. Niner, "Long Journey of Resistance," 18.

50. Lawless, "Indonesian Takeover," 954.

51. U.S. Congress, *Human Rights in East Timor,* 47.

52. Ibid., 1–6.

53. Ibid., 19–21.

54. Ibid., excerpts from 5–14.

55. Ibid., 3–7.

56. Dunn, quoted by U.S. Congress, *Human Rights in East Timor,* 66.

57. Ben Kiernan, "The Demography of Genocide in Southeast Asia: The Death Tolls in Cambodia, 1974–79, and East Timor, 1975–80," *Critical Asian Studies* 35, no. 4 (2003): 585.

Contributors

Jeremy Ball is an assistant professor of history at Dickinson College.

Thomas Borstelmann has been the Elwood N. and Katherine Thompson Distinguished Professor of Modern World History at the University of Nebraska–Lincoln since 2003. Previously, he taught at Cornell University for twelve years. He is most recently the author of *The Cold War and the Color Line: American Race Relations in the Global Arena* (2001) and a coauthor of *Created Equal: A Social and Political History of the United States* (second edition, 2006).

Paul Boyer is the Merle Curti Professor of History Emeritus at the University of Wisconsin–Madison. His books include *Salem Possessed: The Social Origins of Witchcraft* (with Stephen Nissenbaum, 1974); *By the Bomb's Early Light: American Thought and Culture at the Dawn of the Atomic Age* (1985); and *When Time Shall Be No More: Prophecy Belief in Modern American Culture* (1992). He is coauthor of *The Enduring Vision: A History of the American People* (sixth edition, 2007) and editor-in-chief of *The Oxford Companion to United States History* (2001).

Alan P. Dobson is a professor of politics and the director of the Institute for Transatlantic European and American Studies at the University of Dundee, Scotland. He is editor of the *Journal of Transatlantic Studies* and cochairs the Transatlantic Studies Association. He has published extensively on Anglo-American relations, U.S. foreign policy, and the international airline system. His most recent publications are *US Economic Statecraft for Survival 1933–1991* (2002); *Globalisation and Regional Integration: The Origins, Development and Impact of the Single European Aviation Market* (2007); and, with Steve Marsh, *US Foreign Policy since 1945* (2nd edition, 2006).

Jeffrey A. Engel is an assistant professor of history and public policy, associate director of the Scowcroft Institute for International Affairs, and the Evelyn and Ed F. Kruse '49 Faculty Fellow at Texas A&M University's Bush School of Government and Public Service. He is the author of *Cold War at 30,000 Feet: The Anglo-American Fight for Aviation Supremacy* (2007), and is editor of *The China Diary of George H.W. Bush: The Making of a Global President* (2008).

Katherine Carté Engel is an assistant professor in the Department of History at Texas A&M University. She received her Ph.D. in American History from the University of Wisconsin and specializes in the history of the Atlantic world during the eighteenth century, particular transatlantic religious networks. She is also the author of *Pilgrims and Profits: Moravians in the Mid-Atlantic Marketplace* (2008).

Richard S. Kirkendall is the Scott and Dorothy Bullitt Professor Emeritus, University of Washington, Seattle. His most recent book publication is *Harry's Farewell: Interpreting and Teaching the Truman Presidency* (2004).

Hiroshi Kitamura is an assistant professor of history at the College of William and Mary. He specializes in U.S.-foreign relations, with an emphasis on cultural relations between the United States and East Asia. His book on Hollywood's export campaign in the post–World War II period is forthcoming.

Arvid Nelson teaches at the Yale University School of Forestry and Environmental Studies and is the author of *Cold War Ecology: Forests, Farms, and People in the East German Landscape, 1945–1989* (2005).

Michael Oden is an associate professor in the Community and Regional Planning Program of the University of Texas at Austin. During the past decade, he has published numerous reports and essays on economic development and defense adjustment, including *Beyond the Digital Access Divide: Developing Meaningful Measures of Information and Communications Technology Gaps* (2004) and "Post–Cold War Conversion: Gains, Losses and Hidden Changes in the U.S. Economy" in *From Defense to Development? International Perspectives on Realizing the Peace Dividend,* edited by Ann Markusen, Sean DeGiovanna, and Michael C. Leary (2003).

Luís Nuno Rodrigues is an assistant professor of history at the Instituto Superior de Ciências do Trabalho e da Empresa, Lisbon, where he coordinates the graduate program in history, defense, and international relations. He is also a researcher at the Portuguese Institute of International Relations. He was a Fulbright Scholar, and he holds a Ph.D. in American History from the University of Wisconsin. The Portuguese version of his dissertation, on U.S.-Portuguese relations during the Kennedy administration, was published in 2002 and won two national prizes in Portugal. His most recent book analyzes the origins of the American military base in the Azores after World War II.

Anita Seth is a doctoral candidate at Yale University and an organizer with the labor union UNITE HERE. She received her B.A. in international relations from Pomona College in 1995 and her M.A. in history from Yale University in 2001. From 1996 to 1999, she worked with communities in Russia and the United States confronting the environmental and health legacy of Cold War nuclear production.

Catherine McNicol Stock is a professor of history, the chair of the History Department, and the director of the American Studies Program at Connecticut College. She is the author of *Rural Radicalism* (1996) and *Main Street in Crisis: The Great Depression and the Old Middle Class on the Northern Plains* (1997).

Jeremi Suri is a professor of history at the University of Wisconsin–Madison. He is the author of *Henry Kissinger and the American Century* (2007); *The Global Revolutions of 1968* (2006); and *Power and Protest: Global Revolution and the Rise of Detente* (2003). He has also published numerous articles in scholarly journals, magazines, and newspapers.

Charlie Whitham is a lecturer in twentieth-century American history and foreign policy at the University of Wales Institute, Cardiff. He has published on Anglo-American diplomatic and economic relations in the 1930s and 1940s, and his current research is focused on postwar U.S. military-basing policy in Europe and on corporate involvement in economic foreign policy during World War II.

Index

academic proletariat, 68
Academy of Sciences Presidium, 156
Ackermann, Anton, 198, 225n16, 226n19
Act of Union (1707), 173
Adams, Henry Baxter, 10
Adams, Henry, 7
advertising, 39–40, 42f; publicity campaigns for movies, 44
Africa, newly independent nations, 88–89
African Americans: civil rights, 86–88; international inspiration, 88; North Dakota, 262–64; World War II segregation, 80; World War II troop strength, 272n127
African diplomats in Washington, 89
agriculture: Dakotas, 245, 265, 266; East Germany, 203–4, 208, 210; Lenin's policy, 226n20; Siberia, 146–47; U.S. South, 77, 80
Air Force, U.S.: airmen of U.S. Army, 102; base in Portuguese Azores, 282, 298; bases in Dakotas, 238, 250–55; bomber selection, 104–5; desegregation, 261; established, 122; funding levels, 126; ICBM program, 127; Jackson on, 110; Los Angeles as center, 123, 129; missile sites in Dakotas, 255–57; personnel housing, 262–63
Air Research and Development Command, 123

air-conditioning, 80–81
aircraft industry: Los Angeles in 1920s, 119; science and engineering, 120–21; in Siberia, 142. *See also* Boeing Company; Seattle
Akademogorodok, 155–59
Alaskan history, xii–xiii
Albertz, Heinrich, 67
alcohol-related offenses, 181–82
Allen, Raymond B., 108
Allen, William, 105, 106, 112
Alliance Doctrine, 199
Allied occupation: effects of, 210–11; food shortages, 233n110; forestry, 231n74; map of zones, 212
Alvor agreement, 284
America First Committee, 246
America House, West Berlin, 64
American Film Club, 43
Americanism, Dakotans on, 248
Angola: consequences of Cold War intervention, 292–93; independence, 277, 289, 299; investment strategy, 282; Primeiro de Maio, 290; recognizing East Timor, 300; slave trade, 278; superpower diplomacy summarized, 23; U.S. and Portugal, 298; U.S. view, 306; Year of National Reconstruction (1976), 291
Annales school, 10–12, 14, 18, 28n38
anti-ballistic missile system (ABM), 241
anticommunism: Cold War conservatism, 19; Dakotas, 247, 248;

community history, 3
Companhia União Fabril (CUF), 282
Conant, James, 58–59
Congo, 279
Congress, U.S.: East Timor, 309–10;
  seniority system, 83; U.S. South,
  82–83
congressional committees, 83, 309
conservation movement, German, 209
Conservative Party (CDU), East
  German, 199, 237n153
Consolidated Vultee, 121
conspiracy theories, 20
construction trusts, 152, 164n49
Convair, 122, 127
corporations: Cold War era, 78; road to
  globalization, 81
counterfactual scenarios, 77–78, 81
Cuba, 17; in Angola, 277–78, 284, 287,
  288, 292; Operation Carlota, 288
Cuban missile crisis, 240, 258–59
cultural events, Novosibirsk, Siberia,
  146
currency reform in Germany, 236n148

Daiei studio, 37
Dakotas, nuclear weaponry impact
  summarized, 23. See also North
  Dakota; South Dakota
Decolonization Decree (Portugal,
  1974), 299
defense industry: Dakotas, 247; from
  local vantage point, 160; impact
  summarized, 22; Los Angeles, 117;
  Los Angeles boosters, 119–24; Los
  Angeles workers, 128, 130t, 130–33,
  131t; postwar Soviet, 148–50;
  Soviet boosters, 154–55, 160; Soviet
  worker skills, 151–52; strategic
  missions, 119; ties to Moscow, 152
Defense Security Assistance Agency,
  U.S., 310
defense spending, Soviet, Soviet, 141,
  143
defense spending, U.S., 250–51;
  antiterrorism and, 128; levels, 126;
  World War II, 79–80

defense-industry complex, 166n89
Democratic Party, 85, 100–101,
  111–12, 135
desegregation: armed services, 261–62.
  See also segregation
deterritorialization, 241
devolution referendum, 186, 192n74
diplomacy: consequences considered, 4;
  Gaddis on local impact, 16; as
  "Great Game," xvi; impact of, 7;
  linkages, 2; local impact
  summarized, 23–24
diplomatic history: Adams' influence,
  10; after World War II, 12–20;
  Annales approach, 14; in current
  volume, 3; events and crises in, 12;
  evolution of approach, 3–4;
  generations, 18–19;
  historiographical trends, 7–12; how
  and why of policy, 7; intellectual
  revolution in, 2; local features,
  xv–xvi, 24n4; overview, 4–12;
  policy formation, 7; policy impact,
  7; postwar, 14–15; powerful
  individuals, 12; Ranke's influence,
  8; revisionist school, 16–18; strides
  made, 2–3; transnational history, 12
Discovery/Corona spy satellite films,
  126–27
dissident behavior: against land reform,
  201; higher education and, 59;
  Soviet, 158. See also antinuclear
  protests; student protests
documents: access to, 9; broadening
  sources, 9, 10; Ranke on, 8
domestic brutalities, Iran, 66
domestic forces: Bailey on, 14; impact
  of Cold War, 19–20; institutions
  warped, 17, 18–19; Kennan on, 15;
  New Left on, 16–17; realists on,
  15–16; Turner on, 18; Williams on,
  17
domino effect, 305
Douglas Aircraft, 121, 123
Douglas Corporation, 100, 103, 106
Douglas DC-3, 121
Douglas, Donald, 120

drug offenses, 182
Dulles, John Foster, 125
Dutschke, Rudolf "Rudi," 67–69, 70

East Berlin, 60
East German State Planning
   Commission, 204
East Germany: higher education, 60,
   61; land policies summarized, 23,
   222
East Timor: independence, 300, 311;
   Indonesian intervention, 300–302;
   Indonesian invasion impact, 306–11;
   political parties, 299; Portuguese
   departure, 300; right-wing coup,
   299–300; self-determination, 299,
   305; superpower diplomacy
   summarized, 23, 296; U.S. military
   equipment, 303–4, 309–10; U.S.
   policy, 298–99; World War II, 296,
   297–98
ecology, Nazi, 224nn8, 10
economic development: ideological
   competition, 161; Los Angeles, 118,
   119–24; Soviet science research,
   157, 161; state-led, 119
Eisenhower, Dwight D., 19, 90; critics
   of, 111; Dakotas, 250; on military-
   industrial complex, 112; missiles to
   Britain, 170; "New Look" in
   defense, 105, 125; policies
   characterized, 220
electronics sector, defense: Los
   Angeles, 123, 128; Soviet, 142, 145,
   150–51, 154, 160
Elektrosignal factory, 151
elites: New Left on, 17; role of, 21;
   scholarly focus on, 15
Ellsworth Air Force Base, 238, 242
emergency laws, West Germany, 69
emigration patterns: from East to West
   Germany, 204, 208, 230n63; from
   Los Angeles, 133, 134f; U.S. South,
   77, 79, 80. See also rural to urban
   migration
employment: Boeing Company, 106–7;
   Los Angeles defense industry, 128,

130t, 130–33, 131t; Los Angeles
   manufacturing, 118; North Dakota
   militarization, 265; sugar plantation
   wages, 275, 281; wartime
   Novosibirsk, 146–48; women,
   147–48
English-language classrooms, movies
   as, 45
entertainment complex at Los Angeles,
   117, 133–34
entertainment culture, 35, 42–45,
   50–51; content of, 43–45
entertainment, defined, 51n16
environmental concerns: East Germany,
   222–23; Nazis, 197; Soviet Union,
   158
environmental costs, summarized,
   22–23
Espírito Santo Bank, 281
Espírito Santo family, 275, 282, 290
Espírito Santo, António, 285
Espírito Santo, Manuel, 279, 281, 282
essayists, 5
Experimental Flight Institute (LII),
   145–46

Fakel scientific-production association,
   157–58, 159
Falling Down, 134–35
Fargo, North Dakota, 252–54, 266
Farley, Jim, 100, 114n5
farm programs, 24
Farmers Holiday Association, 245, 247
Farmers Union, 245, 247
Faulkner, William, 4, 24n7, 77, 83
Febvre, Lucien, 10, 11, 12
federal government: Dakotas, 242–43,
   244–46, 248–49; Great Depression,
   244; international reach, 91; U.S.
   South, 79–80, 91; views of, 248–49;
   West, 243–44
Federalist Papers, 15
Federation of American Film
   Exhibitors, 43
fighter jets, Soviet, 142, 151
film industry, U.S.: occupied Japan, 34,
   50. See also Hollywood